Literacy, Lives and Learning

'*Literacy, Lives and Learning* is just the kind of study that can lead to sound policy and practice in adult education. As rich in conceptual approach as it is in attention to the details of the lives of learners and classrooms, this book takes an unflinching look at the challenges of the Skills for Life strategy but also shows how those challenges light the way to success.'

Deborah Brandt, University of Wisconsin-Madison, US

What is the relationship between people's lives and their involvement in learning opportunities? *Literacy, Lives and Learning* addresses this question in its examination of adults learning in today's world.

With a focus on language, literacy and numeracy, the authors explore the complex relationship between learning and adults' lives, following a wide range of individual students in a variety of learning situations from college environments to a homeless project and a drug support and aftercare centre.

Based on a major research project and developing a detailed, reflexive and collaborative methodology, *Literacy, Lives and Learning* describes how to undertake such research whilst exploring the literacies in people's lives and their engagement in learning. Illustrated with case studies of individuals and learning sites, this book addresses a number of themes – from how literacy is learned through participation in activities to how barriers such as violence and ill-health impact on learning.

Literacy, Lives and Learning will be of interest to students of applied linguistics as well as to those involved in teaching and learning with adults.

David Barton, **Roz Ivanic**, **Yvon Appleby**, **Rachel Hodge** and **Karin Tusting** have worked together on a range of projects based in the Literacy Research Centre at Lancaster University. Key titles by the authors include *Local Literacies* (Routledge, 1998), *Situated Literacies* (Routledge, 1999) and *Beyond Communities of Practice*.

LITERACIES

Series Editor: David Barton

Lancaster University

Literacy practices are changing rapidly in contemporary society in response to broad social, economic and technological changes: in education, the workplace, the media and in everyday life. This series reflects the burgeoning research and scholarship in the field of literacy studies and its increasingly interdisciplinary nature. The series aims to provide a home for books on reading and writing which consider literacy as a social practice and which situate it within broader institutional contexts. The books develop and draw together work in the field; they aim to be accessible, interdisciplinary and international in scope, and to cover a wide range of social and institutional contexts.

LITERACY, GENDER & ATTAINMENT (forthcoming)

Gemma Moss

HIPHOP LITERACIES

Elaine Richardson

LITERACY IN THE NEW MEDIA AGE

Gunther Cress

CITY LITERACIES

Learning to Read Across Generations and Cultures

Eve Gregory and Ann Williams

LITERACY AND DEVELOPMENT

Ethnographic Perspectives

Edited by Brian V. Street

SITUATED LITERACIES

Theorising Reading and Writing in Context

Edited by David Barton, Mary Hamilton and Roz Ivanic

MULTILITERACIES
Literacy Learning and the Design of Social Futures
Edited by Bill Cope and Mary Kalantzis

GLOBAL LITERACIES AND THE WORLD-WIDE WEB
Edited by G. E. Hawisher and Cynthia L. Selfe

STUDENT WRITING
Access, Regulation, Desire
Theresa M. Lillis

SILICON LITERACIES
Communication, Innovation and Education in the Electronic Age
Edited by Ilana Snyder

AFRICAN AMERICAN LITERACIES
Elaine Richardson

LITERACY IN THE NEW MEDIA AGE
Gunther Kress

LITERACY, LIVES AND LEARNING

First published 2007
by Routledge
2 Park Square, Milton Park, Abingdon, Oxon OX14 4RN

Simultaneously published in the USA and Canada
by Routledge
270 Madison Ave, New York, NY 10016

Routledge is an imprint of the Taylor & Francis Group, an informa business

© 2007 David Barton, Roz Ivanic, Yvon Appleby, Rachel Hodge and
Karin Tusting

Typeset in Baskerville by
Keystroke, 28 High Street, Tettenhall, Wolverhampton
Printed and bound in Great Britain by
Antony Rowe Ltd, Chippenham, Wiltshire

24.99

British Library Cataloguing in Publication Data
A catalogue record for this book is available from the British Library

Library of Congress Cataloging-in-Publication Data
Literacy, lives, and learning / by David Barton ... [et al.].
p. cm.
Includes bibliographical references.
1. Literacy. 2. Functional literacy. 3. Adult education. 4. Continuing education.
I. Barton, David, 1949–
LC149.L49985 2007
302.2′244—dc22
2007016137

ISBN10: 0–415–42485–2 (hbk)
ISBN10: 0–415–42486–0 (pbk)

ISBN13: 978–0–415–42485–1 (hbk)
ISBN13: 978–0–415–42486–8 (pbk)

CONTENTS

FIGURES

ACKNOWLEDGEMENTS

Collaborative research would not be possible without the co-operation of many people, and the authors would like to thank everyone who has participated in the extensive work which has led to this book. The book is centrally about the individuals we encountered in learning environments. We would like to thank all those who have shared their stories and insights with us over the past few years. We could not have met these people without co-operation from all the colleges and other learning settings in which we have been working, and we greatly appreciate the time and involvement of many people from these settings. We have used pseudonyms throughout when referring to people who participated in the research.

At the Lancaster Literacy Research Centre, we would like to thank all of those who have contributed to and supported the work of the Adult Learners' Lives project and the work towards writing this book, particularly Mary Hamilton and Jessica Abrahams. We would like to thank all those whose engagement with the research has contributed to the development of this work: members of the Literacy Research Discussion Group at Lancaster University, the North West Skills for Life Research Forum, and from further afield visitors from the Research in Practice in Adult Literacy network in Canada and from the National Centre for the Study of Adult Learning and Literacy and the Rutgers University Classroom Research Group in the USA.

We have also benefited from discussion with colleagues at meetings of the Research and Practice in Adult Literacy network, the British Association for Applied Linguistics, the British Educational Research Association, the UK Linguistic Ethnography Forum and the Ethnography in Education Research Forum at the University of Pennsylvania. Finally, we would like to extend our appreciation to the National Research and Development Centre for Adult Literacy and Numeracy for funding much of this research, for ongoing dialogue with our partner institutions in NRDC, and for providing important forums for sharing this work regionally and nationally.

1

INTRODUCTION

The relationship between people's lives and their learning is complex. The overall aim of this book is to untangle this complex relationship and to demonstrate what it is like to be participating in formal learning as an adult in today's fast-changing world. Participating in any activity involves learning and this is not necessarily conscious or deliberate. Formal learning takes place in a wide variety of settings, providing a range of learning opportunities. People make individual decisions about whether to attend, to participate, and to engage in activities which are offered. Decisions about participation and engagement are based upon people's histories, their current situations and the possibilities they see for themselves. At the same time people's lives are part of broader currents and people are making decisions within a changing global context which determines what choices they have. This global context is acted out in the particular places where people live; it also exists in the political context of government policies and strategies.

We study the relationship between lives and learning through a detailed examination of people's lives over time in a range of settings. We focus on the learning of literacy and include language and numeracy, but we have a broader interest in all learning. This chapter begins with brief introductions to a range of people who have been participating in formal learning opportunities. This sets the scene, indicating the diversity in people's lives and the complex relationship between lives and learning which this book further explores.

The first person, whom we refer to as Jason, was 31 years old when we first met him. He was single and lived on his own and he was attending a maths class at the local community college. The maths class was offered, free, as part of the high profile Skills for Life strategy in England which offered support for numeracy as well as more traditional support for reading and writing. Jason stopped going to school at 12 years old, spending his time hanging about Liverpool docks and riding the Mersey Ferry. He worked on building sites as a scaffolder and later unloading containers at the docks, just as his father had done. Jason got jobs through a network of local contacts and these were jobs which did not need much reading and writing. A serious hit-and-run road accident left Jason unemployed and with depression. We later worked with him at a tenants' association where he did voluntary work. People in the association had persuaded him to take courses in

1

computing, in maths and in family history. He had helped set up and run their computer, and maintained the association accounts. However, he also lapsed into bouts of drinking and was irregular in his attendance at college courses. Over time we could see the different ways Jason participated in formal learning situations and the unsettledness of his life outside class as he responded to a rapidly changing world around him.

Another person we met at that maths class was Katrina. She was 20 years old at the time of the research and was working as a play worker. She lived at home with her parents, returning home for lunch every day between shifts. Katrina had done a variety of jobs including packing and factory work. Although working hard to study health-care subjects at college, she struggled with telling the time and doing multiplication tables. Katrina attended the maths class to learn topics such as this which she and her teachers felt were holding her back and which were vital for her work. She also wanted to be able to pass her driving test so she could be more independent. In her everyday life we saw the complex ways in which she used maths. For instance, as she was concerned about her weight, Katrina had started to read food packets to work out the calories and fat content of what she was eating. She monitored her weight carefully, noting down any decrease, or increase, from the week before. She worked out ideal body weight in relation to height and then how many calories could be consumed to achieve this. This also meant working out how many calories could be burned off walking to work compared to other activities. We are interested in the ways in which what is offered in classes relates to what people such as Katrina do in their everyday lives.

We also worked with, Susan, a 69-year-old widow who lived alone. She was attending a spelling class. She had six children and was a grandmother and great-grandmother with many family members living nearby. She told us about her life and described going through her primary schooling without her deafness being picked up. This affected her confidence and skills in English. This was made worse as her schooling was interrupted when she was evacuated during the war.

Someone else attending a spelling class, but in a smaller town, was Jack, who ran a successful dairy farm. He had been attending this class for five years. He had had great difficulties with spelling when he started attending the class and was making gradual progress, working with the same volunteer for much of the time.

Other people were attending language classes to improve their English. Sameena from Pakistan had come to England ten years previously to get married, when she was 16 years old. She had two young children and her husband ran a jewellery business here. She finished her secondary schooling in Pakistan and after coming to Britain she attended a community-based English class. Her studies were interrupted whilst she was caring for small children. Three years ago she again attended a community class, and had to 'catch up' on previous learning. When she re-entered education she also attended a First Step childcare course, which she found very demanding as it was not tailored for second language learners. Eventually, after attending college English classes, she opened her own women's clothing business.

English classes have a wide variety of students with very different levels of education. Abdul, from Iraq, came with his wife and two children to Britain a year before we met him. He was in his late forties and had worked as an agronomist. He was highly motivated to learn English so that he could gain employment. He felt that this goal was not in his control as he was waiting for the Home Office to give him permission to stay in Britain and to be able to work. He spent his spare time reading newspapers, books and the dictionary to try to keep learning, watching news coverage on TV, taking the children to the park and town centre and helping them with their science and maths homework. He also attended the BBC Learning Centre in town most days where he was learning, with some tutor support, to use a computer. He said that he had little opportunity to talk to English-speaking people outside the class so felt he did not get enough practice.

There were also people in our study who were not attending college classes. We met Sophie, an 18 year old, at a shelter for young homeless people. She had been expelled from school as a result of repeated assault and arson offences. She became homeless at age 15 and did not do well in her school exams. She had dipped in and out of college and gave up her most recent course, in landscape gardening, when she became pregnant. At the shelter she liked creative and practical activities, but preferred not to attend drugs and alcohol advice sessions. She found the basic skills education she was offered boring and easy. In her own time Sophie read novels and wrote poetry. Towards the end of the study Sophie had just had a baby girl and was in much better health. She was moving on from a mother-and-baby unit to her sister's house for a while, and wanted to find her own flat. She was determined to go back to college, take her GCSE and A-level exams and eventually study veterinary medicine or psychology. Sophie later faced further difficulties with drug dependence and lived with her child in a hostel for homeless single mothers.

Steve was in his early thirties and attending a drug and alcohol rehabilitation centre. He had dyslexia. He told us that he had frequently skipped school from the age of 13 and left officially at 16. He sat some exams but never found out his results. After leaving school, he worked as a joiner. He had been a drug user since his early twenties and had been in and out of prison. He was now committed to sorting his life out and was eager to engage with the educational and support provision provided at the rehabilitation centre, which he perceived as being useful and productive for him.

Jez, who was 17, did not feel ready to attend college but, as a condition of being on probation, was participating in an equivalent course for 16–18 year olds. This was delivered by a private provider. She lived in supported accommodation for young people under the age of 18 years. Jez had an unsettled childhood living with her mum, changing schools frequently and finally leaving home aged 13. She became involved with the local Children's Rights Service, training advocates and helping with their website and information leaflets. She had also just completed a 'runaways project' DVD, acting, filming and editing it. When she reached the age of 16 they were able to employ her for seventeen hours a month but she did a lot more hours than this as a volunteer. Reading and writing were central to all these activities. In her spare time she read novels and loved writing, both her diary and poems. She says she thought she learned to read music before she could read print. She had lots of music books and played the keyboard.

These nine people are just some of those who participated in our study. They represent the rich variety of people who are touched by the Skills for Life strategy. This diversity raises questions about how we talk about people attending Skills for Life courses, and how we characterise this area of education. These issues of terminology, which we will highlight now, run as threads throughout this book and lead to the key issues which we address.

Is there something that these people have in common? How should we talk about them in relation to the particular educational provision of Skills for Life? Many of them dropped out of school or left as early as they could, but not all. Abdul, for instance, attending a language class was highly trained as an agronomist, and there were people with various levels of education in the numeracy and the spelling classes. Many were young people, but not all; many were unemployed, but not all. For some, Skills for Life provision was central to their activities, whilst for others it was on the edge of their concerns or embedded in some other activities. For some, a difficulty with literacy, numeracy or language is the only disadvantage they face. For others, this is one amongst many barriers: being unemployed, homeless, having specific disabilities such as deafness, or having had an interrupted education.

These people do not fit into some neat category. For the most part they are ordinary people who missed out on education for a wide variety of reasons or who need to develop their skills to face new demands, such as in employment or in managing life in a new country. Looking across the three areas of literacy, numeracy and language provision, it is already clear in our data that quite different groups of people attend these classes.

There are shifts in the relative attention paid to these three areas by policy makers and funders, which we trace in the next chapter. There is a tension between treating them as distinct areas and lumping them together as one field of education. We wish to emphasise the distinct nature and contributions of the three fields and how they are responding to extremely diverse learning needs of different individuals and groups of people.

There is also a recurring issue around how to talk about this area of educational provision. At the time of writing it is referred to in England as Skills for Life, though it has been named in different ways since the 1970s in relation to developing policy initiatives and agendas, as documented in Hamilton and Hillier (2006). It has been known generically as basic education and more recently as basic skills, at least within policy discussions. On the ground providers and teachers have not wanted to publicise courses as 'basic' preferring terms such as *English*, or *writing* or *spelling* which they feel are more positive and less stigmatising. One crucial point is that many of the people identified as belonging to priority groups in terms of the strategy are not at some 'basic' level of literacy and numeracy. We have had to make many decisions about terminology in this book; for instance, people in the field generally use the term *numeracy* rather than *mathematics*, and we will do likewise.

4

However, where a class is advertised as a maths class, we will follow the usage of teachers and colleges.

People accessing skills for life provision are usually referred to as *learners* by practitioners and policy makers and this term has common currency in the field of adult education. However, we do not want to lose sight of the fact that much learning takes place outside such courses, as discussed in Chapter 3. An alternative term in some provision is *student* and other organisations we worked with have referred to people in different ways, such as *client*. Similarly, the terms *teacher* and *tutor* are used in different ways in different places, and we use these terms interchangeably, reflecting current debates.

How we talk about these issues and the words we use are not just arbitrary choices; this is an issue of conflicting and competing discourses. People in the Skills for Life priority groups are often referred to in educational discourse as *hard-to-reach*, as if they are invisible, hiding or absent. Therefore understanding and representing their local experiences within a national context is particularly important, showing them from the perspective of their presence in their own lives, rather than of their absence from spaces defined by others. We have been working here with groups which include people in positions of social inequality, many of whom have experienced marginalisation at some points in their lives. *Dropout* and *retention*, like hard-to-reach and learner, are terms common in the prevailing discourse of adult education and lifelong learning. Again, these words view people from the perspective of policy makers and funders. This affects the targets and funding of the college or other organisation which they drop out from, and which cannot reach them or retain them. Such people are constructed as being a problem for the college, to be solved. However, in this study we look from a different perspective: we want to say something about the meaning of learning from the point of view of the people participating, for whom 'dropping out' might well mean 'moving on to something else'.

These terms fit together in a powerful dominant discourse which positions people in narrow educational terms as needing to learn a set of skills. These skills are mapped on to a set of levels to which people are assigned and against which they can then be measured. These levels are used as the basis of targets for colleges and other organisations to achieve. Within this view literacy seems very one-dimensional. It is something which people either have or do not have, and it leads to *deficit* views which define people in terms of what they cannot do. For instance, adults are compared to children in relation to reading levels, in statements such as 'one in six adults do not have the literacy skills of an eleven year old'. A moment's thought should make it clear that adults have broader life experiences, wider vocabularies and more general experience with language, making such comparisons with children inaccurate and invidious. What also happens is that people who are labelled as having problems with literacy are treated in general deficit terms; literacy is used as a marker, or proxy, for other social problems such as poor health or poverty.

We want to provide an alternative richer view to that offered by the dominant discourse on literacy and learning. The deficit view creates a comfort zone in public discussions which the field needs to move out of. It represents an over-simplified way of talking about people which we contest. Our research brings to light aspects of life salient in people's experiences which impact on learning and which are often hidden by not being discussed within current discourses of adult education, such as gender, health, violence and bullying. We want to get beyond common generalisations, public myths and established narratives of people as 'learners' in need of 'functional skills', moving towards more realistic representations of what people do do and can do, and the conditions within which they act.

Our concern with competing discourses develops from the underlying theories we draw upon – theories of language, literacy and numeracy, and of learning. Our framing comes primarily from work in literacy studies, but we believe it is also applicable across the fields of language and numeracy. The book is rooted in an approach that sees literacy, numeracy and language as social practices, rather than just as skills to be learned, unconnected to anything else. This approach entails observing people engaging in these practices in their everyday lives, and listening to what they have to say about these practices and the meanings that they have in their lives. The book provides rich detail about the lives of a wide range of people participating in formal learning. It is based on research in a broad range of situations, including college environments, but also community environments such as a drug support and aftercare centre, a young homeless project and a domestic violence project. We put forward a view and approach that provides an alternative to the skills and deficit discourse.

We take a social practice perspective not only on language, literacy and numeracy, but also on teaching and learning. We explain this perspective in more detail in Chapter 3. This approach has more general implications for understanding the learning experiences of adults and young people in settings other than educational ones. In this book we draw particular attention to the importance of the social elements of the teaching and learning interactions we observed, which can often be overlooked, and to the relationship between learning issues and social issues in the wider context beyond the classroom. The book is concerned with teaching and learning interactions in these sites through the perspectives of individual students, covering their motivations for attending, ways of participating in the classes and experiences of learning. It explores how learning opportunities are created. It looks at what learners bring and what teachers bring to specific situations and illustrates the negotiations which teachers and learners engage in. It emphasises the active role of learners and the broader outcomes of their participation in learning. What learners bring to these settings is analysed in terms of four aspects of their lives: their history, their current practices and identities, their current life circumstances and events, and their imagined futures. By analysing patterns of participation and engagement in learning, the book is able to examine how people's lives shape their learning and how learning shapes their lives in broader ways.

The overarching research question in this book is: what is the relation between people's lives and their participation in learning opportunities? What from their lives do people take to the learning situations and what from the learning situation feeds back into their lives? The themes which are covered include: the range of practices people participate in across their lives, and how they use literacy to get things done; how barriers such as violence and ill-health impact on people's participation in formal learning situations; how literacy is a resource for learning; how literacy is learned through participation; the significance of networks, mediators and brokers; patterns of longitudinal change. The book also acts as an illustration of the detailed, reflexive and collaborative methodology described in Chapter 4. This has included extensive collaboration with practitioners and draws out the implications of this work for pedagogy by proposing a social practice developed with practitioners.

Overall we are interested in how people make decisions and act within the range of possibilities available to them in their lives. In Chapter 2, 'The context of adults' learning', we are concerned with the context which frames what is available for adults and we describe the policies which shaped the possibilities for the people involved in our research. Chapter 3, 'Literacy, lives and learning as social practice', introduces the main theories that frame the research. It begins by describing a social practice perspective on literacy, numeracy and language. It then outlines a four-part framework for an analysis of people's lives in relation to learning, offering a structure which takes into account people's histories and imagined futures as well as their current practices and circumstances. Finally, it describes a social view of learning. The following two chapters then lead on to draw out the implications of these theoretical perspectives for the methodology used in the research. Chapter 4, 'Situating adult learners' lives', describes the wide range of contexts and sites of the research, and explores the significance of people's sense and experience of place. Then chapter 5, 'A collaborative and responsive methodology', explains the overall methodology and the distinctive methods used when working with adults. We describe in detail four examples of how we worked with people in a collaborative and responsive way.

Chapter 6, 'Literacies in people's lives', is the first data chapter. It illustrates the significance of literacy for people in their everyday lives in relation to five case studies. Chapter 7, 'Literacy and learning for life purposes', looks at this issue across all the learners we worked with, before examining the range of uses of literacy in people's lives and how literacy is learned through participation in these activities.

Chapter 8, 'Ways of participating in classes', is concerned with teaching and learning interactions in classes. It describes detailed work in four classrooms, concentrating on focal sessions. It analyses the perspectives of individual students in the classes, covering their motivations for attending and ways of participating in the classes, including their perceptions and strategies for learning. It brings out differences between language, literacy and numeracy classes. Continuing with the same classes, Chapter 9, 'The negotiation of teaching and learning in classes', is concerned with how learning opportunities are created, starting out by contrasting what learners bring and what teachers bring to the situation. It covers the active negotiation which teachers and learners engage in and draws these together to look at how learning opportunities are socially constructed. It emphasises the active role of learners, highlights the conflicting roles of teachers and describes some of the broader outcomes of participating for learners.

The next two chapters are concerned with a broader range of settings, such as the homeless project described above. Chapter 10, 'What people bring to learning settings' describes the people in these settings and concentrates on understanding what learners bring. This is analysed in terms of the four aspects of their lives introduced earlier: their history, their current practices and identities, their current life circumstances and events, and their imagined futures. Chapter 11, 'The negotiation of learning in community settings', examines in more detail how aspects of people's lives shaped their learning. First, it shows how aspects of people's lives shaped their engagement in learning opportunities, identifying common issues such as reluctance to access mainstream education, dipping in and out of educational provision and identifying a 'right time' for learning. Then we turn to patterns of participation in these settings, particularly the use of space and time and the resultant patterns of interaction.

Chapter 12, 'Life careers', uses the idea of people having learning careers, work careers, health careers and others as a way of bringing together the data of previous chapters and taking a longitudinal look at adults' lives over time. The aim is to get a broader understanding of how life histories influence learning and what this leads to. The final chapter, 'Towards a social practice pedagogy', aims to draw out the implications of this work for pedagogy by developing a social practice approach, outlining principles for teaching which takes account of and builds on the resources people bring with them from their lives.

2

THE CONTEXT OF ADULTS' LEARNING

How do people decide to participate in formal learning – to attend a class, to engage with the subject matter, to persist with a course, or to go on to further activities? People act and make choices in relation to the possibilities which are available to them. These are shaped by a nested set of factors, from the broadest global issues about the state of the economy, through to particular government policies, which they may or may not be aware of, down to the ways in which a national policy is mediated locally and to details such as whether a particular class is available on a particular evening in the town in which they live. We therefore need ways to understand how a person's life and choices are situated within a broader social structure, and how these factors interact.

In studying people's lives and their learning, we have had to find ways of representing these two perspectives. In relation to people's lives, working with people in depth over time, we were able to see the unique quality of each individual and how they had made the many independent choices which had shaped their lives. In relation to social structures, it was clear that the conditions within which people made these choices and the possibilities open to them were socially structured. Working with teachers and students in language, literacy and numeracy classes brought to light the constraints within which they acted and the social inequalities structuring our society which affected people's ability to make choices. This is a reworking of the classic question in the social sciences of the relationship between society and the individual, structure and agency, how people act within the constraints and opportunities offered by social structure. We address this more fully in Chapter 3, where we show how social theorists are moving beyond such a dichotomy to develop a variety of approaches to understanding this relationship.

In the current chapter, we outline one key aspect of structure: the government policy in England which has shaped this field, the Skills for Life strategy. Later in the book we develop a framework for understanding people's lives and how they act within the available possibilities at any time. First, we set it in the broader context of adult basic education provision.

Background to adult basic education in England

The Skills for Life Strategy was built upon the foundations of existing work in England in language, literacy and numeracy with adults. Most of the classes were provided in existing colleges and most of the teachers, at least at the beginning, were already working in these areas. It is useful to sketch briefly the history of the field as the tensions and continuities between the strategy and existing practice affected teachers and students and the choices they made. A recent history of the field of adult language, literacy and numeracy (Hamilton and Hillier 2006) has a useful breakdown of the field into three phases before the coming of the Skills for Life era. In the first phase, adult literacy work in England began in earnest in the 1970s. In that period it can be characterised as being largely based on voluntary effort and was seen by many as a temporary phase to 'plug the gaps' left by the school educational system. Issues of access to education, of community development and of social justice were important themes for many practitioners from the beginning and have continued as threads throughout the development of the field. English language work for speakers of other languages was generally seen as a separate field with different teachers and a different ethos, more pedagogically allied to the field of Applied Linguistics and English Language Teaching. Community-based language teaching with the ethos of social integration for ethnic minority people planning to be long-term residents distinguished this work from TEFL (Teaching English as a Foreign Language) with students and workers here for a short term. There was little adult numeracy provision at this time.

In the second phase, in the 1980s, there was more national co-ordination, more courses related to employment and a growing interest in the importance of numeracy. The third phase, in the 1990s, is characterised by a shift of provision into colleges and the field became more formalised as part of the system of further education in England. It became a recognised subject area of further education, controlled by the shifting politics and funding priorities of the further education sector. Throughout this whole period from the 1970s, the teachers in all three disciplines had a strong ethos of focusing on people as adults, summarised in the phrase 'responding to learners' needs'. There was a general suspicion of testing regimes and of any professionalisation of the teaching workforce. There was often a tension between work 'on the ground' and the prodding and pushing of national government agencies. At the same time there was a constant feeling of this being a field which was marginalised and under-funded. Hamilton and Hillier (2006: 8–15) provide more detail on how these phases of development of the field can be characterised by differences in the way the issues are talked about, differences in the role of national agencies and differences in the relative visibility of language, literacy and numeracy.

The development of the Skills for Life strategy

The Skills for Life Strategy came about as a result of a government review of the whole field initiated soon after Labour came into government in 1997. The outcome of this review, *A Fresh Start* (Moser 1999), often known as the Moser Report, proposed a major increase in national funding and outlined a strategy for addressing issues of language, literacy and numeracy, most of which were later implemented in the Skills for Life strategy. The new structures built upon the existing field whilst at the same time challenging much of its general ethos. The strategy can be seen as part of broader government policy aimed at addressing poverty and unemployment. Later we will see examples of how other related government policies shaped the possibilities available to people; for example, in relation to policies affecting young homeless people, young unemployed people and people on drug treatment and testing orders. The receipt of government funding became dependent on the inclusion of Skills for Life courses for these groups of people.

The focus on young people and adults also fitted well into government educational policy. The adult literacy policy followed on from a centrally controlled literacy policy in schools, including a national curriculum and a structured 'literacy hour' each day in primary schools. The national curriculum for adults drew upon the schools curriculum and there are recurrent examples of adult literacy levels being related to school-based levels (as with the comparison of adults with 11-year-old children, mentioned in the previous chapter). This has the effect of eroding the distinctiveness of working with adults rather than with children, eliding issues such as adults' broader life experiences, their self-motivation and the different relationship in which they stand to teachers.

In the earlier periods in the UK, the justification for work in this area was as a response to learners' expressed needs, which were wide ranging and included social and economic issues. The justification of the Skills for Life strategy in terms of broader social policy has always been twofold. At some points there has been a social inclusion justification of enabling participation in society, with basic levels of education being a right. At other times there is an economic justification of upskilling oneself to get and to keep a job, with the acquisition of basic levels of education becoming a duty. The Moser Report justifies this focus on adult literacy and numeracy in terms of both social needs and the economy. By the time we get to the Skills for Life strategy, this has been translated into government policies for social inclusion and for economic competitiveness, with a stronger emphasis on the latter. Which of these two aspects of the broader framing is emphasised is important as it materially affects what courses are available, what the course content is and who can participate in them.

The policy framing shifted in two crucial ways during the period of our research. There was a shift towards focusing on young people, rather than adults, and there were changes in what level of courses were emphasised, with a move away from lower level courses. This has been documented by the National Audit Office (2005) and the Adult Learning Inspectorate (2005) and analysed by Appleby and Bathmaker (2006). Adults with low levels of literacy are no longer the focus of the strategy. Courses not focusing on economic outcomes are not funded. The shift towards the economic justification has continued so that by the end of 2006 this was all that the government funding agency, the Learning and Skills Council, was interested in. It was very clear about its aim: 'The Learning and Skills Council exists to make England better skilled and more competitive. We have a single goal: to improve the skills of England's young people and adults to ensure we have a workforce of world-class standard' (www.lsc.gov.uk/).

The relationship between the three areas of language, literacy and numeracy has also been uneasy. The three areas have different subject matters and quite different profiles of potential students. The original push was for adult literacy provision; interest in numeracy was gradually added. This has often been a question of rhetoric: literacy and numeracy are mentioned together in the same breath but with the interest being primarily in literacy, numeracy being added as an afterthought. There have always been fewer numeracy courses, fewer specialist teachers and less demand for numeracy courses. However, recent evidence from large-scale cohort studies (Bynner and Parsons 2006) has underlined the importance of numeracy in terms of employment, and policy makers have responded emphasising the funding of numeracy.

The attitude towards ESOL (English for Speakers of Other Languages) has always been ambiguous and has been more subject to political concerns around immigration and the seeking of asylum. There is a paragraph on the importance of language in the Moser Report and it is mentioned in the strategy. However, the titles of both the Moser Report and the Skills for Life Strategy named 'literacy and numeracy' without language being mentioned. ESOL policy and provision has largely failed to keep pace with the needs of its diverse and changing cohort. By 2006 language classes were being squeezed by restrictions on what courses could be funded. At the time of writing, people seeking asylum are no longer entitled to access ESOL provision.

The Skills for Life strategy was a high profile, well funded, widely publicised educational intervention which had been a central plank of the government's 2001 election manifesto and which was established at the end of 2001 (DfES 2001a). It was complex and wide ranging, with several components which were all being developed in parallel as our research began. First, a core curriculum was developed, or rather, three separate core curricula for Literacy, Numeracy and ESOL. These were set out in lengthy documents analysing the subject matter of each discipline into a set of levels. Teachers had to 'map' all classroom activities onto these levels. We draw upon examples of the curriculum and mapping later, in Chapter 8. The levels were then related to a set of standards which students had to achieve at each level. Tests were being developed to measure achievement at each of the levels, leading to a set of new qualifications for students. Crucially for the field of basic education, there were 3 levels – Entry 1, Entry 2 and Entry 3 – before Level 1, which was intended to be equivalent to the GCSE grades D–G in England. (GCSE exams are taken at age 16 in England and A-levels at age 18.) Level 2 is seen as equivalent to GCSE grades A–C and Level 3 is A-level standard (as explained at www.qca.org.uk/). Running in parallel to all this, but developed slightly later, new standards for teachers and a new set of teaching qualifications were gradually introduced.

The strategy was driven by national targets based upon the number of people who should pass approved tests in literacy, numeracy and language. Funding for individual colleges and other providers depended on them meeting the targets set by the Learning and Skills Council, the government funding agency. The strategy focused on a set of priority groups, including unemployed people, prisoners, low-skilled employees and other groups 'at risk of social exclusion'. There was also a promotional drive, the 'Gremlins' campaign, which included extensive TV advertising; this ensured that the strategy had a high public profile. The whole strategy was closely controlled by a unit within the Department for Education and Skills, the Adult Basic Skills Strategy Unit, later renamed the Skills for Life Strategy Unit as it broadened out to have more of a focus on young people and on a more general skills agenda. We engage critically with many aspects of this policy throughout the book. We are part of it to the extent that some of the work drawn upon here was originally funded by the government. This work adds the perspective of how the standardised Skills for Life agenda impacts on a diverse group of people.

Skills for Life also grew out of broader concerns about economic competitiveness and the need for a more highly skilled workforce. In the rhetoric of international agencies, the link between literacy levels (both at the individual level and at the country level) and economic well-being is taken for granted. The Organisation for Economic Co-operation and Development (OECD) initiated a comparative survey of adult literacy rates in various industrialised countries. Whilst many of the differences between countries in the International Adult Literacy Survey (IALS) are not in any way statistically significant, the existence of a league table of countries encouraged many of those not at the top of the league (including Britain) to address issues of adult literacy. So Britain's competitiveness in the global economy became inextricably linked to levels of literacy and numeracy of individuals and the field took on a strongly economic imperative.

It was this strategy which funded the educational programmes which the people in our study were being offered. Colleges and other providers were required to change what courses they offered in response to funding criteria. The teachers and managers were responding to the curriculum and to the targets set by the funders and they were attending training events designed to promote the strategy. Teachers and students were working towards qualifications created by the strategy. The students were part of the targets, whether or not they were aware of this.

This has been a sketch of the framework which people we encountered acted within. They see some part of this framework and the parts which are invisible to them also impact on their learning. All these factors come together. So people may be taught in a building which is a hundred years old, by a teacher trained in the 1970s, following curricula and assessment regimes developed in the past few years. Teachers steeped in the ethos of adult learning of responding to learners' individual needs and aspirations may experience tensions when responding to the different agenda and demands of Skills for Life. In this book we are trying to make sense of these conditions and contexts for learning, represented from the perspective of learners' experiences of them. This work is not an evaluation of Skills for Life but it does give some indication of how people see their lives, how a high-profile government policy impinges on their lives and how they act within the possibilities and constraints it offers.

3

LITERACY, LIVES AND LEARNING AS SOCIAL PRACTICE

Introduction

In this chapter we look in more depth at issues raised in the first chapter about how we talk about language, literacy and numeracy, the model of learning which frames the work, and aspects of people's lives we need to take account of. People have conceptualised literacy, numeracy and language, and learning in many different ways. Our key concern in this book is the relationship between people's lives and their learning of literacy, language and numeracy. A social practices perspective makes this relationship explicit. We then use it to develop a social practice pedagogy.

The theoretical perspectives we draw upon to illuminate this relationship are laid out in this chapter. We begin with a social practice perspective on literacy, numeracy and language. We then turn to a four-part framework for an analysis of people's lives in relation to learning, offering a structure which takes into account people's individual histories and imagined futures as well as their current practices and circumstances. Finally, we outline a social view of learning. The following two chapters then lead on to the implications of these theoretical perspectives for the methodology used in the research.

Social practice perspectives on language, literacy and numeracy

Our starting point is that the reading, writing and number work which people do is integrated into their activities in different contexts. This applies to everyday contexts such as home, work and community, and also to educational settings. Each context poses different demands, offers different opportunities, and requires different ways of communicating. People's lives are complex and varied, and the parts played by languages, literacies and numeracies in them equally so. The roles other people take on in literacy, numeracy and language events, the interplay between spoken interaction, reading, writing and using number, the use of resources such as paper, pencils, books and computers, the purposes, and the degree of formality are all shaped by the nature of the events in context and how these unfold.

14

Within the study of literacy this work can be drawn together in what is becoming known as a social practice theory. This provides a coherent framework for thinking about literacy which has implications in all areas of education and which is being taken up and applied to learning in different contexts. A wide range of research in different settings has now been done, including work which we have carried out with our colleagues (Barton and Hamilton 1998; Barton et al. 2000). These studies were specifically of literacy; nevertheless, we see close parallels in the study of language and of numeracy as social practices in the ways in which they are inter-twined in everyday life. They are all part of the symbolic resources and the communicative resources we draw upon.

We use the concept of literacy practices as a powerful way of conceptualising the link between the activities of reading and writing and the social structures in which they are embedded and which they help shape. When we talk about practices, we believe that this perspective offers a useful way for talking about literacy, one which challenges the dominant skills discourse. As we have written elsewhere,

> the central point is that when literacy is talked about in terms of skills, the 'problem' or 'difficulty' is located in the individual people, who are described as having some kind of deficit. A social practice view of literacy accepts that the situation is more complex than that and problems or difficulties are not just to do with people's failings: issues of debt, or needing help with a form, or not being able to navigate a web-site raise issues about the complexity of contemporary life as much as attributes of individual people. . . . Literacy practices are the general cultural ways of utilising written language which people draw upon in their lives. In the simplest sense literacy practices are what people do with literacy. However practices also involve values, attitudes, feelings and social relationships. This includes people's awareness of literacy, constructions of literacy and discourses of literacy, how people talk about and make sense of literacy. These are processes internal to the individual; at the same time, practices are the social processes which connect people with one another, and they include shared cognitions represented in ideologies and social identities.
>
> (Barton 2005: 22)

People are doing all sorts of things in their lives, whether it is baking a cake, paying some bills, or surfing the internet, and in doing these things people draw upon language, literacy and numeracy.

The framework outlined above for literacy can be applied equally well to language and to numeracy. First, language itself is part of most social activities. It is especially important in education to understand that there are different forms or genres of language appropriate to different contexts, and to realise that some forms of language are more valued in some contexts than others (as in Swales 1990). Looking more closely at what people actually do in their lives, it becomes clear that literacy is not the same in all contexts; rather, there are different literacies in different domains of life, such as everyday life, education, or work places. People develop and learn more in these different areas, partly by learning how to use language in more specialised ways. Much of the advanced knowledge of any subject is learning about the specialised genres appropriate to specific aspects of life. And, across literacy, language and numeracy, there is an interplay between what is learned informally and what is taught in formal contexts.

With numeracy there has been some hesitation in viewing this area as a social practice because of the concreteness of the field of knowledge at the centre of numeracy, topics such as counting, measuring and calculation. Nevertheless, if we start from what people do in their everyday lives, it becomes clear that numeracy is a set of social practices. For instance, people have a range of ways of calculating in their everyday lives which fit different activities and which may be quite different from the ways they encounter in classrooms (see Swain et al. 2005; Coben 2006). This means that there are many varieties of language, many literacies and many numeracies, varying across contexts. The literacy and numeracy practices found in betting shops, for instance, are very different from those found in kitchens; people are reading, writing, talking, listening and using numbers for different purposes, with different technologies and with different networks of support in the two places.

Educational contexts are different again, with their own specific ways of speaking, reading, writing and working with numbers. There are many different types of educational context, varying according to what is being taught (for example biology, cake decorating, computing, plumbing, English) and how it is being taught (for example, lectures, simulated work environment, small group activities). As an example, instructions such as 'Identify the main points and ideas, and predict words from context' in the Entry Level 3 reading curriculum (Skill reference Rt/E3.4 in the Adult Literacy Core Curriculum, DfES 2001a: 15) belong to the field of education. They are often taught and tested through exercises with right and wrong answers, such as comprehension questions which involve extracting information. They often involve reading 'educational' texts chosen by the teacher, materials designer or test-maker, such as the 'jobs section' in a newspaper. Such language, literacy and numeracy practices in the classroom are quite unlike those in other contexts. Specialised educational genres and activities such as using worksheets, doing spelling tests or comprehension exercises are quite different from most people's everyday activities. The ways of interacting with such a text in the classroom may be very different from the way in which someone would interact with it for real-life purposes. In everyday life the 'jobs section' is more often scanned for particular information at the moment of needing it, maybe collaboratively with other family members. The 'skill' of reading it thoroughly and then answering comprehension questions on it is largely education-specific. Beyond this, many of the people who come to educational provision read a wide range of entirely different texts in their everyday lives from those used in class, for specific purposes; for instance, reading the weekly *Auto Trader* magazine to keep up to date with the car industry, or health leaflets at the doctor's surgery. Such classroom activities therefore require some extra work to be done by both students and teachers to enable classroom learning to be of use to people in their everyday lives.

Taking this social practices perspective on language, literacy and numeracy involves paying attention first and foremost to the contexts, purposes and practices in which language (spoken and written) and mathematical operations play a part. This is described in more detail elsewhere (for example in Barton and Hamilton 1998; Barton and Hamilton 2000; Ivanič 2004; Papen 2005; Barton 2006b; Coben 2006). This approach is quite different from other, enduring views which see literacy and numeracy primarily as consisting of sets of itemised, transferable skills. Focusing on skills narrows attention to linguistic and mathematical patterns, distinctions and rules, and to 'reading', 'writing' and 'calculating' as if these are processes which can easily be detached from their context. Perhaps the inadequacy of defining language, literacy and numeracy only as sets of skills is best summed up in a point which is fundamental to a social practice view of literacy: 'We don't just "read" and "write": we always read and write something' (Barton 1991: 8; see also Gee 2000–1). This point can be expanded to: We always read and write something, for a particular purpose, in a particular way, in a particular time and place.

Conceptualising language, literacy and numeracy in this way influences the way we carry out research, and helps us to understand and explain what we observe. In our work, we pay attention to how the activities we observe are socially shaped and socially situated, at local and broader levels. This means examining how classroom activities compare and contrast with what we know of students' practices in the rest of their lives, and identifying the views of language, literacy and numeracy which underpin the teaching practices we observe. In relation to the broader social context, we examine the influence of the institutions in which provision is located, the practices typical of that context, and the policies (local and national) within which that provision operates. The implications of this stance for the methodology we adopt are drawn out in more detail in the following two chapters In Chapter 9 we will see how teachers' views of the nature of language, literacy and numeracy underlie tensions in their professional roles when reconciling learners' agendas and policy agendas in relation to learning.

This focus on the social shaping of literacy, language and numeracy learning means that we need to draw not only on theories of language, literacy and numeracy, but also on broader social theories which offer us frameworks for understanding the social world. We now turn to these, focusing first on the approach we have developed to carrying out an analysis of people's lives in relation to learning, and then on the ideas about learning we are drawing on.

People's lives

Through the work that we have been carrying out with people over time, we have developed a framework to explore the various aspects of their lives which are significant in relation to language, literacy and numeracy learning. This framework

17

draws on and links together a range of theoretical ideas and concepts, giving us ways of talking about the social shaping of language, literacy and numeracy while keeping the individual people we have worked with at the centre. The concepts we have drawn on in developing this framework are those which reflect and help us to make sense of the significant patterns identified in our data; the framework is shaped and informed by careful study of the real lives and experiences people have shared with us.

The framework attends to four interrelated aspects of people's lives, reflecting this complexity: their histories, their current identities, their present circumstances and their imagined futures. These are four aspects which have to be taken into account in order to understand people's engagement in formal learning. People bring a particular life history, which shapes the way they engage. They bring with them everything that makes them who they are at that point in time – their current practices, identities, social and cultural capital. They are positioned within contexts, life circumstances which open up some possibilities and close down others. And they have ideas about what lies ahead for them, imagined futures which may be multiple, expansive or highly restricted, with people's expectations, hopes, aspirations and strategies for living being shaped by the other three aspects of their lives. We want to emphasise these four aspects of life: the importance of individual histories; how people have their own 'ways of being', the cluster of social, psychological and affective characteristics which make up their identities; the significance of the circumstances in which they are situated, over which they may have little control; and the importance of people's plans and how they see their future possibilities. The four aspects can be expressed in chronological terms: what has happened in people's pasts, who they are now, what is happening in their lives now, and where they may want to go.

Figure 3.1 illustrates the four aspects in a simple manner, the idea being that each person has a particular combination of practices and identities, with a history behind them and an imagined future towards which they are travelling, situated within a set of current life circumstances and events.

These should not be seen as discrete categories, but as influencing each other and as being related to the outside world. All four aspects interrelate, and all are mediated by the social and cultural contexts within which people have lived and are living. People's current practices are shaped by their life history; people's purposes and goals are influenced by their present circumstances. Different individuals' lives are shaped by such factors to different extents, and socioeconomic factors such as race, class and gender mediate the degrees of determination or freedom people experience – returning us to the issue of the relationship between structure and agency, addressed in the previous chapter. To develop understandings of the complex relationships between lives and learning, it is necessary both to hold in mind these interrelationships and shaping factors and to make an analytic distinction between the four aspects. Focusing on each in turn enables us to draw out the different influences shaping each aspect, and helps us to articulate the factors shaping engagement, participation and learning in relation to people's

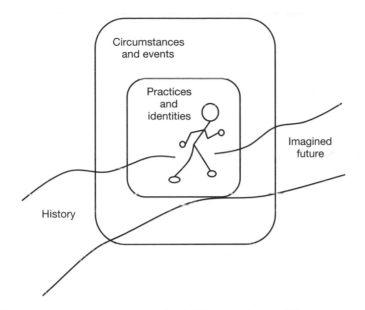

Figure 3.1 Four aspects crucial for linking learning and lives

lives, and the different possibilities, constraints, limitations and boundaries that people are dealing with.

This framework is used in later chapters to help understand people's lives. Chapters 6 and 7 are concerned with people's current practices. Chapter 8 focuses on specific people attending college courses. It analyses their history (i.e. their background), their current practices and circumstances in relation to participating in formal learning, and their imagined futures, expressed in terms of motivations. Chapter 9 examines what people bring to learning contexts: their varied motivations bring together their life histories, their current circumstances and their imagined futures. Chapter 10, which turns to people in a range of community settings, is specifically framed in terms of people's histories, practices and identities, life circumstances and imagined futures.

Theorising people's life histories

People's stories have shown us that they are shaped by and carry with them complex and unique life histories. Examining the relationship between lives and learning does not simply mean looking at what is going on in people's lives at any given moment, but also developing an understanding of 'where they are coming from'. In order to achieve this, conceptual tools are needed which can clarify the interweaving flows and layers of history which people have experienced and which are brought into play in their lives.

One way to think about this is to conceptualise people's life histories as being made up of multiple 'careers', within each of which there are important moments of 'transition'. The concept of 'career' comes from sociology. It was used by Goffman in a broad sense as 'any social strand of any person's course through life' (1961: 127). The idea has been developed in relation to young adults by Bloomer and Hodkinson examining how young people's dispositions to learning changed over time, viewing a career as 'a patterned sequence of roles that is distinguishable as a strand of any person's course through life' (Bloomer and Hodkinson 2000; see also Hodkinson and Sparkes 1997; Merrill 2004).

This is an established tradition in sociological life course studies, particularly in youth studies. Initially focusing on 'careers' in the employment sense of the word, especially the school–work transition, the notion has since been broadened to examine the interplay between other sorts of careers and other transitions. For instance, a large study of youth transitions in a disadvantaged area in north-east England (Cieslik and Simpson 2006) examined young people's school-to-work careers, family careers, housing careers, leisure careers, drug-using careers and criminal careers. They analysed the interactions between these six careers for their interviewees and the significance of points of transition within them (see also Henderson et al. 2007).

Throughout people's multiple careers, key moments of transition can be identified, such as moving in and out of a particular housing situation, or a particular relationship, getting or losing a job, or having or resolving a health crisis. In a broad study of young people's lives, Coles (1995) shows how a transition in one career can significantly impact on another; for instance, becoming homeless leading rapidly to unemployment. He also identifies key strands which influence youth transitions: access to citizenship, shaped by legislation and policy; interactions between young people, their families and professionals; and the structure of localities within which young people make choices at 'critical points'.

Attention to the key transition points of people's histories can be a very revealing way of understanding the relationships between lives and learning. This is directly relevant to language, literacy and numeracy learning and practices. As part of the study of youth transitions mentioned above, Cieslik and Simpson explored the relationships between various types of transitions and literacy, numeracy and language. They show the importance of the context, and of their own personal projects, in relation to the impact of basic skills levels on their other life transitions (Simpson and Cieslik 2007).

The notion of careers therefore gives us a way of exploring the different flows that have made up someone's history which shows the influence of structure and conditions, while also examining the importance of individuals' own actions in shaping their biographies, recalling the relationship between structure and agency discussed in the previous chapter. We utilise this analytical approach in Chapter 12.

A key concept to hold on to in relation to people's histories is the notion of 'hidden' histories. Many aspects of people's life histories and backgrounds can remain hidden – from the class tutor, the researcher, others in the class, or hidden in more general, societal terms. Such hidden histories can have a crucial impact on language, literacy and numeracy learning and practices. For instance, Horsman's work (2000) has shown how domestic and family violence can powerfully frame the possibilities for and barriers to people's learning, while often remaining completely hidden. The methodological implications of attention to 'hidden' aspects of people's histories will be explored in more depth in Chapter 5. We should stress that we are not saying that researchers or educators have a right to uncover hidden aspects of people's lives; rather, learners have the right to decide which aspects of their lives should be acknowledged and which remain confidential.

Theorising people's current practices and identities

Social practices are more than what people do. They also shape who people are, their identities and identifications. Socially shaped notions of identity and identification, such as those developed by Holland et al. (2001) combining ideas from Vygotsky, Bakhtin and Bourdieu, explore ongoing processes of identity formation in social worlds. From these perspectives, people are forming their identities as they engage in specific social practices, in an ongoing process which involves both the discipline and structure of scripted social roles, and the remarkable improvisation and creativity of the individual. Because these identities are in ongoing construction, they can change, and changing identity always involves learning in some way, since this must involve being or doing something new. This gives us a way of exploring how learning is not necessarily just about acquiring new skills or even practices, but can crucially also be about changes in people's identity and representation of self. This learning, which is integral to being and living, is a significant part of the resources that people bring into more formal learning environments and activities.

There are important relationships between the different elements of our analytic framework. With regard to the categories explored so far, people's current practices and identities are shaped by the life histories they have lived through, all the opportunities and constraints which they have experienced in their lives to date. The social practices perspective on language, literacy and numeracy, outlined above, helps us to express this in terms of people acquiring ways of doing things by virtue of the social practices they have engaged in.

A great deal of educational research has been influenced by Pierre Bourdieu's work linking structure and agency. The inter-relationship between past and present is expressed by Bourdieu in the notion of 'habitus', a broad notion which refers to a person's beliefs, dispositions and ways of being, shaped by their past histories (Bourdieu 1977; Reay 2004). This largely unconscious habitus shapes the possibilities that are perceived to be open to any individual within any given socially structured field of activity. Habitus exists in people's ideas and perceptions and it is also embodied – it is in the body, in ways of moving and holding oneself, and in one's emotions. It generates a repertoire of possible actions and also rules out some seen as being impossible. This predisposes an individual to behave in particular ways, particularly those which reproduce the social conditions within which that individual has been produced. But it does not determine those actions. It is shaped by an individual's family and class situation, but also by their own unique life history; the initial habitus acquired through early socialisation processes is constantly restructured by individuals' experiences.

Another concept developed by Bourdieu which has proved useful for us is the distinction between various forms of 'capital'. This is the idea that people accumulate different kinds of capital throughout their lives – economic capital, social capital and cultural capital – which can then be metaphorically 'spent' or 'invested' in pursuing their life projects. Social capital relates to the networks and relationships to which people have access. Cultural capital is made up of such factors as knowledges, skills, education (including qualifications) and habitus (Bourdieu 1986). Access to these different kinds of capital is differentially distributed and reinforces unequal social hierarchies. Bourdieu and Passeron (1977) show how the education system is one of the key mechanisms whereby differential amounts of cultural capital are passed on through the generations. Carrington and Luke (1997) have explored the implications of Bourdieu's notions of capital and habitus for understanding literacy education.

Extensive work by John Bynner and colleagues using cohort studies which follow people across their lives have shown correlations between basic skills and a range of variables, including employment (Bynner and Parsons 1997, 2006). They interpret this in terms of people's access to different forms of capital (Schuller et al. 2004). They also show that educational and work opportunities are very different for people born at different times. These correlational studies provide a starting point for our work in a number of ways. First, they provide hypotheses to explore in our detailed case studies in order to explain these correlations. Second, in examining people's careers and transitions, we want to move beyond dealing just with skills to understand their literacy practices. It may be that the complexity and range of their practices and their forms of engagement in practices are crucial and it is worth exploring the idea of literacy practices as a form of capital, 'literacy capital' (as in Cieslik and Simpson 2007).

The framings of habitus and capital show how people are coming into learning situations with different identities, consisting of a unique, historically and socially shaped habitus and different degrees of access to social and cultural capital. In our analysis, we identify a range of ways in which such identities and practices affect people's literacy, numeracy and language learning and practices, and identify social, cultural and economic factors which shape them.

Theorising people's present circumstances

We want to distinguish current practices and identities from the next category to be examined, that of contexts and circumstances. This third area of the diagram refers to the specific social and personal circumstances people find themselves in, and how these interact with the sorts of learning they can and do engage in at different times. These circumstances need to be considered at both local and broader levels. The immediate circumstances of their lives include such factors as their family and friendship relationships, their living situation, their employment situation, and their caring responsibilities. There are also broader circumstances – such as policy and legislative contexts, economic contexts, and unequal social structures of class, race and gender – which shape people's experiences, opportunities and possible choices. As Bartlett and Holland (2002) argue, selves – 'identities in practice' – form in relation not only to histories, but also to socially organised and historically situated spheres of activity within which practices are embedded, which they call 'figured worlds' (see also Holland et al. 2001).

In anyone's life there are factors which are not necessarily within the control of the individual and yet which have a profound influence on the choices it is possible for them to make at any given time. In our work we have observed that there are unpredictable changes in external circumstances which continually affect people's lives. Similarly, Reder's longitudinal work with literacy learners in the USA identified a pattern common to many of the learners he worked with, whereby factors changing unpredictably – health problems, difficulties with housing, relationship problems – have profound effects on people's learning. He refers to these unexpected external influences on people's lives as turbulence (Reder, forthcoming). The other commitments people are juggling and the activities which structure their days and weeks affect their capability and motivation to engage in formal learning activities. This needs to be taken into account in any studies of persistence, motivation and achievement, as our data will show. Fingeret and Drennon show that the learning journey of literacy learners itself is in 'a state of prolonged tension' (1997: 68) with 'turning points' (ibid.:73). Though this journey is in many ways empowering, it can also be costly in terms of reworking identities and practices which can impact on everyday life, such as shifting relationships with family or friends. Again, it is not merely the existence of circumstances that shapes people's engagement in learning, but crucially people's perceptions of the impact of these circumstances. These perceptions are themselves shaped by and filtered through the historically produced habitus.

Theorising people's imagined futures

The final area of focus is the futures which people imagine for themselves. People's hopes, dreams and expectations play a key role in the ways and extent to which they engage in different learning activities. We have already seen how people's histories, current practices and current circumstances are related. Part of the 'figured worlds' within which people form their identities (Bartlett and Holland 2002, as above) are the futures they imagine for themselves, which shape how they see themselves now and in turn the activities in which they engage. The notions of transitions and careers, described earlier, highlight how people's circumstances can radically change, and this too can affect the futures that they see as being possible for themselves. Learning can only have an impact on people's lives and futures if they perceive that it can do so.

All of these different factors shape people's perceptions of the possibilities they could have in the future, and therefore the way they engage in learning and the pathways they see as emerging from learning. By talking about an imagined future we can include people's specific goals and purposes, but also in a broader sense their hopes, dreams, and ambitions, conscious and unconscious. An imagined future is what people believe to be possible *for them*, and the relative range or narrowness of these perceived possibilities are socially structured. For instance, the possibilities which young people see as available to them at the end of schooling can be very different at different points in history (as the cohort studies mentioned above demonstrate). The idea of an imagined future has been used when thinking about the future of society; for example, in feminist research (such as Bhavnani et al. 2003), and within education in terms of young people's possible futures (as in Ball et al. 1999). The idea is also implicit in radical education, working towards imagined democratic possibilities. People's hopes, aspirations, plans and ideas of possibilities are left out of many models of learning, but they are in the ideas behind courses with names such as new horizons and second chance.

It is important to recognise that the concept of imagined futures incorporates the idea that for some people, the futures which they imagine may be very restricted or, alternatively, unrealistic, and that both of these perspectives can have a significant influence on how someone engages in learning. For instance, someone who has experienced a lifelong history of problems with education and who is currently living in very difficult circumstances may not be in a position to imagine any sort of long-term future, and engagement in learning may therefore seem pointless. This might lead to resistance to any sort of formal learning, or alternatively might lead to a 'compliant' attitude whereby they go along with any choice that is offered to them with little personal investment.

Learning

So far in this chapter we have described the social practices approach to conceptualising literacy, numeracy and language, explaining the importance of seeing these practices as they are situated within people's lives and contexts, but without exploring what we mean by learning. The model described above gives us a way to analyse the different aspects of people's lives, how they are shaped by one another and by social factors and contexts, and how these aspects affect their language, literacy and numeracy practices. Since a key concern of this book is with learning, it is important to also develop a theoretical understanding of what we mean when we talk about learning. This section outlines a range of different models of learning, including models of socially situated learning, models from adult education and models from applied linguistics, to situate the particular perspective we are taking on learning in the rest of the book.

There are many different models of what learning is and how it takes place (explored in more detail in Tusting and Barton 2006). These models are often framed by psychology and focus on learning as being about changes taking place within an isolated individual. More useful for us here are approaches which see learning as a socially situated phenomenon, described and understood in terms of people's ongoing participation in social contexts and interaction. These 'situated' models of learning and cognition (Rogoff and Lave 1984; Lave 1988; Gee 2004) show how learning could be seen as participation and engaging in a social process.

There is a sense in which 'doing' anything, engaging in any social practice, always means 'learning' in the broad sense. Each time someone engages in a practice, whether that practice is brand new to them or whether they have done it many times before, there is some 'learning' going on, because each time you engage in a practice, you reinforce your expertise in it, and also have the possibility to change it slightly. There are also different degrees of comfortableness in and mastery of practices, and 'learning' is about more than just being able or not being able to do something. People engage in practices in different ways. Studies of how people learn practices (Lave and Wenger 1991; Wenger 1998; Barton and Tusting 2005) have demonstrated the essentially social and participatory nature of this learning (see also Kalantzis and Cope's work, 2005, on 'learning by design').

The field of adult education has developed its own theories of learning, much of it driven by the question of whether there is something about working with adults that makes their learning processes distinctively different from those of children. Several characteristics have been identified as being distinctive to adult learning, mainly related to adults being seen as more autonomous than children, more capable of reflection, and having more life experience on which to draw. On this basis, theorists have argued that adults should be seen as being essentially self-directed learners (Candy 1991), as benefiting from reflecting on their own learning or 'learning how to learn' (Smith 1990), and as learning both inside and outside the classroom through processes of informal as well as formal learning (Coffield 2000). The way in which aspects of informality and formality are often intertwined is a key theme in this literature (Colley et al. 2003).

Adults' lives as unique sets of experiences are seen as important resources in models of reflective and experiential learning (Dewey 1933; Kolb 1984), which have become predominant in the field. In all the many theories of reflective learning reviewed in Tusting and Barton (2006), learning is seen as arising from the need to resolve a problem or an issue which people have encountered in their lives. This work relates learning to the real issues which arise for people and insists that learning is always to be understood in a broader context. Reflective learning is seen as a cyclical process, based on and driven by the complexities of each person's experience and broader situation. It is therefore both unique to each individual and socially shaped. Critical reflection on experience is particularly important in models which focus on the transformative potential of adult learning, seeing reflection on experience as the key driver of personal and social transformation (Freire 1972; Mezirow 1990).

There is also a substantial body of research in applied linguistics which provides valuable insights for understanding adult language, literacy and numeracy learning.

As it focuses on language learning, it is concerned with 'learning to' rather than 'learning that', and it pays attention to classroom interaction. In general terms, this research can be summarised as having led to a move away from attempting to identify the most effective method of teaching (after years of attempts to do just that, which consistently came up with contradictory findings) towards attempting to understand the complexity of what is involved in learning. This research has also shown that participation in learning provision can lead to a wide range of types of outcome, some of which may not be discernible until some time after the class has finished; for instance, learning 'content', learning how to learn, learning about language, learning about social relationships, reconstructing identities, and gaining wider social benefits such as increased confidence and autonomy.

This research is summarised in Ivanič and Tseng (2005) and Tseng and Ivanič (2006). They list the multiple factors which have been shown to shape learning in formal situations, including learners' and teachers' beliefs, motivations and goals; the resources learners bring with them from everyday experience; the nature of the curriculum and teaching materials; the political, institutional, socio-cultural and physical contexts; approaches to teaching; the nature of the social interaction in the classroom; and the construction of identities in classroom settings. They suggest that it is more useful to conceptualise teaching, drawing on all these resources, as 'the creation of learning opportunities', from which different learners will benefit in different ways. This conceptualisation emphasises the active role of learners in setting their own agenda, participating in class and engaging in learning opportunities on their own terms. An important conclusion for understanding classrooms is that different people will learn different things from any classroom activity, depending on their own current concerns. A clear example of this comes from Reder's study of English as a Second Language classrooms where, even when working on a worksheet designed to facilitate the learning of something very specific, different students learned quite different things (Reder 2006).

From a range of perspectives, therefore, we can see that learning needs to be conceptualised in a broad and complex fashion. Rather than seeing learning purely as an individual, cognitive phenomenon, it must be seen as involving social interaction and participation, and take into account the interrelationship of many factors in the learning situation. People's own contexts, practices and purposes drive the ways they participate and engage in learning, and therefore must be at the heart of our understanding of learning processes. In any learning situation involving different individuals, each person will bring their own unique pattern of life history, identities and practices, circumstances and imagined future, and actively draw on these resources differently in the learning setting, whether in positive or negative ways. Therefore, they will each engage with what is going on in their own way, and potentially take something different away from that engagement. Chapter 9 focuses on learning events and the collaborative negotiation of learning opportunities and documents broader outcomes of learning.

How lives and learning interact

This book focuses on the way lives and learning interact for adult literacy, numeracy and ESOL learners. We have outlined above a model of literacy, numeracy and language as social practice, showing how context and purpose are key to understanding these practices. We have developed a four-part analytic relational model to describe adults' lives and the different issues they are bringing with them to learning. We have outlined models of learning from various fields, concluding with a social model of learning as participation which recognises the importance of individuals' lives and contexts and sees critical reflection on situated experience as being central.

These reflections show that the relationship between any given learning experience and the rest of adults' lives is crucial. They also raise a range of questions. For instance, if we acknowledge the socially situated nature of literacy and numeracy practices and of learning, what does this mean for learning which takes place in classrooms? In what ways does learning in formal educational settings such as colleges and other learning environments which are 'designed for learning' (Cope and Kalantzis 2000; Kalantzis and Cope 2005) differ from learning which is integral to other practices but not the main focus, and how does it have an impact on people's lives, practices and patterns of participation outside such specialised environments? What, then, are the implications of the significant differences between people's lives, which we have found, in terms of what they learn in a given learning setting, and what is the impact of that learning?

The rest of this book explores these issues in more depth, in relation to the lives of the many adult literacy, numeracy and ESOL students who participated in the research. We will be looking at which aspects of their experience in formal learning situations have been meaningful or useful for people, and which have not. In Chapters 10 and 11 we explore the effects of the different issues and experiences people bring with them on the learning they engage with and, in turn, the effects of that learning. We show the importance of learning being related to social practices that people are engaged in, would like to be engaged in, and care about. We demonstrate the importance of looking at the wider benefits of engaging in learning such as the development of confidence, effects on health and participation in civic life (Schuller et al. 2004). We show the key role of people's identification with, interest in, and desire to participate in particular communities and practices. In Chapter 13 we draw out the implications of this for teaching.

We draw on a rich, complex dataset, gathered over a significant period of time by means of building up relationships with people. Before we go on to explore this data, we now turn to describing the sites where we worked, and then the methods that we used to develop this data, and their methodological rationale.

4

SITUATING ADULT LEARNERS' LIVES

Everyone has a local experience which shapes the possibilities and constraints which they act within. The adults that we worked with came from many backgrounds and had many and varied life experiences. They lived in different communities. They had different experiences of family, health, work and education. People came with different histories and encountered different circumstances. Some had never left the locality they were born in whilst others had travelled considerable distances to form a new life in a new area or country. Some had a sense of permanence in relation to where they lived, whilst others saw their situation as temporary. Others, such as asylum seekers, were experiencing dislocation and disenfranchisement in the locality, unable to share the same rights and access to educational and other provision as most local citizens. Some people were living where they were as a result of patterns of immigration and settlement in the 1960s in response to employment opportunities in specific industries. Where these industries later collapsed, as with the mills in Blackburn, the restricted opportunities available to these people related to the particular places where they were living.

The people we worked with were all involved in some way with educational provision associated with the government's Skills for Life policy initiative. In terms of education, there are national policies, but what is available in a particular place is also related to the history of the place and to factors such as the size of a town. People's experience of a government initiative is mediated by its enactment in a specific situation. In this chapter we situate the people and the research, linking people with the places they live, work and learn in. We describe the research sites and the overall range of people we worked with.

Places, and the spaces that people occupy within them, shape everyday experience and sense of self. People both identify with and are identified by places. People are physically situated within time and place, historically and currently, something which is often central to identity and a sense of belonging. For example, being a 'Scouser' from Liverpool brings a particular history that is rooted in the Mersey River and the docks; both are still an enduring physical presence as well as being embedded in generations of working cultures and practices. Landmarks, phrases, local foods, schools, breweries, football teams and music traditions all contribute to a sense of the local. Local is something that makes an area particular, intimate and known and can include others who associate with the same geographical space and practices connected to it. It can be an important unifying aspect of individuals, of everyday experience and sense making. At the same time it can be something which emphasises difference and which people feel excluded or dislocated from. In this way it acts to create people who are viewed as outsiders and for whom a sense of local is one of being different from others around them. We were interested in how people used language, literacy and numeracy in their everyday lives and how local interests and practices shaped this.

Research sites

The research was located in three different cities in north-west England: Lancaster, Blackburn and Liverpool. They were chosen as being different enough from each other to provide populations of different size, composition and backgrounds. Each has a different economic and social base and each has a different history and identity. Lancaster was selected because it is a small geographically independent city surrounded by rural areas. It is the smallest and least 'deprived' of the three case study areas. Blackburn was chosen as it has a high minority ethnic population and has felt the impact of recent refugee and asylum seekers' dispersal policies. It is connected to the large industrial and manufacturing conurbation of the northwest region. Liverpool was chosen as a major British city which has experienced socioeconomic decline and regeneration. The city has many different communities established throughout its history as a major seafaring port. There were also practical issues underlying our choice: we had carried out related research in Lancaster and Blackburn before (e.g. Barton and Hamilton 1998; Martin-Jones et al. 1993) and between us we had experience of living and teaching in these two cities. We had connections with adult educators in Liverpool which meant it was fairly straightforward to get permission to carry out research in the colleges there.

Lancaster is a small city in north-west England within the county of Lancashire. At the 2001 Census, the urban area of Lancaster was recorded as having a population of 47,000, or 134,000 if the neighbouring town of Morecambe and rural areas are included (see www.lancaster.gov.uk for statistics). The population is growing at a significantly higher rate than other places in the region. Lancaster is generally regarded as a fairly pleasant place to live, offering a relatively high quality of life. According to Home Office statistics Lancaster's levels of reported crime are much lower than the national average. However, these overall statistics mask the existence of pockets of severe deprivation, primarily in areas north of the river dividing the city, which include large council housing estates. Several of these wards feature in the worst 10 per cent for unemployment levels in Britain. This geographical and economic inequality characterises Lancaster, particularly if the neighbouring town of Morecambe is considered.

Lancaster is a university town with 18,000 students living in the area. The dominant employment sector is the service industry and percentages of people working in both health and education are higher than the regional and national averages. The area's traditional employment fields of manufacturing in Lancaster and tourism in Morecambe have declined in the past fifty years, and the rural economy in surrounding areas is also under significant strain.

Lancaster has a minority ethnic distribution close to the regional average and has the feel of a fairly cosmopolitan city for a town of its size, partly because of the international student population attracted by the university. A significant proportion of the English Language provision at the local adult college is related to this, catering for spouses of people studying or working at the university, or for people studying for English language tests with the aim of entering university. Other groups in ESOL classes are people from Lancaster's established community of people of South Asian heritage and people of Chinese backgrounds working in the catering business.

While overall educational performance and work-related training and attainment are on a par with the national average, this is skewed by the existence of large higher education institutions. The large number of university students masks the existence of areas and sectors where educational and training achievements are below average.

Blackburn, with a population of over 140,000, is part of the Blackburn and Darwen Unitary Authority, within the county of Lancashire. The industrial revolution brought momentous changes to Blackburn and at the end of the nineteenth century it had become the cotton weaving capital of the world. During the latter part of the twentieth century the textile industry went into a rapid decline causing mass unemployment, the effect of which is still felt today. The majority of the borough's population is from a white ethnic group (77.9 per cent). There has been, in response initially to the Government's recruitment drives in the 1960s for the textile and service industries, a growing population of residents of Indian and Pakistani origin; a fifth of residents are from Asian ethnic groups (20.9 per cent). Football was and is still a popular recreation. There is a rich music and arts heritage and community arts programmes. The annual multicultural 'Mela' event is the largest of its kind in the region.

Indices of deprivation in 2004 highlighted Blackburn with Darwen's position as one of the most deprived boroughs in north-west England and unemployment levels were high. Rates of long-term illness, infant mortality and mental illness were some of the highest in the north-west and nationally and there was a lower life expectancy than the national average. The Government's more recent dispersal policy led to an increasing number of people seeking asylum and refugee status living in Blackburn; at the time of writing there were approximately 800 people from a wide range of countries. The 2001 Census highlighted that over a third of residents of Blackburn aged 16 to 74 did not have any qualifications, a higher proportion than the national average. School exclusions in the borough are well above the national average and a high proportion of school pupils have statements of educational need.

Liverpool, situated on the mouth of the River Mersey, is a vibrant city of just under half a million people containing many diverse and multicultural communities. It has a proud history and identity as a flourishing and significant passenger and mercantile port. Most of the large North Atlantic passenger liners docked at Liverpool and the huge dockland handled a significant amount of British cargo, anything from bananas to coal. Sailors and ship workers from many countries settled over the years and developed the diverse communities that exist today. The Albert Dock, now a heritage site, is a testament to this history as Napoleonic French prisoners of war built it and today it houses the Maritime Museum with its transatlantic slavery display. Liverpool has been a denominationally divided city with imposing Anglican and Catholic cathedrals overlooking the city and river. The city experienced social unrest resulting in the Toxteth Riots in the 1970s which were attributed to large-scale unemployment and the decline of the dockland communities (Lane 1987).

In recent years Liverpool has seen considerable urban regeneration that has included the waterfront and dockland area. New offices, houses and community buildings have revitalised previously derelict dockland areas and areas of substandard housing. This has had a positive impact on the economic success, fabric and confidence of the city. This re-emerging confidence culminated in Liverpool's successful bid to be European City of Culture in 2008. Although there is much evidence of regeneration, there are many socioeconomic indicators that show Liverpool's continuing underlying problems with higher than average unemployment, below average health and low educational attainment. The loss of employment in manufacturing and the docklands means that unemployment rates in Liverpool are almost twice the national average. Liverpool has proportionally higher Black and Chinese populations than for the North West region as a whole. Other ethnic groups in Liverpool communities include Indian, Pakistani, Bangladeshi and other Asian ethnicities.

These three places represent three contrasting locations in contemporary England and these descriptions are intended to act as reference points when understanding the dynamics of other places. Ideally we would have included a rural location as a fourth site where the dynamics of life possibilities and educational provision are different and could be contrasted with the three areas we worked in.

Working in colleges

The first phase of the research was carried out in college classrooms. We felt that starting in the classroom was an important first step in gaining access to learners, getting to know them in this context and then being able to move from this formal educational setting to their everyday lives. Our access in each area was mediated through local advocates and with their help we responded to the type of provision offered and to the physical constraints of fieldwork. We worked in more detail and often collaboratively with practitioner researchers in their classrooms.

Lancaster has two providers of adult education: a Further Education college situated between Lancaster and Morecambe which caters for 16–19 year olds as well as adults, and the Adult College, a small community college near the centre of Lancaster dedicated to adult education. The two institutions have distinctive local identities, with the FE college being seen as catering more for school-leavers and young people offering vocational courses and A-levels, and the Adult College as offering adult education, leisure and Skills for Life classes to older people. However, there is overlap between the colleges' activities; the majority of students at the FE college are over 19, and the college also offers Skills for Life provision.

The Adult College has a central site in a converted factory building in Lancaster. It also offers courses in more than fifty community locations across North Lancashire. Skills for Life is one of the Adult College's principal programme areas, along with a wide range of general adult education activities on a part-time basis, including Access to Higher Education courses, Counselling, Family Learning, General Studies, ICT, Modern Foreign Languages, Teacher Training and Visual and Performing Arts. It also offers some National Vocational Qualifications in partnership with local employers.

We worked in the Skills for Life department at the Adult College, which provides part-time courses from pre-Entry Level to Level 2 in literacy, numeracy and ESOL. Most courses take place once a week at the Adult College central site, with some provision in community venues across North Lancashire. All the Skills for Life provision was organised on a 'roll-on, roll-off' basis, meaning that students can register at any time of the year, although there was pressure at the time of the project to move towards a termly registration structure.

The college has a reasonably stable population of learners, some who have attended Entry-Level classes for years whilst others pass through onto other courses including pre-GCSE and GCSE classes. Four classes were observed on a weekly basis. These included an ESOL workshop, an English class, an evening spelling class and a maths class. Both the English class and the spelling class consisted mainly of individual tuition supported by volunteers, with the English and maths class also including time for group work. The ESOL workshop used a workshop format, with students sitting at separate tables working on their own or with volunteers.

Blackburn College is a large general college offering a wide range of further and higher education. It is situated in the centre of Blackburn, with over fifty community venues spread across the borough. The college had over 30,000 students at the time of the research and a total budget of £32 million per year. The college curriculum includes courses at all levels from pre-entry to undergraduate and postgraduate degrees. Some 31 per cent of students aged 16 to 18 and 13 per cent of adults studying at the college are from minority ethnic backgrounds.

The college provides a very wide range of literacy and numeracy courses from pre-Entry Level to Level 2. There are discrete courses for adults, learning support embedded within vocational courses, and separate support lessons. There were around 220 adults on discrete literacy courses and 120 adults on numeracy courses, and many more following other courses receive literacy support within their courses. There were over 600 students on ESOL courses. The majority were from the established South Asian ethnic community. Additionally, the recent dispersal policy meant that there were now over 100 asylum seekers from twenty-three different countries. Most courses were based at the college's main site with some held at outreach centres around the local area. Courses were offered at all levels, with most provision being at Entry Level 1 (beginners). Some courses include ICT and there was a work-based programme for learners with a language need. ESOL was also offered as language support within mainstream provision as well as on a one-to-one basis.

In Blackburn College we worked in ESOL classes. Students were mainly recruited at the beginning of the year but could also join if there were vacant places throughout the year. Classes followed a systematic modular syllabus based on the ESOL national curriculum and teachers were encouraged to supplement this by responding to the needs of students in their group. Assessment was rigorous with tests being carried out in formal test conditions; these were added to a portfolio of evidence of skills in speaking, listening, reading and writing. Students came from many different countries and language backgrounds including Angola, Rwanda, Congo, Afghanistan, Hong Kong, Bangladesh, Colombia and Iraq. Some had been in the UK for a while whilst others were refugees and asylum seekers.

Liverpool Community College has three main city centre sites and much of its provision is delivered in over twenty Drop-in Study Centres (DISCs) located in local venues such as libraries or community buildings throughout the city. Overall there were 27,000 students at the time of the research, of whom 22,000 were adult learners and 4,000 aged 14–19. We worked in two DISCs. They offered drop-in classes in literacy, numeracy and IT, often with several classes running in the same space. The two DISCs we worked in appeared to be warm and welcoming places where students seemed to be quite at home. Two classes, one maths and one spelling, were observed on regular weekly basis. This was interspersed with other visits for interviews and working with learners on videoing their class. The maths class consisted of a small group who worked individually with the tutor on worksheets. The tutor skilfully negotiated the content of the worksheet with each individual and then used this as a tool to connect 'maths problems' with what people did in the everyday lives. In the spelling class the tutor used mainly whole-group teaching, often using a flipchart, supported by individual and paired work. Volunteers were not used in the DISCs.

Working in other settings

In the second phase of the research we worked in community provision where literacy and numeracy support was being offered in a variety of different ways. Research participants in all these settings were from social groups which were defined as 'priority groups' in the Skills for Life strategy. We invested a great deal of time building up good relations with people in these sites, explaining our approach to research and negotiating how we would carry it out. This enabled a degree of trust to be established which is crucial for successful research relationships, particularly with organisations who support young people and adults who are vulnerable and on the margins of society in terms of access to educational provision. We gradually got to know each of the research sites and the different ways that language, literacy and numeracy were being taught in them. This was less obvious than in the college classrooms where we had begun the research, as the provision was often hidden or embedded in other services or support provided. We talked to and interviewed managers, tutors and learners as well as observing and taking part in activities as participant observers.

In Lancaster we worked with a drug and alcohol support centre which we will refer to as Pandion Hall. This centre offers one-to-one support as well as group-based and structured learning. Pandion catered for people on court-imposed drug treatment and testing orders which obliged them to have regular structured support, and for people referred by other local agencies dealing with drug and alcohol issues. Support offered included relapse prevention and harm minimisation support groups, complementary therapies and educational courses provided by tutors from the Adult College. Educational activities included literacy, communications and IT, music technology and art, as well as distance literacy and numeracy courses delivered through visits from the staff of the local Learndirect centre. (Learndirect is a government funded network of online learning centres.) The courses on offer had been selected to be of interest to people attending the centre.

In Blackburn we worked with Safeplace, a shelter for young homeless people. Safeplace is a local independent voluntary charity providing emergency night shelter, a longer-term hostel and accommodation as well as an associated day centre. The centre is funded through a mixture of Government, Local Authority and charity funding. Safeplace, in collaboration with other local agencies, has worked with over 4,000 young people in Blackburn over the last fourteen years. Although catering for local needs, the day centre was in the process of changing in response to national funding requirements from being a drop-in centre and safe house with informal education to being an activity-based centre. This meant a more directed and structured approach to learning was being implemented. Changes in the funding available to the centre were resulting in changes in what activities they could put on. Literacy and numeracy teaching was being embedded within activities such as DIY, rock climbing and creativity.

In Liverpool we worked with three organisations which had less formal provision: Big Issue, an organisation for homeless people; Midway Tenants' Association; and Emerge, a domestic violence support group. Big Issue is well known in Britain as an organisation which enables homeless people to earn an income by selling a magazine on the streets. It also offers a range of services for homeless people including accommodation, drug and alcohol support services and a range of educational opportunities. In Liverpool, education was offered in the learning centre based in the main building, at a nearby community college and in various local venues.

Previous funding had enabled the organisation to develop a range of flexible courses that responded to what they described as a 'floating population' who might complete a course over several years with a number of gaps in between. The introduction of the Skills for Life funding was experienced as limiting the organisation's choices to providing discrete literacy and numeracy courses that had to be completed within a tighter time frame. An important issue for the organisation was that of finding tutors who were qualified literacy and numeracy tutors as well as being experienced in working with homeless people. A local police crackdown on homeless people suspected of being drug dealers had also created difficulties as many people were keeping a lower profile or had left the area.

The Midway Tenants' Association is located on an estate near the docks in Liverpool and is run by volunteers. The association supports people on the estate with practical tasks such as sorting out rent problems or reporting anti-social behaviour, as well as encouraging people to participate in literacy, numeracy and IT courses. The office, housed in a ground floor flat, offers IT courses and free internet access to encourage people who would not attend college or other types of formal provision to participate in structured learning opportunities and to gain confidence. They provide information about local courses and support people to get to these courses. The Emerge domestic violence support group also works out in the community offering both some learning opportunities itself and support for those trying to attend college. It is housed in a church hall in the centre of a large estate on the outskirts of Liverpool, a place that has experienced a great deal of poverty and social isolation. The organisation, run by local volunteers, is committed to supporting women who have experienced domestic violence by providing safety and new opportunities, including learning.

The educational provision in these quite different sites ranged from being educational programmes provided by college-based specialists, through to informal learning by participation in the activities of the organisation. The aim was to have a set of contrasting sites in terms of learners and in terms of forms of provision. To summarise the sites, from the most formal to the least formal, these were:

- *Pandion Hall in Lancaster,* a drug and alcohol support centre which offered clients both one-to-one support and a group Structured Day Programme.
- *The Big Issue in Liverpool,* an organisation for the homeless which offered educational provision including literacy, numeracy and IT.
- *Safeplace in Blackburn,* a shelter for young homeless people, and an associated day centre which had always offered informal educational provision on a needs-driven basis.
- *Midway Tenants' Association in Liverpool,* run by volunteers, which supported people, both through participation in the association's everyday activities, and through attending college programmes where appropriate.
- *Emerge, a domestic violence support group in Liverpool,* which as part of its activities supported women's attendance at college and other courses.

Some of the data in later chapters are also taken from an Entry to Employment programme (known as E2E) put on by a private provider in Blackburn in a purpose-built suite of classrooms. This is a government-funded programme primarily for 16–18 year olds which mixes basic skills, vocational work and personal and social development. It aims to prepare young people for work. This falls between being a college site and a community site and in many ways the site we worked in had the atmosphere of a workplace (see Hodge 2005). We also draw upon data from a workplace-based Skills for Life and computing class.

Local lives and responsive research

In each of these sites, nationally occurring social issues such as homelessness, drug and alcohol use, violence and housing were responded to in a local context. For example, Pandion Hall made support and learning available for drug and alcohol users in Lancaster using local resources. In a similar way, Safeplace was a local response to the most disenfranchised young homeless people in Blackburn, who were rejected by other local provision with tighter entry criteria based on records of past behaviour. In Liverpool, Big Issue's work was negatively affected by local policing policy, which attempted to 'clean the streets' of drugs by focusing on homeless people. Both the tenants' association and the domestic violence support organisation depended on local knowledge and local networks to carry out their work.

For each of these organisations working with vulnerable people, often with complex and turbulent lives, support relies upon local knowledge and awareness of what issues are important individually and within a community, historically, currently and in the future. Each organisation is responsive to local contexts whilst being part of larger scale social or education policy initiatives. National policy is mediated through local networks, local organisations and crucially impacts upon individual lives; lives that are situated and bounded by local communities even if this is experienced as being outside of them. To understand literacy practices as socially situated means that we need to understand what this means in people's lives and how this is experienced as local and temporal.

All the organisations were part of a changing environment where literacy and numeracy had recently become higher profile. This meant that money became available to them through Skills for Life funding, but also that their educational provision was scrutinised more closely and so they had to respond and change what they offered. It is also important to stress that although they counted as part of the Skills for Life priority groups, the range of knowledge and abilities people demonstrated in terms of literacy and numeracy was quite broad. We want to show this range and variety and, as stated earlier, to point out that many of the people in these sites were not at some 'basic' level of literacy and numeracy.

What people experience locally is also connected to, and is directly shaped by regional, national and international events and policies. For example, as a result of policy related to a widening skills agenda, even small charities such as Safeplace needed to provide evidence of more formal educational initiatives in order to secure further funding. National policy, however, is also interpreted and situated regionally and locally. Its implementation responds to human resources, perceived needs, target allocation and money available regionally and locally; there is interplay between national, regional and local concerns. These factors shape what provision is available, where it is located and the extent to which it is part of formal educational opportunities.

In each of these places there was a different range of possibilities available to people. For instance, in Lancaster formal educational provision was offered by the adult college near the centre of town and in the local further education college, a short bus ride away. The colleges offered on-site courses, as well as putting on courses such as family learning in local community sites, and working in the prison and in the Young Offenders Institution. There were also other providers such as the YMCA and the WEA. Other organisations signposted the existence of language, literacy and numeracy courses, such as Job Centre Plus, a government agency designed to move people from welfare to work, and the Connexions service, a national government-funded advice and guidance service for young people, designed to help them make and manage educational and training choices. Others such as the Traveller Education Service and the Community Learning Network project focused on particular groups and areas in making available accessible provision responsive to people's local needs and circumstances. Further information about particular cities can be found in reports of local mapping of provision carried out by practitioners (Burgess 2004 for Lancaster; Kennedy and Crosby 2004 for Liverpool).

These then are the research sites within the three cities in north-west England where we carried out the research and which are intended to act as reference points for understanding other places. We now turn to details of the research methodology.

5

A COLLABORATIVE AND RESPONSIVE METHODOLOGY

In order to address the research questions outlined in Chapter 1, we need a methodology which takes account of the complexity of people's lives and which enables us to build up a picture of people's lives in relation to the learning of literacy, numeracy and language. Our approach is to get as close as possible to the detail of people's lives, drawing on qualitative social science research methodology (Denzin and Lincoln 2005; Silverman 2001, 2005) and in particular ethnographic approaches to understanding social phenomena.

An ethnographic approach involves detailed, local study of people's practices, where the researcher spends time in particular communities and uses a variety of methods to develop a rich and complex picture of their lives (Atkinson and Hammersley 1994; Green and Bloome 1997; Hymes 1996; Rampton et al. 2004; Tusting and Barton 2005). Ethnographic research seeks to understand the meaning in participants' practices from their own perspectives. It looks for patterns and systematicity in situated practice across cases, but also remains sensitive to the uniqueness and distinctiveness of each setting. These local understandings are situated in their relation to broader social structures and processes, which can highlight significant differences between people's own perspectives and the official discourses, assumptions and definitions which relate to them. Ethnographic work responds to the unpredictable realities of each situation, working with initial 'sensitising concepts' rather than closing down the research design from the outset. As Strathern puts it, there is 'no other way . . . of grasping what the ethnographic method grasps, namely how to make room for the unpredictable' (2000: 286).

Theory, data and interpretation feed into each other as the research continues. Ethnographic representations attempt to produce a holistic picture of the complexity of the situation through writing and other means, while recognising that lived experience is never reducible to any representation of it. Finally, ethnographic researchers always attempt to remain sensitive to their own role as participants in the research, constraining their idiosyncrasies with systematic fieldwork strategies, but also recognising the importance of their own positioning and resources in understanding and interpreting the data. It is therefore essential to make explicit our theoretical position and how this shapes our research principles and our overall methodology as well as the specific methods used in the research. It is crucial to explain how we generated the data in order for readers to understand what the data represents, and any claims we make from it.

To draw upon the richness and complexity of people's lives and social practices we used many tools common in qualitative research. These included participant observation with detailed field notes; in-depth and repeated interviews, both structured and unstructured; case studies which focused on particular issues in detail and over time; photography and video – recording people's practices and working with people to record their own; collecting images and documents, as well as examples of free writing, poems and rap. In short we used a qualitative multi-method approach. This enabled us to gather different types of data and allowed us to see complexity, multiple values, different positions, opposing perceptions, and different identities in different contexts. It allowed for shared meaning making and shared knowledge production that depended on participation built through dialogue and the establishment of research relationships.

In this chapter we draw attention to two particular aspects of this approach: that it is collaborative and that it is responsive. We see these as basic principles of a methodology of situated practice, for reasons related both to the validity of the research and to its ethical stance. To study situated practice entails not only understanding what is going on, but also explaining the meanings of what is involved for those engaging in the practice. This cannot be achieved without collaboration with research participants. In addition, each instance of situated practice is unique in its complexity, so pre-planning of research can only take you so far. Responsiveness to the realities of the situation as they are encountered is essential if the realities of the practice are to be reflected in the research. Finally, from an ethical perspective, working collaboratively with participants and responding to their needs and perspectives is at the heart of a person-respecting approach to social scientific research. The relationship between researcher and participants is key if research is to be not just ethically conducted, but potentially empowering for participants (Cameron et al. 1992). Using four examples from our research we illustrate how being collaborative and being responsive worked out with different people in different contexts.

A collaborative methodology

A collaborative way of working acknowledges that knowledge does not exist in one place or with one person simply to be discovered. There are differing knowledges that are partial, contingent and situated. The examples given later in this chapter show the potential for situated practice research to uncover different perspectives and deeper meanings through shared meaning making in co-research and collaboration.

Research itself is a practice that is situated in the lives of all those involved. It is not a disembodied, or situation-less action, which produces untainted 'universal knowledge' of people's lives. It is co-constructed, negotiated, dynamic and partial.

The researcher is always a part of the research that is taking place. A reflexive awareness and analysis of the effects of this needs to be systematically integrated at each stage of the research, from design through analysis to writing (Davies 1999).

A collaborative approach which recognises this situatedness opens the process up to include many active participants who can be both contributors and beneficiaries (as for example in the Adult ESL research carried out by Auerbach et al. 1996). This collaboration runs throughout the research process, from the early stages of planning the research, gaining access and establishing collaborative research relationships in the field, right through to on-going analysis, dissemination and writing up.

Within this approach, practitioner research is an important element as it acknowledges, draws on and makes available the experiences, resources and understandings of those directly situated in the area of study. Practitioner research, built upon collaboration, dialogue and critical inquiry, can produce research that is reflective and recognises and develops existing practitioner knowledges (Cochran-Smith and Lytle 1993). It ensures the research will be grounded, relevant and useful to the situation that is being researched, thus closing the gap between research and practice within the production of knowledge (Middlewood et al. 1999). It blurs the distinction between researchers and researched and enables different roles at different times. (See Hamilton and Wilson 2005 for accounts of a range of practitioner-researcher projects. Belfiore et al. 2004 present a range of interlinked workplace literacy research projects and a reflective conversation around the authors' experience of collaborative practitioner research.)

A collaborative approach has the potential to create a shared view, rather than one solely authored by the researchers, which allows for reflection, verification and elaboration. For instance, in each site initial analysis and reports were taken back and discussed with research participants, including learners and practitioners, for their comments and responses, which fed back into later versions. This multi-voiced approach helped test the local validity of the research and its findings and enabled participants to develop their own practices in response to their engagement with the research.

A responsive methodology

There is, of course, a sense in which all research is 'responsive'. By a responsive methodology here, we mean that we developed a flexible approach to researching the sites in which we worked. While we addressed the same broad research questions in each site, the means we used to do so varied in ways appropriate to the settings concerned. As appropriate in an ethnographic approach as described above, we adapted our research methods flexibly, in response to the realities we encountered in the field.

In our research we wanted to know about people's practices – both in their everyday lives and in the classes they attended. We looked at different types of learning provision and learning opportunities as well as how people used literacy, numeracy and language in their everyday lives. Whilst the focus of the research was the same, the way that we carried it out was different in each site. Because the people and the provision we were studying were situated locally we had to respond to this, accounting for differences in time and place. Each college was organised differently and each class we worked in was set up quite differently; to address the same research question in each site, different methods were necessary in the different settings. The ESOL classes in Blackburn, and the people who attended, were different to the people who attended the English class in Lancaster. Some of the people in the Blackburn class were dealing with recent experiences of displacement and violence as well as current racism in their lives whilst many of the learners in the Lancaster classes had been attending classes in a stable environment for several years. This was also different to the Liverpool classes which provided localised drop-in learning opportunities. Being responsive to particular situations was essential in the community sites. These sites varied greatly and most involved vulnerable learners. Access and successful conduct of the research depended on sensitivity to participants' realities and situations.

People's lives are multifaceted, changeable and complex. To capture some of this we had to be able to respond to individuals and their lives in a variety of ways, developing a range of flexible methods that could be used and adapted to a variety of contexts. Examples of this are the order in which we undertook different forms of data collection, such as whether participant observations came before or after in-depth interviews, or the degree of structure to an interview, or whether or not data was audio recorded. These varied across different sites and with different people.

Crucially, the research was responsive to the interests and needs of practitioners and other participants. So, for instance, in the colleges the research had to be seen to be of some use to the college management, to the class teachers and to the students. During the course of the research we were also able to be responsive to opportunities which arose to involve other people and to initiate smaller sub-projects. Particular methods were selected, added to and abandoned as circumstances indicated. In many cases several different methods were used together or sequentially to collect information. Some were formally set up in advance, such as a video project and a photography project, whilst others were more responsive as the situation or circumstance changed. The approach can be summarised as: to be flexible, responsive, reciprocal and respectful of people and the circumstances of their lives, whilst at the same time remaining focused on the overarching research questions.

Collaborative research in practice

We now provide some examples to illustrate some of the different ways in which we worked collaboratively, responding to the diverse contexts in which we were carrying out research and to the life histories of the people we were researching. The first two examples cover working with adults in different learning environments. We begin with an example of working with an individual within one of the research settings, describing how a researcher worked one to one with Suzanne who was attending a domestic violence support group. In the second example we discuss working with a group of young people attending a day centre for young homeless people. We then move on to two examples of working closely with practitioners in colleges, demonstrating how they can participate in research contributing their situated knowledge and understanding. In one example we discuss the practitioner research of a maths teacher, Kay, showing the significance of practitioner research and inquiry in generating new insights located in practice. In the final example we discuss working collaboratively with a language teacher, Wynne, who provided access and support in the classroom as well as helping with emerging and ongoing analysis.

Example 1: Working one to one over time

Our first example here shows working one to one using a range of methods which include life history, participant observation, repeated interviews, telephone contact, home visits and field notes.

We worked with Suzanne for over two years, a white 41-year-old woman who lived with her small daughter. She had found many strategies for managing to live independently in a small community near the city centre, despite many difficulties she has experienced in her life. She grew up in a large, poor, sometimes violent family. Following this she experienced a violent marriage and many obstacles to her attempts at learning. Fearing for her daughter's safety, Suzanne left her husband and with the help of a local domestic violence support group, which we will refer to as Emerge, had been living independently for two years. Struggling to manage sole parenting and a home with difficulties reading and writing and limited support networks, Suzanne attended several types of learning provision supported by members of Emerge. She attended an assertiveness training course and an art workshop where her daughter was looked after in the crèche. This was her first experience of formal learning since leaving school at 15 years of age.

We had already established good links with Emerge and had carried out a practitioner research project there (Ivanič et al. 2004). The management group of Emerge were positive about Suzanne becoming involved in the research as they felt it would help them understand how they could support women's learning better. They felt this careful approach was ethically important, as many women who have experienced domestic violence are frequently subjects of a variety of external and often negative 'professional gazes'. They did not want the research to add to any feeling of surveillance in the women's lives.

In the assertiveness class Suzanne struggled with the written content of the course and this experience left her feeling inadequate and confirmed for her that she was 'stupid'. A turning point came when she met Jenny Horsman (www.jenny horsman.com), the Canadian writer, educator and activist whose work was mentioned in Chapter 3. This meeting had been organised by us as part of the reciprocal relationship within the research, which provided a way of bringing together practitioners, researchers and activists working in this area. Attending this meeting directly inspired Suzanne to tell her story and when the class terminated Suzanne agreed to continue meeting to do this. This was something she had been unable to do herself and for the first time in her life she was able to record her experiences. She also hoped that by putting her story on Emerge's website other women might learn from her experience.

We discussed issues of safety, ownership and ethics, as for Suzanne this was potentially a life threatening issue. She was comfortable that the conversations were recorded, chose a pseudonym, and we discussed carefully what informed consent meant. This was particularly important, as the data was part of a research study where findings would be widely disseminated nationally. Also, professionals had written many reports and official texts about Suzanne: these were texts which she had no access to, no ownership of, and was unable to read herself. Violence is part of everyday experience and by recognising this we wanted to include it within our research and examine the ways this often invisible aspect of people's lives affects their learning.

Suzanne recorded her story over an eighteen-month period between March 2004 and September 2005, meeting at Emerge at the beginning, and later at her home. As Suzanne's story unfolded she described her experiences of violence, both as a child and as an adult, and how being unable to read and write related to this. Suzanne explained the control her husband had exerted over her because she couldn't do bills or read household information. She had no independence and was socially isolated. She described the difficulties she experienced after leaving him. Living independently she worried that she might give her daughter food poisoning, as she couldn't read the instructions on food packets, and that she was unable to manage her money. She also felt under surveillance from what she referred to as 'the authorities' (social workers, lawyers and Sure Start workers) who she thought would equate her problems with reading and writing with lack of enough parenting skills to bring her daughter up adequately. She was able to show us copies of documents and describe in detail the textually mediated bureaucratic systems through her own, almost always, negative experience of them.

At her home Suzanne described the literacy practices she used and was developing for herself. This included a system she operated with a volunteer for keeping appointments on a simple calendar, food shopping based on brand and content recognition, using a cash card to save handling cash and having legal documents read by an Emerge advocate. In addition Suzanne was teaching herself, and her daughter, simple words from the junk mail that came through her door, recognising words such as 'Pizza' from the leaflet picture and television adverts. She had also bought a computer so that she could learn and practise at home. Although she was able to use and develop some literacy and numeracy skills she knew that she needed to learn more to be able to get paid work. She described the difficulties she encountered in her attempts to learn literacy skills, where her experiences of violence were not acknowledged, and in the assertiveness class, that acknowledged the violence in her life, but was unable to support her literacy needs.

As well as improving her literacy and numeracy Suzanne wanted to gain more confidence and social skills, attributes she lacked because of her isolation. Being involved in the research increased her confidence to such a degree that, supported by one of the Emerge workers, Suzanne gave a short speech at the organisation's launch attended by nearly eighty people. This speech was tape recorded as part of our 'data' from a wobbly pub table and the field notes from the event recorded Suzanne joining in the belly dancing that followed. Having built a research relationship that was valued by her, and the organisation, it led to an invitation to attend, join in and record her achievements, in what was a very new public context for her. It was possible, from this, to give her the script of her first public speech and celebrate her first belly dance!

Through keeping in touch by phone and the occasional visit, Suzanne continued to contribute to the research by describing how she has learned new skills and attempted, so far unsuccessfully, to find work. She says that she valued being part of the research and participating in a research relationship that helped her record her story. This story is now on Emerge's website.

Example 2: Research with a group of homeless young people

Our second example illustrates how working in a group setting, particularly with vulnerable young people, required us to take account of the young people and the situation they were in. It demanded careful negotiation with the organisation that provided support to produce research that reflected the lives of the young people but that did not negatively reflect on the work of the organisation, affecting any future funding.

We worked with a group of young homeless people. To do this we used a range of methods that included field notes, one to one and group interviews, working with photos and images, participant observation, interviews and collecting materials. We carried out the research with these young people at the day centre of Safeplace, over a six month period. This was at a time when, in response to funding requirements related to education and progression, the learning environment and culture was changing from an informal 'drop-in' centre with integrated learning moving towards a more structured, evidence-based approach to learning activities with measurable outcomes. The research aimed to explore the impact of this shift on young people's participation in formal learning opportunities, a matter of great concern to the management. The research was responsive and collaborative in that all research activities were negotiated with participants. Managers, staff and young people carried out some of their own research in a photography project.

As a result of the challenges they had faced in life, these young people's trust had to be earned. Time was needed to get to know each other, build up friendly relationships and learn how to be with each other. Working in this careful way was crucial to the success of the research. This meant several weeks of being at the day centre generally chatting, playing games, helping out with washing up, serving lunch etc. In this way we got to know young people and staff and we began to understand some of their current interests and issues and where learning fitted with these. This period was in itself active research through participant observation. Notes were not taken while at the centre, as this was felt to be too intrusive, but were written up as soon as possible afterwards. At the start there was not a blueprint of how to explore young people's perspectives of life and learning. Rather we expected this to evolve as we got to know them and their situation and as opportunities presented themselves. For example, informal chats with a performance artist working in the centre led us to plan a photography project. Involving a creative person who was already had the trust and respect of those young people was key to the success of that research activity.

The photography project serves to highlight the challenges and issues faced in this research context. It was planned as a five-week project with six young people that aimed to document their feelings and views associated with places and activities in their everyday lives. It had multiple and, as we will see, potentially conflicting purposes. First, it enabled the researcher to get to know the participants more before giving them one-to-one interviews. Second, it involved them as researchers of their own realities related to everyday life and learning. Third, it served managers' purposes of running an interesting activity with a small group of particularly vulnerable young people and then using it to provide evidence to funders of a learning activity.

Photography offered the possibility for the most vulnerable young people to be more involved in the research and was more collaborative than just relying on interviews and observations, allowing for their own perspectives and voice to shape the research. Taking photos was an easy and enjoyable research method which was attractive to them.

However, we had to be very flexible in order to manage the research and to fully utilise the data. Responsiveness was needed to changing conditions. For example, some of them missed sessions or were late finishing their project because of living with drug and alcohol dependence as well as other circumstances. This meant we had to add two weeks on to the project to complete properly and include everyone.

There were also difficulties in trying to serve the multiple purposes of the project. Most of the young people did not want their individual photographs or writing to be identified so they agreed to prepare a general display by the group. This was intended to be a collaborative exercise but the young people showed little interest in this, only checking that the final product, mainly done by the researchers, met with their approval. The idea of the display was for the young people to exhibit their views on life and learning and also to showcase an educational activity to funders. These two agendas conflicted, as revealed when the manager did not accept the final display. We had to amend it, making compromises on content and language (e.g. no swear words). These young people's voices were quite volatile and negative about some aspects of their lives and encounters with society, but the manager felt the need to present something more positive and 'polite' to funders.

Also the written display of young people's volatile spoken words jarred with staff. One staff member explained that this was because they continually worked hard to help young people to manage language choices depending on the context they were in, both informal and formal, and the display seemed to undermine this. We learned from our mistakes and wrong assumptions.

It took very careful negotiation with all participants to manage and make such compromises in order to be sensitive to the needs and agendas of the managers, who were trying to secure further funding, the staff, and the young people who wanted to have their say but not necessarily in the format of a public display. Most of these young people had experienced let down and rejection by adults who come and go in their lives. It was vital that they understood what they could expect from us and how long we would be around for. The staff and young people wanted to maintain contact after the research was completed, which was managed by dropping in for lunch from time to time.

Practitioner research

Practitioner research is important in several key areas of research from a situated practice approach. First, it values practitioner knowledge within the context of literacy teaching and learning, seeing this knowledge as situated in practice. It acknowledges the agency of practitioners and their ability to contribute to knowledge generation through research. This approach is different to research that is imposed upon practitioners and learners, where researchers 'helicopter' in, collect and analyse the data, then reinterpret findings back into practice. Instead it values a collaborative approach that draws upon the professional knowledge and insight which teachers and learners bring.

Second, by working collaboratively with practitioner researchers it is possible to make a closer link to the practices that are being researched. Instead of entering the field and testing existing hypotheses, this approach allows the research questions themselves to be developed within the context of research; that is, for the research questions to be situated in the practice being researched. This allows for more nuanced research that is located more precisely in practitioners' and learners' experiences. Therefore, situated experiences inform the research, rather than only being interpreted through an externally imposed research lens. Collaboration between practitioners and researchers also helps to facilitate access, to support fieldwork and data collection and in disseminating findings.

Third, this approach actively supports the agency of practitioners and learners involved. Often practitioners say they are disconnected from, and feel judged by, research that does not represent their knowledge, experience or voice. This is a potential outcome of 'research on' practitioners. We suggest rather 'research with' which allows practitioner knowledge, experience and voice to be included and heard more widely. Practitioner research encourages reflective practice and the generation of research evidence based upon existing practitioner knowledge, which benefits individuals, institutions and the field more widely.

Two practitioners from each college site worked with us for a year with one day a week remission from teaching. The six practitioner researchers received research training and support, contributing to the research project as well as their own professional development (Ivanič et al. 2004). They provided an invaluable link to the practice as this phase of our observations and interviews was carried out in their classrooms. They not only provided the link for us to get to know the learners in their class, but they also enabled this to happen in a safe environment where people would be supported to give proper informed consent and discuss any reservations they might have about being involved. It was a reciprocal relationship where their practice perspective provided important insights on emerging data and findings that enabled us to link the analysis more closely to what was happening in the classroom. From the research perspective they benefited from the time to reflect on their practice, something not often available to busy practitioners. They all felt, even though some were very experienced, that their practice improved by seeing learners as whole people who used literacy, numeracy and language in their everyday lives, not just in class.

Examples of working with practitioner researchers

Example 3: Practitioner as researcher

Kay was an experienced practitioner who taught maths and more recently had trained as an ESOL teacher. She had written and developed many literacy and numeracy materials for Liverpool Community College prior to the coming of the Skills for Life framework and was a well-respected and well-liked colleague and member of staff. Kay described herself as quiet. From observation and discussion, she was very reflective about her practice as a teacher of adults who mainly come from economically and socially deprived communities. Kay wanted the opportunity to think more about her practice rather than rely on existing ways of doing things. She was enthusiastic, although nervous, about becoming a practitioner researcher within the project.

Kay's maths class was one of the focal classrooms described in Chapter 8. As part of the project she was paid one day a week release time to carry out her own related research and she became increasingly interested in the links between the students' everyday uses and meanings of literacy and numeracy and what she taught them in class. Although much of her teaching was 'student centred', Kay said that she had not had the time or support to think about what this link, between everyday and class learning, meant for her practice as a maths tutor. With support of the full-time researcher, Kay designed and carried out her own practitioner research project on how maths shapes lives (see Ivanič et al. 2004).

Kay observed that many people found maths difficult because they could not translate from their everyday strategies for managing number to abstract concepts they found in the maths class. For example, people had ways of dividing up a bill at Pizza Hut between friends in their everyday lives, but they found grasping fractions or percentages difficult in the classroom. Kay wanted to understand people's everyday strategies in more detail to see if she could use insights from these everyday practices in her classroom teaching. She interviewed several people in the Drop-in Study Centre to understand the range of strategies people might use, asking about past learning histories and present uses and feelings about numeracy. From these interviews Kay constructed a short questionnaire that asked about the strategies that people used in their everyday lives to manage their money and household task such as shopping or decorating.

The findings provided important information that focused on what people could do rather than on what they could not, which is often the focus in the more formal setting of a classroom. Kay used these insights practically in her classroom by making more explicit links between how people used numeracy in their everyday life and what they learned in the classroom. She felt that the questionnaire had given her a useful tool, enabling her to find out this information about people's everyday lives, which would help their learning. Kay also felt that her research had provided her with a way of seeing people that she taught as whole people: 'as three-dimensional beings with a road behind and ahead'. She felt that through the research the classroom began to feel more open and democratic, more reflective of people's lives: 'By respecting people's own methods and understanding, the questionnaire helped to put these on the agenda and reinforce people's confidence in their abilities'. Kay felt the research had given her a way of opening up opportunities for people to situate learning more firmly in their lives.

Example 4: Practitioner as research consultant

We consulted with ESOL managers at Blackburn College to explore the possibility of carrying out research there. The main concerns of ESOL teachers there were around the difficulties of responding to the particular social needs of young students seeking asylum. The research specifically explored the relationship between language learning needs and broader social needs with young, secondary-school-educated students in the beginners Entry Level 1 class who were from a wide range of countries and had only recently arrived in Britain. This was in the context of the impact of the recently introduced government dispersal policy which had led to a rapid increase of people being sent by the Home Office to Blackburn. Educational and other social organisations found themselves ill prepared for this sudden change in policy.

Carefully negotiated access, facilitated by strong existing links and identification of the site-specific research question, was key groundwork. The ownership and importance attached to the research by the ESOL practitioners was crucial to the success of the study. The research happened at a point when morale was low because of restructuring of provision in the college. Other recent research they had been involved in, where they had had no meaningful ownership, had left them feeling wary and protective of their students and themselves.

The research activities were weekly participant observation of classes over half a term, audio recording of two consecutive classes with teacher reflections, collection of learning materials from each class, preliminary mini-interviews with all students in the class, main interviews with seven of the students (in the language of their choice where possible), photographs and student writing from a photography project (with the students as researchers documenting their feelings about living in Blackburn), audio recording and notes of photography project feedback, and notes from regular meetings and informal conversations with the teacher.

This range of research activities and the order in which they were carried out was not a pre-planned blueprint but rather evolved out of initial negotiation of the research with the class teacher, Wynne. Her co-operation and level of interest presented the opportunity for a collaborative approach working closely with her and the students. Establishing exactly how she wanted to be involved was important. Unlike Kay, described above, she did not feel she had time to carry out co-research, analysis or writing. Nevertheless, she felt ownership of the study and was interested to take on a role as ongoing consultant and advisor.

This led to setting up weekly meetings paying her as a research advisor/consultant to plan and reflect on activities, analysis, writing up the research and later running dissemination events together. The framework for the research, that is, the plan to interview students and carry out observation of classes and audio-record if possible, was set out in the draft proposal following our initial meetings. She became very interested when she realised that we wanted to work closely with her in deciding on research activities and how to carry them out. This was central to a negotiated research process. We built up a relationship of mutual trust and respect for our different knowledge and expertise. Wynne brought local knowledge, her experience and her understanding of the students. Her concerns and questions related to teaching these students. The researcher brought research experience, a background of living in Blackburn and teaching ESOL there and links to the research community. Wynne was able to influence the researcher's role. For example, we had not assumed any involvement in the classroom, but she preferred the researcher to participate as well as observing, as she felt the students would benefit and there would be an atmosphere of researching with them rather than on them.

Wynne's involvement strengthened every aspect of the research. Her commitment to the students ensured that they felt ownership of the research. This led us to make changes to the planned framework. Rather than explaining the methodology, it allowed us to discuss it and make joint decisions about what research activities to carry out and how. For example, rather than choosing seven students to interview, Wynne felt that it would only work if all twelve members of the class were involved. For this reason she suggested brief mini-interviews with every student parallel to their tutorials with her. These initial interviews not only ensured everyone's involvement but allowed the researcher to build rapport with each student, gain informed consent, and check out areas they would be happy to talk around and which language they would prefer to be interviewed in.

She was able to set boundaries such as not using video as she felt it inappropriate with these particular students and she herself was not comfortable with it. She felt free to guide on any detail of activities. Wynne's interest also led to her suggesting additional activities, which had not been planned initially, to integrate the research into teaching and learning, thus enriching the students' learning opportunities. For instance, we devised a photography project in which the students could take photos to represent their feelings about living in Blackburn. Wynne exploited this to generate student discussions, individual presentations and student writing. She said that she had never seen the students produce so much spontaneous spoken and written language before.

Withdrawing from the research was difficult, as we had built up very friendly relationships with the students. Wynne was able to facilitate this by suggesting the researcher dropped in from time to time and setting up email contact in the IT sessions. Our close working relationship meant that we were able to offer each other and the students' mutual support when one of the students, Faisullah, who had been very involved in the research, took his own life. We were also able to take the tough decision to include Faisullah's story in our study, as it was directly relevant and disturbingly showed the importance of the issues we were exploring, that is, that social issues have a huge impact on the ability of these learners to realise their potential.

Being able to pay for Wynne's consultancy during the dissemination phase strengthened the links between research and practice. It greatly increased the credibility of the research with senior management within the college, as well as with practitioners, managers and policy makers both regionally and country wide. It led to concrete change in responding to the needs of these learners such as providing common room space, addressing progression by strengthening links with mainstream courses, and creating a post for a liaison worker to assist students to manage their social issues.

Overview

Using the methodologies described here and working in the sites described in the previous chapter, overall, 282 people participated in the research: 134 were students and the remainder tutors, managers and other support workers. The electronic database from the project consists of 403 data files, which include 198 audio recorded interviews as well as extensive field notes and other data. Where we worked in depth with people in learning programmes, this ranged from carrying out several interviews over a six-month period to keeping in touch with the person and their learning for more than two years. We maintained contact with fifty-three people who represent the longitudinal cohort of the study.

Chapter 6 presents case studies of five of the people we worked with in depth, examining their everyday literacy practices. Chapter 7 draws on the range of data from across the sites. It analyses and examines in detail the range of literacy practices people were involved in, as part of their everyday lives out of class, focusing on how people used literacy to get things done in their lives, how they used literacy to learn, and how literacy is developed through everyday activities.

Chapters 8 and 9 focus on instances of relatively formal provision for adults, that is, classes offered in college settings, rather than other contexts. Each of these classes was researched by one of the research team. We gained an in-depth understanding of the regular patterns and practices of each class, and recorded one session for more detailed analysis, referred to below as *the focal session*. In Blackburn and Lancaster, the research involved frequent participation in the class, where possible attending every week in order to understand the routines and activities of the class as an insider. We kept records of what happened in these sessions in detailed field notes, written within twenty-four hours of the visit. In the two classes in Liverpool, the students collaborated with the teacher and the researcher in the production of a video over a four-week period to record a session as a focus for discussion.

We studied not only the characteristics of each of these forms of provision but also how it was experienced by a selection of participants in it, spanning thirty-seven learners overall. We asked learners about their intentions, their perceptions of what was happening, their perceptions of what they gained, and how these factors related to their everyday lives. We juxtaposed the learners' perceptions with our own observations of the classes, and with teachers' accounts of what they were doing in the classes and why. In each class, at least four learners were selected for more detailed interviews about what they had learned, both from the class in general and from the focal session. We recorded the perspectives of the class tutors through interviews, field notes and taped peer discussions. Some of the class tutors were co-researchers working in partnership with us on documenting these classes.

The data collected in this way was analysed in a three-stage process. First, each researcher individually interpreted the data for their classes, annotating it for emerging themes. Each case showed the ways in which learning is shaped by the characteristics of the specific social context, and how it differs from person to person, depending on the life histories, beliefs, motivations and resources which they bring with them to the same learning–teaching event. The case studies produced as a result of this work reveal the complexity of factors which teachers need to be aware of and to which they need to be responsive. The four case studies presented in Chapter 8 give a flavour of this complexity. The case studies were shared across the research team, and themes identified collectively were then used as categories for a second round of analysis. The team then generated a set of provisional findings from the analysis. These were checked against the data in order to see how far they were supported by the individual cases and to identify specific details to exemplify each. This process led to the refinement of the findings, and the headings which we use in Chapters 8 and 9.

In the community sites reported on in Chapters 10 and 11, we spent time getting to know and understand each of the research sites and the kinds of literacy and numeracy learning that was taking place, as described above. We interviewed staff and service users, both informally, recorded through field notes, and using more formal semi-structured interviews, audio-recorded, transcribed and analysed. This involved regular visits (twenty to twenty-five visits per site over the course of the year), over fifty formally recorded interviews, and many more informal conversations recorded in field notes. We developed other methods as appropriate to the settings, in dialogue with participants. As we have outlined above, this approach to research relies on developing detailed local understandings in collaboration with research participants. Therefore, we first produced detailed reports on each of these sites which were fed back to the sites and discussed with participants. These have acted as background papers when preparing further reports. Understanding the lives of people in the specific sites was an important step in making sense of the data.

6

LITERACIES IN PEOPLE'S LIVES

Introduction

This is the first of two chapters which focus on people's everyday literacy practices, what people do with literacy to manage and enjoy their lives, what opportunities, demands and constraints they face in relation to their literacy practices. The chapters examine the significance of literacy for these people in three distinct ways: what people use literacy for in their everyday lives, how literacy is a resource for learning, and how literacy is learned through participation in activities. The primary focus in these two chapters is literacy, although there is some mention of numeracy and language. This chapter provides five short vignettes, showing how people who attended classes were involved in a wide range of literacy events and practices outside class. In the following chapter we look across data from all the learners we worked with to discuss different ways people used literacy for different life purposes.

The people we studied used and learned literacy for many purposes outside their classes, as part of their varied lives as workers, family members and members of different communities. Attending literacy classes is in most cases a temporary and transitory supplement to their situated experiences of using and learning literacies. This chapter focuses on these uses of literacy in the everyday lives of five people, on how they use literacy to learn about things they are interested in, and how they extend and develop their literacies through participating in literacy events in their lives outside college. For these vignettes we have chosen women and men of different ages with diverse life circumstances and experiences to highlight the many ways in which people are using literacy, language and numeracy in their everyday lives.

Katrina

Katrina has already been introduced in Chapter 1. She was 20 years old at the time of the research and was working as a play worker in a private business providing nursery provision and after-school care. She lived at home with her parents, returning home for lunch every day between shifts. Katrina had had a variety of jobs including packing and factory work but said that she preferred work that is local and liked to work with people. Although working hard to study health-care subjects at Level 2, she struggled with telling the time and doing multiplication tables. Katrina attended the maths class to learn these basic skills, which she and her tutors felt were holding her back. Her dad had been unable to help with multiplication tables. Katrina wanted to learn these skills, which were vital for work, and to be able to pass her driving test so she could be independent.

Literacy and numeracy for life purposes

Katrina used literacy and numeracy for everyday activities such as reading the bus timetable, reading instructions and finding out what was on in her city. She didn't read papers or novels and gained most of her information online and in chat rooms. She described herself as having few friends but she and her friend Daisy spent a lot of time chatting on the internet about their favourite singers and film stars. She and Daisy communicated frequently using instant messaging and sometimes email, as Daisy did not work and often slept at different times from Katrina. They kept in touch by texting each other frequently.

As she was concerned about her weight, Katrina started to read food packets to work out the calories and fat content of what she was eating. She watched her weight carefully, noting down any decrease, or increase, from the week before. This process involved many calculations, including working out an ideal body weight in relation to height and then how many calories could be consumed to achieve this. This also meant working out how many calories could be burned off walking to work.

Katrina also used the computer for most of her leisure activities. She said that she could not afford to go out much as she received the minimum wage and had to pay board and her contribution to the family's broadband. Her computer was in her bedroom, where she downloaded music and films, watched them and then joined chat rooms to discuss them. She was very aware of the dangers of meeting people on the web and was careful not to give out too much personal information whilst enjoying the social aspect of talking to new people. She described this as being important to her as she was not very confident socially, she did not have many friends, and she did not enjoy going out to clubs and pubs.

Literacy for finding out and learning about things

Katrina used the internet to find out information about wrestling, as following the sport was a family hobby. She looked up the websites of well-known wrestling stars to find out more about them and when they were fighting locally. She also found this information from wrestling magazines that her dad read. She liked to find out detailed information behind the public faces in the ring, discovering favourite hobbies or foods of the stars.

Katrina read adverts to find out about how to lose weight and through a friend's recommendation went to a local Weight Watchers class. When her parents went on holiday, leaving her on her own for the first time, Katrina used the internet and her mother's cook book to work out how to feed herself. She was not sure about quantities and timings. Although she said she could read the information she found it hard to work out the sequence of steps. She also said measuring was hard, both working out what was required and actually weighing ingredients out. This shows how reading on its own is not always sufficient as a way of learning, particularly for learning how to do something. Some written texts are most useful when they accompany action and there are other people to talk through what they mean.

Literacy learning through participation in everyday events

Katrina had tried to learn left from right herself, so she would not have to admit she did not know it, and in the end her mum had taught her by explaining that right was the 'hand you make the sign of the cross with'. Katrina was confident about using digital literacy, more than reading the written language she found in books or in the classroom. She had confidence in her ability generally and had isolated the skills that she needed to progress. Although she described herself as a poor speller, she did not see this as a difficulty that would impede her progress at work or in her everyday life. At work she developed strategies for dealing with record keeping by looking at how words had been spelled in previous pages, looking at where children's names were displayed and asking for acceptably difficult words such as 'diarrhoea' to be spelled.

In her everyday life, Katrina was not worried about formal conventions as this extract from her email shows:

HEY YVON
>
>*ITS ME KATRINA!! :-)*
>
> *sorry i havent been in touch i have had bad family prombles i got ya script well part of the books thing u are doing. good news i have passed my NVQ LEVEL 2 PLAYWORKER i havent got my ceftican yet but will soon any way i am not well i have a blocked nose and blocked ears and my throat hurts me when i talk or eat somethink so i have been haveing hot lemma and going 2 bed theres last couple of weeks i have got 2 got 2 go the doctors on wed 7th and see if he can do anythink 2 help me . Work has been ok i still have 2 go in of the easter hoildays and look after the older children it doenst me because there off school that i am off work i have taken this wed off because i am getting sky digtial tv of my 21 birthday present off my parents i know my birthday isnt till november but its £200 of the boxs than £50 of the boxs 2 be put in and than u have 2 pay £15 up front of the bill it will be £15 a month so i am going 2 be paiding £15 of the internet and £15 a month of the sky ditigal so i used my smart brain and that leaves we will £22.05 i will tell when i see u i know it looks all werid here but i will tell u in person when i see ya*

Using a mixture of text language and the 'softer' conventions of emailing Katrina was able to express herself clearly and articulately in her everyday life writing. Katrina associated the computer with learning that she was interested in, and information that related to her life and interests. As such it did not seem to present a textual barrier around 'right' and 'wrong' forms of spelling, rather a flexible and personal method to communicate textually with others. Within this she was learning new technical skills to do with computers, which use literacy as well as offering the fun of reading about favourite film or wrestling stars.

Alan

Alan was in his fifties when we met him in an English class at the Adult College in Lancaster, where he had been attending classes for some years. Alan had trained and worked as a plumber in his youth, and had worked on building sites in the local area, including Lancaster University when it was being constructed. He enjoyed making things, particularly model aeroplanes. He was highly skilled in practical matters, and proud of his ability to make items as required; for instance, he could construct the small pieces he needed for his plane engines from scrap metal. Many of his stories about his life included reference to items he had made from scratch: fixing a neighbour's gutter with a piece of cast iron, or mending a workshop coping saw by adapting a welding rod. He had a real interest in how things worked, and appreciated high quality items which worked well. He lived with his parents, both of whom were in poor health and needed his assistance in practical matters.

He had spent several extended periods of time in hospital following a breakdown in his mid-twenties, and was taking a range of medication, some of which had unpleasant side effects. He felt the treatments he received in hospital, particularly electroconvulsive therapy, were not effective and had left him with permanent damage to his memory. He had also experienced discrimination from people locally who knew he had spent time in the hospital, saying that people had treated him 'like a vegetable', and had refused to acknowledge what he was capable of doing.

He worked in what used to be the hospital's industrial therapy unit, now a workshop providing supported employment for people with mental health needs, housed on a local industrial estate. He enjoyed working with his hands and feeling he was doing something of practical use. At the time of the research he was working gluing prescription pads together. He preferred doing this to a desk or computer-based job, which he did not see as 'real work'. He was critical of people who 'just sit there all day and push buttons'.

Literacy for life purposes

Many of Alan's uses of literacy were in connection with his passion for making model aeroplanes. He made these models from elaborate plans, which he carried around with him in his notebook. He wrote letters to model shops to obtain plans handbooks and to *Aeromodeller* magazine, which he regularly read. His sister helped him print pages from the internet about the planes he wanted to make. At one point his planes were displayed in a local museum, and making up the display involved a great deal of reading, writing, and collaboration with others. Plans and texts such as these combine complex visual representations with written labels, titles, explanations and descriptions; a very different type of reading from many of the reading passages in Alan's classroom tasks designed for literacy learning.

His room at home was full of books. In addition to books and magazines about model aeroplanes, he owned a variety of information books. He reads for pleasure, both non-fiction and fiction, including war stories and information books. He kept his collection of books in a bookshelf which he had made himself, pictured in Figure 6.1.

Figure 6.1 Alan's bookshelf

Alan used literacy for personal communication too, writing regular letters to pen-friends. However, he said that he did not get the privacy from his parents to write at home, so wanted to do this at college. He kept in regular touch with a pen-friend called Millie, telling her about what he was doing at work and how his life was going. He frequently created beautiful hand-made cards, which he sent to tutors and friends. He belonged to the choir at church, a form of social participation which necessitates a considerable amount of reading, not only of the hymn book but also of messages, circulars and other forms of communication which organised and synchronised activities (as discussed in Tusting 2000).

Literacy for finding out and learning about things

Alan read the books and magazines described above not only for the pleasure of it, but also specifically to find out how to do things. He used *Aeromodeller* magazine, library books, his own book collection, and detailed plans which he obtained from the model shop and from the internet to find out how to make his aeroplanes. For example, one day he was reading an old *Aeromodeller* magazine in connection with the Tiger Moth that he was working on. There was an article about Tiger Moths with a picture of a man who was flying a model in the 1950s, coupled with an intricate blueprint for the plane, a mass of tiny lines which covered the page. Alan read these complicated plans several times to make sense of them, then had them blown up and stuck on the walls in his room, so that he could keep reading them over and over again, in order not to miss anything important. He also had a rather elderly copy of *Model Aero Engines*, a manual about engines, full of technical illustrations, which he kept with him and read often.

Alan also used books to help him to do things other than make model aeroplanes. For example, he had an interest in butterflies and some time ago a friend from the local Butterfly House had passed on some specimens which had died. Alan had found information about how to preserve them in formaldehyde in one of his books and put together a display, using one of his father's old insulin syringes. He also taught himself to use a micrometer screw gauge, after someone had given him an old imperial gauge as a gift, using a book from the library to work out how to use it: how many thousandths of an inch a full turn of the screw was, how precise it was and how to use it to make clocks.

Literacy learning through participation in everyday events

Using reading and writing to get things done and to find out information provides many opportunities for developing and expanding literacy capabilities – learning by doing, rather than learning by being taught. Through the substantial amount of reading he was engaged in, Alan's reading capabilities were constantly being augmented. His vocabulary increased – albeit within a fairly limited semantic field of technical terminology associated with making model aeroplanes, but not exclusively restricted to this. Another example of literacy learning through participation in literacy events was when Alan was involved in a lot of Christmas activities with the church, as a result of which he learnt how to spell 'Christmas'.

Alan also learnt how to engage in literacy practices by watching his sister, for example when using the computer. She sometimes took the mouse and did whatever needed to be done herself. Alan found this irritating, as he felt she was invading his space, but he also learnt by seeing what she was doing, which he could later do himself.

Jez

At the age of 17 Jez was referred to the Entry to Employment programme through her Youth Offending Team Worker to fulfil a condition of her 'licence' after a conviction. She lived in supported accommodation for young people under the age of 18 years. She had had an unsettled childhood living with her mother, changing schools frequently, finally leaving home aged 13, then spending time in reception centres and in care. This unsettled and unhappy early life experience led her into habitual offending from the age of 10. Jez had a very difficult time at school, gaining little and being repeatedly excluded. Jez's experience of going to college was disastrous because she continued to be bullied by people she had been at school with and who moved on to college with her, which is how she in turn began to bully others.

Literacy for life purposes

Jez's activities outside of the educational programme revealed her social and creative potential. After she had put in a complaint to Lancashire Children's Rights Service, they involved her in training advocates. Realising her artistic ability they asked her to help them with their website and information leaflets and at the time of the interview she had just completed a 'runaways project' DVD, acting, filming and editing it. When she reached the age of 16 they were able to employ her for 17 hours a month and she did more hours as a volunteer. Reading and writing were central to all these activities. Her careful, skilled, sensitive artistic expression displayed a contrasting, more hidden side to her personality than that of the brash, intimidating person that she often seemed to be.

She had a wide range of interests and in her spare time read regularly, mainly romance and horror stories. She loved writing, both her diary and poems. She found it easier to manage her peer relationships by communicating her feelings through writing than she did through speaking:

> I struggle expressing what I'm on about [when speaking] and I start waffling on about crap . . . so I'll throw it [what she has written] down on someone's head. They'll read it and then they come back and they're like 'we understand, we'll leave you to it'.

She said she thought that she had learned to read music before she could read. She had lots of music books and played the keyboard.

Literacy for finding out and learning about things

Adil, the accommodation manager, let Jez use the internet at the house to pursue her interests even though they were not really allowed to:

> Adil knows I'm very smart on computers . . . If I want to do something I have to know the ins and outs of it otherwise I won't do it.

She used the internet for finding out information and learning about topics she was interested in. She was clearly inspired by her grandfather. He had his own website with the family tree and a game he had built, and had written books, including one on card games which was published.

Literacy learning through participation in everyday literacy events

Jez learns literacy through her participation in these activities in which she is using literacy to get things done. She broadens her uses of literacy through her close relationship with her grandfather, who shares his activities with her, and thereby 'scaffolds' her ability to do what he does (Bruner 1985). In addition, she shares her skills with others in the house, helping them learn what she can do, and simultaneously helping them develop their reading and writing through participation in these activities. When people become interested in what she is doing, she teaches them, for example, how to play keyboard or how to do needlework.

Paula

Paula, in her early thirties, had come to the UK two years previously as a refugee from Colombia and was attending an ESOL class when we first met her. She had permanent residence status in Britain and lived with her two children who attended primary school. Paula was highly motivated to make a new life for herself and her family. However the displacement she and her children had faced meant that she went through periods of depression and ill health from time to time. She received support from Sure Start and she joined a self-help group to help her cope with her children's emotional and behavioural difficulties. Paula wanted to learn English as quickly as possible in order to gain employment in child care or as a teacher's assistant. She enjoyed going to aerobics when she could afford it and was learning to drive. She applied for and was chosen to take part in a council 'Community Leadership' scheme.

Literacy and numeracy for life purposes

Paula took the initiative in trying to improve her own situation and was not deterred by the literacy demands this brought with it, but she also often encountered obstacles which were beyond her control. For example she paid £200 on the train to London for an urgent trip to the British Embassy to arrange a travel visa because she did not know about the early trains being expensive. She lacked the cultural knowledge to find out what information she could access and read about variable fares.

As a student herself and as a mother of two primary school children, Paula and her children spent time every evening helping each other with homework. Her 11-year-old son would help her with pronunciation and spelling, which he teased her about, and she would help him with maths and other subjects. She would also read stories in Spanish with the children as she was afraid they would lose the ability to read in their home language. Paula had an old computer at home but she found it very frustrating as it often crashed and she could not afford repairs.

Paula was using literacy to learn to drive. Again she was in a reciprocal learning situation as she was also using Spanish and English literacy for teaching her driving instructor Spanish, which paid for her lessons.

Keeping in touch with her extended family and friends involved writing emails and texts in both Spanish and English as well as telephoning. She travelled to Spain to visit her mother once a year and used reading, writing and numeracy for calculating fares, booking tickets and finding her way around airports in both countries.

Literacy for finding out and learning about things

Paula was an avid learner. She was, at times, enrolled on three courses at once IT, psychology and childcare – though during times of depression she would drop out of learning altogether. On her own initiative she looked for books on child development in the local library to prepare for applying for work as a teacher's assistant, telling us: 'Always, always I am trying to learn'. Paula also engaged in a range of literacy practices in order to try to become a childminder. On her own initiative she went to a Jobcentre where she was given information about a childcare course and an application form. She filled it in and posted it and was offered a place straight away, whereas at college she had filled in forms for a childcare course and at the library for a computer course and two months later was still waiting for a reply.

Paula obtained and read a lot of information about the health and safety requirements for making her house childminding friendly. However, reading this information was not sufficient: it did not resolve the problem that she could not afford to pay for these modifications to be made. With help from Sure Start she filled in forms to get criminal clearance so she could do voluntary work and childminding. However, completing the right paperwork was not sufficient: after waiting three months she got a reply saying that they could not give her clearance since she had not been able to verify her address for the last five years – something which was impossible since she had only been in the country for two years. Paula also had to obtain a hygiene certificate and do first aid to prepare for childminding work. She was worrying about needing to prepare a CV.

Literacy learning through participation in everyday events

Apart from using literacy in everyday events such as shopping, travelling and going to doctors and health clinics, Paula also learned literacy through her involvement in a Community Leadership Programme. Her name appeared on the agenda of the local Asylum Support Multi-Agency Forum, in an item on updating a community leadership programme. This made it very obvious that this person was not 'just' an ESOL student, but was also an active member of the community, with all the language, literacy and numeracy demands which that entailed.

Tommy

Tommy was in his mid-fifties and was working part time as a caretaker in a church hall. He lived on his own and suffered recurring back and hearing problems after twenty years as a heavy metal worker. He was attending a spelling class to improve his spelling, something he said he had never learned at school. He said he could not write a cheque or spell 'sausages' when writing his shopping list, 'which embarrasses me'. He was keen on computers and he visited his local library frequently, usually to find books or information about his latest hobby, gardening.

Literacy and numeracy for life purposes

Tommy had bought his own house and managed to run a car on his part-time wages. His experience of careful management and budgeting meant that he could help other family members with this too. He wrote his own shopping lists as he did not mind writing for himself when he was the only one to read it, but he had avoided writing cheques before he had gone to the spelling class, as it was a cause of embarrassment.

Tommy labelled and organised his large tape and CD music collection, which ran into several boxes and hundreds of discs. He was in the process of changing the albums from tape to CD and then cataloguing them on his computer. This was something he said would take a long time but would be satisfying. He read computer magazines about desk-top publishing and graphics to help with this process.

Literacy for finding out and learning about things

Tommy explained that he wanted to work part time so that he had enough time to enjoy his leisure interests. Over the years he said he had tried lots of hobbies and interests such as astronomy, deep-sea fishing and computers. For each of these he had bought equipment and had read the various magazines and trade journals to find out the best buys and professional tips. Most of the equipment and magazines were now in the back bedroom as his interests had moved on. He still maintained an interest in computers and was proud that he had bought some of the early ones that were available, taking them to bits and rebuilding them to find out how they worked. He built several for family members out of parts that he got at computer fairs and from second-hand machines. To achieve this, practical work and reading about computers had been inextricably intertwined: Tommy would not have read about computers without having one to work on, and he would not have been able to work on them without reading magazines and information books and leaflets. When Tommy used the internet it was to visit the chat rooms for the Dungeons and Dragons computer games that he played. He explained that these operated at different levels and players could improve their scores by working out the clues and by swapping information in this way. He had an extensive collection of these fantasy games.

Tommy used the library and internet for finding out information, as well as asking people. For example, he was keen to grow vegetables. He had looked up courgettes in a vegetable book in the library and checked on the internet but he could not get two pieces of information that he needed. One was how to pronounce the word and the other was how to fertilise them. For both pieces of information Tommy asked people in the spelling class and on receiving several varying pieces of information asked the researcher for her opinion. Having read that courgettes were part of the cucumber family he wanted to know whether there were male and female plants and whether he had to fertilise the female plants by hand. He also wanted to check that he had understood the best growing conditions, including feeding and position, as well as how to prepare and eat the vegetable when it had grown. Not only did he find lots of information but this also provided a way for Tommy to talk to others in his class about something which was mutually interesting.

Literacy learning through participation in everyday events

At work Tommy and his colleague kept a calendar diary of shift changes and holidays when they had to cover each other. There were lists of telephone numbers displayed in the small caretakers' office for council, amenities and emergency numbers including the police. Every time we visited Tommy at work he was reading science-fiction novels and, later, writing. He was an avid library goer and often complained that the new library building was unattractive and difficult to use. For him the main success of a library was having all three volumes in a series available, rather than bright colours and wide aisles. Tommy had developed a supportive relationship with Cheri, another student on one of his courses. Although she had left to attend a nearby GCSE course, they had maintained an online friendship, sometimes emailing each other daily.

Summary

In this chapter we have illustrated the literacies in people's lives beyond college through vignettes of five people with contrasting life histories and current circumstances. These vignettes show how literacies fit into the bigger picture of each person's life: their interests, the demands placed upon them, their identities and their imagined futures; their sense of who they are and who they want to become. These examples bring out clearly how this varies from person to person, and they exemplify the richness and diversity of literacies, even in the lives of such a small number of people. In particular, they clothe in detail the point we made in Chapter 1: that the people we worked with, while all attending 'Skills for Life' provision of various sorts, were in many ways leading highly literate lives. However, each of the five cases is very specific and inevitably gives a partial picture of the range of ways in which literacy mediates social life. In the next chapter therefore we take a more comprehensive look at the roles and uses of literacy in people's everyday lives, providing examples and discussion from across the full range of our data.

7

LITERACY AND LEARNING FOR LIFE PURPOSES

Looking across all the people we worked with, this chapter examines the significance of literacy for people's lives. In the first part of this chapter we focus on literacy practices for different life purposes. The other two sections then focus on the connections between literacy and learning in everyday life: first, the use of literacy to find out and learn, covering topics as wide ranging as family history and medical conditions; and second, the way in which literacy itself is developed other than through literacy classes.

In describing literacy practices for life purposes Barton and Hamilton developed an analytical framework which showed 'vernacular literacies' as serving six functions: organising life, personal communication, private leisure, documenting life, sense making, and social participation (1998: 247–50). We found that the literacy practices in the lives of the people we interviewed were serving similar functions and we draw upon and develop this here. We were interested in vernacular literacies in the sense of those literacy practices in which were shaped by people's engagement in the passions and pursuits of their personal lives, but not all literacy practices in life beyond formal classes are of this type. We were also interested in the literacy practices in which the people we studied were forced to engage through their encounters with bureaucracy, and in those which were generated by their employment.

Literacy practices for dealing with major life issues

Literacy plays a central role in negotiating and maintaining relationships with institutions. There were major legal and life-threatening issues concerning some of the young people seeking asylum, young people at E2E and at Safeplace, which involved them, involuntarily, in literacy practices which could have serious consequences. The examples below show the degree to which civil life is permeated with complex literacy demands. More significantly, they show that being able to meet these literacy demands does not solve problems. Economic, social and political factors, the (non)co-operation of bureaucratic authorities, and cultural knowledge are what really make the difference to people's life chances.

ESOL students seeking asylum received important documents from the Home Office and solicitors which even many native speakers would have difficulty in understanding. For example, Lisette, one of the ESOL students at Blackburn college, had to complete a complex application for hardship support and to obtain letters of support from a doctor and solicitor. Letters sent to her about removal of benefits and housing and other legal documents were sent to the wrong address which put her case in jeopardy. Lisette had to ask Wynne to explain what the questions meant on a questionnaire sent by a solicitor. Abdul, introduced in Chapter 1, wanted to write a letter to the Home Office about the legal status of his family but the local Member of Parliament advised against this and to 'lie low'. The literacy practices involved in such critical issues involve not just being able to read and complete the forms, but also to understand how to act strategically in order to manage complex relationships with the system.

Stevie, who attended the Safeplace day centre, had received an anonymous word-processed letter which was very ugly and threatening, pointing out details about his childhood that only someone close to him would have known and basically saying they would 'get him and his life would be ended'. The staff at Safeplace told him he should go to the police. Just as Lisette had used networks of support for the literacy demands placed upon her, so Stevie shared this threatening letter with people he trusted in order to get the moral support he needed to make sense of it and manage it.

For Dee, an E2E student, sometimes everyday life worries were distracting such as a big court case her mother was going through related to her younger sister having been kidnapped the year before. She was close to her family but at the same time she felt the need to be more independent and was trying to find a place in a young people's accommodation scheme. These aspects of everyday life involved her in reading correspondence from the court and from the solicitor and coming to terms with its implications, and filling in forms for accommodation. She had support for this from her Liaison Worker at Entry to Employment classes as she needed her reference. These are all shared rather than individual practices and involve a lot of moral support as well as literacy support.

Literacy practices for getting things done

Literacy mediates all aspects of people's lives. People use reading and writing to keep household affairs such as shopping and finances running smoothly, to set up storage and record-keeping systems, in relation to health and well-being, to arrange their leisure activities, their work and their study. The following examples show the variety and complexity of these literacy practices in the lives of the adults in our study.

Household

Cordelia, who studied English and maths at the Adult College in Lancaster, left most of the paperwork involved in running the house to her boyfriend. He wrote it down but they talked it through together. She worked with him on the household budget, working out what she had spent money on in the course of the day. She didn't have a bank account, but he did. She got benefits and paid most of the bills. They had just started to discuss money and budgets, working out how much they had coming in, how much needed to go out on regular expenses such as rent and TV, and how much was left that was theirs to spend.

Abdul interpreted for his wife when she was in hospital which would have involved a range of literacy practices such as reading the instructions for taking medicines, signs and information. He dealt with all the school communications and helped his children with their homework. This help was reciprocal in the same way as it was for Paula (see Chapter 6) with her children; his son helped him with spoken English.

The people we interviewed also mentioned demands in their lives which they felt they could not fulfil because of a lack of language, literacy and numeracy. For example, Soraya from Iran was not sure how to get extra maths help for her son. She saw a private advert in a shop window and answered it but it was too expensive. She felt that she could not support his study because of her lack of language and English literacy. He got some study support from the library. She had to tell him, 'We can't help you. If you need something you can go [to the library].'

Jane, whom we met in a spelling class at the Adult College, looked after her husband's interests by finding creative ways of doing things cheaply, and felt that this was her contribution to the household finances. For instance, she was much better than her husband at booking their holidays, often to far away places such as Jamaica and the USA. Despite her husband's skills – he had always been good at spelling and maths – he did not understand how to go about booking holidays and even struggled to take messages when the travel agent rang. It was Jane herself who found travel bargains and organised itineraries. She found special offers on Ceefax, and worked out ways of travelling cheaper than organised packages by booking independently. Others mentioned using guide books and the internet to organise holidays.

Jane used literacy to organise her family's private leisure; for example, using a newspaper to book tickets to a Bruce Springsteen concert at the cricket ground in Manchester. When she phoned up to ask about hotel accommodation, she was given a couple of website addresses. They had a computer at home, used mainly by her 22-year-old son. She had only been on the internet once, when he had left it on; when it had started asking her for credit card details, she decided that she should leave it alone!

Work

Mark, a bricklayer who attended a spelling class at the Adult College, had to keep accounts as a self-employed person. He kept records, receipts and tax vouchers together in a box and sorted them out once a year when he prepared his accounts for his tax return. This was a big job which he broke down by doing an hour or so on it at a time over a few weekends. These organising tasks are examples of how working life is textually mediated, and of the uses of literacy in the lives of adults who attend classes. More examples are given in Chapter 12.

Literacy practices for personal communication

Writing is one of the main ways in which people can maintain relationships with family, friends and contacts at work. Even though they were all involved in some way with language, literacy or numeracy provision, many of the people who participated in this research were using a range of literacy practices for the purposes of personal communication.

For Angie, writing was an essential means of maintaining contact with her children. When we met her at Safeplace, she was 19 years old, and had had two children taken from her and put into care. She said,

> My son's nearly two now . . . it's still hard but it'll get easier as time goes by . . . it's mainly just like his birthday and Christmas that it hurts. I can write him a letter and send him a card. I've got to give it to social services. Just like if they write me a letter they've got to give it to social services. The social worker tells me how he's doing sometimes which is helpful so I know he's alright.

All the young asylum-seeker students, some of the younger ESOL students from the Asian community, and all the young people in Safeplace and Entry to Employment used texting for personal communication as it is cheaper than phone calls. In this way they kept in touch with family members or friends in other towns in the UK. People's values and identities related to language use varied even in one family. For example, Sameena (see Chapter 1) texted her husband in Urdu (which she said annoyed him) and he replied in English, and she texted her children in English. For Soraya and Sameena letter writing was a thing of the past. With cheaper rates, they now use the telephone (at least weekly) to keep contact with their relatives in Iran and Pakistan – they said that they need to hear their voices. The younger members of their families used email more, and were more proficient with it. Writing gave others an opportunity to develop relationships with friends. Dee wrote regularly to a pen-friend in Australia.

Several of the people we met wanted to use email for communication with family and friends but had limited access at home because of the cost. Lisette wrote emails at the local library. (None of these computer-literate young asylum seekers have computers at home – they were not allowed to even if they could, as they were only allowed to spend money on basic food and clothing.) She, Abdul and the other asylum seekers from the ESOL class kept in touch with news from their countries through the internet.

In the context of work Mark, being self-employed, had to communicate with the companies and individuals who employed him, which he did mainly through email from his home computer. These examples show how essential literacy still is to maintaining personal contact, and that it serves this function for people who are attending Skills for Life classes, just as much as for others. The examples also show how personal communication is becoming increasingly technologised, with more and more people using email and texting to maintain personal and business relationships. However, these new literacy practices are dependent on access to the technology, as is made startlingly apparent by the difficulties faced by people living in poverty and by asylum seekers who are not allowed to buy computers.

Literacy practices for leisure and pleasure

Even though many of the people we met in our research were attending language, literacy and numeracy classes, and others were considered as being 'in need of basic skills', many of them engaged in reading and writing in their leisure time. This included reading fiction and novels; reading to keep informed of world affairs; reading out of interest; reading and writing associated with hobbies, games and travel; communicating with friends as an enjoyable way to spend time; using reading and writing to make sense of life around them and their own identities; and creative writing.

Several people mentioned reading for pleasure: novels, magazines, newspapers, religious literature and information books. For example Martina, from Angola, liked reading novels in French and magazines in English, and she obtained Portuguese versions of Jehovah's Witness publications from a friend in London. She said these are not just about religion but also have interesting information about world affairs. Some people mentioned the pleasure they get from being intellectually challenged through her own reading at home. Martina really enjoyed studying at home for her business studies course, which also involves some philosophy and politics. Young people at Safeplace displayed their identities through the way they engaged with the books which were brought into the centre, related to their expressed interests. It was a chance for them to join and visit the library with the library outreach worker, as several of them had been previously barred. At the Entry to Employment programme, Sean, who did not enjoy the literacy class, clearly enjoyed reading for pleasure. We saw him reading a book on spiders when he was supposed to be doing art and craft and the teacher asked him to put it away. Tommy (see Chapter 6) preferred the evening shift at work as it gave him time in the day to follow his own interests, and allowed him time to read at work too, in between opening the door for visitors.

Several of the people we met used literacy to support their hobbies and interests. However, such leisure pursuits are beyond the means of some: the young people at Safeplace could not afford items such as music magazines and had very little chance to access the computer in their current circumstances.

For some of the people we interviewed, leisure, hobbies and other aspects of life were indistinguishable. Sameena kept her own cookery book where she collected recipes – some written in Urdu and some in English depending on the cultural origin of the recipe. Abdul read gardening books in the library, then he used the information to develop his small garden at the front of his house – the best-looking garden on their street in a run-down area. Thomas, who attended an English class at the Adult College in Lancaster, lived in an old pub which he had bought derelict, renovated and made into a highly successful business. He tended to avoid reading and writing out of class, but one year he used his college class to put a 'CV' together for the house, covering its history, appearance and particularly period features, to send off to television companies to see whether they might be interested in using it as a location for filming. While this literacy practice was for work purposes, he enjoyed it in such a way that 'work' and 'leisure' were intertwined.

Travel was a leisure activity for some of the people in our study, as with the example of Jane, mentioned above, although many could not afford holidays. We have already discussed the literacy practices entailed in organising holidays; but beyond the practicalities of planning, travel itself involves a wide range of language, literacy and numeracy practices, such as following maps, reading guidebooks and soaking in textually mediated aspects of life in the new environment. Many Asian ESOL students like Sameena travel to Pakistan and India every two or three years, which involves literacy practices for being in a world that is textually mediated mainly in Urdu or Hindi rather than mainly in English.

We observed and gained understanding of a range of literacy practices which the young people in the entry to employment programme class engaged in as part of their private leisure interests. They had a variety of passions and talents in which they engaged in their everyday lives, and many of these had literacy and numeracy practices associated with them. For example, Charlie read to her neighbours' children on a regular basis, which belied the lack of confidence and unsettled behaviour she showed in her literacy class. Both Sameera and Mani were drawing on other languages and literacies, Urdu and Arabic, at mosque school, skills and experiences that are hidden in their basic skills classes. Young people revealed with articulate ease their particular 'life world' expertise which positioned them very differently from the unconfident learners they sometimes appeared to be in formal learning contexts. Sean had expert knowledge of spiders. Jo was a film buff, an articulate film critic and a cook with some professional training behind him. He followed recipes when cooking at the young people's accommodation he lived in.

Literacy practices link identities, culture and place. For example, Abdul, Martina and Soraya all watched a lot of TV and videos on channels from their own countries (Iraq, Angola and Iran) as well as the mainstream UK channels. For the young people in Safeplace and Entry to Employment, texting, a signature part of youth culture in particular, was as much a leisure activity as a need for communication. For example, Jez (see Chapter 6) described sending silly texts back and forth with other students in class. Texting was the main leisure activity for many of the young people at the centre, since financial considerations put many other activities beyond their reach.

Literacy practices for self-expression

Many of the people in the study used reading and writing to make sense of life around them and their own identity, particularly the younger ones. For instance, Dee and Jez were creative writers using poetry and letter writing as vehicles of self-expression and for management of life issues and of their emotions. Dee wrote poems, often with detailed explanations about the meaning of particular lines, on:

> anything and everything from everyday life to . . . just your feelings really . . . I think of something and I'll wake up in the middle of the night and can't sleep so I'll write a poem . . . Because whatever I'm feeling it gets it out . . . my friends always says to me a problem shared is a problem halved and yeah it's true.

At the Entry to Employment arts and craft class, making Valentine's plaques and cards gave the young people the opportunity to write freely and spontaneously, with humour or emotion, some of them using the different languages in their linguistic repertoire. Interestingly, the girls' verses were lewd and humorous whereas the boys' verses were more romantic and sensitive. Jamal wrote a romantic piece in Urdu for Yasmin which she translated for us. Seb, who had been disengaged for most of the card-making session, showing little interest in the art work, finally wrote a particularly creative, sensitive piece of writing for his card. However, neither Jez nor the young people in the art and craft class will ever be credited for this personal writing in any literacy test. Seb explained that he had been writing poetry since the age of 12. He, Dee and Jez and others had complete freedom to write poetry at home without the fear of not producing correct grammar, showing their well-developed skills as creative writers, which again is 'hidden', not built on and unaccounted for in the literacy tests.

The use of writing for self-expression, managing emotions and making sense of experience was not limited to the young people in community provision. Soraya wrote poems to express her sadness when she first came to Britain from Iran as an asylum seeker. Once she became a bit more settled she no longer did that. She did not want to show these to us as she thought it would upset her. Jane wrote creative pieces or poems about events that were important to her, such as going to concerts and Ronald Reagan dying. Martina created her own proverbs in Portuguese. She explained that the proverbs were to help her to keep strong and live in the right way, and to remember what is really important during the bleak and difficult time when she arrived in England alone aged 16 and lost all her family in Angola. Paula when asked in the ESOL class to write sentences to practise the structure *can/can't* did not produce the expected drills such as 'I can drive' but used the activity as a way of expressing her feelings at that time in her newly acquired language:

> I can't understand English people at all.
> I can cry easily.

I can't leave England at the moment.
I can't forget my good friends.
I can't speak Chinese but I would like to learn.
I can meet with my friends but not with my family.

As these examples show, literacy played a major role in the leisure lives and in the expression of emotions of many of the people we interviewed. Even though most of them had chosen to attend Skills for Life provision, and others were considered 'at risk' as regards their language, literacy and numeracy, their lives were rich with uses of reading and writing of their own choice. In some cases, this reading and writing 'for its own sake' was not just a pastime, but helped people to make sense of life and to establish a sense of who they were and who they wanted to become.

Literacy practices for social participation

The reading and writing associated with Jez's voluntary work for the children's rights charity, described above, are examples of literacy practices for social participation. Other people we interviewed provided evidence of participation in a wide range of forms of community, religious and political activity, all of which in one way or another involved the use of language, literacy and/or numeracy.

Mark and his girlfriend had an allotment and were encouraged to become joint Chairs of the local Horticultural Association, which gave them the task of organising the village summer show. Mark described some of what this role involved:

> That involves organising meetings, chairing the Committee meetings, sorting out judges for the Show and venues, taking the minutes, that kind of thing . . . We just, we asked if we could have a list of what each job was, and got a little piece of paper and it was like booking the judges, printing schedules, that kind of thing, and got handed the official minute book, and just left to it . . . We sorted [the show] out for I think it's the 6th August and got everything . . . contacted the school, cos we're having it at the school, made sure everyone was available, the secretary and everyone, and then found out that it clashed with [another local] Show.

These responsibilities brought with them a lot of paperwork, which he and his girlfriend did together.

Lee, from Safeplace, who had previously been very disruptive, had, through creative arts workshops, not only produced a substantial body of creative work but also taken on responsibilities for mounting exhibitions and fundraising. Most importantly he had drawn several other previously disengaged young people into the activities.

> He's helping loads with Safeplace Enterprises. He's been made the president because he's the only one who actually stays behind and he'll

work on the computer doing posters and things like that and he's been going off in his own time, going to Radio Lancashire and to the Telegraph for advertising, things like that, he's very resourceful is Lee. (Safeplace worker)

Martina, Paula and Ferdinand all went to different churches and engaged in the literacy practices of singing hymns and reading the bible, information and notices in English language. Lisette went to a French-speaking congregation further away with an Angolan pastor which was run as a sister church to the English Methodist Church. She was in a choir and was also a member of a women's organisation, with whom she attended a conference. Her participation in the church and membership of the women's organisation continued to be a life line and main network of support when she had to go underground after rejection of her application for right to remain in Britain.

An example of literacy practices associated with political activity is Abdul, from Iraq, who went to Manchester to vote in the 2005 Iraq elections. He received written information and a website address for instructions about how to get there and what to do. These required him to read in English, not just as an exercise, but for a fundamental social purpose. These examples show that attending classes, or being identified as 'at risk' and potential beneficiaries of the Skills for Life strategy, does not mean that people lead illiterate lives. In fact, they participate in a wide range of activities, most of which are textually mediated and some of which involve complex and demanding communicative practices.

Literacy for finding out and for learning

In addition to all the uses of language, literacy and numeracy we have described and exemplified in the previous sections, language, literacy and numeracy are tools for learning about anything and everything, in and out of school. This is why there is so much emphasis especially on literacy in schools and colleges: it is the main vehicle through which the teaching and learning of, for example, history, biology, or almost any school or college subject takes place (as discussed in Smith 2005; Fowler 2007; Ivanič and Satchwell 2007). The people we worked with revealed their uses of literacy for informal and formal learning around a wide range of topics. In this section we give a selection of these to exemplify this crucial function of literacy, and to show how people who are designated as needing help in terms of Skills for Life are already using literacy for other types of learning in other domains of their lives.

In some cases, language, literacy and/or numeracy for finding out information and for learning was connected to other pursuits. For example, Mark and his partner liked to travel independently, booking only the first couple of nights' accommodation. They researched their trips in advance, nowadays using the internet – it used to be using guide books and Youth Hostel Association information books. Momo and Darren, from E2E, had a lot of knowledge about cars and bikes, much of which they gained from reading the related magazines regularly. Soraya needed information on child development and health and picked up leaflets wherever she went.

We found that reading for information and learning in people's everyday lives was often a collaborative activity, or would have been better if it had been collaborative. For example, Dee searched the local press and the internet at the Jobcentre to find out about work opportunities. However, she was left to read through all the information on the computer screen on her own and would have benefited from someone helping her to scan for the jobs which might have suited her. Tommy also used a combination of the library, internet and his peers for finding out information.

Several of the people we interviewed talked of seeking out information on topics of vital concern to them. For example, Jane read counselling books and self-help books to help make sense of her life. She had recently been reading a book by the celebrity self-help guru Dr Phil McGraw, and felt she needed to put into practice some of his recommendations. Several of the young people at Safeplace, when they were presented with a selection of library books, chose information books to find out more about topics of their own individual interest, which included cannabis, pregnancy, marriage and Islam. Thomas wanted to research, learn about and understand his dyslexia and anxiety. He felt that developing an understanding of his problems gave him some relief, and every little bit of relief was 'one notch under my belt', so it was important to him. He has a lot of underlying concerns and worries, particularly relating to his mental health, and was concerned that he had been asked by his health professionals how he would feel if this was 'as good as it gets'. He often tried to find ways to understand what was going on: 'I've diagnosed myself quite a lot, because you had to, because you felt so out of place, and you felt that you looked out of place.' His daughters downloaded a lot of material for him from the internet about his conditions and printed it up, but he found a mass of printed material was just a lot of white lines to him.

At Safeplace there is a wide range of advice and information leaflets on life issues targeted at young people, some rather dull nationally produced NHS leaflets but most more visually attractive which are locally produced, some by the young people themselves.

> I look at the information box in the corner with comfy chairs – loads of stuff targeted at young people on sexual health, drugs and alcohol, education and training, personal safety etc. There is a colourful, cartoon 'rules of the house' poster that the young people themselves had made, entitled 'Moshi says . . .'. Amy says they produced it with 'Art in Action' [a local community arts organisation] saying that this was much more effective in giving information and getting them to accept how to live in the house than something more official and boring looking. She tells me they pick up stuff which was visually appealing with characters but tend to ignore anything that looked boring. Sophie is lying on the chairs

reading 'Turning Point', a handbook with advice for young people on independent living which the young people themselves produced with Art in Action.

(Extract from researcher's field notes)

A few of the people we interviewed were already studying on courses other than their language, literacy and numeracy courses, or were trying to find out about college courses they would like to take. For example, Paula read course materials about child development on her childcare course. Abdul read leaflets about the agricultural college as he was interested in doing a higher level agronomy course. However, the information was not enough. He was not confident to manage all the literacies of travel and what he would read at the college and did not realise the importance of going early enough so he left it too late to enrol. Everyday literacy practices have to be accompanied by cultural knowledge. There was a double-edged sword of opportunities for initiative on the one hand and constraints on the other, especially for people for whom English was being learned as an additional language.

Literacy learning outside the classroom

Not only do people use literacy in a wide range of contexts outside literacy classes but they also can and do learn and develop their reading and writing outside classes, often without the help of teachers. Most literacy learning in classes involves being shown or told about the structure of written words and sentences, having practice in understanding and using written texts and, less often, writing them. This section shows how people are learning literacy practices through participating in them, not just through sitting in classes or other integrated provision. There are three themes within the section. First, the research indicates how many people were learning through doing subconsciously, with no intention to learn nor awareness that they were developing their literacy capabilities, but were nonetheless doing so. Second, there were examples of people taking steps to increase their literacy capabilities outside the remit of a literacy class. Third, there were examples of how family members and others close to them were actively helping people to improve their literacy capabilities, scaffolding and supporting their development though shared activities.

Literacy learning through participation in everyday literacy events

The participants in our study were 'learners' not just in the sense of being enrolled in classes, but also in that learning is part and parcel of doing. For example, Mark developed the literacy practices involved in his new role as a foreman through trial and error:

KT: *Any training related to that?*
MA: *No. No. No. It's just . . . you can look after this job. Get on with it. [laughs]*
KT: *Right. Right. And how did you learn how to do that?*
MA: *[pause] Um, I think a bit from experience. With being self employed, there's always a bit of, you have to look after your own sort of work, so, it's just like doing that but with a lot more people.*

When he became chairperson of his village horticultural society, as described above, he was thrown 'in at the deep end' and had to learn the literacy practices for committee meetings by doing them as best he could.

Tommy used literacy for his own purposes in his everyday life, and was confident about reading and about finding out information linked to his interests and hobbies. He developed his literacy capabilities through these everyday events, particularly those associated with his hobbies and leisure pursuits. He felt he would probably always be 'getting into something else' that caught his fancy, and hence his literacy capabilities would be reinforced and augmented through use.

Learning at the Safeplace day centre is for managing and enjoying everyday life and is about getting on with people, anger management, preparing good cheap food, DIY and expressing themselves creatively, all factors which impact on their well-being. Learning is linked to everyday social and emotional issues, such as safe sex. Learning and the developing of basic literacy and numeracy skills for those who want or need this is only relevant to young people and workers as part of this life-enhancing endeavour based on what young people want or agree to.

Dave, a youth worker, described how the young people at the Safeplace day centre learn how to follow instructions through activities such as rock climbing where they have to listen and learn in order to survive. He says they need constant encouragement to be able to hold on to what they have achieved and to grow in confidence.

> The next day they might be cooking a boiled egg and be giving up on themselves so I say 'Ok, you're losing it. Well what about yesterday all you did then', and when they make that link they can have the confidence to follow instructions.

But these particularly vulnerable young people shy away from participating in activities when outsiders come on to their territory, as this threatens their confidence and ownership of their space and their creative work, which results in lost opportunities for literacy development.

> Ali tells me that next week Granada Studios are coming in to film a programme called 'Books on the Edges' and that young people from [another project] are coming up as the Safeplace young people would not be confident on someone else's territory. She tells me later that this was disastrous as the other young people had been encouraged to finish the

story started by the Safeplace young people who were reluctant to participate and finish it themselves. '. . . great TV but the young people felt excluded on their own territory'.

(Extract from researcher's field notes)

If this opportunity had been more sensitively handled it might have been a valuable opportunity for literacy development through a purposeful and creative leisure activity.

People taking their own initiative to develop their capabilities

Tommy described enjoying reading and using a dictionary to improve and extend his use of vocabulary – this was for spoken as well as written language. This was similar for Abdul, Martina, Sameena and Soraya who developed a real interest in grammar, which became a sort of leisure activity that they enjoyed at home. Cordelia used strategies to link home and college; for instance, writing words down that she got stuck on at home and bringing them in to work on in her spelling programme.

Through his spelling class, Tommy discovered that he enjoyed imaginative writing and constructing stories. Previously he described much of his reading as technical information gathering and saw himself as someone who was not very imaginative. He was very proud of his writing, which received much praise from Debbie, the tutor, and others who read what he had written. He began to see himself as someone who was able to write imaginatively and in a sustained way. In short he began to see himself as a writer. He wrote at work and at home about people and places from his everyday life.

Martina, from Angola, liked reading novels in French and magazines in English, which helped her languages to develop. Abdul's family's opportunities to use and develop literacies through their own initiative were severely constrained when the National Asylum Support Service inspected their home and disallowed the computer a friend had given the children, on the basis that they are only allowed basic food and clothing. This denial of basic human rights and freedom meant that their three children had to queue at the library to do homework and Abdul could not help them as much as at home.

Collaboration and networks of support for literacy development

The research showed that many of the people we interviewed had networks of support or significant others who not only helped them with the literacy aspects of their lives, but also helped them develop their own literacy capabilities. For example, Jane would write letters with her husband; he would spell the words and she would do the handwriting.

We saw earlier that Cordelia left most of the paperwork involved in running the house to her boyfriend but they worked out what was involved together, so that if anything ever happened to him she would have an idea how to do it. Her boyfriend worked it out on a piece of paper and broke everything down, and they talked about what she needed to do in the post office. This was not something that came from what they had learned in college, but something they had decided to do together. She said that she would always need someone to show her how it all works. She did not want to go out and do things with money without her boyfriend there to protect her, saying she would be frightened she would lose the purse and the money.

Dee did not achieve GCSE qualifications, but at the entry to employment programme she was assessed at Level 2 Literacy and Numeracy. She said she got to this level mainly because of support from her mother:

> I think my Mum's learned me a lot more than anybody else at school. I used to get the books and do it at home, the teacher would wonder how come you'd done so much work and they think they never done it in the lesson they never take much notice of me anyway . . . in school you can't do it, you can't concentrate, it's the noises, too many people . . . My Mum actually used to do the work herself [with me] if we got some exam papers.

The young people at the entry to employment programme used a range of outside support networks of family and friends. Sameera, Mani and the other Asian young people lived in settled Asian communities and Mani in particular drew on support from the local community centre for job-seeking. Peer support was vital to them and most of them mentioned the importance of friendships, as another student, Jodie, mentioned both generally and in relation to developing her writing skills. Several others mentioned the importance of support they received with the literacy demands of everyday life from people in their family and community networks, such as Sameera's sister. Jodie worked on her literacy skills with a friend and Dee's and Mani's proactive job seeking utilised their own and community resources.

Such scaffolding and support was evident in work as well as at home. Mark's way of keeping accounts was not something he learned to do in college; instead, when he got his first job after his apprenticeship, the man he was working with gave him the number of an accountant, he went to see her and she gave him the forms he needed and showed him how to keep his books.

Summary

This chapter has shown, first, how people who attend Skills for Life classes often have rich literacy lives beyond the classroom which can remain hidden and not built on in learning. They have powerful reasons for reading and writing arising from the demands made on them by the state and other institutions, their responsibilities, their relationships, and their passions. In these, reading is often inseparable from writing; they are not separate 'skills' but integrated in the fulfilment of a social purpose. Secondly, it has shown how some of the people we interviewed use literacy for learning and for finding out information as part of their everyday lives: literacy for learning is not confined to educational settings. Finally, we have evidence of how people develop their literacy capabilities independently of formal teaching: they learn by doing, they use strategies to teach themselves, and they draw on networks of support to scaffold their learning. People bring these resources and starting points to class with them, as foundations on which tutors can develop and build.

8

WAYS OF PARTICIPATING
IN CLASSES

In this book, we are examining the relationship between people's lives and their learning. Having demonstrated in the previous chapters the wide range of literacy practices that the people we worked with were dealing with in their lives, and the range of purposes that these served, we will now turn to examining the ways people engaged with literacy, numeracy and language provision. In this chapter, detailed case studies will show how participation in classes related to people's lives outside class, particularly their motivations for attending and to their backgrounds. In the next chapter, we will draw out themes from across the data to show the interaction of learning and lives by demonstrating the influence of what learners and teachers bring to classes and how the learning–teaching event is constructed as a social space.

We present four case studies of college classes in this chapter: two literacy classes, a numeracy class and an ESOL class. For each, we describe the teaching and learning interaction in the class, describing a focal session in detail, and present profiles of individual students, some of whom have already been introduced in earlier chapters. The examples have been selected for their diversity, with different types of class in different colleges being studied. They also cover different types of provision, including a drop-in centre open to people at all levels, a class set up according to level, and one-to-one tuition with volunteer tutors. There are also differences in that they take place in different cities, there are different patterns of gender relations and different life circumstances. In the six profiles, we describe people's backgrounds, identifying their motivations for attending provision and the way they participated in teaching and learning interactions in the class, drawing out perceptions of and strategies for learning. The profiles show how such factors interact in people's lives impacting on their learning, and how widely one set of circumstances can vary from another.

The Liverpool maths class

As described in Chapter 4, Liverpool Community College delivers a large programme of adult learning through a mixture of city sites and local Drop-in

Study Centres (DISCs). The DISCs are located within communities, with the aim of making adult learning accessible and responsive to local needs. The class we studied was advertised as a maths class (rather than numeracy) offering a two-hour session in the DISC in Redbrick Community College, an old Victorian building in the heart of the dockland area of Liverpool. The DISC space was an open-plan room situated on the second floor. It contained an office, two teaching spaces, filing cabinets and teaching resources. Our first impression was that it seemed cramped and noisy but it was a space that students clearly felt very comfortable in. They moved around with confidence and a sense of ownership.

The teacher was Kay, who was introduced in Chapter 4. Students ranged between Entry Level 1 and Level 2 according to the Numeracy National Curriculum. They worked on worksheet materials chosen in consultation with Kay to be at the level appropriate to them. As this was a drop-in session, students were free to attend when they wanted. Generally everyone attended the whole session from beginning to end, taking a collective coffee break halfway through. Students sat around a group of tables in the middle section of the room, surrounded by filing cabinets with an old CD player on top, which often played classical music softly in the background. There were maths artefacts in the space including posters showing multiplication tables, number posters, sets of scales and tape measures. At the other end of the room, a small group studying English met at the same time.

The focal session

Five students attended the focal session: Jason, Katrina, Sarah, Ella and Vicky. Kay greeted each person individually as they arrived and checked that they knew what they were going to do. They chatted about 'public' information such as other study, work and their children as individuals entered. The group helped to arrange the video camera to record the session, which Yvon, the researcher, operated, and then continued with their usual lesson structure. Kay prepared the tables and set out materials whilst the students collected their worksheets and learning plan folders.

The students appeared at first sight to be working individually on their own curriculum-referenced worksheets at a wide range of levels. Jason was working on fractions using work sheets at Entry Level 3 and Level 1. Katrina was doing multiplication at Entry Levels 1 and 2. Sarah was working on area and measurement at Level 1 and Ella was doing averages at the same level. Vicky was doing statistical analysis for her GCSE psychology course work. They were using calculators, tape measures, pencils, pens, notebooks and folders, alongside the worksheets, and were recording what they were doing by keeping a learning plan in their own file. There was a high level of engagement with the tasks on the worksheets. What was not so obvious at first sight is that Kay had contextualised these worksheet tasks in terms of each student's own wider interests, and in terms of the meanings and uses of number which had emerged when she had asked them questions such as: 'Why do you want to work on area?'

The room was hot and noisy with the phone continually ringing and the administrative worker responding to the calls. The English class also generated a continual low hum and there was noise from other parts of the building. Nevertheless, everyone in the maths group concentrated on their worksheet, ignoring all the noise. While students focused on their worksheets, Kay moved around the room, guiding, demonstrating and helping students to achieve the tasks on the worksheet. Her manner was quiet, respectful, calm, responsive and reassuring. She stood, knelt, bent, smiled a lot and laughed. She predominantly interacted with students on an individual basis, either responding to student requests or standing by a student and waited to be shown their work. She marked, or showed calculations in pencil and discussed follow-on topics or worksheets with each person. When responding to a request for help, Kay spent several minutes looking at the worksheet and discussing the difficulty. Through dialogue, she demonstrated how the answer was calculated, using her hands and arms to show size, proportion or area. The student either recalculated with her there or showed they could manage on their own.

The lesson worked as a shared but individual enterprise. Students looked at each other, talked to each other and engaged socially, negotiating roles of provider or recipient of knowledge and understanding. Sarah used a tape measure for her worksheet on measurement and in between measuring the desk, a cup and her hand she mimed measuring her waist and her bust. The group, including Kay, joined in a light-hearted discussion about measuring their bodies. Katrina and Jason discussed what part of the head should be measured for a head measurement. After social interactions such as this, individuals returned to work on their worksheets whilst Kay continued moving around the room.

Student profile 1: Jason

Background. We now focus on an individual student, Jason, who was introduced in the first chapter; he was a single, unemployed man who lived in Liverpool and who worked as a volunteer at a local tenants association.

Motivations for attending the class. Jason explained how he viewed learning maths now:

> I'm hoping to get qualifications or something out of maths. Like when I went to school I was in the first year, I sort of went but . . . when you look at maths now I want to learn something.

He described wanting to learn to overcome general feelings about being scared of maths and also to master particular topics he identified such as fractions, subtraction and addition. He appreciated the learning about measuring that was occurring and thought this was useful for buying a shirt or for clothes. He also thought knowing numbers would help him with his voluntary work in the Tenants'

Association; for example, in using numbers on the phone or sending a fax. Jason said that he understood money, in terms of how much he had in his pocket and what items cost in the shop. It was the link between the abstract concept of fractions and the everyday concept of dividing that he was learning and Kay was teaching him.

Jason felt that he was learning many new skills and knowledge that interconnected for him. He felt that Kay's teaching was different from his previous negative school experience and he was excited and now enjoyed the whole and interconnected process of learning:

> As I say we were having a good laugh and a joke about everything in maths. Maths now, as I explained it, I never went to school, but maths now, it's just like teaching, that's what it is the teacher's learning us and I'm learning. I'm probably learning faster. As I say it's just getting involved in everything. Same as when I go to college for computers, that's another useful thing you know. Take maths, that's probably like the keyboard, it's got all numbers and then looking up the internet. And with English as well, because I'm learning English as well, that comes up the same as on a computer.

Participation in learning. In the focal session, Kay responded to Jason's learning agenda and placed it within the curriculum framework for Entry level 3. She reported in her pre-session notes that Jason planned to continue with fractions both cancelling down and making a fraction in a context. Her post-session comments recorded that Jason cancelled fractions confidently but was not quite sure about fractions in context and he therefore needed more practical examples.

Jason explained that he felt he learned best on his own, even when in a group setting. He described the videoed session as successful in these terms:

> Well, I thought the class was good because everyone was doing their own individual work, I tend to stay on my own . . . by myself in my own project. I was doing fractions.

The video recording showed that Jason interacted in the measuring episode enjoying the fun, some of which was directed at him as the only male. Observation notes recorded that Jason interacted socially with others in the group who responded in a friendly and interested way. The social interaction, as well as the maths skills, was part of Jason's sense of what he was learning and of his increase in confidence:

> My confidence now has gone up. I used to be a very shy person. I wouldn't do nothing, I used to hide away in one corner and now you meet everyone.

The Liverpool spelling class

The spelling class was held as a two-hour morning session at Deepside DISC, housed in two rooms within the newly refurbished public library. Deepside is situated on the outskirts of Liverpool's city centre, about four miles out. The area is made up of mainly post-war corporation housing, new build and regeneration projects. The access to the library was both hidden and unattractive, with litter and rubbish in the alleyway leading to its entrance. In contrast, the library itself was new, warm and inviting with many posters in the entrance.

The main DISC room was a large newly furbished open-plan teaching and learning space. It had an array of about twenty computers at one end of the room where the IT tutor taught a range of courses. This was always busy, with students working on their own with the support of the tutor. The middle section had the reception desk and file cabinets. The end section had tables grouped together to make a large space for about a dozen students. In this space there was a white board and flip chart at the front, with both numeracy and literacy artefacts including scales, multiplication table posters, dictionaries and files around the area. The student filing cabinets were on one side of this space with the tea and coffee and photocopier on the other side.

The spelling class catered for students with different knowledge and confidence levels of English and spelling. Debbie, the tutor, taught the class at one end of the room with the IT course running at the other end, against a backdrop of a constantly ringing telephone and people dropping in for information.

The focal session

The group worked collaboratively on videoing a focal session of the spelling class. Debbie welcomed each student individually as they entered and asked about homework, discussing any additional writing they had done, and asking about jobs, children and families. As the group settled, people chatted to each other while getting out folders, worksheets, pens, paper and dictionaries. Eight people attended, sitting to accommodate Tommy and Susan, two hearing-impaired students, who sat at the front.

Debbie worked mainly from the flipchart, which was at one end of the table and the focal point of the class, writing key words and phrases that she talked about and demonstrated. Her delivery was to the whole group, encouraging participation and involvement without putting anyone on the spot. Although clearly in charge, standing at the front using the flipchart, Debbie also came across as a warm human being who readily shared her passion for her subject and for the student's own subjectivities and understandings. She skilfully engaged with the group, keeping their attention through the use of jokes, interjections and responses to comments that they made. By referring to her own, sometimes negative, experiences of learning, she created a space where students were encouraged not to be fearful of learning new things, or of making mistakes.

The lesson started by recapping the previous lesson on prefixes, checking for understanding and any homework generated from it. She gave examples of a root word 'willing', the prefixes 'un' that made a new word 'unwilling', and asked students to give examples to show their own understanding. Then she demonstrated suffixes on the flip chart, explaining that 'pre' meant before and 'suffix' after. She wrote common examples on the flip chart, using a column to show the root word, the suffix being added, and the new word it made, and encouraged students to come up and add answers to the tasks she had set. Students then worked on worksheets, either individually or in pairs, filling in beginning and ends of words from memory or by using a dictionary.

As the students became more confident, recognising words that they knew and being able to identify suffixes and prefixes, they related this to a general awareness of language and how it was made up. They were interested in the Greek and Roman roots of the English language. Tommy, Elizabeth and Susan were enthusiastic, relating this knowledge to doing crosswords. Responding to this enthusiasm, Debbie departed from her prepared material to talk about grammar. Most of the students found this confusing. Debbie's post-lesson evaluation made reference to this in a critical self-reflection about the difficulty of the materials she used and going too far for the students' understanding. Debbie recovered by explaining that grammar was something that they could do another class on, but they should concentrate on suffixes and prefixes for the time being. She discussed the possibility of a future class on grammar and both Tommy and Susan registered an interest, saying they had not really understood what they had just done but would like to learn.

Towards the end of the class time Debbie asked who would like a worksheet to practise suffixes at home. Most in the group wanted one. She also asked who would like ten words to write a story for homework. Tommy was very enthusiastic and Debbie read out ten words which those who wanted to wrote down.

Student profile 2: Susan

Background. Susan was 69 years old, a widow who lived alone. She had six children and was a grandmother and great-grandmother with many family members living nearby. She had been attending the spelling class to improve her spelling. She described going through her primary schooling without her deafness being picked up. This affected her confidence and skills in English. This was made worse as her schooling was interrupted by the war when she was evacuated to Chester. Although she said that she was a shy and naive child, she described herself now as being more confident. Susan talked about her limited writing practice when bringing up her six children:

> I never put pen to paper, I'd be seeing to their needs and they were hardly ever off school so any little note I wrote was they were off sick, that's it.

No more words, and sign it. Then I'd sign my family allowance book once a week and then I'd sign my pension.

Motivation for attending the class. Susan joined the spelling class after she had joined the IT course at the DISC and found she struggled with spelling. She had been given a computer by the family and wanted to know how to use it, keeping up with her grandchildren and helping with their homework. Susan described her motivation for coming as:

> I hope to learn a lot of my spelling because when I joined the ICT I realised I couldn't spell the shortest word, it had all gone out of my head.

By joining the class Susan had widened her understanding and appreciation of English language. When asked in the pre-class interview if she knew what she was going to do, she replied:

> No, because we were doing the prefixes, which I enjoy. I think English is fascinating and it's a subject that you can go on and on with. The more you find out about it the more interesting it becomes. I think that's the way learning should be, isn't it?

Susan spoke a lot about finding pleasure, enjoyment and fun in learning about language and spelling. Although she enjoyed the social aspect of the group, this was not always easy because of her hearing impairment. The video showed how she would engage with both Debbie and other members of the class when she could hear, but would work on her worksheet when she could not. She described enjoying the challenge of learning, of acquiring new skills both through her own enquiry and through instruction. She saw her quest for the truth and under-standing as potentially difficult:

> I've got to have the truth and I need to be told a bit. I'm a bit of nuisance really.

Susan showed through her classroom interactions and her worksheets that she acquired knowledge and understanding about suffixes – something she enjoyed. She also felt this was useful to her:

> Well actually you know I can grasp, I can see the difference when I've done the word and added on the end, so it's making the word a bit longer. So, it's enabling me to spell a bit better.

Her positive relationship with Debbie was important to Susan in providing what she described as a 'nurturing environment' for this learning to take place.

Participation in learning. The teacher, Debbie, showed in her notes on Susan that she was aware of the reflective nature of Susan's learning and how although she came to learn something specific – spelling – her interest and learning had broadened out. Debbie described small notes that Susan wrote in her homework indicating her learning: 'I didn't think I understood this but I know I do now.' This showed it was important for Susan to understand her own learning progress and not simply to be measured externally.

The Blackburn ESOL class

The Entry Level 3 ESOL class was a two-hour morning class held four times a week and it followed the ESOL National Curriculum in a modular scheme. The classes were held in a large, pleasantly refurbished, grand Victorian building adjacent to the main college campus in the centre of town. In addition to ESOL, there were mainstream courses held here with a wide student mix, which brought a lively atmosphere to the environment. The class was held in a spacious room with high ceilings. Students worked on tables arranged in a horseshoe facing the teacher's table with a blackboard behind and an OHP to the side. There was a photocopier in the room which was used by other teachers who came and went just before lessons started.

There were up to twelve students in the class, which the teacher, Duncan, saw as falling into two distinct social groups. There was an 'urgent' group, made up of students seeking asylum from a wide range of countries, who lived with a sense of uncertainty and not belonging, and were desperate to learn English in order to quickly build up a life here. And there was a 'non-urgent' group of young South Asian women who lived in extended families in a stable community. Though some of this group wanted to seek paid employment, there was not the same desperation about this in terms of survival in society.

The class worked together, all following the same learning activities which were decided by the teacher and were teacher-directed. It was a fairly formal but relaxed and friendly learning environment. Students were mainly focused on the learning tasks with minimal 'off-task' interaction, except at the beginning and end of lessons.

Typically the two-hour session began by the teacher explaining to the whole group which main grammar points would be covered in the session and carrying out introductory activities with the whole group which were teacher-directed, using materials from the main source textbook, *Headway*. The rest of the session was a combination of pair work or small group work, with some individual work on a common exercise and whole-group feedback, working on exercises related to the grammar points being learned, which were photocopied from the textbook. Each of the four aspects of language – speaking, listening, writing and reading – was practised in some way related to the task. The lesson concluded with a review of what had been learned in the session, which the teacher wrote on the board and the students copied on to their record sheets.

The focal class

The focal lesson was observed six months into the course. The session was based on the widely used ESOL textbook *Headway*. They were studying E3 Unit 12: Verb Patterns, which had a magazine feature story as the central text. There were ten students, from a range of countries: Pakistan, Angola, India, Iraq and Iran. Duncan signalled the start of the class by greeting students once most had arrived. He rearranged their seating arrangements, asking students he perceived as 'stronger' to sit with weaker students and pairing students of different linguistic backgrounds together. He explained that the main purpose of the lesson was 'to look at some grammar', and that he wanted to start with some reading, but that there would be a chance to speak more later.

He gave out the magazine feature story cut up into pieces and asked students, in pairs, to read the pieces and then put them in the correct order. The students were very engaged and there was a buzz of 'on-task' conversation. Sameena and Abdul and another pair completed the task easily; other students found it more difficult. Then Duncan gave the students a photocopy of the complete text and asked them to check their text ordering. He then asked students what type of text it was. Abdul answered: 'report . . . something that really happened'. Others were answering at the same time and Duncan did not hear his answer. After this discussion, Duncan read through the feature story, with little expression, seeming to use the text more as a vehicle for learning vocabulary and grammar structures rather than as an interesting story in its own right. He stopped frequently to elicit meanings of words he thought might be unfamiliar to the students, allowing them to help each other.

Then came two comprehension exercises: a whole group exercise followed by pair work. Duncan moved around the room from group to group, sometimes perching on the table or crouching down near a student, checking that they were managing the task, encouraging them by asking questions to help them get to the answer, and rarely providing them with an answer. Student interactions were almost all on-task and there was concentrated engagement with the exercise. Duncan asked different students to give feedback on the answers from the comprehension exercise to the whole group. He continually gave praise and encouragement for correct answers, and handled incorrect answers in a positive and sensitive way, sometimes referring them to the other students for them to decide.

The next activity was a whole-group session on a range of verb patterns. Duncan explained each of these in turn and elicited examples from the students, continually asking questions to check that they understood. He elicited the meaning of the word 'pattern' from the students, referring to patterns on their clothes. He then elicited examples for the other verb patterns from them on the board, using different coloured pens to highlight various structures. Then he asked the students to read the text individually and to tell the group when they had identified an example of the first verb pattern. He asked them to complete the exercise in pairs, and check with their partner if they wanted to. Sameena and Abdul were paired up, and although Sameena repeatedly asked Abdul for answers, which he gave correctly, she appeared not to accept these. She continued to struggle to find the right answers on her own. As a result, Abdul was not able to check and confirm that he was right, until finally he asked Duncan a question which brought him over.

Duncan asked students to prepare for homework by looking at a worksheet. He gave examples illustrating the exercises related to familiar situations at college, and drew cartoons on the board. Finally, he asked the students to review what they had learned in the lesson. They shouted out various answers such as 'new words', 'about let and make', 'infinitive and -ing form', 'about adventure Tony in jungle', 'about adjective infinitives'. Finally, Duncan wrote on the board 'verb patterns', and students wrote this on their record sheets.

Student profile 3: Abdul

Background. Abdul had come with his wife and two children to Britain from Iraq one year previously. He is in his late forties and worked as an agronomist. He was highly motivated to learn English so that he could gain employment. He felt that this goal was 'not in my control' as he was waiting for a decision from the Home Office. He would have liked to continue his agriculture studies at university but in the meantime he was willing to take any job. These days he felt he is doing very little. He spends his spare time reading newspapers, books and the dictionary to try to keep learning, watching coverage of the Iraq war on TV, taking the children to the park and town centre and helping them with their science and maths homework. He also attends the BBC Learning Centre in town most days where he was learning, with some tutor support, to use a computer. He said he had little opportunity to talk to English-speaking people outside the class so felt he did not get enough practice.

Motivations for attending the class. Abdul had a higher level of literacy than speaking and could, for example, read and understand letters he received from the Home Office. He said that his main reason for coming to the ESOL class was because he had difficulty in speaking English and understanding different accents. He wanted to learn how to 'speak very quickly [fluently] and correctly'. He had both a global and a local perspective which reflected the uncertainty about his future:

> The main reason [I come] I think English is an international language. Everywhere you go if you speak English, you can manage your affairs . . .
> If I want to stay in England I should learn English, for everyday life.

He felt unsure of his progress saying: 'I don't feel it' and 'I am not fully confident at speaking', but at the same time said 'I haven't any problems'. Though this seems contradictory, perhaps he was indicating that he had enough English to get by in everyday life but at the same time needed to keep positive and keep his dignity despite the challenges. The way he described how the focal class went also suggests this. He said that the class was 'not very difficult' and that 'if I understand the language, I can order the story'. Our class observations show that in fact the class was very difficult for him. Duncan's perception was that Abdul, as a mature, well-educated person who had little status in his new situation, needed to show that he was intellectually equal to the challenge of learning English even if he could not speak it so well.

When Abdul was asked what he liked best about the lesson, he said that he was 'interested in grammar'. It was clear that as well as the intellectual enjoyment he experienced, he perceived the usefulness of this kind of lesson as giving him more underpinning knowledge of English which would enable him to make correct grammatical choices when speaking: 'learning about . . . how arrange words in a sentence'.

Participation in learning. Abdul came to the class with a strong educational background, knowledge about and interest in the English language. He liked working in groups, he said, for both learning and friendship. He liked Duncan's teaching style saying that it was 'more detailed and higher level' and that there were 'high expectations here of students', which he saw as positive. He liked the way Duncan 'asks first before telling answers' and that he 'learned by Duncan's explanations'. Abdul had a high awareness of language and a particular interest in and enjoyment of grammar which he demonstrated by the frequent questions he asked in class; for example, referring to the subtext of the feature headline '500 kilos plus and four metres long', he said: 'Excuse me . . . in this we haven't verb . . . what does this mean? . . . I understand. It's possible to have sentence without verb?' Duncan explained that this is allowed in journalistic style. Abdul acknowledged that 'grammar is not everything'. He was a very quiet, unassuming man and sometimes seemed to 'disappear' within the group. Duncan failed to hear Abdul's correct answers on several occasions during the focal lesson. This happened in moments of high engagement when several students were speaking at once. Abdul was one of only two men in the class and at times seems to be 'submerged' by both the gender imbalance and his quiet personality. On the other hand, it was clear that despite this he felt well supported in class and completely free to ask questions and contribute whenever he wanted to: ' [it doesn't matter] how much I ask questions, they don't worry about my questions . . . they explain me in detail'.

Abdul found the article studied in the focal class 'interesting . . . because adventure'. He explained, and the researcher observed, some of his learning strategies in this lesson and more generally: he made up his own examples of the structure they were learning and checked with Duncan whether it was right; he wrote down words he didn't know; he made links with words he had read outside. For example, he linked '500 kilos plus' from the text to 'Jobcentre Plus' which he had seen in the town centre, asking what this meant. He learned with other students in group work, both checking and asking at the same time, for example (about how to order the story correctly): 'I think it's this one, which one is?' He showed the researcher how he read the cut-up text to put it in order, reading the last line first, possibly linked to the way he read Arabic. Duncan, who had worked in Saudi Arabia, commented that he formed letters and lines of letters 'in a Middle Eastern style with a right to left perspective'.

Abdul did suggest some factors that impeded his learning such as 'sometimes no time in class'. As Duncan explained, Abdul learned more slowly than most in the class, but he employed strategies such as frequently asking and checking with Duncan and other students and working at home. On more than one occasion Abdul seemed to know the correct answer but was not able to articulate an answer before Duncan turned from him to ask another student. Working with a very strong student could be an impediment for him, as well as a support. He said of the 're-ordering the text' task with Sameena, 'she didn't let me do anything'.

Student profile 4: Sameena

Background. Sameena had come to England from Pakistan ten years previously to get married at the age of 16. She had two young children and her husband ran a jewellery business in England. She had finished her secondary schooling in Pakistan and after coming to Britain she attended a community-based ESOL class. Her studies were interrupted when she was caring for small children, then three years ago she again attended a community class, moving up in her classes and being at Entry Level 3 at the time of our research. She felt she lost ground with the interruption of bringing up children and had to 'catch up' on previous learning. When she re-entered education she also attended a First Step childcare course, which she found very demanding as it was not tailored for ESOL learners. She was a very confident learner and had a very positive experience of both schooling and ESOL learning. She said she felt confident coming to classes in Britain because her teacher 'spoke my language' and also gave her support with her childcare course.

Motivations for attending the class. Sameena was highly motivated to learn English: 'I need practice . . . desperately I want to do job.' Learning English had already made a big difference to her life. Her relationship with her husband seemed to be central to her feelings about this. He had encouraged her, and Sameena's new-found social confidence had brought them happiness and a closer relationship: 'Big thing this one, my husband is happy, I am happy.' Sameena spoke of her husband passing on to her many jobs requiring English which he used to do himself. She was very assertive and confident in using English outside the class: 'I ring them, I ask for information . . . I don't want every time my husband's help, I want to do by myself.' She had not allowed the negativity of some in the community to undermine her, though it caused her some embarrassment when they asked her if she was still going to college. Their perception that she knew enough, 'You can understand and make yourself understand [understood]', was very different from her husband's 'No, you go, you in future speak good English', and her own perception: 'I said I want to a job or anything in the futures and this English is not enough . . . takes many years, I said it's a different language a lot of grammar in

91

there.' On the other hand, she felt a sense of progress and achievement in that she could now socialise with her husband's friends. Still her main goal was to learn enough English to be able to continue her childcare studies and get a job. She felt she needed practice and did not get it much at home, and felt that the two-hour class did not give her enough either.

Sameena was learning patterns of language that she saw as a crucial framework for learning to speak English. 'I like grammar, is very big thing to speak good English.' She explained that this was useful outside because if, for instance, she used the present tense correctly, people understood what she wanted to say. As she explained above, she was also experiencing the pleasure of intellectual challenge and gaining confidence both socially and as a learner.

Participation in learning. Sameena enjoyed the ESOL class and saw it as a social as well as a learning group. She had good friends there from her own community and liked to meet people from other countries. She especially liked grammar and 'word patterns'. Sameena said of the article they read that it was a 'nice story'. She found Duncan's style of teaching helps her to learn: 'He doesn't answer straight away, he is try to make me think and very like it use my brain'. In reference to her confusion on a grammar point of when to use 'ask' or 'tell', which other students pointed out to her, she showed her confidence and assertiveness in learning: 'I'm not shy, oh I'm wrong and leave it, I always ask him why.' She suggested that her level of comfort and confidence again stemmed from Duncan's style of teaching and communicating with her: 'He never said *no* [something we also observed about how he deals with incorrect answers], always he answers very friendly, easily.' She explained the benefits of group work: 'I speak a lot with her . . . I ask meaning.' As Duncan said, we observed that she was a very co-operative and pleasant student. She worked in a pair with Abdul, discussed above, and gently helped him find the answers in the whole-group feedback as he was quite slow. But at the same time, her confidence and higher level of skills did cause an impediment to him in the re-ordering exercise.

Sameena clearly articulated how she learned from the focal text 'depending on the task': reading 'main points quickly but if questions I am reading slowly'; finding answers by locating key words she already understood, such as finding the word 'wear' then working out the answer to the question 'What did the guide make him wear and why?' Her previous learning also helped her to order the story as she had read this particular story in another class and had awareness of layout, knowing that bold type indicates a heading. She said that it was necessary to read all the bits first before starting to order: 'If we didn't read . . . then decide is hard.' Some other students did not employ these strategies or have the understanding of layout that Sameena had and so struggled more with the task. She used a highlighter pen so that she could quickly find the answer in the whole group feedback. She mentioned how she came to understand a difficult grammar rule on choice and obligation – the use of 'let' and 'make': 'I was confused . . . then I use brain . . . I did lots of time again and again one thing . . . I like this style.' She seemed to suggest a combination of thinking and practice to achieve learning. She mentioned Duncan's acting out scenarios and drawing as aids to understanding words and word patterns in this lesson, such as the cartoons of happy and sad faces he drew to illustrate the difference between 'choice' and 'obligation'. In talking around how she did the grammar exercise in class, she said doing it herself is the best way for her to learn: 'I don't want to copy another person . . . . do on my own . . . then check together.' She said that changing partners was important as there was the temptation to use a shared language with some students. She again showed how strongly she took charge of her own learning. If she did not understand something at home, she asked her husband or underlined it and the next day asked Duncan, but that did not go far enough for her: 'But I want to put in sentence, in *my* sentence.' Similarly she liked to use the dictionary herself so 'I understand meaning', and to her daughter who wanted to help her she said, 'No, I want to do my own!'

The Lancaster spelling class

This class took place weekly on a mid-week evening in the Adult College. It was held in the 'Skills for Life Centre', a large refurbished classroom which had been opened at the start of that academic year and was still relatively new, well-presented and well-equipped. The room was lined with shelves and pigeon-holes full of literacy and numeracy resources, with a bank of new computers around the walls. The class lasted two hours with a short coffee break in between. The first hour consisted of people working either individually or with a volunteer tutor on work specific to their individual learning plan. The second hour was a tutor-led group session. Here we focus on describing two one-to-one sessions where students worked with volunteers; this provides a contrast with the tutor-led sessions in classes described previously.

This spelling class is an established class which has been held at the same time for several years. It covered a range of levels from beginners through to Level 1. Most of the students in the class were working people and there was a majority of men. The class had two components: group work led by the class tutors, and individual work by students alone or with volunteer tutors. Group work sometimes focused on specific spelling patterns ('ai' words for instance) but often involved more general work, such as reading the college newsletter together and picking out spellings and grammar points. In individual work time, students focused on work which had been prepared for them by tutors or volunteers on the basis of their individual learning plans. Many students were working towards a spelling certificate from a national awarding body and had particular topics to cover, such as knowledge of specific word patterns. Most also used an ongoing 'spelling support programme' which involved recording new words one week, working out strategies to spell them and practising them following the technique of 'look, cover, write, check', being tested on them the next week, and using them in dictation two weeks later. The analysis below focuses on two students' patterns of participation in one-to-one sessions with their volunteer tutors.

Student profile 5: Jack

Background. Jack was a dairy farmer who ran a large farm in the local area. He had been attending this class for five years, having arrived as an Entry Level learner, and had been working with the same volunteer, Hannah, for much of that time. Hannah was a retired school teacher. She took most of the responsibility for planning out Jack's individual work, based on the individual learning plan that they worked through together, although the class tutors kept a check on what was being covered.

Focal session. The focal session began with general chat. Jack had had travellers staying on his land without permission, a recurrent problem for him, and was discussing a newspaper story about this issue. The session 'proper' began when Hannah explained to Jack what she had planned for them to do in the session.

The lesson started with practice of a sample of 'Dolch words' (the most commonly used words in English) and some social sight vocabulary reading. These were activities which Jack and Hannah practised regularly together. They started off by filling in the date at the top of the piece of paper, leading to a discussion of Jack's activities that day. He had been artificially inseminating cows, and explained that his computer provides the date automatically when the cow number is punched in. Hannah then tested him on a sample of Dolch words, reading them out first alone and then in sentences, and occasionally linking them with real events that had been happening (for example, linking the word 'saw' back to the discussion about travellers). When Jack made a spelling mistake, Hannah hinted with phrases like 'just nearly' and Jack self-corrected. They also teased each other; they have been working together for several years now and have developed a jokey, friendly relationship. Social sight vocabulary was then tested with Jack reading out a number of common social words – way in, exit, etc. – which he did quickly and with assurance as if this was something he had done many times before.

They then moved on to a worksheet exercise about prefixes and suffixes, which Hannah had prepared, in which he was asked to select from a choice of prefixes and suffixes to add to words on the sheet (e.g. 'happy' – add 'un' to make it 'unhappy'). Jack worked quietly writing these down for a long time with Hannah saying nothing. When he had finished, he read them out to her, and when they were both satisfied that he had them right, Hannah asked Jack to put them in his file under the appropriate curriculum reference. While doing this, they came across a list of months, which they had decided not to practise writing because Jack never uses them in real life. Hannah quickly tested his reading knowledge of them by asking him to read them out, which again he did confidently and quickly.

They then moved on to doing an activity which Hannah had prepared to practise map-reading. She had brought in a map of Lancaster. First she asked him whether he ever came in to Lancaster for his work. It turned out that he did not: there was no point in coming to the Lancaster auction any more, since dairy cows at the end of their life were now bought at a fixed price by the government. They talked through what the map represented and then Hannah asked Jack to point out where he went to school, teasing him gently when she found it was in a prestigious area of town that she had not realised he was 'posh'.

After working with the map, they went on to practising some words from Jack's own everyday life which they had worked on many times before. Hannah promised him that this would be the last time they did it. She removed one word, 'concentrates', from the list they had used before, having discovered that this is a word he never actually has to write. She asked him to test himself on the words using the 'look, cover, write, check' method. Looking at the words prompted more discussion about his farming work; for instance, talking about whether he still grew maize or not. Once Jack had tested himself, Hannah asked him to check through that he was 'comfortable' with them all. She then read out some sentences they had worked on before, using unusual words, and asked him to write them down, checking the spellings as he did so.

The next activity was to look at a paper Hannah had brought in: a notice that the council had sent her about some works that were to happen at the end of her road. This time Jack teased her, about living at the 'posh end'. There was a punctuation mistake throughout the leaflet – 'it's' for 'its' – and Hannah asked Jack to find it, chatting to the other people in the classroom as he looked for it.

Finally, Hannah asked Jack to write five sentences on the computer, using the words from his everyday life that he had been practising. He called Hannah over once in a while for assistance, but for the most part worked independently on this. When he had completed some sentences, Hannah checked them with him and talked through how to correct a misspelt word before he continued working. The last time she went over to check they shifted the conversation back to farming and he explained to her how silaging works.

At the end of class, Jack and Hannah filled in together the sheet recording the work done in the class. They referred to Hannah's lesson notes to do this, and Hannah prompted Jack as to what to write. They talked about whether he would attend in July, which depended on the silaging, and briefly discussed the activities that had happened in the group session, Hannah drawing attention to the progress Jack had made in the past year.

Motivations for attending the class. Jack had been a successful farmer and businessman for many years, and was not impeded in this by his reading and writing capabilities. Where paperwork was necessary for the farm, his wife assisted him. So coming to class was not so much about opening up new opportunities for him in his everyday life as about addressing something which had been an issue in his life for a long time, as an 'extra' activity. He was spurred on to come to the class when his father saw an advert for the classes in the local doctor's surgery. This came shortly after his son had said something about him not being able to read and write, which he said had 'annoyed' him.

In interviews Jack told us how the learning he did in class had some impact on his everyday life. He felt he was getting benefits from coming. His reading and writing had both improved significantly. The main difference for him was that he used to feel pressured when writing in front of someone, and would rush and make a mess of it. Now, he found he had the confidence to calm down and slow down even when someone was watching, and this helped him not to make mistakes.

Though his wife dealt with most of the paperwork related to the farm, if something came up when she was not there, Jack dealt with it himself. Hannah tried to ensure that at least some of the activities used words which would be useful to him in everyday life, which was why they practised the farm words towards the end. However, they found that in fact much of the business Jack transacted at the farm was done over the telephone, or by ticking boxes in forms, so he did not actually need to know how to write down many of the words they worked on together. As Hannah learned more about the writing Jack needed to do in everyday life, she tailored his work to it. This was why, for instance, they had not continued to test his spelling of 'concentrates'. Jack said the classes had helped his confidence in dealing with farm paperwork.

Other areas he now felt more confident about include going out driving with a map and being able to find his way to new places, though he always used to and still did sit down with a map to plan his journey by writing down junction numbers. He also read more at home, and particularly on holiday, than he used to. The practice of reading for pleasure was something new that he had developed through coming to class.

The class had also given him more confidence in general terms. He had initially expected the class to be full of teenagers and was surprised to find a group of people of varying ages, many around his own age, which gave him a feeling of being less 'different' than he had previously expected. There were social benefits associated with attending class, giving him the opportunity to socialise with people outside the farming world. This had been particularly significant during the foot-and-mouth crisis in 2001, when Jack had had to remain completely isolated from the rest of the farming community.

Participation in learning. The session was made up of short chunks of relatively discrete word-focused tasks, with few links made between them. This meant that Jack's participation in the session involved engagement in a wide range of different learning opportunities, including writing dates, Dolch words, social sight vocabulary, affixes, months of the year, map reading, and 'farm words', among others. He also engaged in a variety of strategies to support his learning, including 'look, cover, write, check', keeping track of where he was on a task using check marks, checking the accuracy of his own spelling by developing a 'feel' for the words, using a word processor and keyboard, and organising papers in filing folders. Volunteer and student shared knowledge of 'the routine', with shared understandings of what tasks consisted of as a result of having engaged in similar activities for some time. There was little explicit explanation of tasks, which were referred to simply by shorthand labels which both understand: 'your Dolch words', 'your social sight', 'your farm words'.

The focal session was characterised by constant praise and reinforcement. Each time Jack got something right, Hannah made a point of praising him. This constant focus on his success and progress helped him to reshape his understanding of himself as a successful learner, which contributed to the development of his confidence in his ability described above. There was also a constant interweaving of on-task talk and off-task talk, which was usually about what was going on in Jack's and Hannah's lives. They shared talk about memories and experiences, both memories of what had happened in previous sessions and memories about life beyond the classes. This was a deliberate strategy on Hannah's part, who saw this provision of social support as being part of her role as a volunteer, and it was an important part of the social benefits that Jack reported gaining from the classes. He was also positioned as being an expert, particularly in some of the off-task conversations, as he explained to Hannah some of the 'insider knowledge' he had about how farming works that he was bringing to the session.

Student profile 6: Alfonso

Background. Alfonso was from the Dominican Republic, where he had married an English woman who he met when she was there on holiday. She settled there with him, and they had two children. The family came over to England three years earlier. He had been working with Diana, his volunteer tutor, for a few months. At the time of this recording she had been volunteering at the college for about a year and a half, training first as a literacy volunteer tutor and now engaged in ESOL volunteer training. They were good friends and talked a lot about what was going on in each others' lives, but this normally took place during social time. In class time, they focused very much on the topic covered in the session. Diana took most of the responsibility for planning out Alfonso's one-to-one work on the basis of his individual learning plan, though the class teachers kept a check on what they were doing.

Focal session. The focal session began with Diana checking through Alfonso's work-done-sheet to see when he last came and what was covered. She then told him about her plans for the session. He had taken home a book about Winston Churchill from the library to read, so they began by talking about what he had learned from reading that. Diana suggested Alfonso pick a section to read so that she could check his pronunciation. He read aloud from the book for some time, and Diana corrected his pronunciation whenever he made an error. Where there was a cultural reference that she thought he might not understand, or where he asked what something meant, Diana explained it. This reading aloud took up the major part of the recorded session. Once he had finished reading the book aloud, and Diana had checked whether he enjoyed it or not, they moved on to writing his individual learning plan. This happened very quickly and was largely directed by Diana, suggesting goals for the plan on the basis of what she already knew about Alfonso's goals for learning.

Diana had prepared pronunciation exercises from a pronunciation book with associated tapes: *Ship or Sheep*. They had the book available in class but Alfonso had the tapes at home. They worked through a written exercise together practising different pronunciations of 'c'. They then started another pronunciation exercise but Diana decided the tapes were necessary for this one so curtailed it. They worked through another exercise where he had to distinguish between words with similar sounds (such as 'mouth' and 'mouse'). After a quick check where Alfonso read aloud the ordinal numbers in sequence, they played a game involving questions about the positioning of horses in a race, to practise his use of ordinal numbers. Finally they both went over to the library to select another book for him to read at home.

Motivations for attending the class. Alfonso was very keen to learn and develop in general terms. He was motivated to get as many certificates and qualifications as he could, and enjoyed spending time learning and studying. When he first came to England, he and his wife had both planned to work part time and look after their two children part time. However, it proved easier for his wife to find work and he ended up being at home full time with the children. He was not happy in this situation. He liked to be active, and found it difficult being in the house all the time. It was also hard for him to learn English and develop social networks. Eventually he and his wife decided on a trial separation, which was when he began living on his own, working and studying and meeting new people. He now worked five days a week. When he was not at work, he was studying. He followed a chef's course at the local Further Education college one day a week, after which he spent a couple of hours in the learning centre there where he had been doing learndirect courses. On Tuesday evenings he took driving lessons, on Wednesdays came to the spelling class, and on Thursdays went to a maths class.

Alfonso first found out about the Adult College courses from the newspaper. Initially he came enquiring about ESOL classes and was not sure about Adult Basic Education, but he enjoyed the spelling classes and learned a lot. The spelling classes were seen as appropriate for him because while his spoken English is quite good, he had learned it all by speaking and listening and did not know how to spell words. He also wanted to work on his pronunciation, and felt that learning how to spell words will help with that. He enjoyed coming to classes, both because he was very keen on learning, and because he got to meet new people and chat to them.

Given Alfonso's high levels of motivation regarding any sort of learning, the first and most significant impact of his learning on his everyday life was that simply engaging in the process and in the classes improved his quality of life. He was also very motivated to improve his spoken English and pronunciation and saw the focus on spelling in this class as helping him with that. Again it was hard to say which specific aspects of this particular interaction were useful to him in his everyday life, but he found any sort of learning positive and useful.

Participation in learning. The main task, reading the Winston Churchill text, was worked on for a long time, and took up the majority of the time of the session. This was a longer activity than most of those observed taking place during the one-to-one sessions. The reading of the book was used for multiple teaching purposes, including to practise punctuation, to provide examples of spelling words, and to develop Alfonso's cultural knowledge. Diana was keen to help him integrate in British society and tried to select tasks for him that would both help him with this and contribute to the subject-specific learning opportunities he wanted to work on, such as pronunciation. She drew upon her background as an historian to inform him about British culture and history.

Repetition of words was used as a tool for ensuring correct pronunciation, and Diana made sure that the pronunciation of every word was correct before moving on to the next. Whenever a pronunciation error was encountered there was a common pattern. First Diana corrected the pronunciation, and Alfonso repeated after her. Then, when Diana was happy with his pronunciation, she explained the meaning. She seemed to assess, through prosody or other non-verbal cues, when only a pronunciation correction was needed and when the word's meaning should be explained too.

The principal subject-specific learning opportunities for Alfonso here were to practise and correct the pronunciation of the various words encountered while reading the Churchill book aloud. Embedded in this was explanation of the meaning of the words he did not know, and some review of spelling rules and patterns, such as the silent 'e' rule. The pronunciation exercises later give him the opportunity to practise different pronunciations of the letter 'c', different ways of spelling the sound /k/, and the th/s sound distinction, as well as the pronunciation of some difficult words like 'ocean'. He also practised reading ordinal numbers aloud and listening comprehension of ordinal numbers, including their use in question forms.

In addition to subject-specific learning opportunities, Alfonso and Diana discussed strategies for learning new words, including writing lists of new vocabulary. They also engaged in educational practices, including reading aloud and filling in an individual learning plan. There was very little conversation in this session about Alfonso's everyday life. Both volunteer tutor and student remained focused on the different tasks that were being worked on. Nevertheless, relationships of trust and friendliness were demonstrated between them, and a lot of laughter and joking was woven around the task-focused interaction. There was also not the same level of ongoing reassurance and praise seen in other volunteer–student sessions which have been recorded. Instead, there was explicit acknowledgement several times of what Alfonso had learned, through summarising and through Diana picking out and highlighting particularly significant difficult points he had mastered.

In the next chapter we broaden the discussion out to include discussion of data from all the classrooms studied.

9

THE NEGOTIATION OF TEACHING AND LEARNING IN CLASSES

In this chapter we draw on the detailed accounts of individuals described in the previous chapter and combine them with data from other classes and on all thirty-seven students studied in detail in the classroom phase of the research. We focus on what adult learners bring to their classes, the teachers' contributions, and then how these two factors are negotiated in the social space of the classroom. We identify five aspects of learning and teaching as 'social spaces'. These are: the dynamic dialogue between students' and tutors' contributions; the importance of social relationships; the negotiation of learning opportunities through the fine-tuning of elements of learning–teaching interactions such as pace, formality and structure; the role of learners as active agents in this negotiation; and the broader outcomes of attendance at educational provision, such as social confidence, which emerge from this negotiated process.

What adult learners bring to their classes

In this section we discuss three main issues. The most significant of these is adult learners' varied motivations for attending educational provision. We also summarise how learners differ in terms of their life histories and current life circumstances, and indicate the nature of the strengths, experience and varied expertise people bring with them to their classes. This and the previous chapter show how varied the lives of adult learners of language, literacy and numeracy are, even those who are attending the same classes. The point of emphasising the complexity and diversity of what people bring to their classes is to illustrate what teachers need to take into account in order to fine-tune their teaching to their learners. For those involved in national frameworks such as Skills for Life, the data illustrates the nature of the challenge faced when contextualising national frameworks to individual circumstances.

Motivations for attending educational provision

The Skills for Life strategy makes a strong connection between learning, qualifications and employability. One tutor said: 'Gone is the sense that you can come to college because you enjoy it. Even in the non-vocational courses there is constant pressure for progression, progression.' Qualifications and employment are the main goals for many learners, especially those for whom English is an additional language. Alfonso from the previous chapter is a classic example of someone seeking to develop their language and gain qualifications in order to get better work and settle in the country: a motivation more common for ESOL than literacy and numeracy learning. All the students seeking asylum in the Blackburn Entry ESOL class had similar motivations to Alfonso. Abdul and Sameena both had clear ideas about what they wanted to do in the future. Abdul, like other recently arrived students, was very unsure of the learning route and the possible options, which suggests that there is a gap in addressing these students' learning needs as a whole. He was learning English but not getting the information and advice he needed in order to move towards his goal as quickly as possible.

However, motivations could not always be tied in to gaining qualifications and increasing employability. Susan said at age 69 she would not work again. Cheri, one of the students in the Liverpool maths class, doubted whether she would be able to hold down a job because she had been diagnosed with and was being treated for bi-polar disorder. Jason aspired to find work, but thought he would probably do voluntary work for a while. Jack had a well-established job that he was happy with and good at, which was not affected by his reading and writing capabilities. He did not come to class for reasons related to work, but to boost his own confidence and to address something which had been an issue in his life for a long time.

We found that the students have many other motivations related to their everyday lives. Some of the learners are going to classes for general interest, some as a way of managing mental health issues, some for skills in non-paid voluntary work, and only some to help with employment. For some the motivation was to become confident in areas that they had failed in at school, or had missed through non-attendance. These sorts of 'educational' motivations included individual small goals, for instance learning how to spell correctly a commonly misspelled word, or big goals, such as Cheri's ambition to achieve GCSE maths. Several of the Lancaster students' motivations related to increasing their confidence in everyday life, rather than seeking to develop their employability, for reasons partly related to mental health problems they were dealing with. Reasons for coming to class included supporting or enabling others as well as helping oneself. Susan wanted to help her grandchildren, and Jason to help people who belonged to the tenants' association he worked for. One tutor pointed out the significance of age differences in learners' differing motivations. Many learners held several types of motivation simultaneously; their own long/short term individual ones, including factors such as gaining confidence, as well as external ones such as learning fractions or completing a national test, getting a certificate or doing another course.

Learners' motivations often change over time. One tutor pointed out that people often say their reason for coming to class is to address specific difficulties with spelling, because this is something visible and self-diagnosable, but that they do not know enough about the structure of language to identify other issues, for instance: 'My sentence structure is poor.' Once they start coming to class, broader issues emerge and they identify other motivations. One student said: 'I don't know what I need to know, because I don't know what there is to know.' Sameena set out with mainly educational motivations but an unexpected outcome for her was the effect her learning had on her already happy relationship with her husband. They came to share a broader range of activities such as watching films in English or with English subtitles and socialising together with English-speaking friends with whom previously only her husband had communicated. Her motivations for learning English became, as a result, social as well as educational.

Learners often had to overcome considerable difficulties in order to attend, and displayed a high degree of commitment once they had done so. In spite of what often appeared to be quite bad conditions for learning – noisy or badly furnished classrooms, inconvenient locations or unsocial hours – the learners sustained their initial motivation to come to class, and participated actively when they were there. This suggests that, if the learning environment is good, it can ameliorate the effects of a poor physical environment.

Life histories and current life circumstances

There were differences not just between, say, the ESOL class and the spelling class, where differences in the aims of the class itself would be likely to attract different learners, but also within each class. Differences are not just attributable to obvious characteristics such as country of origin or entry placement score, but were much more individual, dependent on the personal characteristics and life opportunities of each person. It was not just a question of a 'spiky profile' of current capabilities. Other physical, material, social and affective aspects of people's lives were equally relevant to this diversity, particularly their sense of independence, feelings of fear or willingness to take risks, and the extent to which they felt affected by negative prior educational experiences. Differences between people include those related to mental health issues, physical disabilities and home circumstances. People vary in their concentration span, and in their comfort with working independently or in groups. The complexity and diversity of these individual circumstances showed the difficulty of attempting to tailor provision to particular groups; even within a narrowly defined group, individual differences are likely to be greater than similarities.

There is a marked difference between many ESOL students, particularly refugees and asylum seekers, and other literacy and numeracy students. This group have, on the whole, higher levels of confidence in educational settings, having had, in many cases, positive experiences of education in their home countries. Compared with other learners, people in this group are often experiencing downward mobility. Many are well qualified or have high academic potential, yet even 'fast tracking' will not lead to jobs of the financial and social status they had or could expect in the countries they came from.

The strengths, experience and varied expertise of adult learners

Adult learners not only face difficulties in their lives but also bring a wide variety of capabilities, resources and strengths to their classes. In the Entry Level spelling class in Lancaster, tutors made a point of establishing that all students are 'experts' in something, and the tutor knew enough about the students' everyday lives to know what each person is expert in. This ensured that they were not positioned simply as 'basic skills learners' but as fully rounded adults. For example, as shown in the previous chapter, Hannah selected Jack's words to practise according to his expertise in farming, and often discussed his everyday life during the session. She adapted their activities according to his feedback on whether or not they reflect what he is doing in everyday life.

Teachers' contributions to the learning–teaching event

We observed teachers in their interaction with students in the classroom: how they responded to them, and how they adapted the curriculum to their needs. We talked to them about their teaching, what led them to certain decisions, what they were pleased with and what troubled them. We identified key factors which they were bringing with them to their practice: responsiveness to learners as individuals, and the views of language, literacy and numeracy underlying their practice. We also became aware of tensions between two types of professionalism which they brought to their work. We discuss these in the following sections.

Responsiveness to learners as individuals

We observed many tutors listening closely to what learners were saying, both out loud and between the lines, seeing learners as complex individuals with a past, a present and a future, and responding to them as such. We observed tutors working to sustain the motivation which brought students to the class, to find new challenges which would maintain their enthusiasm. Many teachers knew not only about the difficulties learners faced but also about their cultural resources, dispositions, propensities, capabilities, strengths and the expertise they have in their everyday life. They often referred to these factors and based their teaching on them. Learners would bring items in or discuss things they had seen which the tutor might be interested in. The tutors also discussed events from their own lives, sometimes connected to the learners' interests and experiences, and by doing so established a symmetry in the teacher–learner relationship.

The more tutors understood about each individual, the more they were able to fine-tune their teaching to them, adjusting both the content of an activity and their management of the interaction to give the learners maximum opportunities for learning. For example, in the Blackburn ESOL class the teacher, Duncan, adapted his style of wit to suit students from diverse cultural backgrounds. Duncan's understanding of Abdul's prior education, of his experience as a learner and his existing knowledge of English (that his written language was stronger than his spoken language) allowed him to set the right level of learning challenge and support to address Abdul's learning needs. Duncan's awareness of social dynamics, such as cultural and religious differences between Muslim students from the South Asian community and students seeking asylum from other countries, was important in helping him to foster a co-operative learning environment of mutual peer support.

In the Liverpool maths class, the teacher, Kay, worked with one of the students, Katrina, to understand the relevance of learning her multiplication tables in relation to the work that she wanted to do and the difficulties that she was experiencing. The meaning of 'times tables' was translated into concrete experiences; for example, measuring baby bottles, nappy changing timetables and shopping. Although Katrina was studying at NVQ Level 2, her maths needs were at Entry Level 1/2. The way that Kay bridged the gap with concrete and everyday task-based understanding did not threaten Katrina's other subject knowledge. Topics such as shopping formed a baseline of everyday activities which Katrina already knew about and was proficient in. Kay also worked with Jason's expressed fear about maths. Although he was working consistently well at Entry Level 3 and Level 1, Kay understood the need to work on his confidence as well as the skills involved. Again she located much of the understanding of the concepts covered in his concrete experience with the Tenants' Association. It therefore made sense to him and he wanted to learn to be better at what he did there.

Teaching was most engaging when learning activities were chosen or adapted to learners' individual goals, personal interests or immediate lives. This was true even where there was a common learning aim, as in the ESOL classes. What was important was a student's sense that the teaching was focused on them rather than just on the coverage of content. In some of the classes we observed, however, the class activities did not seem to be directly linked to learners' goals. This resulted mainly from the teacher's efforts to follow a curriculum framework too closely and being solely guided by the curriculum specifications, the assessment targets and the level descriptors. This often led them to concentrate their efforts on explicit attention to formal aspects of language or literacy, as we will demonstrate in examples, below. Overall, these examples show that tutors' responsiveness to adults' unique circumstances and preferences is a crucial resource in these classes. Researching their own practice seemed to heighten tutors' awareness of the importance of listening to learners and thinking about them as people with lives beyond the classroom as well as within it.

Views of the nature of language, literacy and numeracy

As has been noted in Chapter 3, participants in learning–teaching events bring with them conscious or subconscious beliefs about the nature of learning and teaching, and about the nature of language, literacy and numeracy. We observed learning and teaching practices which appeared to be based on a variety of views about the nature of language, literacy and numeracy, and recorded similarly varied views in our interviews with teachers and learners. Even though most lessons appeared to be relaxed and sociable, our observations suggested that language, literacy and numeracy were frequently being treated as skills isolated from social practices. Many of the activities learners were undertaking involved a focus on linguistic form or abstract numerical calculations, often based around worksheets. In spite of many learners' goals being formulated in terms of social purposes for speaking, reading, writing and calculating, there was comparatively little attention in some classes to the practical use of language, literacy and numeracy to get things done.

A view of language, literacy and numeracy as technical skills manifested itself in the high premium on 'correctness' which was in evidence in many situations. Correctness was emphasised and reinforced as a central value in many different ways across the different contexts, possibly to the detriment of other values such as expressiveness, fluency, speed, effectiveness for purpose, communicativeness, or sociality. It manifests itself in activities which focus on form rather than meaning, in a building-block approach whereby a learner cannot move on until a prior stage has been achieved, in repetition and insistence on accuracy. This could lead to a limited view of what counts as success, or progress. This emphasis on correctness is linked to a view of literacy and numeracy as competence, and a focus on the formal set procedures of numerical calculations, rather than understanding literacies and numeracies as social practices which are concerned with meanings and use.

For example, the Lancaster Spelling class, while responsive to students' needs, showed (particularly in the group work) a predominantly skills oriented understanding of language and literacy from both learners and teachers, with a focus on correctness. Teachers in group work broke tasks down into simple steps, repeating the same point several times, the goal clearly being for learners to achieve correctness. Texts were used mainly as examples of relevant points, rather than for content. In one-to-one sessions Hannah selected small decontextualised tasks for Jack to practise: Dolch words, spelling tests, prefixes and suffixes. The main focus of the text Diana and Alfonso worked with was correctness of pronunciation; although broader 'cultural knowledge' was drawn out of it as well, this was more incidental to the interaction. Decontextualised pronunciation exercises were also used.

There was a strong grammar focus in the Entry Level 3 ESOL class in Blackburn. The tutor said that ESOL teachers feel that the ESOL assessment criteria demand a fairly hierarchical step-by-step approach to covering the curriculum. Abdul,

Sameena and other students all mention the importance for them of producing 'correct' English which is clearly a main motivation for attending the class. However, their goal to learn, as soon as possible, to speak English fluently enough to join other courses and seek employment does not seem to be sufficiently addressed by this hierarchical approach and suggests the need for opportunities to practise more free, spontaneous use of English. The materials used in the class are mainly textbook-based and there is very little time and support for the development of specific materials and resources which would help these students to gain information and knowledge about the cultures of the society they are living in. However, the predominantly textbook-based materials are mediated by the respectful and sensitive inter-personal approach of the teacher, as described below.

It is not clear why teachers are privileging correctness (of, for example, spelling, grammar, letter formation, punctuation, apostrophe use) over fluency or fitness for purpose. It may be because it is what they themselves believe in, because of the influence of the curriculum, because this is what students say they want, because of demands made by employers and teachers of other courses, and/or because of the washback effect of assessment criteria. One tutor said that the new curriculum and auditing requirements have significantly influenced this, saying that they used to focus more on the uses of literacy in everyday life 'pre-curriculum'. Another emphasised multiple pressure from the funding bodies and 'the Government' to show 'progression, progression, progression: always learning new things, never time to consolidate'. A volunteer tutor who was a retired teacher found the core curriculum 'very unfriendly' and hard to work with. However, one experienced tutor thought that it was not the curriculum itself but people's interpretations of it that are preventing them from treating language, literacy and numeracy as social practices and making their teaching relevant to real-life situations, perhaps under the influence of what they perceive to be institutional and inspection expectations. This evidence suggests that there is a need for further research on the effects of the new curriculum on practice, and perhaps further training of teachers about ways in which the curriculum can be integrated into a pedagogy which focuses on language, literacy and numeracy as practices fulfilling social purposes.

We did not observe many activities which involved students in continuous writing. This is significant considering that, in the country as a whole, many people's motivations for attending includes the wish to improve their writing. In the spelling classes we observed, there was frequent writing, but this was usually of individual words or notes about spelling. Activities which did involve continuous writing were mainly exercises to practise the use of a formal feature, rather than writing for meaning or purpose. This implied a view of literacy as knowledge about the linguistic rules and patterns of written language, rather than as creative self-expression, or purposeful communication of content. However, we did observe writing by some students working with volunteers during the 'individual work' part of a class in which students wrote on topics of their own choice, mainly exploring issues which were central to their own life and identity. In one case this continuous writing was only included at the student's insistence, and then only as a 'reward' for completing what was considered to be 'real work' – that is, a worksheet that practised formal features of written language.

A view of language, literacy and numeracy as social practices, embedded in everyday purposeful activities, was evident when tutors chose or adapted learning activities to relate to learners' individual goals, personal interests or immediate lives. In doing so they were fulfilling the Skills for Life strategy recommendation that 'each individual learner's . . . own set of priorities and requirements . . . must be the starting point of their learning programme development' (DfES 2001a: 9; DfES 2001b: 8). The learner's context, aims, everyday informal knowledge and approaches to learning are often hard to mesh with the knowledge and skills which are codified in the national core curriculum. Tutors were sometimes able to translate between these different 'knowledges', contextualising curriculum content to make sure that learners get what they want whilst satisfying the institutional requirements to 'deliver' the curriculum. This process of translation required listening to the learner as a whole and making pragmatic decisions. At best, tutors were taking account of everything they knew about learners' lives in order to help them to engage with learning. For example, in the numeracy drop-in and in some one-to-one sessions the tutors encouraged and discussed engaging in language, literacy and/or numeracy practices for social purposes associated with the class itself or in everyday life. Individual tutors sometimes followed a student-initiated topic rather than sticking to a planned activity. In the Liverpool maths class, Kay often started from the students' own images and understandings of numerical ideas, rather than trying to redirect them towards her own understandings. Students appeared to be most engaged when tutors sought the relevance of what they were teaching to the learners' everyday lives, but this was often in passing, rather than a central part of the curriculum.

Tutors may have developed these views of the nature of language, literacy and numeracy, and of how they are learned, through their training, through their education before becoming professionals, through their independent reading, through years of experience, through a personal commitment to a particular view of the field, or some combination of these. For some tutors, there seemed to be a coherent and deep-seated philosophy underpinning their practice based on these factors. Others appeared not to have such a well-established teaching philosophy, which could lead them to experience as yet unresolved contradictions in their practice.

Tensions between two types of professionalism

Our research showed that tutors bring two types of professionalism to their work. First, as adult educators, many tutors bring the sort of responsiveness to learners as individuals which we described above, often informed by an understanding of and commitment to social justice issues. Many tutors saw their capacity to listen to learners in order to fine-tune their teaching to make it relevant to people's lives as a crucial factor in their professional identity: a 'responsive professionalism'.

Second, tutors bring training in the content of the core curriculum, and professional knowledge of the requirements of the Skills for Life strategy. These requirements include delivering the core curriculum, meeting targets in terms of recruitment, retention and achievement, and administering the specified forms of assessment. This aspect of tutors' professionalism involves the ability to fulfil their institution's commitments through adherence to procedures and completion of the associated paperwork. While on the one hand this 'new professionalism' was helping tutors to make their teaching more systematic than it had been before, on the other hand some tutors were finding it crowded out the 'responsive professionalism' which had previously been the cornerstone of their practice. The way the core curriculum is presented in terms of itemised skills, knowledge and understanding is also, we suggest, making it more difficult for tutors to conceptualise language, literacy and numeracy as social practices.

We found that tutors were often faced with a tension between these two types of professionalism. Often the requirements of the curriculum and institutional constraints made it difficult for them to put students' individual interests and motivations at the centre of their teaching. For example, they experienced a tension between a perceived requirement to 'teach to the test', and being able to serve the needs of students who wanted to work on their writing. We found many examples of such tensions in our interviews with the teachers.

Learning–teaching events as social spaces

A dynamic dialogue between students' and teachers' contributions

Our research shows that learning opportunities emerge from dialogue between what students bring to classes and what their tutors bring. This dialogue evolves and changes over time, as tutors listen to students' accounts of their purposes, their desires, their lives and their perspectives on learning. There is an ongoing, deepening dynamic between these different contributions to the classroom, facilitated by the 'responsive-to-learners' type of professionalism we identified in the previous section. It is dependent on time to talk, and time to listen.

In this section we discuss four key aspects of this dynamic, all of which underline the social nature of learning–teaching events. First, under the heading 'The importance of social relationships', we discuss the types of social relationship which both facilitate the development of dialogue and emerge from it. Second, under 'The negotiation of learning opportunities', we discuss the aspects of learning–teaching events which need to be negotiated as part of this dialogue. Third, we discuss the importance of learners being active agents in their own learning. Finally, under the heading 'The broader outcomes from attending classes', we mention some of the wider, social benefits of participation in classes which students gained in addition to knowledge, skills and qualifications.

The importance of social relationships

A major part of providing successful learning opportunities was creating a supportive atmosphere – a 'safe space' for people, many of whom had had negative experiences of learning at school. Students responded positively to opportunities to engage with one another socially. Being treated with respect and equality as adults was, for many, in stark contrast to their perception of how they had been treated at school. Teachers paid a great deal of attention to establishing, sustaining and supporting relationships of warmth and trust in the classroom, and learners appeared to be relaxed and happy and enjoying class. Having an adult relationship with a tutor was important in overcoming the sense of inferiority experienced by those previously labelled 'unsuccessful learners'. Many talked about enjoying coming to class because of 'all the friendly people'. This relationship encouraged wider benefits of learning beyond curriculum knowledge and the achievement of qualifications. In this section we discuss in more detail issues which will resonate with the experience of the majority of teachers: how personal relationships in the classes we observed made students feel better about themselves and contributed to their engagement and participation in learning in the classroom.

Personal relationships were crucial to engaging people in learning. We cannot emphasise strongly enough how important we found this factor in the dynamics of the classrooms we studied. Nor can we ignore how important a factor it was to students, who in interviews consistently privileged these social relationships as being crucial for successful learning. Social aspects of learning were viewed by both learners and tutors as fundamental to the provision of learning opportunities. Teachers paid close attention to such social aspects by, for example, the way they introduced a new student to the class. One teacher commented that some people came to class whose greatest need could be defined not in terms of literacy skills, but in terms of social factors such as making relationships with people, and that lack of opportunity for social relationships can impede learning.

Personal relationships were valued, supported and acknowledged in all classes, albeit in different ways. For example, in the Liverpool spelling class the personal relationships were important for Susan, who valued being treated as a proper person by a teacher not looked down on by them. For Cheri a good relationship with her teacher enabled her to attend whilst managing her bi-polar disorder. She was quite categorical that without this relationship she would have dropped out. In the Wednesday one-to-one tuition in Lancaster, the relationships between Jack and his volunteer tutor, Hannah, and Alfonso and his volunteer tutor, Diana, were warm, friendly and well-established. The tutors both drew on their understandings coming out of their friendships with their students to guide what they do in class.

The building of such relationships depended to a large extent on respect and trust between learners and teachers, the teacher's commitment and professionalism, and the teacher's authenticity of response as a person, rather than solely from within their teaching role. This could mean a wide spectrum of things, ranging from a more conventional, structured personal style to a more physical and emotional one. Duncan took a fairly formal, teacher-directed approach but had a relaxed and friendly relationship with the students, treating them as equals, as educated adults. Abdul, Sameena and others interviewed said that they respected and trusted him as a teacher, as they felt they were learning and progressing well. They mentioned his consistency and fairness and his high expectations of them, expecting them to learn as much as they could for themselves, facilitating rather than spoon-feeding them, which gave them confidence. Duncan treated them as individuals even though he was taking a 'whole-class' teaching approach, taking account of their individual needs and personalities, such as always taking time to respond to Abdul's frequent detailed questions about grammar. In the maths class in Liverpool the nature of the social relationship was vital for Jason and Katrina. Both had received support from others to get to the point where they could attend college to build this relationship. What these all had in common was the sense that the teachers cared personally about their students' success and well-being. This mattered as much as the nature of the curriculum, the physical characteristics of the environment and resources, or the teaching approach adopted.

The classroom acted as an arena for the social construction of the identities of students and tutors. Furniture layout, body language, tone of voice, form of address, organisation of groups, and the structure of activities all have subject positions inscribed in them. Learners can be positioned as competent adults, as 'experts', as learners, or as people with a deficit. We noticed many examples of tutors re-positioning learners as experts in their jobs or in some aspect of what they did in their everyday lives. This was part of seeing learners as people with other aspects to their identity beyond membership of the class. In some activities, however, learners were positioned as people with 'difficulties' or 'problems' – usually not overtly, but implicitly, by the choice of examples, by the illustrations, or by the tone of instructions on worksheets. In many instances we observed, the tutors tried to counter any negative positioning inherent in materials or learning tasks by the way they directed the activity. Class participants were positioned and positioned themselves in different ways, often shifting positioning within one class. As we will discuss further at the end of this chapter, a changed sense of their own identity is one of the outcomes which participants might take away from learning–teaching events. The ways classroom interaction and other factors in the learning–teaching event position learners are therefore important considerations for teachers.

The classes we observed could be described as 'learning communities' in which the participants had built up shared understandings of what it means to be a member of the community, of how to participate, of what tasks consist of, of what counts as the beginning and end of a class, and of the routines and rituals associated with class time. A class culture of peer friendship, support, a joint endeavour to learn and common learning goals provides a relaxed, positive learning environment. Such 'learning communities' were established as a result of having engaged in similar activities for some time, through trust, fun and commitment by tutors and learners. A learning community is transitory, lasting for the life of a class, and is also linked to the local community where the class is situated. Relationships had an impact on sustaining the learning community as well as supporting the individual members of it.

We identified a distinction between developing individual confidence and developing 'social confidence'. Social confidence is associated with, but not the same as, individual confidence. It concerns not just a person's confidence in what s/he can do (for example 'I can achieve Level One maths'), but in who s/he is and who s/he can be in relation to others. It was encouraged in listening to each other talk about learning, in talking about home life and other factors which mattered, and in sharing things that were affecting learning. Whether the method of learning was individual, paired or group, learning to be socially confident was valued highly by students. This is particularly relevant to most ESOL students. They generally have a high level of self-esteem in relation to their educational achievement, but low social confidence because of their lack of English language capability and their positioning in society.

Classes all maintained a serious intent, but within this, learning was conducted in relaxed, friendly and enjoyable ways. There was lots of humour, laughter and play; the students found learning fun. This is an important factor in countering previous negative experiences of learning as embarrassing and painful. In the Lancaster class there was a marked use of humour to deconstruct teacher authority. Jokes about social conventions and teacher authority served to shift positioning and break down unequal power relations between tutors and students. Learning activities were sometimes akin to play, especially those which emerged spontaneously.

The importance of personal relationships was apparent also in the amount of praise, encouragement and minimising of error evident in the classes. Tutors provided a lot of encouragement to learners to participate in class, to try things and to see their progress positively. However, there was no associated cost for choosing not to participate or take risks. Most tutors responded to student contributions with praise and reinforcement for everything successful, or even nearly successful. Some tutors' responses were exclusively positive. Even in a situation where the student made an error, the way many tutors responded to it was to avoid reference to the error, to comment on something which was nearly right, thereby building up the learners' trust that they would not be exposed to failure.

Tutors were on the whole tolerant of off-task discussion in English or in other languages, seeing it as a way in which students can gain confidence, can make links between their lives outside class and what they are learning, and can participate as 'experts'. In the Liverpool classes, we noticed that tutors used social talk, talk about the everyday and talk about themselves as bridging between formal and informal elements of lessons. Sometimes this is tutor-led, as in Debbie's admission that she had 'messed the lesson up' by getting 'carried away', and sometimes it was student-led as in Sarah's measuring episode. Humour, jokes, mimicry and play-acting were also mechanisms for moving between one and the other.

By contrast, we observed that lack of attention to social factors may impede learning. Instances we observed of social factors which had potential to impede learning included personality clashes, gender imbalances, and the dominance of confident, vocal students over quieter ones. One tutor commented that team teaching can help to avert personality clashes between teachers and students. Some students appeared to be denied learning opportunities by being in a minority group in a class, or just by being shy or reserved in their style of participation.

The negotiation of learning opportunities

Within the sort of supportive environment described above, learners and teachers can collaborate to maximise learning opportunities for everyone concerned. This involves making joint decisions about content, methods, style, formality, structure, pace, tone, and the materials and activities of the classroom. The tutor's task is to negotiate these in interaction with all concerned, to fine-tune them according to the individuals involved, to be flexible and responsive to ongoing changes in configurations of purposes and preferences, and – as we emphasise in the following section – to be responsive to the learners' own agency in these processes. We saw many examples of these sorts of negotiations, some of which we include here.

Teaching which maximised the availability of learning opportunities seemed to develop in negotiation between learners and teachers. It was not only carefully planned, but was also responsive – both to individuals and to the group as a whole – and emergent from the ongoing interaction. This involved collaboration, dialogue and flexibility around the content, method and mode of delivery. Pre-planned schemes of work are often recommended as good practice, but the flexibility to respond dynamically to learners' changing needs and interests is also essential. Teachers were frequently adapting their plans in order to accommodate the particular circumstances of learners' lives, for example by being flexible about timekeeping and ensuring that the scheduling of classes was responsive to students' needs.

We observed tutors adjusting their teaching out of sensitivity to mental health difficulties or learning difficulties, stepping tasks down to give students oppor- tunities to succeed, and using different means to get across the same points: checking student understanding in different ways, and constant repetition and review. Gauging the appropriate amount of support without stepping the task down so much that students are no longer challenged is a difficult balance. We observed tutors making fine-grained decisions to ensure they did not scaffold students so much that they were no longer learning anything new. For example, at the times when Duncan elicited Abdul's contributions in the group and answered his questions on grammar this could be seen as a successful provision of learning opportunities. When Abdul and Sameena were left floundering without the necessary support in the pair work the learning was not so successful. When Duncan spent a long time trying to help another student understand a point in the whole-group feedback, it may have been a learning opportunity for her but those

112

who already understood may have felt held back, which two of the students suggested sometimes happens in this group. The balance between challenge and support was largely achieved by the tutors we observed, but there were moments when it appeared students might have been able to respond had they been given a little more time before the task was broken down.

We observed many instances of tutors moving skilfully between formality and informality, structure and flexibility, interweaving personal and task-based talk, fine-tuning their individual or group interactions according to the reactions of students. Formality and informality are often intertwined. We noticed that in quite informal settings (such as a relaxed, friendly atmosphere at a small table) the nature of the work could be formal (such as worksheets about language forms or abstract numerical operations). For example, in an Entry Level 1–3 English class in Lancaster, structured worksheets were used during the one-to-one part of the session, which had an informal, conversational atmosphere. In the Blackburn ESOL class, Duncan took a formal approach to teaching grammar using an ESOL textbook, closely controlling the learning activities. At the same time, his good sense of humour and appreciation of his students and their enjoyment and engagement with the tasks created a 'buzz' and a relaxed, informal atmosphere. Students were chatting freely, either in English or in their shared languages whilst doing the learning tasks. This can be interpreted in terms of Bernstein's concepts of classification and framing (Bernstein 1996): the curriculum content was strongly classified, but by being mediated informally, it was weakly framed.

Formal, structured teaching methods and materials were not straightforwardly positive or negative features of these classes. Some students found a degree of formality reassuring, giving them a sense of order, structure, purpose, challenge and achievement. Formality can provide security and familiarity: this is what many learners expect of classes. Many ESOL students had thrived and achieved well in their own countries going through very formal systems of schooling. However, structure could become counter-productive if it squeezed out individual responsiveness and links to worlds beyond the classroom. Formal procedures and ground rules were reminiscent of the school practices which some students associated with previous fear and failure.

Classes and one-to-one tuition sessions varied in the pace and nature of activities. Some spent a long time over a single point, repeating and checking until everyone appeared to understand it. Some used many different activities to present and reinforce the same content. On the other hand, a single activity often had multiple uses and multiple outcomes, either for the class as a whole, or for an individual learner. These different or additional learning opportunities were often driven by tutors' ingenuity in adapting or extending activities to suit individual and emerging needs and possibilities, but also by the students' own motivations for attending.

Students as active agents in their own learning

Our observations have shown that many learners reinterpret what they encounter in classrooms to create learning opportunities for themselves. Whatever the nature of the provision, they work actively to 'make something of it' according to their own agenda, and to take ownership of their own learning experiences. This may be a characteristic which is specific to adult learning as compared with child learning. Most of the students we observed had strong views about their learning: about what their goals were, and how these would best be met. However, some students did not display the same degree of agency and might have benefited from discussion and encouragement of them taking a more active role. Recognising the possibility of learners taking a more active part in shaping learning–teaching events presents a challenge to views which see teaching as primarily about transmission of knowledge with teachers taking the main responsibility for planning what will be learnt.

In the Liverpool drop-in maths class the learners were supported to choose the topic area and worksheet that they wanted to work on. For example, Sarah wanted to learn 'area' as she wanted to know how to measure for a bedroom carpet, or the amount of wood for an alcove shelf. In the interview she said that her dad had always done this and she wanted to learn to do it herself. Jason said he wanted to do fractions because he found them hard. He chose the level of worksheet – a 'harder' or 'easier' one depending on his confidence level. He decided the pace and called Kay when he wanted to check or move on. Katrina, in discussion with Kay, said she wanted to learn the basics like 'times tables', as she knew these were important and she could not do them. She said this would help her with her money and with her job. Her pace was very slow and she had to keep asking Kay for help, but in all her interviews and observations she displayed an enormous sense of being an active agent. She felt that she would succeed if she tried hard enough. She did not seem to be daunted by her lack of skill as she worked up to Entry Level 1.

Students have the ultimate option of attending or not attending, attending but tuning out, or attending and engaging in the event. Participation and engagement, therefore, are crucial factors within students' control, and a crucial aim for tutors is to encourage and facilitate them. We observed that engagement was most apparent when tasks were personally meaningful to students, in the sense that they could see the relevance of the task to their own lives, and when they were exercising choice and control over what they were doing. However, we observed a surprisingly high level of engagement even in tasks for which the rationale was not immediately apparent. Good learning can happen in what on the surface look like bad conditions. For example, in the Liverpool drop-in maths class students worked assiduously on worksheets – not what some might see as a particularly engaging activity – because of the way they were framed and mediated by the tutor, Kay, and because of their trust in her. These adult learners seemed to have a high degree of tolerance for uncertainty as to the ultimate purpose of activities. Even when there was considerable mismatch between the class activities and the students' motivations to attend, we observed high levels of engagement, especially when the motivation was very urgent, as in the case of asylum seekers and refugees.

We observed students participating in discussion about what and how they were learning, being involved in democratic decision-making about how courses were run, and negotiating their own pace. Many learners were active in understanding how they were learning, taking ownership and making choices. Some tutors also encouraged critique from their learners, further boosting learners' sense of agency and control. Students taking control of their own learning through dialogue in this way depends on tutors taking account of the wider perspective of students' lives and capabilities beyond the classroom, and recognising the importance of social relationships in the class, as discussed above.

In the Liverpool drop-in spelling class Susan developed a good relationship with her tutor, Debbie. This supported her learning outside the class. She often wrote little notes in her homework for Debbie telling her how she felt about learning, for example: 'That was hard and I didn't understand but I think I do now.' She often stayed behind to talk to Debbie about what she was reading or writing, or her delight in learning about language, and Debbie gave up her own unpaid time for such meetings. Tommy took an active role in developing his interest in creative writing, writing more than required and also discussing this with Debbie. He decided from this positive experience to sign up for a creative writing course following the spelling class. Tommy linked this experience of learning with other learning experiences in his everyday life where he got books out of the library to teach himself about astronomy, photography or sea fishing. Cheri also took the initiative in developing a relationship with Debbie that supported her learning. With this support she explored writing poetry, which she brought for Debbie to see. Debbie also used this space to discuss her progress in her maths course, so these interactions were also about learning more generally. Elizabeth explained that by using the 'look, cover, write, check' method that she had learned in class, she was practising words herself, constructing her own methods for learning outside the classroom. Sameena, Abdul and most of the other students responded to the strongly teacher-directed learning environment of the Blackburn ESOL class by taking charge of their own learning within the framework offered, through their contributions in whole-group and pair work, their questions to each other and to Duncan and the use of their individual learning strategies.

We gathered evidence of learners gaining benefits which went beyond what the teacher had intended or planned. For example, what the students learned in the Blackburn ESOL class went way beyond the main aims of learning new grammatical structures that seemed to be the major focus. What they were ostensibly learning was a grammatical framework or scaffolding that can underpin learning to speak English, but they were also developing reading, writing, speaking and listening skills in the process. In the focal lesson Duncan used the central text as a 'vehicle' for learning grammar rather than to be read as an interesting story. He purposely read it with little expression directing their focus to concentrate on learning new words and verb patterns. Despite this, Abdul, Sameena and other

115

students said they liked the article because they found the story 'interesting because I like people', 'adventure', 'nice'. It was through their *own* reading for the comprehension exercise that they came to appreciate the story. The lesson was around a written text but there was as much speaking as reading, though this was mainly focused on comprehension and grammar related to the text. In the end of lesson review, although Duncan wrote on the board and the students recorded on their sheets 'verb patterns', the students identified other learning such as 'we did [comprehension] exercises about [what] happens', 'describing text', and 'new words'.

A particular arena in which students could take control was the pacing of their work. Many of the students, particularly in Kay's class, reported liking worksheets, as they gave them control over the pace they worked at. Using worksheets enabled learners in the maths class to talk and then return to task. This was felt to be distinctly different from a school regime of learning. In many classes the students responded to worksheets and Individual Learning Plans positively. They felt these gave them some sense of ownership and involvement in choosing their pace of learning and in their progress, especially when these were used more flexibly and personally than just as a 'record of work done', and when the plans were used to facilitate discussion about the individual learner, not just to collect data. The type of teaching, whether individual or group, seemed to matter less than the students feeling they were learning at their own pace and could participate in discussion about how they were learning.

Broader outcomes from attending classes

'Content' learning is privileged by curricula, but it is inextricably bound up with other types of learning, such as learning how to learn, learning about language, learning about social relations, the reconstruction of social identities, and wider benefits of learning such as increases in confidence and physical and psychological well-being. In the classes we observed, these other forms of learning were in evidence, and emerged as essential factors in the success of the classes. Curriculum targets were by no means always considered to be the most important outcome, except in relation to gaining employment. For example, in both of the Liverpool DISC classes the learners explained that gaining confidence, managing their health, meeting other people, learning things they did not know and making up for skills not learned at school were more important than achieving curriculum targets.

An important outcome of participation in language, literacy and numeracy education is an increase in 'social confidence', as described above. This is not only to do with demonstrating competence, which might be done in isolation, but also a change in self-perception, a conscious awareness of competence, and a sense of confidence in interacting with others (for further discussion of the wider benefits of participation in educational provision see, for example, Eldred et al. 2004; Vorhaus 2001; Schuller et al. 2004). Tutors seemed to be aware of the value of their classes in building social confidence, and many of the things we observed them doing or saying were indirectly contributing to this. For example, Jack in the Lancaster spelling class learnt that he is not 'different' and that there are other people of a similar age to him who have similar learning needs. This was very important in terms of changing his self-image and boosting his confidence.

We observed many instances of students learning about how to benefit from attending classes. For example, in all the Lancaster classes observed, including others not reported here, learners are not only learning content, but learning about classroom practices by participating in them, such as patterns of interaction in groups, and classroom rituals (filling in 'Work Done sheets', etc.).

Students often came to classes with one goal, but gained something more, different or unexpected. As we pointed out in the section on 'motivation', Sameena's initial motivations were educational, and the positive effect her learning had on her relationship with her husband was unexpected. They now share a broader range of activities such as watching films in English or with English subtitles and socialising together with English-speaking friends that previously only her husband communicated with. Her motivations for learning English are now, as a result, social as well as educational. Abdul and Sameena were learning not only English language but also about a new learning culture in a new country. They were learning about this society and about the wider world from their teacher, their peers and to some extent through learning materials, though a broader range including 'real' and locally contextualised materials/resources would have made this even more effective. Sameena and other female South Asian ESOL students were learning to learn with male learners, not a norm associated with their cultural background and previous educational experience. In Lancaster, a student came to a spelling class to work on form-filling so she could apply for a passport. She got the passport, took her first holiday abroad, and enjoyed it so much that she stopped coming to class because she was too busy working at a second job in order to earn money to pay for more holidays. This is an example of the direct economic benefit of attending classes. It had a huge impact on the learner's life, but was not measurable in terms of standard achievement targets or passing tests and in fact since she did not complete her course she would show up on college records as a 'drop-out'.

Summary

These two chapters have addressed the key issue of this book, the relationship between people's lives and their engagement in learning, in literacy, numeracy and language classes in colleges. We have described the wide range of life histories and motivations which students bring to classes. We have explored what teachers bring, including their responsiveness to the learners as individuals, their views of the nature of language, literacy and numeracy, and the ways these could lead to developing tensions between two conflicting visions of what professionalism as a tutor meant for them. Finally, we have suggested that the construction of learning opportunities in classrooms such as these emerges from a dynamic dialogue between what learners' and teachers' contribute. In the classes in which we worked, this dynamic could be characterised in terms of supportive social relationships and negotiated learning opportunities, with students having an active role to play in this negotiation process. Through engaging in this dynamic relationship, broader outcomes of learning emerge for people's lives, including increased social confidence, some of which were unexpected by both students and teachers concerned. In later chapters, we will argue for a social practice approach to pedagogy which recognises and builds on this negotiated process. We first turn to others sites, beyond formal classrooms.

10

WHAT PEOPLE BRING TO LEARNING SETTINGS

In Chapters 8 and 9 we concentrated on people attending courses in colleges. We now turn to people in the community settings described in Chapter 4. These were a drug and alcohol support centre, organisations for homeless people, a tenants association and a domestic violence support group. We are interested in the relationship between lives and learning in these settings where education is not the main aim but where there is some educational provision. There are two distinct aspects to the analysis. First, in this chapter we describe the characteristics of people's lives in these settings. The next chapter then looks in more detail at how these characteristics influence and shape the learning in which they participate and at patterns of participation and engagement in learning in these settings.

In this chapter we take up an issue introduced in the previous two chapters: the diversity and complexity of the lives of students in language, literacy and numeracy provision. This was particularly apparent and salient for the people attending provision in community settings, affecting not only their learning, but also their propensity to participate in educational provision at all. We describe what people bring to the settings in terms of the framework introduced in Chapter 3. This analyses people's lives in terms of four aspects: their history, their current identities, their current life circumstances, and their imagined futures. This provides a framework for understanding how to link language, literacy and numeracy learning to people's lives. In Chapter 3 we illustrated these four aspects in a simple manner, the idea being that each person has a particular combination of practices and identities, with a history behind them and an imagined future towards which they are travelling, situated within a set of current life circumstances and events.

Here we apply this framework to describe the range of people we worked with in these settings. Looking across all the data, we identify two particular areas where their histories affected their learning in formal situations: histories involving pain, trauma, violence and ill-health; and negative previous experiences of education and of authority. In terms of current practices, people had skills, competencies and talents which were often unrecognised and ignored. Often their ways of interacting were in conflict with discourses of education and their ways of structuring everyday life did not fit into the rhythms assumed to be appropriate for formal education.

119

Many felt excluded from what they referred to as normal society. In terms of life circumstances, they often had multiple interacting constraints on their lives, juggling multiple roles and responsibilities and complex relationships. In terms of imagined futures, their engagement in learning was driven by broader life purposes, which changed over time and could be quite conventional in nature. Overall, people's underlying search for well-being was a profoundly important motivator for them, and one which could either draw them in to formal learning or pull them away.

To give a sense of the rich data that has generated these findings, we begin each section with a profile of one of the people we worked with. The profiles are based on repeated interviews and were written at the end of the data collection. While each of the four people profiled, Sophie, Caroline, Jason and Steve, has been selected to illustrate one of these four areas, their profiles also demonstrate the ways the topics interact. These profiles are then used as a basis for discussion of the full range of data which we have collected, drawing out those aspects of people's lives which seem to us particularly relevant to the relationships between life and learning.

History

We introduced Sophie in Chapter 1 as an 18 year old who came to a shelter for homeless young people. Here is a more detailed profile of her:

> **Sophie** was a regular attender at Safeplace, the shelter for young homeless people. She had had an unsettled family situation as her mother, a teacher, was drug and alcohol dependent. She is very bright but hated school, often absconded, and was expelled as a result of repeated assault and arson offences. She eventually became homeless at age 15 and as a result underachieved in her GCSE exams. Because of the difficulty of studying whilst homeless and coping with substance misuse, she has dipped in and out of college. She had to give up her most recent course, in landscape gardening, when she became pregnant.
>
> For some time she lived in the Safeplace hostel and came to the associated day centre every day for somewhere to go, to meet friends, chill and get help, support and food. She says she learns things at the day centre without realising it. She likes creative and practical activities, but prefers not to attend drugs/alcohol advice sessions and finds the basic skills stuff boring and easy. However, for a while new funding rules meant that she was not supposed to stay or eat at the centre unless she agreed to take part in the education sessions provided, until these rules were re-negotiated.
>
> Sophie is a reader, and her favourite author is Virginia Andrews (who writes in graphic detail about child abuse), saying: 'Like it's like real life . . . I can relate to the people, like the stuff that's going on.' She likes to

write Haiku poetry in English and in French, and freer style poetry, especially when she is going through a bad patch.

Sophie guards her privacy well and it is not easy to know what is dream and what reality in her life. She showed Rachel one poem about anorexia which she said she had written for a friend but which was clearly related to herself.

Towards the end of the study Sophie had just had a baby girl, was is in much better health, and was moving on from a mother-and-baby unit to her sister's for a while, eventually hoping to find her own flat. She was determined to go back to college, take her GCSEs and A-levels and eventually study veterinary medicine or psychology. The staff were all hoping that she would be able to manage to look after her baby with continuing support, but they were also worried about her

These notes show how people are bringing their whole history with them when they enter these community settings. Each person has a distinct and individual history, but there are patterns in the lives of the learners we worked with in community settings which have particular impacts on their learning and which give rise to common themes.

As we have already noted above, any profile is a partial picture of a person. People come with a wide range of backgrounds and histories, and generalisations about trends can be misleading if they are thought to apply to everyone's particular history. Nevertheless, common patterns of socially organised inequalities have been documented. As mentioned in Chapter 3, large-scale cohort studies demonstrate how literacy and numeracy difficulties correlate closely with measures of social exclusion such as unemployment, poverty, poor health and overcrowded housing conditions. Most of the people we worked with in these community settings had lived their lives at the sharp end of such social inequalities and this is reflected in some common patterns in the histories they carried with them. We identify two areas where their histories affected their learning in formal situations: histories of pain, trauma, violence and ill-health; and negative previous experiences of education and of authority.

Histories of pain, trauma, violence and ill-health

Like Sophie, many of the people we worked with had come from unsettled and shifting family backgrounds, which often included violence and physical or mental abuse. This was particularly true of the young people at the homeless shelter, most of whom had had periods of living in care. It was also true of the women at the domestic violence support group. Where people had experienced periods of homelessness, this was often associated with incidents of violence, particularly where people had spent time living in hostels. Drug and alcohol misuse and associated health and social problems were common factors, most obviously in the drug and alcohol support centre data, but also in the homeless shelter, the domestic violence support group and Big Issue work where alcohol and drugs were often described by people as being part of their coping strategies for survival. Where people were bringing histories involving pain, trauma, violence and ill-health, these could form significant barriers to engagement in learning, which we explore in more detail below.

Negative previous experiences of education and of authority

Like Sophie, many people had experienced very negative previous experiences of education. People reported extensive physical and emotional bullying, both from teachers and from other pupils. Experiences of humiliation were described, like those of Steve, profiled later, who was expected to read aloud in English classes despite finding this very difficult because of dyslexia which was not diagnosed until after he left school. Many people felt they had been positioned as 'thick' or as 'failures' in their experience of school. School work was described as 'too hard' or as 'boring'. Many had coped by removing themselves from school, skipping individual lessons, whole subjects or full days, or dropping out completely. Where people had come from difficult home situations, characterised by violence or abuse, this had often led to behaviour which was unacceptable within the school environment such as Sophie's assault and arson offences, leading to disciplinary action and eventually suspensions or exclusions. Where home situations were mobile and shifting, this had led to periods of discontinuous and interrupted schooling for some, which had caused further problems. People described feeling very different from other pupils who were not dealing with the same issues, and this feeling of not belonging also led to skipping school and spending time in situations where they felt more at ease, such as with groups of friends instead.

A related point is that many of these people had had negative experiences with authority throughout much of their lives. Encounters with authority at home, at school, through social services and through the criminal justice system had often involved sanctions and disciplinary procedures which were experienced by many as unjust impositions. This was especially true of those people who had come from family situations characterised by violence and mental or physical abuse, for whom any authority tended to be met with deep distrust and wariness.

At the homeless shelter in particular, where they felt safe and valued, most of the young people displayed resentment of impersonal authority, rigidity and control, especially when this was seen to be displayed without respect and understanding. This was a recurrent problem for them, which they had experienced in many official and institutional contexts, particularly the job centre, the police station and school. At the same time, these people are dependent on the services and benefits associated with these settings, so cannot escape them, and often display levels of frustration and anger which colour their emotional experience. Similar feelings, although to a less extreme extent, were described by many at the drug and alcohol support centre, particularly by people who were there on drug treatment and testing orders, and who had to manage many contacts and appointments with various agencies, including probation, the community drug team, social services and the job centre (an issue which we will return to below).

Current practices and identities

Caroline has not been mentioned so far. Here is part of the profile of her which was written at the end of data collection.

> **Caroline**, in her forties, attends the Structured Day Programme at Pandion Hall regularly. She enjoyed school, was in the top class, and always got good reports, but got fed up with it in her last year, when she was doing exams and wanted to leave. By then she had started to go out and drink. She got married aged 20 and had two children. She trained and got a job as a secretary, but had to leave because of childcare requirements and thereafter only had what she calls 'daft jobs', such as factory work. The family moved to a new area when their marriage ran into difficulties, but the problems continued and her husband eventually left. Caroline met someone else whom she married and had three children with, but he drank and was violent throughout the marriage and eventually they divorced.
>
> After the divorce, Caroline says she had her worst time. She used to drop the kids off at school and then spend the day in a shelter on the local promenade. 'I used to drink all day in the shelters, bottles of cider. I was always pissed up, just going with anybody, messing about, a lot of that. And ended up in hospital, and at the police station.' After a while, she noticed she was bruising very easily and bleeding a lot. She went to the doctor's, who referred her to the local alcohol detox unit. She has been in the detox unit about twenty times. At some times, her health has been very poor. She has been in short-term residential rehab, which was not successful for her, and a longer-term structured residential in another part of the country. This was better for the four months she was there, but she had to face all the same issues when she returned home. She finds the programme at Pandion much better, because she can carry on with support, rather than being just stuck at home. The structure and the activities give her something to think about other than drinking, and she says it has 'saved my life'.
>
> Caroline has always been interested in learning, and likes having something to do. She had previously tried going to college, but found this very difficult. She found the people there described lives that were very different from hers: 'people that are talking about their families, and going for meals, and golfing, and stuff like that'. She couldn't say she had a problem with drink, because they didn't. College staff did ask her if she was drinking, and she said a bit, but didn't want to tell them she had a

problem with it. As a result of feeling this pressure, she used to feel scared, so would take a bottle with her so that she could drink at college. She had also gone on courses at a local employment training centre, but had encountered similar difficulties dealing with those she referred to as 'normal people'. Despite these difficulties, she persevered and got her European Computer Driving License, but did not want to continue at college. At Pandion Hall, in contrast, she can come and learn without feeling under pressure about her drinking. If she has lapses and is drinking, people will understand why, she will not have to pretend she has been ill. And because she feels secure, she no longer feels the need to drink. 'I don't drink when I come here. I don't want to.'

Caroline came in to the centre every day when she could, doing courses in IT, art, creative writing and music technology, and having acupuncture on a Friday. She also started doing learndirect courses there, including numeracy and IT. Eventually she would like to gain the qualifications needed to get back into office work. Despite her previous negative experience of college, once her confidence had developed, she felt able to sign up to do a course at a local community college. This was possible for her partly because the tutor would be someone she had already been working with in the Structured Day Programme and whom she knew and trusted, partly because a friend from the same programme would be going, and partly because the site felt different to her from the local FE college, particularly as it was not full of disruptive teenagers.

It is clear from this example that there were some aspects of how Caroline saw herself and how she led her life which were helping her make the changes she wanted to in her life, whilst others were creating barriers. People's current practices and identities were important in affecting how they approached formal learning. The skills, competencies, passions and talents which people had were either acknowledged and taken up in the learning situations or were ignored or unrecognised. At the same time, how people saw themselves and how they conducted their lives created conflicts and barriers with the educational opportunities they were offered.

Skills, competences, passions and talents

The first resource that people brought to learning as part of who they were was a wide variety of skills, competences, talents and passions, including literacies unrelated to the curriculum. At the drug and alcohol support centre, people shared their multiple skills, often supporting one another with practical activities such as fixing each other's cars, domestic appliances or computers, or engaging in complex negotiations with agencies such as Social Services or probation. Many of them, too, enjoyed and became skilled in the creative arts activities offered as part of the structured day programme, particularly visual arts, creative writing and music

technology. Several people described this in terms of having discovered unexpected 'hidden talents', or passions and interests from earlier on in their lives which
they felt had been set aside or even trampled on by everything else they were
dealing with. This was particularly important in contributing to the development
of people's self-esteem, by placing value on an aspect of themselves which had not
been valued before.

At the tenants' association, volunteers used a range of literacy, numeracy and
language skills to carry out their support roles, including taking minutes, making
fliers, gathering new information, keeping records, supporting people with form-
filling, letter writing or finding out who to contact to make a complaint, and
running a bonus ball scheme around the estate (and organising a children's outing
with the funds raised), which required extensive literacy and numeracy skills. While
some of these had been taught through formal courses, most were acquired and
passed on informally as volunteers participated in the association's activities.

People's skills and competences were often not reflected in the qualifications that
they had. The majority of people we worked with in these settings had left school
with no or very few qualifications (although this was not true of some clients at the
drug and alcohol support centre who had qualifications up to degree level and
beyond). However, this did not necessarily mean that they had no academic
abilities. Sophie is a good example of this, with her enjoyment of reading and of
writing poetry – even in a foreign language – not being reflected in her current
paper qualifications. The other young people at the homeless shelter had a range
of literacy skills from minimal word recognition through to GCSE-level.

Conflict with discourses of education

Part of people's identities and practices were the discourses which they brought
with them, that is, their ways of talking and ways of interacting. These were shaped
by their whole histories. Often, there were clashes between these different ways of
talking and interacting in the settings. For instance, the discourse of young people
at the homeless shelter was very different from the discourse of formal education,
which in many ways was alien to them, and within which they had been positioned
as failures. Staff drew on informal discourses when interacting with the young
people. But this raised issues when the centre changed from being a 'drop-in'
centre to being a 'centre for educational activities', when the 'activities' had to be
re-framed if the service users were to accept them, as discussed below. Given that
many people had these negative associations with education, we found that
learning and, particularly, participating in formal structured learning meant more
to people than just acquiring new skills. It could mean entering a different culture
or taking on a whole new identity, a process that could be experienced as difficult
and sometimes even as dangerous. One client at the drug and alcohol support
centre, who had attended university, described having lived two parallel lives
associated with two different identities: his identity as a mature student and his

identity as a drinker. This eventually became too difficult for him to sustain and he did not complete his degree.

Ways of structuring everyday life

In addition to identities, people also brought with them habits and practices which challenged some of the assumptions of more structured provision. One important goal of the programme at the drug and alcohol support centre was to provide people with a regular routine in their day, to replace the habits associated with the addiction they were dealing with. Otherwise, clients described how they would have had an 'empty hole' in their lives which would have been hard to fill and, they felt, made it more likely for them to go back to using their substance of choice. Many attenders, especially those at the start of their involvement with the programme, said that they did not really care what the content of the educational provision was; the most important factor for them was that they had something positive to get up and out for each day. As one client explained:

> It's something to get up out of bed for in the morning. I find I'm getting up in the morning and living a useful day. [. . .] By coming in every day it's getting me into a routine which I've not been in for a long time. And that's getting up in the morning, washing, shaving, dressing and getting out. So that when the time comes when hopefully I'll get back to work it's not going to be completely alien to me.

Service users spoke in very positive terms about the programme, explaining that it took time and support to introduce structure into lives which had previously often been very unstructured.

Similarly, the young people attending the homeless shelter had often come from unsettled and shifting home situations and unstable living conditions, and were dealing with unpredictable life events. Sustaining the regularity of going to college or engaging in a structured course with deadlines was hard to co-ordinate, and they would often 'dip in and out' of activities as these were feasible for them. Many of the women's lives at the domestic violence support group had been structured around the imperatives of their own and their family's survival in violent relationships, which took priority over other activities and made regular attendance elsewhere difficult.

The practices people were bringing with them did not fit in well with the expectations of formal learning programmes. It is important to recognise, however, that an apparent lack of structure in people's lives, often described by outsiders as 'chaotic', is closely related to the life circumstances and events that they are dealing with on a daily basis. For many of the people we worked with, their lives were not so much chaotic as very complex. They were constantly juggling unpredictable demands which could make the introduction of learning activities on any regular basis difficult. This was particularly true where people's lives were regulated by several different systems of social support. (See the section on roles and responsibilities, later in this chapter.)

Feelings of exclusion from so-called 'normal' culture

People bring with them particular identities and cultures which shape their experience of learning. Caroline's experience of college as representing a culture which excluded her is a common one, described by many of the people we worked with. Steve, profiled later, explained that 'a lot of people with drug problems have this thing about "normality" and what normality is and being part of it'. At the drug and alcohol support centre, one of the most important benefits people described was being with people who had been dealing with similar issues, rather than, as Caroline describes, having to hide what was going on or to try to explain it to people who did not understand.

The young people at the homeless shelter felt particularly marginalised by the difference between their lives and the lives of young college students. As a worker there told us,

> If you look around nowadays it's very important for young people to be wearing the right clothes and look the part . . . you can't do that on forty pounds a week in your own little bedsit, kipping on someone else's floor. But when you go down to the college a lot of them live at home with parents who can afford to buy the latest stuff, they can afford to go out at weekends, they're taking driving lessons, going on holidays. They can get a part-time job at the weekends, go home and have their tea, they've got their own bed and their clothes get washed and ironed for them and if they haven't got money they can hopefully get some off their parents. Our young people, a lot of them have nowhere to live, no one's washing their clothes, nobody's making their tea, you know. It does affect whether or not they attend training or work or education because they haven't got the confidence and they're struggling with their own mental health and they just feel down, feeling absolutely awful.

One of the crucial ways the domestic violence support group offered support to women who had experienced domestic violence was in helping them to see that they were not alone in their experiences. For those who were attending college, while learning support was available for them, they found additional support was also necessary to help them deal with the difficulties they were experiencing, which were largely invisible within the college system. Vendors at Big Issue told of the 'regular' lives they had had in the past, and the catalysts – illness, relationship breakdown, drug and alcohol addiction, leaving the armed forces – which had led to these lives 'falling apart'.

And while this distinction was not made in quite the same way at the tenants' association, the members were nevertheless proud that they were doing it for themselves, making a clear distinction between those on the estate and those from the outside. They were guarding their independence fiercely and resisting outside interference wherever possible.

Current life circumstances and events

Jason is a 31-year-old man introduced in Chapter 1. Here are more details of his life.

> **Jason** stopped attending school at the age of 12 and hung about the docks with older employed members of his family. After a YTS course on a building site he worked as a labourer and then as a container operator. He did jobs that did not require reading and writing. A hit-and-run accident left him unemployed and with depression. He has been unable to work since then.
>
> Members of his local tenants' association persuaded Jason to have a go at learning. He started courses in computers, maths and family history. Although lacking in confidence, Jason passed his national test in maths at Level 2, travelled to Ireland with family members to research his family history and has undertaken several computer courses. He was positive about learning: 'It's learning anything, life is great, it's just learning and learning and learning. It's exciting.' He enjoyed the challenge of learning new skills, and aspired to study to become a Blue Badge Guide, telling people about the history of his local area.
>
> Jason used his new skills in his voluntary work at the tenants' association helping to set up and run the computer and internet, as well as keeping the accounts. He also enrolled on a Tourism NVQ course. However, he was not able to start this as his drinking pattern of 'going on benders' increased. He attended a computer course, as it was necessary for his work at the tenants' association, but he was not able to manage the regularity of other formal learning. In the last two years Jason has moved from being enthusiastic about learning to habitually drinking, and is currently not engaging in organised learning activities. Although committed to the tenants' association, he has been unable to sustain his work with them because of his depression and drinking. The other members, who have issues they are dealing with in their own lives, understand this and he is welcome to participate again if and when he chooses to.
>
> Jason appears in the college records as a 'non-attender'. But the tenants' association provides a non-judgemental learning environment where he can succeed over time with support, at the points in his life when he chooses to do so.

Jason's story shows the complex lives people led, the constraints on their lives, the many interacting roles and responsibilities they had and the many relationships which they were part of. External circumstances meant that many of the people lived what we have referred to earlier as turbulent lives, where they often described events they had little control over.

Multiple interacting constraints

People experienced multiple constraints when engaging with conventionally structured learning activities. These constraints were of different kinds: physical, social, emotional and practical. It was the interaction of these multiple constraints which constructed barriers for people. Having left school early, Jason was successfully employed for some time, initially through family contacts. At this point, the fact that he had not been at school since the age of 12 was not problematic for him. Nor was it seen as unusual or stigmatised by people in his immediate social circle. It was after his accident, which caused physical constraints on his activities, that this aspect of his history became an issue, as he was no longer able to do manual work which did not require any reading and writing. At the same time, broader social constraints had a role to play in his opportunities, as local employment in the docks and construction trades where he had experience were dwindling. These factors contributed to the onset of depression, and in turn to him using alcohol as a coping strategy, both of which became constraints on his engagement. Despite these constraints, Jason found a route through the tenants' association which was positive for him for some time, supporting him to gain qualifications and skills which could assist him to move towards the sort of life and employment he was striving for.

Jason's hit-and-run accident shows the importance of unpredictable events in shaping people's lives. Where people are already managing multiple constraints, such an event can have more significant consequences than where people have fewer existing issues to deal with. Sophie's story gives another good example of this, where her pregnancy forced her to give up a landscape gardening course. It also shows how such unpredictable events can have both negative and positive effects at different points: after having the baby Sophie moved to live in a more supportive environment with her sister and seemed to be doing well. Such unpredictable changes characterised the daily lives of many of the people we worked with. Events such as sudden health problems, court decisions, family problems or housing difficulties could all lead to spiralling consequences, with people who had been very committed to learning suddenly finding it difficult or impossible. Practical issues, including financial ones, could also prove severe barriers to learning. Caroline, profiled above, would have liked to come into the centre every day, but could only afford a bus pass on the first week of her fortnightly benefits payment.

Multiple roles and responsibilities

People in these settings had multiple roles and responsibilities, many of which had to be prioritised over engaging with learning opportunities. People managing caring responsibilities, such as childcare, parent care or care of a sick partner, had to prioritise these, particularly where they had few financial or social resources to draw on. If your childcare is provided by a family member who falls ill or goes away suddenly, or you have no support and you cannot afford to pay for any, you have no choice but to stay with that child. On the other hand, responsibilities such as caring for a child or supporting your community also had the potential to act as 'pull' factors back into learning, where people perceived this learning as being something which could contribute to or offer support with fulfilling their responsibilities. At the tenants' association, volunteers were engaged in a range of commitments within their local community, and their engagement in learning was primarily in order to carry these out effectively and successfully.

Similarly, people who were involved with multiple agencies, such as the people on drug treatment and testing orders mentioned above, or many of the women at the domestic violence support group who were engaged with social services and the legal system, did not have a choice about many of the appointments they had to keep during the week. Suzanne, profiled in Chapter 5, was living alone with her daughter for the first time, with support from social services. She was involved in a complicated court case to retain custody of her daughter, which involved dealing with a range of professionals, among them psychologists, solicitors, social workers for herself and her daughter, support workers, NSPCC representatives and Sure Start co-ordinators. When appointments and arrangements with these people clashed with learning opportunities, it is clear that the learning opportunities had to take second place.

Relationships

The relationships that people had, both within and outside the community sites, had a significant impact on their engagement with learning. Being able to come in for 'a brew and a chat' was an important feature of the homeless shelter, the domestic violence support group, the drug and alcohol support centre and the tenants' association. The relationships people built up at the drug and alcohol support centre, both with staff and with other clients, played a crucial part in supporting them. The range of services available to people interacted to form a climate in which learning could take place within a network of support. People talked about the importance of the staff being available to them all the time, the egalitarian relationships that were built up, which are described in more detail below, and, as has been mentioned already, the importance of being with other people with similar issues who understand what they are going through.

People also bring with them relationships from outside the setting. Some of these can have positive effects on their engagement in learning, and some can have the reverse. At the homeless shelter, the young people brought with them a complex social structure of relationships and identities. The presence or absence of particular groups of people shaped others' willingness to engage with the activities that were offered. They appreciated being in a space with others who shared their experiences, such as homelessness, pregnancy or the drug culture. While they valued the positive support this offered, this could also have negative effects. As staff told us:

> It does drag them down [group involvement]. One lad got a job and the others kept coming saying: Come on, let's go – so he did and lost his job ... All your friends don't want to do things, and they just want to get wrecked every night. (Safeplace worker)
>
> Falling in with a peer group of like mind, which accentuates how they are feeling, as though there isn't anything for them and that they are fairly worthless so they generally have a low opinion of themselves and their position ... and that they expect almost nothing at all. (Connexions adviser – a one-to-one support worker for 13 to 19 year olds addressing social and educational issues)

Jason found a great deal of support for his learning from the people in the tenants' association, and this support was one of the factors that made his engagement possible. However, he also had support of a different kind from friends he socialised with. When his depression worsened, this was the support he chose for a while, rather than that which related to learning activities.

This takes us to the final aspect of people's lives, which is concerned with the crucial importance of people's own purposes and desires in whether and when they choose to engage in organised learning activities.

Imagined futures

Steve was introduced in Chapter 1 as being in his thirties and attending a drug and alcohol support centre.

> **Steve** has negative memories of his secondary schooling, describing the teaching as having been authoritarian, clinical and abrupt. He has dyslexia but received no support for it at school, and remembers getting into trouble for his reactions when people laughed at him reading aloud. He is very critical of 'old-fashioned schoolteacher types', who feel that taking on a strict or authoritarian role is part of their job. In his experience of talking to people who have had problems with drugs and alcohol, they have often gone through this kind of schooling. He frequently skipped school from the age of 13 and left officially at 16. He sat some exams but does not know the results. He worked as a joiner for a while, locally and in London.
>
> By his early twenties, he had started dabbling in hard drugs with friends, which led to addiction. He rapidly lost interest in work and made money by other means. Finally, after stealing money he was sent to prison for three years. He maintained his habit in prison, so needed to 'score' straight after getting out. Within weeks he had committed another

robbery and was sent down again, this time for five years. Steve says this was 'basically what saved my life, really; it changed things forever for me'. He chose to spend this time getting himself sorted out, did some courses, and signed up for a residential rehab in the south of England.

When he came out of jail he went to London for a fresh start. He stayed clean there for a year, but had to come back suddenly when his mother fell ill. Surrounded by old acquaintances, he soon started using again. Then his girlfriend had a baby and they moved down to London, wanting to get back to the good work he had done before. But their drug use continued, he was arrested, and their son was taken away by Social Services and placed with his girlfriend's mother. Steve and his girlfriend returned to the local area to be close to their son; since when, ironically enough considering this is where he had always had problems before, he has 'got my shit together'. He and his girlfriend got married, they have had another baby, and he has got involved in setting up a user group to support local people using drugs.

Steve's writing skills are poor, related to his dyslexia. However, he was very reluctant to engage with discrete literacy provision. This was not a priority in his life, he did not see any immediate use for it, and the strong negative associations he retained regarding 'study' from his school days made him unlikely to choose to spend his time in this way. He was, however, eager to engage with provision – both educational and support provision – which *he* perceived as being useful and productive for him. He found the support he received from the Structured Day Programme to be absolutely vital, because it was there whenever he needed it, and because it was a 'safe place' where he could engage in structured activities without risking bumping into old acquaintances.

He expressed his future goal as to have 'just a clean, healthy life really. The rest of it I'll make, and mould, and manufacture . . . My goals are to just maintain what I'm doing, and try and achieve something, whatever it be, however small or big, to achieve something.' By the end of our study he was working as a community research assistant for a local university.

Steve's sense of a possible future, of what he might become and how he could achieve it, was crucial to his engagement in learning. In this section we introduce the fourth component of people's lives which affects their learning. It is concerned with their purposes, aspirations, hopes and desires, and we refer to this as their imagined futures. People's imagined futures create and constrain what they see as possible. People's plans changed as they saw different possibilities for themselves, and the sites we worked in were important catalysts for this.

Engagement in learning driven by broader life purposes

We found that the different individuals we worked with had many and varied reasons for engaging in educational provision. These could be very different in the different sites. People attending the drug and alcohol support centre were for the most part engaged in a process of transition, and this shaped their relationship to learning. Where literacy and numeracy learning were seen as important or useful to them and their goals, as with Caroline earlier, who wanted eventually to get back into office work, they were taken up. For other people, introducing structure of any kind was perceived by them to be useful for their development, and so for a while they attended all the courses that were offered, but with quite a different motivation. Recognition of the diversity of factors that people want from engaging in learning is crucial when working in these settings.

'Conventional' long-term aspirations

Nearly everyone we talked to described their long-term aspirations in conventional terms: a settled home, a family, a good job, happy relationships – although these aspirations were often held in tension with the concept of 'normality' in a culture which, they felt, excluded 'people like us', as mentioned earlier. At the homeless shelter, all but one of the interviewees cited these as being their significant goals in life. But these longer-term goals often took a secondary place to more immediate and urgent priorities. At the homeless shelter, for instance, the principal purpose for many was immediate survival. Most of them in the medium term wanted to train and to prepare themselves for work, and most of them had dipped in and out of vocational study and training at college or with other providers. However, most have found this difficult to sustain, experiencing difficulties related to unstable living arrangements, drug use, and all sorts of more immediate priorities linked to their current circumstances that we have described above.

Purposes and desires change over time

People's purposes and desires are not fixed, but change over time. As people's life circumstances changed, the relative priority of their goals could shift rapidly, and the place of literacy and numeracy learning within these could shift too. At the Big Issue, survival was the vendors' major concern, and this meant different things to different people: a hostel bed, money for drugs or alcohol, clean needles or a chance to attend a detox programme. Learning came secondary to these issues. People's purposes and desires could also change as a result of the learning and support activities they were engaging with in these settings. As they built up confidence and self-esteem, they might begin to consider options which they did not feel were open to them before, such as Caroline, who ended up attending a mainstream college class only months after explaining to us how she did not think she would ever go back to college.

The search for well-being

One constant, however, was the search for *well-being* which shaped people's choices. The young people at the homeless shelter were looking for a place to stay where they felt happy, safe and settled. They often moved around a lot to escape shifting relationships, noise, disruption and violence. This mobility was not in itself their goal, but was a function of their search for settledness and well-being. Safety and happiness had a much greater priority for people than formal learning achievements. Where engaging in learning challenged their safety and happiness, it was not taken up. This included examples we came across where attending college became very uncomfortable, or when learning activities offered at the centre were perceived as being too formal, school-like and off-putting. When a woman attending an assertiveness training course run by the domestic violence support group felt she had exposed too much of her personal history at the first session, she was too uncomfortable to return the following week.

In the next chapter, we turn to examining how these aspects of people's lives play out in the ways they participate in learning opportunities in these settings.

11

THE NEGOTIATION OF LEARNING IN COMMUNITY SETTINGS

In this chapter we look in more detail at how the aspects of people's lives covered in Chapter 10 shaped their learning in these settings. We examine the dynamics of the individual sites, their distinct purposes and people's patterns of participation in them, and we show how aspects of people's lives shape the provision. First, we turn to how aspects of people's lives shaped their engagement in learning opportunities, identifying issues such as their reluctance to access mainstream education, how they dipped in and out of educational provision and how they identified a 'right time' for learning. Then we turn to patterns of participation in these settings, examining the use of space and time and the resultant patterns of interaction.

How lives shaped participation and engagement in learning

The characteristics of people's lives covered in Chapter 10 combine to shape their responses to and feelings about participating in formal learning. There were common factors influencing choices and ability to participate.

Reluctance to access mainstream provision

A key point to recognise is that in these settings, people were for the most part unwilling and unlikely to access mainstream college provision, or indeed community provision which appeared similar to mainstream college provision. Negative previous experiences of education and negative experiences with authority meant that what they perceived as hierarchical formal learning environments were very off-putting. Feelings of exclusion from so-called 'normal' culture made it very challenging for many to contemplate participating in college activities or taking on a new identity as a college student. Mainstream college provision is normally provided on a daily or weekly basis, and this could be problematic for people whose lives were not structured in this regular way, or who were dealing with a range of unpredictable life circumstances and events which might have to be prioritised over learning. These difficulties were reinforced where people were in relationships, whether with partners, family members, friends or peer groups, which were not supportive to learning.

This is not to say that people in these groups would never access mainstream college provision. Some clients of the drug and alcohol support centre day programme went on to mainstream courses at the local community college, including Caroline, profiled earlier, who only a few months before had explained how unlikely she felt it was that she would ever attend college. In the previous year, twelve clients had gone on to college and this was seen by the support centre as a significant achievement. This was in a setting where support was available for moving on to mainstream courses, and where the same teachers from the college were teaching the mainstream and the community classes, so clients felt supported by the existing positive relationships they had built up. Some of the mainstream classes were even running in the support centre's building, making the step that much easier to take. This was also a college where the principal was supportive in continuing with community provision, even at times when the numbers were low, which paid off in the long run both in terms of people's progress and in terms of their progression. Brian, another client, is a good example of this progression. He went from doing a creative writing class as part of the structured day programme, to doing an evening creative writing class with the same tutor on the same site which was part of the mainstream provision, to an introductory counselling course on the main college site and eventually a diploma course which he considered vocational training, planning to work as a counsellor himself eventually.

Accessing mainstream provision required support. As part of their core activities the domestic violence centre offered bridging support to women to attend college. This included childcare, financial support for travel and, most importantly, being accompanied by other women for the first few sessions. At Safeplace the Connexions adviser accompanied young people through the application process for college, but they did not have the resources to sustain this bridging support.

Emotional experiences influence learning

People in these settings were regularly dealing with difficult or overwhelming mental, emotional and physical experiences in response to events in their lives which could profoundly influence their whole learning experience. This could happen for a range of reasons; for instance, if elements of the learning environment recalled people's previous negative experiences of education or authority, or other traumatic or painful events from their histories; or if they brought with them difficult or challenging current life circumstances and events. (For more on this see Jenny Horsman's (2000) study in Canada where she identifies both the prevalence of trauma and violence in the lives of women attending literacy education, and the devastating impact these life experiences can have on people's learning.)

The teachers and learning providers we worked with were sensitive to such issues and had developed ways of dealing with them in the classroom. This might mean being ready to change the lesson plan very quickly, in order directly to address the issue at hand. But equally, it might mean being prepared to sit outside with a cup of tea and give people some space, rather than launching straight into activities. Tutors with no experience in this area need to be provided with training which will give them confidence in making such decisions, an issue which we return to later.

'Dipping in and out'

Many of the people in these sites 'dipped in and out' of learning. This was particularly true of people attending the homeless shelter who, as we have already mentioned above, would often attend for a short period of time before other circumstances got in the way. While on college records this would appear as a 'drop out', within the context of that young person's life it wasn't necessarily failure. Attending college, even for a short time, could be a significant and important step for them, given the histories they were carrying with them, the circumstances they were dealing with and the multiple life goals they were addressing. This is well illustrated by a summary of a case history from the Connexions adviser at the homeless shelter:

> One young person I was working with was a heroin addict. He had a lot of support from Safeplace. He had a really unsettled lifestyle but had some support from a 'leaving care' worker. He then got thrown out of his hostel and went to NACRO for training which didn't work out. But at that time he stopped being a heroin addict so he had moved a million miles because he was completely down and out when I first met him. He then managed to get his own flat, attended college for a while but something went wrong and he was asked to leave. Statistically he has not moved on and not achieved and on our system he is 19, still unemployed and failed. But I can see that a lot of input from a lot of people has achieved a lot in his case.

Where the experience of attending college was a positive one for people, it could challenge conceptions of a normality which excluded them or a new identity which they could not take on, and perhaps lead them to engage for longer the next time. But where the experience was negative, it could make them less likely to engage in the future. With this group in particular, having support and encouragement for small steps could make a big difference to their future choices within the context of their lives as a whole.

Another example is that of Jason, earlier, who appeared in college records as a 'non-completer'. However, he had had a very positive experience of learning, had continued to engage in informal learning in the tenants' association and as a co-researcher, and made a significant contribution to the work of the association and to our research. His progression routes at the end of our study were unclear, as his return to drinking had led to difficulty in managing his learning and life. Nevertheless, the support from other volunteers at the tenants' association was still open to him, and his positive experiences of and attitude to learning meant that it was entirely possible that he would return to it in the future, when the time was right for him.

The 'right time'

This idea that learning opportunities needed to be made available at the 'right time' in a given individual's life if they were to be taken up effectively was a common one among the people we worked with. This 'right time' emerged from a combination of their life experiences, their purposes and goals and the priority of learning within them at this point, the support that was available for them for making potentially difficult changes, and the learning opportunities that they had access to. Sophie's immediate priority needs were for safety, support and company, rather than for formalised learning. While she had tried to engage in formal learning, this had been difficult for her to sustain whilst living with homelessness. She had clear life goals, but at the end of our study engaging in formal learning was not seen as a priority to help her to meet them. She needed ongoing support through her rapidly changing life circumstances, from people who were able to spend time with her, build trust and positive relationships and understand how she represented herself, her realities, her wants and her needs. With sensitivity, the supportive people in her life could encourage her to move towards her own 'right time' for learning; but this is essentially a subjective experience, so she is ultimately the only person who can really recognise and engage with it.

This interaction of history, circumstances and purposes meant that the relative priority of literacy, numeracy and language learning – or indeed of learning in general – varied a great deal, both between people and over the course of any individual's life. Where these were not aligned, developing the motivation to engage in formal learning was less likely. Since Sophie's underachievement at school does not necessarily indicate basic skills needs, it is unlikely that literacy and numeracy learning will be her top priority when her 'right time' comes. Steve gives a different perspective of this, from that of someone who does have what would be classed as basic skills needs. He explained how, despite having dyslexia and not feeling confident in writing, literacy learning was of very low priority for him in relation to his overall life goals, which had been first and foremost to get and stay clean, and second to 'make, mould and manufacture' the other factors that he wanted to achieve.

In summary, the characteristics of people's lives – their histories, their current identities and life circumstances, and the shifting goals and purposes they have for their futures – interact to shape their engagement in and experience of learning. In community settings such as these in particular, people are often unlikely or unwilling to access mainstream provision, especially if this resembles school. They may be dealing with difficult and overwhelming emotional and physical experiences, which may be relatively invisible to practitioners, but nevertheless shape the possibilities for their engagement in learning. They often 'dip in and out' of learning; from the perspective of provision this might be classed as failure, but within the context of their lives might be a very positive step. And for learning to be successful and positive, it had to be made available at the 'right time' for that individual, a subjective experience which emerges from the interaction of the characteristics they bring with them and the support and opportunities available to them at that point.

This takes us to the next aspect of the analysis: the dynamics of the different sites we worked in, how the sites were distinctive in their purposes and yet we observed similarities in the patterns of participation. This then leads on to how characteristics of people's lives shaped the forms of provision to support people.

What goes on in the sites: purposes

Each site had a set of principal purposes which were not primarily educational and which shaped the patterns of participation there. These purposes shaped the priority and visibility of formal literacy and numeracy learning in these places, from an explicit role at the drug and alcohol support centre to a more indirect, though important one at the domestic violence support group, where people were learning as it became necessary in carrying out their responsibilities.

The principal purpose of the programme at the drug and alcohol support centre was to offer support for drug and alcohol users and ex-users. This included people who had been given drug treatment and testing orders, obliging them to have regular structured support. The centre provided a variety of approaches, including one-to-one support and a structured day programme of activities. These included relapse prevention and harm minimisation support groups, complementary therapies, and educational courses provided by tutors from the local adult community college, such as Music Technology, Art and Skills for Life. Once a week, staff from the local learndirect centre visited and supported people who were doing courses online, including literacy, numeracy and ICT, but also courses such as web design. After signing up for these, several clients also spent time at the learndirect centre in town. Again, engagement in learning was driven by the needs of the clients. The courses that had been put on as part of the day programme had been selected in consultation, and were chosen primarily because they were likely to be of interest to people attending the centre. While people were initially encouraged to attend all the courses to try them out, they were then free to choose which ones they continued to go to, in negotiation with staff. The principal priority was meeting their own particular needs and wants.

The Big Issue in Liverpool worked with people who were vendors of the Big Issue magazine. The principal purpose of the organisation is to provide opportunities for people facing homelessness to help themselves, first through selling the

magazine, and second through empowering them to change their lives by supporting them around issues of housing, employment and education, and helping them
develop self-esteem, self-confidence and independence. At the organisation's
Liverpool base, training and education for vendors had for some years included
literacy and numeracy, delivered in a flexible way responsive to vendors' needs.
With the introduction of Skills for Life funding, discrete maths and English classes
were offered, with the incentive of an extra fifteen magazines to sell for attending.
The organisation also offered music and IT classes.

At the homeless shelter, the principal purpose was to offer support to young
homeless people. The priority issue was ensuring their survival and well-being,
making sure they had a safe place to come to and a safe place to live. Once this
was established, staff worked with the young people on individual action plans,
including addressing accommodation issues, drug and alcohol use, and planning
for the future. These young people were learning all the time, but often this was
not phrased in explicitly educational terms. For some young people, their action
plan included engaging in formal learning, such as attending college; and educational activities formed part of what was going on at the day centre. But everything was framed in terms of meeting the particular needs of the young people
involved, with learning being focused on to the extent that this was appropriate for
these individuals.

The principal purpose of the tenants' association was to offer support to residents of the estate with practical issues, particularly relating to their housing. For
volunteers, the association offered support with educational and development
issues, which included both supporting people to attend formal courses and
supporting their learning through participation in the activities of the organisation.

The principal purpose of the domestic violence support group was to offer
advice and support to women who were or had been in situations of domestic and
family violence, and to raise awareness of these issues in the community and in
legislation. The group sought to be an alternative to official support services run
by professionals, which the organiser, Jacqui, felt disempowered women. The
organisation, run from a local church hall, offered drop-in support sessions and
activities including an assertiveness training course, a men's stress management
course and a telephone support and advice service. As part of their support
activities, the group worked with women attending college, including for some
vocational Skills for Life classes. Education and training were seen as part of the
way women receiving support could develop their confidence and self-esteem, and
the possibilities open to them for paid employment and new opportunities.

What goes on in sites: patterns of participation

Staff and volunteers in all these different community settings made it a priority to
foster and develop a supportive, informal, relaxed atmosphere. They appreciated
the issues that clients and service users might have with authority, structure and
formality, described previously, and worked to develop each site as a 'safe place'

in which social interaction and developing mutually supportive relationships were as important as any more structured activity which might be going on. This was achieved through particular patterns of the use of space, the use of time and the interactions in the sites, which built up supportive and informal relationships between people.

Use of space

In each of these sites, spaces were available both for structured activities and for less structured social interaction. At the drug and alcohol support centre, group activities took place in several rooms. A large room with a central table and chairs, decorated with clients' art works, was used for group discussions and activities not requiring the use of computers. The room behind this, of a similar size, was lined with broadband-equipped computers and mixing decks, and was used for music technology and IT classes and as a drop-in computer resource room. There were also local newspapers and information leaflets and the room served as an informal space for people to relax in. The entry hall held a signing-in book and led onto the staff office, so had institutional functions, but also served as a place for people to wait, chat and circulate. At the end of a corridor with one-to-one rooms and an office leading off it came a kitchen, where clients and staff made tea and coffee and talked, and beyond this a small and comfortable room primarily used for complementary therapies.

The key place for informal interaction, though, was outside the centre itself, in a small space outside the back door leading onto the yard. A corrugated plastic roof offered some scant protection from the elements, and chairs were arranged in a small group. This was where people congregated for a cup of tea or coffee and often a smoke. Clients told us that one of the key supports that the centre offered was a space to come and 'have a brew and a fag' and 'just have a chat and a laugh' in a non-pressured environment. It was an egalitarian space, where community workers, tutors, management and administrative staff met on an equal footing with service users to talk about everyday life, and was therefore a key site for the development of informal patterns of interaction and positive relationships. Staff told us that some of their most important work was done in that small space outside the back door.

All of the other sites we worked in had similar spaces for unstructured social interaction. The day centre for young homeless people was housed in a converted electricity station. In a corner near the door were a sofa and some armchairs, where a few of the young people would normally be sitting relaxing, with a brew area on the other side of the entrance for making tea and coffee. The tables in the middle of the room were used both as a place for organised activities and as a space for sitting, chatting, drinking tea, eating lunch, playing games and planning activities. The centre also had a kitchen at one end and office space at the other, along with a quiet room, toilets, showers and a store room; but most of the space was unstructured enough so that the young people could wander about in it and use it as they chose to.

The tenants' association was sited in a first floor flat in a maisonette on the estate. It contained an office room with telephones and computer facilities, a bedroom with an internet computer and a kitchen. The kitchen was a crucial resource for the association; people were continually dropping in on an informal basis. Teas and coffees were constantly being produced and there would normally be people sitting around on easy chairs in the office, discussing everyday activities. The domestic violence support group was based in a local church hall, providing a safe and supportive environment both for women coming to the centre and for those who provide the service. It was in a single room, with a phone line and a computer available. When training events and meetings were not happening, the room functioned as a drop-in when staff are available, with people sitting around on easy chairs talking. The Big Issue was housed in a large building in Liverpool city centre. It contained a magazine collection point for vendors and offices downstairs. Upstairs were a computer suite, several classrooms, a kitchen, a music room and several additional training rooms. As at the drug and alcohol support centre, there was a space outside the door where smokers assembled and chatted. The informal space here was the office, which was always open. At Training 2000, the young people congregated outside, if it was fine, or in the canteen and around the entrance and stairs in bad weather. All these spaces for unstructured social interaction allowed for the de-emphasis of the institutional identity of the sites and the development of informal interpersonal interactions and relationships.

Another key point is that in most of these settings, ownership of the space was visibly demonstrated by the use of clients' own work in displays decorating the sites. The homeless shelter is a particularly interesting example here, showing a tension between the use of space to display ownership and the use of space to construct a particular atmosphere. When we began our work, the day centre was filled with artwork done by the young people: glass painting on the windows, banners, collages from magazines up the stairs, artwork and posters. This produced a large, vibrant and colourful space, clearly marked as being owned by the young people themselves. But staff decided to redecorate to produce a calmer, more minimalist environment, partly because they were working with a particularly challenging group of young people at that time and felt that this would help to quieten the atmosphere. However, the young people rejected this new look and the staff realised the importance of the young people marking the space in their own style. Colourful and visually attractive advice and information leaflets on life issues produced by the young people themselves were made available, contrasting with rather duller-looking nationally produced ones, and locally produced centre information such as a 'rules of the house' poster produced with a local community arts organisation were prominently displayed.

Finally, and significantly, attention was paid to security in all the sites where this was an issue, an important part of constructing the various settings as 'safe places'. Access to the drug and alcohol support centre was through a locked door. Staff served as gatekeepers, and if people appeared to have been drinking or taking drugs they would be turned away. The tenants' association rooms were protected by a large steel door. The church hall where the domestic violence support group was sited was used for many activities, making it possible for people to visit the organisation without making it obvious why they were there, and access to the hall was controlled through an intercom by the caretaker. Access to the upstairs space at the Big Issue was controlled through a security door, with notices on it warning that this was a drug-free space. Access to the day centre for young homeless was through a single door, which people who had been barred were not permitted to enter. This might not seem on the face of it to be an issue directly relevant to learning. But where people were living in circumstances in which they might be actively under threat, focusing on learning activities could only happen when they felt sure that the space they were in was secure and where learning would not be disrupted.

Use of time

In similar ways to the existence of unstructured social space, unstructured social time was a common feature of all these settings. Time was made available in the social spaces just to chat and interact. Clients at the drug and alcohol support centre talked about the importance of having somewhere in their lives without pressure, where they could sit, chat, have a laugh and be peaceful without feeling pressured to do anything. Staff also saw this time as important and made it clear that some of their most important work happened during this time. Similarly, time spent chatting was an important element of what went on at the domestic violence support group, at the tenants' association and at Big Issue.

Where the setting offered structured activities, these often had relaxed starting times. At the drug and alcohol support centre, though classes were advertised as starting at a particular time, they often began later, after people had come in, settled down and had a brew and a smoke. During this time, the class tutor would normally sit outside and talk to people, giving them the opportunity to assess the clients' current state of mind and their feelings, and to be responsive to that once the class began. At the homeless shelter, activities might be going on for some time in one corner of the space before the young people would express interest or feel ready to join in. The same was true on a longer-term basis, where people were not pressured to begin formal course-related activities straight away. Once these relationships were established, people were happier about focusing on learning activities, where these were relevant to their own purposes.

Another time issue was making support available to people for as much time as possible, within the resource constraints of the organisation. The homeless shelter offered 24-hour support for those young people who were staying in its emergency accommodation, and the day centre was available to young people on a drop-in basis during its opening hours. And many of the clients at the drug and alcohol support centre appreciated being able to come in for support whenever they needed to, in addition to their classes and appointments.

Patterns of interaction

In all these settings, the style of interaction was predominantly informal. Staff and clients addressed each other by first names. There were implicit and explicit ground rules about what sorts of interaction were appropriate. These differed in the different settings; for instance, swearing was frowned upon at the homeless shelter, which had a younger clientele, but less so at the drug and alcohol support centre. But in all of them showing respect, by listening to one another and avoiding displays of anger or irritation, was important.

At the homeless shelter, an interesting manifestation of this informality was that care had to be taken to avoid presenting what was going on to people in a formal, structured way. When they had the day's programme displayed as a list of 'activities', some young people refused to be involved – 'we're not doing "activities"'. When the list was presented as 'what's happening today', there was much less resistance. This relates to the young people's previous negative experiences with structured education and with authority, described earlier. As one staff member put it:

> The way we work with them is like we never say: 'we're going to have a cooking session'. We might say: 'Do you fancy a barbecue?' Then we might joke about the crap in sausages and show them how to cook them ... They often have a mental block about instructions as they associate these with authority. They find authority difficult either because they have had bad memories of abuse of authority or the opposite – they have never ever been disciplined by anybody and have brought themselves up more or less.

The change in decor mentioned above was associated with a change in the name of the centre, from a 'drop-in centre' to an 'educationally based day centre', related to changing funding requirements. This led to a difficult period of adjustment. The manager told us:

> It's better now but it's been a difficult time. The culture changed overnight because we not only changed the décor but also the language such as naming the Safeplace day centre an 'educational activity centre' which sounds formal and you know these young people don't do 'education' so we've changed the words and we've not used the word 'education' ... It's about words that people feel comfortable with.

In all these settings, there was an attempt to develop relationships between staff and clients that were egalitarian, rather than authoritarian. This worked out differently in different places. The tenants' association saw themselves as representing the local voice against external officialdom, and there was already little social distance between volunteers and people coming to the centre. Similarly, the domestic violence support group was set up as a support service offered by people who had themselves had experience of domestic and family violence. The Big Issue and the drug and alcohol support centre were staffed by professionals in community work, which set up more distance between staff and clients; however, explicit attempts were made to minimise this. For instance, at the drug and alcohol support centre staff made efforts to talk with clients about their own problems and current issues and seek advice from them, partly to challenge the idea that so-called 'normal' people don't have problems to deal with and to ensure that clients were themselves positioned as competent people with contributions to make. As one client told us,

> I've found the staff very supportive, really. Wherever I've been before, there's been a very definite staff–client divide. But here, the staff tend to treat you like an individual rather than: 'Oh, an alcoholic, and all alcoholics are the same, and typical alcoholic, and . . .' You know, we're all just treated like individuals, which is great.

At the homeless shelter, this development of egalitarian relationships was complicated somewhat by the difference in age between staff and young people. At the homeless shelter, the staff took on not only supportive but also disciplinary roles; for instance, when the young people challenged the ground rules of interaction at the centre, or in discussions challenging aspects of their behaviour, such as gambling. They attempted to strike a careful balance between setting boundaries and maintaining positive relationships.

And as a result of building up this knowledge and understanding of people as individuals, staff were able to be responsive to people's immediate concerns and experiences, the changing responses to histories, events and circumstances that people were bringing with them to the setting. Where centres were offering structured learning activities, this might mean: leaving an extra few minutes before starting an activity, to give people a chance to 'get their head together'; having extra breaks during activities; or allowing people to choose not to participate that day, or to engage in peripheral ways, such as playing Solitaire during an IT or music technology class. Bertie, one of the clients at the drug and alcohol support centre, told us that the courses were great because of the lack of pressure associated with them. This seemed to be one of the only times and places in his life at that moment where this was the case, where he could unwind and forget about difficulties that he was currently facing. And it is telling that as described earlier, from a programme of very fluctuating numbers attending formal provision, in one year twelve people went on to mainstream college provision. These were all people who would have been unlikely, for all the reasons outlined previously, to have done so without this interim stage.

How lives shaped provision

The features of provision identified earlier are shaped by the concern of all the workers in these sites that what they provided should be driven by the needs of their clients, rather than solely by external targets. The informal patterns of participation and the trusting and respectful relationships built up with people as individuals were central to the achievement of the principal purposes of the sites. This approach was necessary precisely because of everything that clients and service users were bringing with them from their lives.

With regard to learning, this approach implied that agendas for learning had to be flexible, and respond to the changing circumstances and needs of clients. The Connexions adviser at the homeless shelter explained how it was necessary in his view for all those supporting vulnerable young people to be prepared to 'go the extra mile' and to 'walk alongside' that young person for as long as it takes. Where the settings offered formal, structured learning, it was important that this was delivered in a flexible, responsive way. In many of the sites, the principal learning that was going on was happening informally, through participation; and this was true even when there was more structured learning also available. For instance, Steve explained to us how, although he was profoundly reluctant to attend dedicated literacy provision at the drug and alcohol rehabilitation centre, he was happy to be able to bring in a piece of writing he had to do for work and go through it with one of the centre staff.

A key issue, particularly in relation to literacy, numeracy and language learning, was that this localised, needs-driven approach could clash with the agendas and priorities of funders and institutions. For instance, there were instances where staff felt they were under pressure to persuade clients to undergo basic skills diagnostic testing. Where this was not a priority for the client concerned, where it evoked previous negative memories of testing, where it was inappropriate given their level of literacy, or where it was experienced as an institutional imposition before trusting relationships had been built up, this could be counter-productive, even leading to clients leaving the provision.

A related point is that some of the structures and frameworks of formal educational provision were inappropriate for the needs of this client group. At the drug and alcohol support centre, much of the formal literacy and numeracy provision clients were engaging in was offered by learndirect, a government-funded distance learning programme. In order for these courses to be funded, they had to be completed within a certain period of time. But as a result of all the issues raised earlier, particularly the turbulent unpredictability of the life events people were often dealing with and the fact that many did not lead lives structured around regular routines, clients would often start a course but not complete it within the specified period. This was demoralising for the client, who had again been positioned as a failure within the educational system, and for staff, who might have spent a long time supporting that client to be ready to try engaging in education again. Clients would then understandably be reluctant to try another learndirect course, as this had reinforced their negative experiences of education. This underlines the importance of considering carefully the sorts of timescales for learning which are realistic for different groups of people.

At the Big Issue, the initial impact of the Skills for Life strategy was perceived as a shift from a locally produced, flexible literacy programme relating primarily to vendors' concerns, to one based on the national curriculum. Previously, literacy and numeracy had been embedded in a wider essential skills curriculum that had fewer time constraints and assessment requirements, and a general approach described by the manager as 'a person-centred style of community education, looking at the whole person'. This was the approach with which they had experienced the most success with this client group, and they were resisting a felt shift away from this towards a model structuring learning from the outside by means of the national curriculum and assessment framework.

The national teaching standards also had an impact on the provision here. The manager felt that the most important quality in the teachers they employed was the ability to work with this client group, rather than having a Level 4 qualification; but this qualification was now becoming a requirement, limiting the already small potential pool of teachers they had available to them. This is a particularly significant issue in these community settings, where provision is far more fragile than in a college setting, cover is not readily available, and unexpected difficulties such as having one person off sick can make the provision fall apart. For instance, as we started our work with Big Issue, the Basic Skills tutor – who had built up excellent relationships with clients and was rated very highly by the management – fell ill, and it proved impossible to replace her. Sustainability of provision is a very important issue in these settings.

In general terms, where literacy, numeracy and language provision was happening in partnership between Skills for Life specialists and community staff, it was important for tutors coming in from college settings to understand and respect the importance of the patterns of interaction that were practised in the site, which were often quite different from those in colleges. Although there might be no visible, immediate outcomes of the relaxed social interaction that was central to all these settings, it underpinned and made possible everything else that was going on. It helped when literacy and numeracy specialists understood the reasons for this and were able to participate in it. This also underlines the importance of community workers understanding clients' language, literacy and numeracy needs.

These six chapters have presented data about people's literacies, their lives and their learning. In the next chapter we bring this together by examining lives over time, using the concept of people having a set of interlinking 'careers'.

12

LIFE CAREERS

So far we have described what is going on at a particular point in time, when learners are engaging in provision in college or community settings. In this chapter we want to bring together the data of previous chapters and broaden the perspective to take a longitudinal look at adults' lives over time. We want to get an understanding of how life histories influence learning and what this leads to. This brings together both retrospective work, interviewing learners about their histories, and longitudinal work, keeping in touch with people over time to see how their lives develop. As explained earlier, we carried out retrospective interviewing with most of the people we worked with across the diverse settings and kept in longitudinal contact for up to three years with around fifty people. We will describe people's lives over time in terms of multiple 'careers', a concept introduced in Chapter 3.

Lives as multiple careers

Lives consist of a variety of different careers, one of which is a learning career. Learning careers run alongside and overlap with other careers in people's lives: health careers, family careers, friendship careers, employment careers, leisure careers, crime careers. Any one of these can be the main focus of attention. Here we are going to focus on learning careers and how other careers impact on this to demonstrate the usefulness of taking this longer-term view, looking at changes in people's lives over time and their relationship to learning. To illustrate this we look at one person's life over time, that of Barbra, a 53-year-old woman who worked part time as a care assistant at a day centre for the elderly. We met Barbra when she was attending a workplace-based Skills for Life class, billed as 'Computing for the Terrified'. We will highlight her multiple careers and how these interconnect. We will draw on Barbra's story to exemplify our points, but these have come from an analysis of the dataset as a whole, to which we will refer for other examples of interconnected careers.

Work career

We begin with her work career. Barbra's work career began when, aged 14, she started as a Saturday girl at a hairdressing salon. When she left school, she became indentured as an apprentice at the same salon. Barbra herself had not been particularly interested in hairdressing, but her mother, who Barbra described as having been a dominant, strong character, had encouraged her to go into this field, as it was something that she had wanted to do but had not been able to.

Barbra's real interest was in nursing, and she was thrilled at the age of 18 to be accepted for training at a local hospital, after passing their entrance examination. She even got as far as buying the nurse's uniform. However, her parents separated at around this time, and her father became depressed, which put pressure on Barbra to stay at home with him rather than to leave for the residential training. So she continued working as a hairdresser, in a range of salons around the area, as well as doing some work for herself. One of her regular jobs was at a local home for the elderly, and it was the manager of this home who said she had 'a way with the elderly', and should perhaps consider going into this field. So when the day centre first opened in 1988, she was interviewed for one of the first six jobs, and was awarded it, out of a field of four hundred candidates. She has worked there ever since. She felt that working at the day centre had enabled her to use the skills she learned as a hairdresser, both technically and in terms of dealing with people, whilst also fulfilling to an extent her initial desire to go into nursing.

A diagram of this career helps to illustrate the highs and lows Barbra experienced through her work career. The diagram represents Barbra's life through time from

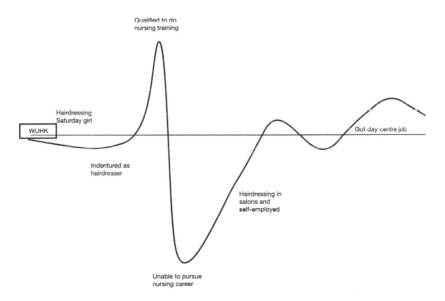

Figure 12.1 Barbra's work career. The horizontal axis indicates her life over time, from birth to age 53 years.

her childhood through to the time when we met her at age 53 years. The vertical axis represents an interpretation of the highs and lows of Barbra's emotions around the events, as she described them to us in our conversations. While this representation is inevitably impressionistic, it nevertheless portrays the broad pattern of events. Building up this diagram in Figures 12.1 to 12.5 by adding in different careers provides a useful way of demonstrating the complexity of Barbra's multiple careers and the important points at which they were interlinked.

Family career

The description of Barbra's work career already shows the importance of events in her family career affecting her working life, with her mother encouraging her into hairdressing, her father's needs overriding her desire to go into nursing, and family responsibilities forcing her to take breaks from her day centre work. A more detailed representation of her family career shows how the highs and lows of this career map closely onto those of her work. We can see from the diagram in Figure 12.2 how her family career had been marked by the highs and lows of having children, marriages beginning and ending and caring responsibilities for elderly relatives have shaped the possibilities for her work career. She had to have a break in her service at the day centre to care for her father after he became ill, and worked part time while bringing up her two children alone. Now that the children were older and her daughter had left home, she still had family responsibilities, as she was caring for elderly relatives.

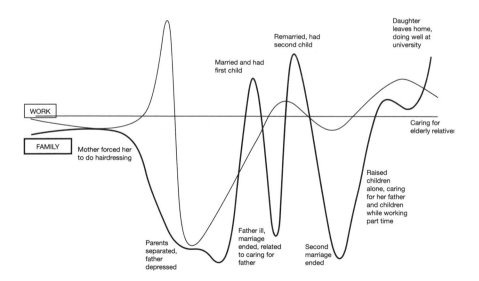

Figure 12.2 Barbra's family career

Health career

The discussion so far has been missing out one very important career in Barbra's life: that of her health. At the age of 9, she suffered a serious head injury in a bus accident, and she felt that the repercussions from this affected her life ever since. She was very ill for two years, and felt that although she was still able to attend some school, she did not benefit from education at this point and was forever catching up afterwards, particularly since she only just missed out on getting into the grammar school at her 11-plus exam. She suffered severe bullying at school, related to the scarring on her face from the accident. She felt that these experiences left her with anxiety, and there were times where this had been a real problem for her. She also wondered whether the difficulties she experienced with concentration might be related to the accident. She felt that this anxiety and lack of confidence had held her back from achieving some of the things she might otherwise have done in her life, such as gaining more qualifications and moving on in her work career, doing something that she saw as being more 'for myself'.

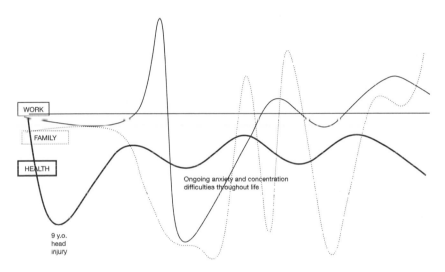

Figure 12.3 Barbra's health career

Leisure career

One important strand in Barbra's story is what we will call here her leisure and creative career. This was a very significant part of her identity. She described herself as being 'artistically inclined', and this was one of the first ways she introduced herself to us. This manifested itself in her life in various ways. She was

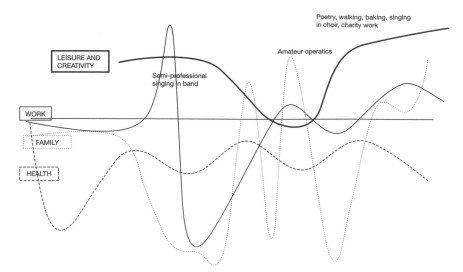

Figure 12.4 Barbra's leisure and creativity career

a singer and performer, and in her late teens and early twenties sang semi-pro-fessionally in a band, travelling around the local area for gigs – something of an additional career to her hairdressing work, as well as a leisure activity. Later in life she was a member of the local amateur operatic society, and for the 18 years had sung in a local choir, a significant commitment with weekly rehearsals and a very disciplined approach. With the choir she has travelled the country singing and attending festivals. They also did concerts for charity, which she described as community projects. She also went to modern sequence dance classes, wrote poetry, went fell walking and enjoyed baking. And she had recently started to attend a local Alpha course, an introduction to Christianity. She was drawn to 'anything creative'. This leisure and creativity career had been an unfailingly positive thread for Barbra, offering an important balance when her other careers hit difficult patches.

Learning career

Finally, we turn to the central theme of this book and add one more line to the complexity of the diagram in Figure 12.5, that of Barbra's learning career. The understanding of her other careers developed here helps to explain and to situate the events and choices that shaped her formal learning choices. We can see how the impact of the accident in her health career had a very detrimental effect on her school career, losing two years of schooling, and suffering bullying on her return to school. We can see the high of her successful qualification to enter the nursing college being followed by the low of her father's needs coming first in her family

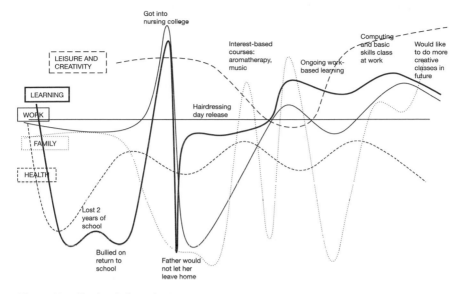

Figure 12.5 Barbra's learning career

career. This theme of putting the family first continued, as she felt that when she was left to bring up the children alone, she should have stayed at home and done a college course relating to her interests, rather than continuing working. But the need to support the family, coupled with her underlying anxiety which she related back to her head injury, prevented her from taking that risk, which she felt stopped her from doing 'something more interesting and beneficial to me, both financially and creatively'. Instead, she pursued day release courses as part of her hairdressing training, and later, developed her interests in creative and performance work by taking part-time courses in aromatherapy and music. Her entry into the caring profession brought with it an ongoing programme of work-based training, including NVQs, dementia awareness, health and safety, food hygiene, diversity, manual handling and group dynamics, held in colleges in the local area. She enjoyed this training, as it allowed her to meet other people, get out of the centre, and become more aware of her own strengths and weaknesses. She found through this that one of her particular strengths was in standing up and making presentations, an example of her experience in her leisure career as a singer and performer carrying through to her learning. In the future, she would like to have the opportunity to do more creative courses, mentioning a wide range including performing arts, floristry, art appreciation, music appreciation, fine art, pottery and creative writing.

She chose to participate in the Computing for the Terrified course not because she was particularly interested in ICT, but because she felt that using computers was inevitably going to become more and more a part of her job as a care worker, and it was therefore part of her professional development. However, throughout the course she felt hemmed in by the course structure, and preferred to take the opportunity to use the computers to play with the paintbox programme or to word process her poetry. We can see from the description of her leisure career why these factors were more important to her than learning to lay letters out correctly or engage in some of the other exercises, although she did do this too. She felt quite vulnerable in the group educational setting, partly because it recalled bad experiences of school for her at an emotional level, and partly because she felt pressured to keep up, straining her concentration span. She felt she would have preferred to work at her own pace, and to fathom out problems herself or with one-to-one help. All of these features of her engagement with the course make much more sense in the perspective of her other careers, and the interactions between them.

Relationship between careers: lives and learning

A look at Barbra's life and how her different careers intersect illustrates that people engage in and respond to learning differently over time. For instance, in relation to work learning is sometimes to do with getting specific jobs. Barbra, for example, needed to train to be a nurse, she needed to be indentured and do day release to train to be a hairdresser, and she had more training when she got a care assistant job. The work and learning careers of Barbra and other people we worked with show that changes in people's work lives affect their learning, and vice versa; and learning affects their progression, to other sorts of learning, other sorts of jobs, into and out of work, and into and out of paid and voluntary work.

Being in work offers more opportunities for learning. Barbra attended a range of training courses through day care centre, including the Basic Skills and computing course through which we met her. Some of these she would not have tried outside work. This was also true of other people. Katrina had done courses in computing and in childcare, and was currently working on another work-related course. Sarah, a student from Liverpool, was following a teaching assistant course. Helen, from the Lancaster spelling class, had done health and hygiene courses associated with working in a pub.

Many people we worked with had a strong perceived need to be proficient in IT, and an understanding that 'everyone' will need to be able to use computers eventually, whatever their job, which came through in widely varying different settings. This was a strong motivator for people to get involved in doing courses in the workplace. Mohammed, an ESOL student, sees going on computer courses as 'the key' to progressing to a good job. 'If you can speak English and you can't do it work with computer, many job is cleaning and factory, and I not want that for the future.' Barbra, Isabel and Anne, who all attended the Computing for the Terrified class, said that they were doing a course in Basic Skills and computing because they thought IT would be increasingly needed in their work. People talked about the possibilities of using IT in the workplace, but also about the non-work-related possibilities: being able to use computers with their families; adding 'strings to their bows' which might be useful later on. Here we see how work, learning, family and leisure careers intersect.

Learning can have a later as well as a more immediate impact on people's lives. People bring with them different resources from their life and learning histories and are able to draw on them when the right point comes. For example, Barbra drew on her work related to beauty therapy and aromatherapy trainings in her care work. Jez drew on her creative talents to help the Children's Rights service with their website and leaflets. Ammara, another ESOL student, drew on her skills and background in social sciences to talk to the children with behavioural difficulties in the nursery where she worked as a volunteer about truancy and the importance of education. This helped her to maintain her self-respect and to cope with her negative feelings related to her husband not allowing her to continue her education and career after marriage. This is the social and educational capital which people draw upon at later stages in their lives. These are examples of important aspects of learning which only becomes visible in longitudinal work which takes account of people's multiple and intersecting careers.

Informal and social learning

Both paid work and voluntary work offer possibilities not only for organised learning but also for informal learning from other people. This is particularly important when the demands of work change. For example, Barbra found that the demands of working at the day care centre had changed significantly since she first started. Clients now had more complex needs and the paperwork demands were changing in many ways. All the staff helped each other out in managing the form-filling etc, and they learned from each other. Javed, an ESOL student, reported that most of his development in oral English came from the considerable time he spent interacting with other people whilst doing his many voluntary jobs including work in a hospice, a community centre and a garage. At the hospice he had a reciprocal informal helping arrangement with a university student who wanted to learn Urdu, who helped him both with his English language and his integration into English culture. There were many examples of this sort of support.

Organised learning was seen by many people as a supportive and helpful activity to engage in when legal and health problems made work impossible. Lisette, unable to work for legal reasons, got bored and lonely, and found attending college helped her to deal with this. Martina finds that the ESOL class fulfilled a crucial social and emotional need, as well as a learning function, in 'trying to keep myself busy'. Again, we see an intersecting of different life careers: health, learning, legal and social.

Learning outside the workplace

People were often taking up opportunities for learning despite their work commitments according to their wider interests and needs beyond work. Frederick and Mahmood both attended ESOL classes in the evening as they were doing or looking for casual work in the daytime. There were also various examples of people engaging in organised learning only when they stopped working: people who had done shift work, or who simply did not have time when working, engaged in formal learning when they retired, or when they were signed off work sick. The times in people's lives for learning and their times for working are not always in synchrony. After he was signed off work for mental health reasons, Michael started coming to college to do courses in subjects he was interested in, including psychology, science, local history and counselling. He came to the literacy class where we met him after he had been struggling with note-taking for an A-level human physiology course. He gained a great deal of enjoyment from the learning, finding that having something to think about helped him with his stress and anxiety, and a great deal of pride in achieving certificates, when he had previously always thought he was stupid.

Transitions, turbulence and critical points

The relationship between learning and other careers is more complex than simply relating learning and work. Working with people in the way that we have has allowed us to develop better understandings of the interrelationship between people's learning careers and the broader influence of their lives as a whole.

Transitions

Transitions are common life changes, such as going from school to work or leaving home. Particular transition times such as going from school to work are very important for learning. Barbra's story shows the importance of key points of transition in her employment and learning career, and how other factors influenced these. Transition from school into work was heavily influenced by her strong-minded mother's desire for her to be a hairdresser and then her father's unwillingness for her to leave home following her parents' separation. This directly shaped the sort of learning she engaged in. Learning issues frequently arise in times of transition.

Social relationships often played a key role in transitions. Many people we encountered had got work through social relationships; for instance, Sameena, who helped her husband with his jewellery business and then later opened her own women's clothing business through community contacts and family support. Jack worked on the family farm from his childhood onwards, eventually inheriting it. Max, a carer, first heard about jobs at the day centre through being key holder for a meeting which met in the local day centre for twelve years, and so getting to know the staff there and the way things worked. Mark explained how as a bricklayer you start off by going round different building sites asking people for work, until you built up a reputation locally and were in the networks. There are examples of people who left jobs because of social commitments or stayed in work because of networks of social support. Mohammed was only able to take up a late night cleaning job he found outside the local area because he was able to get a lift from a friend. Mahmood found that his job in a sewing factory had expanded his social network and socialising with workmates had helped him feel part of the team.

Transitions in learning and work sometimes came at what people differently perceived as 'the right time' for them, which may not always have seemed logical to others such as teachers or family members. Despite her high level of ability, Dee did not achieve GCSE qualifications. She explained that her coursework had been torn up by someone who had a grudge against her so she never sat her exams. Her tutors seemed perplexed as to why she had not been able to gain a qualification and move on quickly to the next stage; one said that 'she could do anything she put her mind to'. We have provided several other examples of people identifying the right time in the previous chapter.

Turbulence

The idea of turbulence, which we introduced in Chapter 3, is the result of external events which affect people's lives. As well as the common transitions we referred to earlier events happen in people's lives that are outside of their control, changing their lives suddenly and unpredictably. Barbra's work life changed with her divorce and with her father's illness. When people had come from difficult home situations, this had often caused behaviour which led to exclusion from school, as with Sophie, who eventually became homeless at the age of 15 and as a result under-achieved in her school exams.

There are many examples in our data of unexpected health problems altering people's lives, such as people having to stop or change work following accidents, and many stress-related health problems. Sophie's substance misuse led to her dipping in and out of college and she had to give up her landscape gardening course for health and safety reasons when she became pregnant. Many people, especially women and including Barbra, Sophie and Sameena, had to leave or change jobs or interrupt learning to enable them to care for others. Jason's serious accident left him unemployed and with depression, but then he was encouraged take up learning opportunities at the tenants' association and did voluntary work. But change for the worse also came later as his drinking led to irregular attendance at college. Mark had to stop work temporarily after injuring his back, and was concerned about what would have happened if his back had been damaged more severely.

Periods of turbulence in people's lives often left them feeling that they could not fit in with others in mainstream learning, such as in college. We have already described how Caroline found that other students she referred to as 'normal people' talked about lives that were very different to hers, leading her to feel she had to hide her drinking and, ironically, causing her to drink more. The young people at the homeless shelter often had very similar experiences to this.

The wider political and economic situation can change people's opportunities for better or worse. Barbra's work opportunities changed for the better when the expansion of the day care system as part of a government initiative opened up caring work possibilities for her which she had always wanted. David, a Hungarian ESOL student, was able to become a full-time student in Lancaster when Hungary joined the European Union. The effects of the global situation applied particularly to the people such as Ferdinand and Lisette in ESOL classes who were refugees or seeking asylum, whose whole lives are framed within traumatic global political circumstances, out of their control, which have brought them to the UK. Both Ferdinand and Lisette, who were here for five years and had their appeals turned down, lived as 'non citizens' for two years, dependent on charity, unable to be repatriated and with no rights to any education or to work, health care and housing. With these two ideas of transitions and turbulence we turn to how these can lead to critical points in people's lives.

Critical points

In relation to transitions and turbulence, people could sometimes identify moments of radical change in their lives. Barbra's story has a number of critical points at which her life changed radically. The first of these was the accident when she was 9 years old. This transformed her school experience, and the ongoing anxiety she still feels shaped what she was willing to do in terms of employment and training throughout her life. She felt that if she had had more confidence she would have pursued her creative talents through education and employment, not just through her leisure career. The second was getting into nursing college, but being unable to go because of her dad's health. The third was her divorce, which coincided with having to care for her father. Fourth, there was the opening of the day centre, which enabled her to use her considerable expertise with people in the caring environment she had wanted to work in initially. Again we see the importance of social networks in making this a critical point; it was through knowing someone through hairdressing who managed another care centre that this opportunity opened up for her.

Critical points in Sophie's life which impacted on her learning were being excluded from school, becoming homeless and coping with substance abuse which meant she dipped in and out of college, and becoming pregnant and needing to give up her landscape gardening course. In Jason's life, the critical points which impacted on his learning were leaving school age 12 years, joining the tenants' association and lapsing into drinking which interfered with his college education. For Susan, her deafness not being picked up at primary school and being evacuated during the war impacted heavily on her learning. These critical points, often sudden, often outside of people's control, which opened up some possibilities and closed down others, were to be found in each individual's life history, and were often the deciding factor for them as to which sorts of learning opportunities they engaged in at what point in time.

A sense of progression

This way of looking at the complexity of people's lives through exploring their life careers leads to a richer, more nuanced understanding of the different meanings of 'progression'. The dominant discourse in the literacy, numeracy and language field is often one of progression to further education, higher qualifications and better jobs. Barbra's story illustrates that if you understand what is going on in people's lives over time it becomes clear that this is one of many possibilities. Different sorts of support are needed for different types of progression, which might involve going backwards in some careers in response to other events going on in people's lives. For example, Barbra moved from being a self-employed small business woman to working part time as a care assistant. Within the dominant discourse of progression, this could be seen as a regressive step. But from the perspective of Barbra's life narrative, this move gets her back to the caring profession she originally wanted to go into.

There are also many examples in our data of people finding fulfilment and making a contribution to society through voluntary and community work or caring work. They view this as progression in terms of their lives, even though it is not progression into paid employment. Examples of this include Jason working at the tenant's association and Jez working for the children's rights organisation.

Summary

This chapter has explored what can be gained from studying learners' lives over time, that is, gaining a longitudinal understanding of learners' lives in relationship to their learning careers, and exploring how these interconnect in a complex way with their other life careers such as work, health and family. Life is made up of transitions; these, as well as other factors such as family expectations regarding work, directly shape the sort of learning people engage in. Taking a longitudinal look using the concept of careers has allowed us to develop better understandings of how the broader influence of people's lives as a whole has impacted on learning. It seems clear that people engage with learning better when they follow their own motivations and fit learning into their own purposes, which may or may not just be directly work related, and where their learning is self-directed (Tusting and Barton 2006).

13

TOWARDS A SOCIAL PRACTICE PEDAGOGY

This book has described and analysed the relationship between lives and learning for people in a range of different types of literacy, numeracy and language provision. In this final chapter, we turn to explore the implications of this work for pedagogy.

Drawing upon a social practice approach and the research reported in Chapters 6 to 12 we have worked in collaboration with many practitioners to develop elements of a social practice pedagogy, that is, principles for teaching which take account of the resources which people bring with them from their lives. We describe five aspects of a social practice framework for adult literacy, numeracy and language teaching. These provide a way of thinking about the complexities that exist in all adult teaching and learning environments. (They are developed further in Appleby and Barton 2007, which is a guide for practitioners and link up to other social approaches to pedagogy, such as Kalantzis and Cope 2005.) Picking up on issues raised in Chapter 1, this framework contributes to an alternative discourse of teaching and learning.

This approach does not offer a ready-made template for teaching, as it recognises that each learning environment and each tutor is different. Instead, it acknowledges the value of practitioner and learner enquiry. While research by outsiders, particularly if done collaboratively with practitioners, can make specific contributions to addressing certain dilemmas around policy and practice, a social practices approach suggests that practitioners and learners are well placed to ask questions and find answers themselves as part of the ongoing teaching and learning endeavour. Teachers have professional knowledge and experience they bring to practice, which can be applied to practitioner enquiry. They are the ones who make policy work through their practice in the classroom. They are therefore in a good position to know the significant questions that need to be asked or the issues that need to be explored. This can be seen in the examples of practitioner research people carried out in this research, which benefited their practice and fed into their colleges.

Experienced teachers are often implicitly use these tactics already. When focused on explicitly and made central to teacher training and professional development, they form a powerful approach to teaching and learning. This both draws upon and strengthens individual and collective practitioner knowledge and confidence.

The five aspects of a social practice pedagogy are:

- *Researching everyday practices*: Teachers and students can investigate their changing language, literacy and numeracy practices and the learning practices around them.
- *Taking account of learners' lives*: People are complex: they have histories, identities, current circumstances and imagined futures. We need to engage with all these different aspects in a teaching and learning relationship.
- *Learning by participation*: Using authentic materials, in tasks for real purposes, helps to make links between learning and literacy, numeracy and language in people's everyday lives.
- *Learning in safe, supported contexts*: A social practice pedagogy recognises and values social and affective aspects of learning, including physical and emotional safety.
- *Locating literacy learning in other forms of meaning-making*: This approach recognises and works with different literacies that include oral and visual ways of communicating.

Here we look at how these principles can be applied in teaching and learning. We describe what we mean by each, explaining why it is an important element of the social practice approach.

Researching everyday practices

In our research, teachers and learners questioned what language, literacy and numeracy are, and what part they play in people's lives exploring their different meanings and uses. Investigation through enquiry is a valuable way to do this as it enables us to look at factors in a more focused and systematic way. It is also something that we already have experience of, as we use methods associated with enquiry to find out information in our daily and professional lives.

Both learners and teachers use methods of enquiry inside and outside the classroom as part of their everyday practices. Teachers often rely on their pro-fessional knowledge to answer questions that arise in their practice. These questions might include: is individual work more effective than group work in my spelling class; or, is working on an individual learning plan the best use of time in the classroom? Learners use a similar enquiry-based system asking questions such as: will this course give me what I need to help my children with their homework?

This method can be developed to investigate both literacy and learning practices inside and outside the classroom, drawing upon the experience and insight of both the learner and teacher. We saw an example of this in Chapter 5 where the maths teacher, Kay, used a simple questionnaire to understand how people used numeracy in their everyday lives. Her reflection on teaching maths inside the classroom showed she did not have a way of finding out how her students used numeracy outside of it. As a second example, Wynne decided to use a research activity around her ESOL students' photographs, to develop speaking, listening, reading and writing activities. She was astounded at how much they gained from the opportunity for 'real communication' in English and the amount of language they were able to produce in this space from talking and writing about their own photos on living in Blackburn. Wynne learned much more about her students in the process. A third example is the way Jason, a student in the same maths class, investigated some of the literacy practices in his life. By becoming aware of some of his everyday practices, his confidence grew to seeing himself as someone who used numeracy frequently not simply as someone who could not do maths. Whilst other aspects of his life remained turbulent, impacting upon his participation, he nevertheless changed how he saw himself as a maths and literacy learner.

Taking account of learners' lives

As we have seen throughout the data and especially in Chapters 10 and 11, everyone has a unique combination of experience, interests and needs. Although we talk of groups of people as 'learners' or 'students' it is important to recognise that these groups are made up of individuals with different backgrounds, different current circumstances and different hopes for the future. Some people have stable lives whilst others have experienced dislocation or difficulties, either as children or as adults. Some are dealing with issues around their physical or mental health. Others feel that their identity, race, ethnic origin or faith group marks them out as different.

In some areas of targeted provision we may know that people are dealing with alcohol or substance misuse, homelessness, violence or mental health issues. In other areas this may not be visible and yet people may be trying to cope with these same issues in their lives. Taking account of learners' lives means that we need to be aware of what is happening to them and connect this with what they want to learn and how best they are able to learn it. For example, if we know that someone has an addiction and is going to the methadone clinic on Tuesday afternoon, it explains why they are absent from class. If we know that someone is being made homeless, this will account for lapses in concentration and uncompleted home-work. We do not need to know everything about learners, and there may be things they do not want us to know, but we must recognise that there are aspects of each person's life, which, on the one hand, could be drawn upon to enhance learning, or on the other may act as substantial barriers.

Many people value the social aspects of the teaching and learning relationship, being recognised as people with a life outside the classroom. Like any relationship this is built upon communication and trust. A teacher who understands and works with the complexity of people's lives is more able to link learning in class with life outside it, making learning more positive and meaningful. When people feel that their interests, talents and skills are recognised in the classroom, this encourages them to use and practise new skills in a variety of settings outside the classroom. It is also vital that people who come to learn are not just seen as learners; they often support the learning of others. Many of the parents we worked with were consciously teaching their children. Where a learner is unable to succeed, perhaps because of external factors, the teacher will be able to limit damage to self-esteem and possibly encourage returning to learn in the future.

Two examples of this are the stories of Dee and Abdul. Dee, like many other young people, was dealing with the aftermath of bad school experiences and continuing disruption in her life. Whilst her teachers were able to understand some of these issues, they struggled to provide enough opportunity for self-expression and free writing, which they recognised as being beneficial to her. It was hard to provide the different types of learning that Dee needed within a system that focused mainly on outcomes for employment. The example of Abdul also shows the tension between teaching knowledge, in this case language, whilst acknowledging everyday experiences of learner's in the classroom. The ESOL class he attended fitted with his expectation of what teaching grammar should be, but also shows how he had to develop his own strategies for learning within it. There was little recognition for the difficulties that he faced as an asylum seeker in practising his language in a sometimes-hostile environment, and the impact this might have in his learning.

Learning by participation

Most learning occurs in everyday life in real situations and it is often done while participating in activities with other people. Even when learners are working on an individual task, for example a maths worksheet, there is much interaction between people. This includes asking for and offering advice and help. Learning is about being involved with others as well as being individually engaged.

An important part of encouraging participation is to use materials that relate to people's everyday purposes and activities. This acknowledges that learners have existing skills and knowledge on which to build. Using authentic materials for real purposes encourages participation as people see the value in learning material that is 'really useful' to them rather than abstract information or skills. Whether this is a newspaper brought into the class or travel information from the internet, what is important is the way it is used. A social practice approach recognises the different uses, purposes and meanings of literacy, numeracy and language, acknowledging that they often cross from one domain to another (Appleby and Hamilton 2005). This understanding supports literacy teaching and learning that makes and develops these connections. An example of this we observed is working with a learner to write a letter of complaint to the newspaper about the intended closure of a local market. If this is something the learner feels strongly about and has significance in their lives, it makes materials authentic.

Using authentic materials for real tasks makes us question what is authentic for the people who come to learn. We cannot simply rely on existing materials that assume all learners to be the same. Learners are diverse; they speak many languages and dialects, have different work and hobbies, different amounts of money and health and different social networks. Using a set of examples may be authentic for one learner but not for another. An example of this is Jack, the dairy farmer, working with a volunteer linking his learning with his farming life. The use of materials based upon his experience gave Jack both a sense of safety in the classroom and motivation through relevance to his everyday life.

We suggest two possibilities for using existing materials and resources; there are of course others. The first is 'tailoring' and the second is 'translating'. Tailoring is using existing materials but linking them closely with the individual's life so that the subject content applies to the learner's everyday experience. Jack's learning is a good example of this. His support tutor talked to him and listened carefully to what was going on in Jack's life. This then became the basis for tailoring the materials and resources she used. She changed the vocabulary he was learning, rejecting those words that were not relevant, and she used Jack's own words as the basis of his computer work. Much of the subject content of Jack's learning was tailored to his identity and interests around farming.

Translating is applying experience or understanding from individual life to more general materials so that learners are able to translate their previous experience to the task in hand. Kay's use of the maths worksheets is a good example of translating. She translated the skills that Sarah wanted to learn in her everyday life onto the worksheet about measurement. She was able to translate application of number into a real context in Sarah's life. Kay did not adapt the worksheet but translated the meaning into everyday use, which Sarah was able to understand. The same applied to her work with Katrina and the nappy-changing rotas. Kay was able to translate multiplication tables into an everyday setting and then go back to the maths worksheet with this everyday understanding in mind.

Learning in safe supported contexts

People identify a variety of reasons for wanting to learn. Some people talk about improving particular skills, such as spelling. For others, although they do not use such terms, learning is about broadening the range of practices they participate in. It could be about keeping up with technology, such as taking a computer course to help children and grandchildren. Or they may want to get out of the house to meet people, to gain more confidence or to learn new social skills. For some people it could be a mixture of all these. It is important to recognise what people's initial reasons for coming are, and how they may change as a result of attending.

As we have noted, people also bring with them many different experiences that need to be taken into account. For some, negative experience at school shapes any future learning, as it produces feelings of fear, intimidation and panic. Many adult learners describe having been made to look stupid, bullied and even physically threatened whilst at school. It is important to show clearly that each person in a class is valued, will be listened to and will be treated with respect. Some people bring experience of violence, of threat and of intimidation. Refugees and people seeking asylum may have encountered extreme violence, brutality and displacement. They may also be dealing with current violence, fear and threat associated with racism. Women, and to a lesser extent men, may be dealing with personal or family violence. These experiences may affect regular attendance, the ability to concentrate or the confidence to socially interact with others.

For people living in poverty, in bad housing, with health issues or communicating in a second or third language it is easy to become socially isolated. Some adults lack the skills and confidence to participate in learning in classes because it is a social activity. Making sure that the social aspect of learning is non-judgemental and includes all learners is important to establish and maintain in a learning environment. Many learners' experiences remain hidden, as they are not recognised as educational issues or classroom concerns. Understanding what people are dealing with outside the classroom offers pointers on how learning can be supported in the classroom.

There have been many examples to illustrate this. The example of Susan in the spelling class shows how a safe learning environment was essential for her to be able to learn. Her previous negative experiences of learning, related to a hearing impairment, left her with spelling difficulties and a lack of confidence in learning. The relationship between Susan and her teacher was key to finding practical strategies to enable her participation and enjoyment in learning. In spite of this though she found group work difficult, because of her hearing, and preferred worksheets and paired tasks. Debbie the teacher often spent additional time, outside of allocated teaching time, to support Susan's independent learning, which she did outside of classroom time to catch up.

Locating literacy learning in other forms of meaning making

In everyday life, literacy and numeracy are often part of signs which incorporate other forms of meaning making. Spoken language practices are important: people often receive and share information by talking with others, as well as by reading. Texts read outside the classroom are often articulated with visual meanings. For instance, road signs incorporate both textual and graphical semiotics, which people 'read' together to generate meanings. Magazines and websites are multimodal texts, in which people read meaning both from the written text and from the other semiotics incorporated into the page. Literacy learning in everyday life incorporates engagement with many other forms of meaning making.

Recognising that people have existing oral and visual skills, and interests, encourages us to think about the ways that we communicate and make sense of the world, and how this can be incorporated in learning. Acknowledging people's existing understanding provides a strong foundation for developing new knowledge and skills. Acknowledging different forms of communication and learning outside the classroom makes it easier for learners to be confident about what is being 'added on' inside the classroom. Incorporating oral and visual methods in the classroom also provides the potential for fun and creative learning.

People make sense of the world, both on their own and in groups in their everyday lives. For example, individuals find out information about a hobby such as gardening, or use computer chatrooms as a social activity. Some people like working in a classroom group, as they learn from others making them feel more confident. Others, such as Jason, from the maths class earlier, prefer to work mainly on their own. Jason did enjoy joining in with group activities but liked having the choice to participate when he felt socially confident and not under pressure to do so.

Many adults understand how people learn, both inside and outside the classroom, and where teachers take account of this, learners feel valued and enjoy learning. Recognising the importance of talking and seeing also helps to develop the social aspects of learning in class. There were several examples which demonstrate how oral, visual and communicative skills used in everyday life can be drawn upon in teaching and learning literacy, numeracy and language. For example, Amna, a bilingual literacy learner, used stories and games to develop speaking and listening skills for herself and for her children. She understood how she was being taught then used these methods to help her children learn, becoming herself both learner and teacher. By using forms of meaning associated with everyday social practices Amna was able to move between teaching and learning, where one reinforced the other.

Implications and challenges of this approach

Finding out information about people's lives is not straightforward. It needs to be approached carefully and ethically, enabling learners to fully understand and have a choice in the process. Practitioner research and learner enquiry needs to achieve a careful balance between asking questions, observation, reflection and achieving what people come to learn. Teaching and learning resources need to be developed and used in a variety of ways. This may require finding new information and in some cases learning new skills. Sufficient time and resources need to be available to be able to talk and listen carefully in order to match people's diverse reasons for coming to learn with what is on offer. There are training, mentoring and support implications for developing the skills for practitioner and learner enquiry, and also for developing people and classroom management skills for recognising and supporting the social and emotional aspects of people's everyday lives in learning.

Social practices pedagogy and sustained impact

The real strength of a social practices pedagogy which includes learner and practitioner enquiry is what it contributes to sustained positive change. This will depend on what is possible or desirable from the perspectives of participants and those who work with them in each context. A good example of positive change from this research is that of Wynne, the ESOL manager, who was involved in setting up a student photography project as part of collaborative research. This led to her introducing new staff development sessions which focused on strategies for linking language learning to everyday life practices and using learner enquiry. She invited college managers to a high profile dissemination event, which led to funding being released for increased social facilities and new initiatives in linking ESOL students with mainstream college courses.

Practice is set within educational structures. Sometimes these present opportunities, sometimes they present constraints and frequently they create a tension between the two. For example, Wynne wanted to use as many authentic materials as possible such as health and local information leaflets to help her students to use language to manage their lives outside the classroom; but she was under pressure to work as quickly as possible to put them through the national test, a qualification which many of them also wanted. These are complex agendas for practitioners to manage. A social practices approach, linking lives and learning, enables us to understand what the tensions are between people's lives and classroom learning, and between teaching which is responsive to learners and teaching structured by a curriculum. It can support realistic reflection on what is possible, practical and positive to aim for in teaching adult literacy, language and numeracy. It approaches literacy not as a set of skills to be taught in a disembodied way in the classroom but as part of people's everyday lives.

We believe that the principles of social practice pedagogy and critical reflection which underpin good practice generally should be an essential part of initial teacher training and continuing staff development for both teachers and managers. Exploring the connection between lives and learning that is at the heart of this approach provides ways of working with people to make a better fit between what they learn and achieve in the classroom and what they learn and use at work, in families, social networks and communities.

REFERENCES

Appleby, Y. and A.M. Bathmaker (2006) 'The new skills agenda: increased lifelong learning or new sites of inequality?' *British Educational Research Journal*, 32: 703–17.

Appleby, Y. and D. Barton (2007) *Responding to People's Lives in Adult Language, Literacy and Numeracy Teaching*. London: National Research and Development Centre for Adult Literacy and Numeracy.

Appleby, Y. and M. Hamilton (2005) 'Literacy as social practice: Travelling between everyday and other forms of learning.' *Lifelong Learning: Contexts and Concepts*. P. Sutherland and J. Crowther (eds). London: Routledge.

Atkinson, P. and M. Hammersley (1994) 'Ethnography and participant observation.' *Handbook of Qualitative Research*. N. Denzin and Y. Lincoln (eds). Thousand Oaks, CA: Sage, 249–261.

Auerbach, E. with B. Barahona, J. Midy, F. Vaquerano, A. Zambrano and J. Arnaud (1996) *Adult ESL/Literacy: From the Community To the Community: A Guidebook for Participatory Literacy Training*. Mahwah, NJ: Lawrence Erlbaum Associates.

Ball S.J., S. Macrae and M. Maguire (1999) 'Young lives, diverse choices and imagined futures in an education and training market.' *International Journal of Inclusive Education*, 3(3): 195–224.

Bartlett, L. and D. Holland (2002) 'Theorizing the space of literacy practices.' *Ways of Knowing Journal*, 2(1): 10–22.

Barton, D. (1991) 'The social nature of writing.' *Writing in the Community*. D. Barton and R. Ivanic (eds). Newbury Park, London and New Delhi: Sage: 1–13.

Barton, D. (2006) 'The significance of a social practice view of language, literacy and numeracy.' *Adult Literacy, Numeracy and Language: Policy, Practice and Research*. L. Tett, M. Hamilton and Y. Hillier (eds). Milton Keynes: Open University Press, 21–30.

Barton, D. and M. Hamilton (1998) *Local Literacies: Reading and Writing in One Community*. London: Routledge.

Barton, D. and M. Hamilton (2000) 'Literacy practices.' *Situated Literacies*. D. Barton, M. Hamilton and R. Ivanič (eds). London and New York: Routledge, 7–15.

Barton, D. and K. Tusting (eds) (2005) *Beyond Communities of Practice: Language, Power and Social Context*. Cambridge: Cambridge University Press.

Barton, D., M. Hamilton and R. Ivanič (eds) (2000) *Situated Literacies*. London: Routledge.

Belfiore, M.E., T.A. Defoe, S. Folinsbee, J. Hunter and N.S. Jackson (2004) *Reading Work: Literacies in the New Workplace*. Mahwah, NJ: Lawrence Erlbaum Associates.

Bernstein, B. (1996) *Pedagogy, Symbolic Control and Identity: Theory, Research, Critique*. London: Taylor & Francis.

Bhavnani, K., J. Foran and P. Kurian (2003) *Feminist Futures: Reimagining Women, Culture and Development*. New York: Zed Books.

Bloomer, M. and P. Hodkinson (2000) 'Learning careers: continuity and change in young people's dispositions to learning.' *British Educational Research Journal*, 26(5): 528–597.

Bourdieu, P. (1977) *Outline of a Theory of Practice*. Cambridge: Cambridge University Press.

Bourdieu, P. (1986) 'The forms of capital.' *Handbook of Theory and Research for the Sociology of Education*. J. G. Richardson (ed.). Oxford: Greenwood Publishing Group.

Bourdieu, P. and J.-C. Passeron (1977) *Reproduction in Education, Society and Culture*. London and Beverly Hills: Sage.

Bruner, J. (1985) 'Vygotsky: a historical and conceptual perspective.' *Culture, Communication and Cognition: Vygotskian Perspectives*. J. V. Wertsch (ed.). Cambridge: Cambridge University Press.

Burgess, G. (2004). '"Is that not literacy, helping parents to help children?" Mapping Basic Skills provision in the Lancaster area.' *Working Paper No. 5*. Lancaster: Lancaster Literacy Research Centre.

Bynner, J. and S. Parsons (1997) *It Doesn't Get Any Better: The Impact of Poor Basic Skills on the Lives of 37 Year Olds*. London: Basic Skills Agency.

Bynner, J. and S. Parsons (2006) *New Light on Literacy and Numeracy*. London: National Research and Development Centre for Adult Literacy and Numeracy.

Cameron, D., E. Frazer, P. Harvey, M.B.H. Rampton and K. Richardson (1992) *Researching Language: Issues of Power and Method*. London and New York: Routledge.

Candy, P.C. (1991) *Self-direction for Lifelong Learning: A Comprehensive Guide to Theory and Practice*. San Francisco: Jossey-Bass.

Carrington, V. and A. Luke (1997) 'Literacy and Bourdieu's sociological theory: a reframing.' *Language and Education*, 11(2): 96–112.

Cieslik, M. and D. Simpson (2006) 'Skills for Life: Basic skills and marginal transitions from school-to-work.' *Journal of Youth Studies*, 9(2): 213–229.

Cieslik, M. and D. Simpson (2007) 'Basic skills, literacy and transitions to adulthood'. Working paper. University of Teesside.

Coben, D. (2006) 'The politics of numeracy: how might a sociocultural approach inform policy on adult numeracy education?' *Adult Literacy, Numeracy and Language: Policy, Practice and Research*. L. Tett, M. Hamilton and Y. Hillier (eds). Milton Keynes: Open University Press, 96–107.

Cochran-Smith, M. and S.L. Lytle (1993) *Inside Outside: Teacher Research and Knowledge*. New York and London: Teachers College Press.

Coles, B. (1995) *Youth and Social Policy*. London: UCL Press.

Colley, H., P. Hodkinson and J. Malcolm (2003) *Informality and Formality in Learning*. London: Learning and Skills Development Agency.

Cope, B. and M. Kalantzis (2000) *Multiliteracies: Literacy Learning and the Design of Social Futures*. London and New York: Routledge.

Davies, C.A. (1999). *Reflexive Ethnography: A Guide to Researching Selves and Others*. London and New York: Routledge.

Denzin, N.K. and Y.S. Lincoln (2005) *The Sage Handbook of Qualitative Research* (3rd edn). Thousand Oaks, CA and London: Sage.

Dewey, J. (1933) *How We Think: A Restatement of the Relation of Reflective Thinking to the Educative Process*. New York: D.C. Heath.

Department for Education and Skills (2001a) *Adult Literacy Core Curriculum*. London: Cambridge Training and Development Ltd on behalf of The Basic Skills Agency.

Department for Education and Skills (2001b) *Adult Numeracy Core Curriculum*. London: Cambridge Training and Development Ltd on behalf of The Basic Skills Agency.

Department for Education and Skills (2001c) *Skills for Life: The National Strategy for Improving Adult Literacy and Numeracy Skills*. London: Department for Education and Skills.

Eldred, J., J. Ward, Y. Dutton and K. Snowdon (2004) *Catching Confidence*. Leicester: NIACE.

Fingeret, H.A. and C. Drennon (1997) *Literacy for Life: Adult Learners, New Practices*. New York: Teachers College Press.

Fowler, Z. (2007) 'Demanding literacy and literacy demands: Contexts for functional skills.' *14–19 Skills Bulletin* (in press).

Freire, P. (1972) *Pedagogy of the Oppressed*. London: Penguin.

Gee, J.P. (2000–1) 'Identity as an analytic lens for research in education.' *Review of Research in Education*, 25: 99–125.

Gee, J.P. (2004) *Situated Language and Learning: A Critique of Traditional Schooling*. London and New York: Routledge.

Goffman, E. (1961) *Asylums*. Harmondsworth: Penguin.

Green, J. and D. Bloome (1997) 'Ethnography and ethnographers of and in education: A situated perspective.' *Handbook of Research on Teaching Literacy through the Communicative and Visual Arts*. J. Flood, S. Heath and D. Lapp (eds). New York: Macmillan, 181–202.

Hamilton, M. and Y. Hillier (2006) *Changing Faces of Adult Literacy, Language and Numeracy: A Critical History*. Stoke-on-Trent and Sterling: Trentham Books.

Hamilton, M. and A. Wilson (eds) (2005) *New Ways of Engaging New Learners: Lessons From Round One of the Practitioner-led Research Initiative*. London: National Research and Development Centre for Adult Literacy and Numeracy.

Henderson, S., J. Holland, S. McGrellis, S. Sharpe and R. Thomson (2007) *Inventing Adulthoods: A Biographical Approach to Youth Transitions*. London: Thousand Oaks, CA, and New Delhi: Sage.

Hodge, R. (2005) 'Learning and life transitions of young people on and Entry to Employment (E2E) programme.' *Working Paper No. 11*. Lancaster: Lancaster Literacy Research Centre.

Hodkinson, P. and A.C. Sparkes (1997) 'Careership: a sociological theory of career decision making.' *British Journal of Sociology of Education*, 18(1): 29–44.

Holland, D., W. Lachicotte Jr., D. Skinner and C. Cain (2001) *Identity and Agency in Cultural Worlds*. Cambridge, MA, and London: Harvard University Press.

Horsman, J. (2000) *Too Scared to Learn: Women, Violence and Education*. Mahwah, NJ, and London: Lawrence Erlbaum Associates.

Hymes, D. (1996) *Ethnography, Linguistics, Narrative Inequality*. London: Taylor and Francis.

Ivanič, R. (2004) 'Discourses of writing and learning to write.' *Language and Education*, 18(3): 220–245.

Ivanič, R. and C. Satchwell (2007) 'The textuality of learning contexts.' *Pedagogy, Culture and Society* (in press).

Ivanič, R. and M.-I. L. Tseng (2005) *Understanding the Relationships Between Learning and Teaching: An Analysis of the Contribution of Applied Linguistics*. London: National Research and Development Centre for Adult Literacy and Numeracy.

Ivanič, R., D. Beck, G. Burgess, K. Gilbert, R. Hodson, A. Hudson and C. Woods (2004) *Listening to Learners: Practitioner Research on the Adult Learners' Lives Project*. London: National Research and Development Centre for Adult Literacy and Numeracy.

Kalantzis, M. and B. Cope (2005) *Learning By Design*. Melbourne: Common Ground.

Kennedy, K. and N. Crosby (2004) 'Mapping Skills for Life in Liverpool.' *Working Paper No. 6.* Lancaster: Lancaster Literacy Research Centre.

Kolb, D. (1984) *Experiential Learning: Experience as the Source of Learning and Development.* New Jersey: Prentice Hall.

Lane, A. (1987) *Liverpool: Gateway of Empire.* London: Lawrence and Wishart.

Lave, J. (1988) *Cognition in Practice: Mind, Mathematics and Culture in Everyday Life.* Cambridge: Cambridge University Press.

Lave, J. and E. Wenger (1991) *Situated Learning: Legitimate Peripheral Participation.* Cambridge: Cambridge University Press.

Martin-Jones, M., R. Ivanič and D. Barton (1993) *Bilingual Resources in Primary Classroom Interaction: Final Report to Economic and Social Research Council.* Lancaster University, Centre for Language in Social Life Papers, 53.

Merrill, B. (2004) 'Biographies, class and learning: The experiences of adult learners.' *Pedagogy, Culture and Society,* 12(1): 73–93.

Mezirow, J. (ed.) (1990) *Fostering Critical Reflection in Adulthood.* San Francisco: Jossey-Bass.

Middlewood, D., M. Coleman and J. Lumby (1999) *Practitioner Research in Education: Making a Difference.* London: Paul Chapman Publishing.

Moser, C. (1999) *A Fresh Start: Improving Literacy and Numeracy.* The Report of the working group chaired by Sir Claus Moser, London: DfEE.

Papen, U. (2005) *Adult Literacy as Social Practice: More than Skills.* London: RoutledgeFalmer.

Rampton, B., K. Tusting, J. Maybin, R. Barwell, A. Creese and V. Lytra (2004) *UK Linguistic Ethnography: A Discussion Paper.* London: UK Linguistic Ethnography Forum. Available online at www.ling-ethnog.org.uk/documents/discussion_paper_jan_05.pdf.

Reay, D. (2004) '"It's all becoming a habitus": beyond the habitual use of habitus in educational research.' *British Journal of Sociology of Education,* 25(4): 431–444.

Reder, S. (2006) Presentation, RaPAL Conference, Glasgow.

Reder, S. (forthcoming) *Dropping Out and Moving On: Life, Literacy and Development Among High School Dropouts.* Cambridge, MA: Harvard University Press.

Rogoff, B. and J. Lave (1984) *Everyday Cognition: Its Development in Social Context.* Cambridge, MA: Harvard University Press.

Schuller, T., J. Preston, C. Hammond, A. Brassett-Grundy and J. Bynner (2004) *The Benefits of Learning. The Impact of Education on Health, Family Life and Social Capital.* London: RoutledgeFalmer.

Silverman, D. (2001) *Interpreting Qualitative Data: Methods for Analysing Talk, Text and Interaction.* London: Sage.

Silverman, D. (2005) *Doing Qualitative Research.* London: Sage.

Simpson, D. and M. Cieslik (2007) 'The role of basic skills and transitions to adulthood.' *YOUNG (Nordic Journal of Youth Research),* 15: (in press).

Smith, J. (2005) 'Mobilising everyday literacy practices within the Curricula.' *Journal of Vocational Education and Training,* 57(3): 319–334.

Smith, R. M. (ed.) (1990) *Learning to Learn Across the Lifespan.* San Francisco: Jossey-Bass.

Strathern, M. (2000) 'Accountability . . . and ethnography.' *Audit Cultures: Anthropological Studies in Accountability, Ethics and the Academy.* Strathern, M. (ed.). London and New York: Routledge, 279–304.

Swain, J., E. Baker, D. Holder., B. Newmarch and D. Coben (2005) *Making Numeracy Teaching Meaningful to Adult Learners.* London: National Research and Development Centre for Adult Literacy and Numeracy.

Swales, J.M. (1990) *Genre Analysis: English in Academic and Research Settings*. Cambridge: Cambridge University Press.

Tseng, M.L. and R. Ivanič, R. (2006) 'Recognizing complexity in adult literacy research and practice.' *Understanding the Language Classroom*. Gieve, S. and Miller, I. (eds). Basingstoke: Palgrave Macmillan, 136–162.

Tusting, K. (2000) 'Written intertextuality and the construction of Catholic identity in a parish community: an ethnographic study.' Unpublished PhD thesis. Department of Linguistics and Modern English Language, Lancaster University.

Tusting, K. and D. Barton (2005) 'Community-based local literacies research.' *Multidisciplinary Perspectives on Literacy Research* (2nd edn). R. Beach, J. Green, M. Kamil and T. Shanahan (eds). Cresskill, NJ: Hampton Press Inc., 243–264.

Tusting, K. and D. Barton (2006) *Models of Adult Learning: A Literature Review*. London: National Research and Development Centre for Adult Literacy and Numeracy.

Vorhaus, J. (2001). 'Lifelong learning and personal autonomy: a response to John Field.' *College Research Journal*, 4/3 (summer).

Wenger, E. (1998) *Communities of Practice: Learning, Meaning, and Identity*. Cambridge: Cambridge University Press.

www.jennyhorsman.com   last accessed on 28 August 2007
www.lancaster.gov.uk   last accessed on 28 August 2007
www.lsc.gov.uk   last accessed on 28 August 2007
www.qca.org.uk   last accessed on 28 August 2007

INDEX

173

Dyslexia and Stress

Second edition

Dyslexia and Stress

Second edition

Edited by

T.R. Miles, OBE, PhD
Emeritus Professor of Psychology, University of Wales, Bangor

W
WHURR PUBLISHERS
LONDON AND PHILADELPHIA

© 2004 Whurr Publishers

First published 2004 by
Whurr Publishers Ltd
19b Compton Terrace, London N1 2UN, England
325 Chestnut Street, Philadelphia PA19106, USA

British Library Cataloguing in Publication Data

A catalogue record for this book is available from the British
Library.

ISBN 1 86156 383 3

Contents

Sheena Harrison

Foreword

One of the worst aspects of being dyslexic is the vicious circle caused by stress. As soon as I make a mistake I panic, and because I panic I make more mistakes.

In spite of my good fortune in having an interesting and, on the whole, fulfilled working life, there are many days when I feel that I am only just keeping abreast of the stress that is a result of my own inadequacies. For instance, just a simple request such as being asked to write the Foreword to a book, which would be water off a duck's back to many people, fills me with fear. My heart sinks visualizing the dozens of versions of the Foreword I shall have to write before I am satisfied, all the time convinced that each version is wrong.

However, I am happy to write the Foreword for this book to share the feelings of frustration and despair that I am sure many of my fellow dyslexics have suffered when doing something as simple as, say, driving a car.

Map-reading, filling out forms, reading aloud, reading road signs are just a few of a long list of things that I find really frustrating. However, with good luck and a great deal of hard work I have managed to master my job.

I remember one experience last summer, which was probably the most frustrating, stressful experience that I have ever had in my whole life.

I was working at the Chichester Festival Theatre in *Relative Values*, and the night before the matinée days I usually stayed in Sussex instead of commuting back to London. On this occasion I was staying with a friend 5 miles outside Chichester, about a 20-minute journey from the theatre. I had been there twice before with my sister, who had helped me find the way, and there had been a full moon so the landmarks were more visible. On this night, however, I was on my own, I was very tired and it was very dark. My first mistake was to turn right instead of left a mile or two after setting out. Eventually, after about 2 hours, I was so lost that I was desperately pounding my fist on the wheel, and even if I did see a signpost I couldn't read it or remember if I had seen it before.

I was so distraught that I was screaming at the top of my voice. I don't ever remember feeling so frustrated, except when I was a child and I was asked to look up words in the dictionary! If I could find the road to London at least I could go home.

I was just turning round, in the hope of finding a hotel, when I saw a signpost to Chichester, but once again I found myself driving up and down an endless series of country lanes, which were even more indistinguishable than the last. About an hour later, tears running down my face and still lost, I saw a young man parking his car, hooted and screeched to a halt to catch him before he disappeared into the night.

'I beg you to help me!', I gasped. 'I'm lost – I've been lost for 3 hours! I'm looking for School Lane and I can't find it.'

'It's there,' he said, calmly pointing into the dark. I couldn't believe it.

Had I not feared I would make a mistake, I'm sure I would not have done so, but I allowed the stress of the situation to get the better of me.

Susan Hampshire

Preface to the first edition

The literature available on stress in general is extensive (for sources see, in particular, Varma, 1973, 1993) and there is also plenty of evidence from case studies that dyslexics experience more than their fair share of stress (see, for example, Simpson, 1980. Hampshire, 1981; Miles, 1993a, b; Edwards, 1994). As far as we know, however, this is the first book that has attempted to study stress in dyslexia in its own right.

The aim of the book is to increase people's awareness of the stresses that dyslexics undergo and to encourage reflection on ways in which these stresses can be avoided.

There will, of course, be scope in the future for systematic comparisons between dyslexics and non-dyslexics in respect of stress levels, and in particular for the use of physiological measures. Our present purpose, however, is more limited; it is rather that of putting the notion of stress in dyslexia 'on the map' and showing that it is a topic that merits further investigation.

To achieve this we decided that what was needed was a 'personal' approach in which colleagues with experience of dyslexia were asked to contribute chapters. We did not expect them to report systematic experiments but rather to describe the kinds of situation which the dyslexics of their acquaintance regularly found to be stressful. We also thought it important that there should be contributions from people who were themselves dyslexic, because there is clearly no substitute for first-hand experience.

We were extremely pleased when Susan Hampshire agreed to write the Foreword, and we particularly appreciate the way in which she has chosen to share with us the details of a hideously stressful experience which occurred many years after she became famous.

Chapter 1 is a letter from Karen Dodd. Karen is the mother of a dyslexic girl, now at secondary school, and she sets the stage for the rest of the book by calling attention to the appalling stresses that can arise when parents who approach their child's teachers are shown indifference and sometimes downright hostility We have shortened her letter slightly but otherwise have reproduced it as it was written.

The next chapter [now Chapter 20 in this revised edition], written by Angela Fawcett, contains an account of the struggles – and the later successes – of her son, Matthew, along with some other very telling case studies. Besides being the mother of a dyslexic son, however, Angela is also one of the most prominent dyslexia researchers in the UK, and her work with Dr Rod Nicolson is internationally known. We therefore encouraged her not to limit her contribution to a discussion of individuals but to say something about her own research and in particular about ways in which it might contribute to our understanding of stress.

The next four chapters are arranged on an 'age' basis. Chapter 3 [now Chapter 2], written by Patience Thomson, is entitled 'Stress factors in early education'; in Chapter 4 Steve Chinn and Maryrose Crossman describe their experiences of stress in dyslexic teenagers; in Chapter 5 [now Chapter 4] Dorothy Gilroy writes about stresses among college students; and in Chapter 6 [now Chapter 5] Gerald Hales deals with stresses in the workplace.

Chapter 7, written by Peter Congdon, returns to the issue of stress in children, and indicates some of the problems that can arise in the case of highly gifted dyslexics, whilst in Chapter 8 Roger Saunders straddles the different age levels by writing about stresses within the family. The setting for Roger's work has been in the United States of America, but dyslexia is no respecter of national boundaries and his conclusions are clearly applicable in many different parts of the world.

Chapter 9 [Chapters 12 to 16 in this edition] is entitled 'The dyslexics speak for themselves'. The contributors are Michael Newby, Joy Aldridge, Brother Matthew Sasse, Sheena Harrison and Janet Coker. We thought it best to record their contributions as they wrote them, rather than attempt to change style, grammar or spelling. We believe that, had we attempted such changes, something of the personality of the writer would have been lost in the process. Our special thanks are due both to them and to Susan Hampshire for their willingness not only to re-live some highly traumatic experiences but to do so via the written word – a task that, as some of them make clear, can itself be extremely stressful.

In the final chapter we attempt as editors to take stock of the book as a whole and to formulate some tentative conclusions.

We should like to end this introduction with a word of warning. As their brief was to deal with stress, the contributors have quite properly spent time calling attention to things that can go wrong. Our worry is that this may present too gloomy a picture! Let it be remembered, then, that things that our contributors claim to have noticed in some dyslexics will not necessarily apply to all dyslexics; this would be far too pessimistic a conclusion. For example, just because there are dyslexics who, as a result of their dyslexia, do not make friends easily, it would be a serious mistake to jump to the conclusion that no

dyslexic ever makes friends easily. What our contributors mention are essentially risks – the dyslexic tends to be at risk more than others to possible sources of stress, and in the interests of realism it was essential in a book of this kind not to minimize these risks. Our main message, nevertheless, is one of optimism: there is ample evidence that in the right environment dyslexics can lead happy and productive lives. It is our belief that with increased public awareness many of the situations that cause them to feel stress can be avoided; indeed, if it had not been so there would have been little point in writing this book.

Tim Miles
Ved Varma
January 1995

References

Edwards J (1994) The Scars of Dyslexia. London: Cassell.

Hampshire S (1981) Susan's Story. London: Sidgwick & Jackson.

Miles TR (1993a) Dyslexia: The Pattern of Difficulties. London: Whurr.

Miles TR (1993b) Understanding Dyslexia. Bath: Amethyst Books.

Simpson E (1980) Reversals. A Personal Account of Victory over Dyslexia. London: Gollancz.

Varma VP (ed.) (1973) Stresses in Children. London: London University Press.

Varma VP (1993) Coping With Unhappy Children. London: Cassell.

Preface to the second edition

It was my much respected friend and colleague, Dr Ved Varma, who first suggested to me that the two of us should co-edit a book entitled *Dyslexia and Stress,* and I readily concurred. Sadly, for health reasons, it has not been possible for Ved to collaborate in the editing of this second edition. However, I should like to take this opportunity of paying tribute, not only to his far-sightedness in suggesting that we edit such a book, but for his sensitive awareness of the stresses experienced not only by people with dyslexia but by the many other people with whom he made contact during his profes-sional life. He could not have been an easier person to work with.

Of the contributions that appeared in the first edition, those by Karen Dodd, Gerald Hales, Peter Congdon, Roger Saunders, Sheena Harrison and Janet Coker have remained as they were. The other contributors to the first edition (Angela Fawcett, Patience Thomson, Steve Chinn, Dorothy Gilroy, Michael Newby, Joy Aldridge and Brother Matthew Sasse) have modified their original contributions, in some cases quite substantially.

Among the new contributors are five dyslexics: Morag Kiziewicz, Dave Alexander, Brenda Millward, Michael Lea and Julian Cox. Morag describes her experiences as the Support Tutor to the dyslexic students at the University of Bath, while Dave, Brenda, Michael and Julian describe the ways in which dyslexia has affected their lives - in Julian's case with tragic results. The other new contributors are Lindsay Peer and Melanie Jameson. Lindsay was Education Director at the British Dyslexia Association (BDA) and has had the opportunity to observe all kinds of stresses undergone by families who have come into contact with the BDA; Melanie has worked for the Adult Dyslexia Organisation (ADO) and has unique experience of the ways in which people with dyslexia can be disadvantaged within the legal system.

I, of course, had to ask myself whether all these contributors were speaking with one voice - and, if they were not, whether I should take any

steps to interfere. I had no hesitation in deciding that editorial interference was unnecessary. Certainly there are differences of emphasis between one chapter and another – just as there are differences between one dyslexic and another; but although much more remains to be discovered about the *causes* of dyslexia there can be little room for dispute about its manifestations.

Finally, there was the issue of whether I should attempt any editing of the spelling, style or punctuation of the dyslexic contributors. I found that, perhaps thanks to spell-checkers, spelling errors were relatively few. I did, however, find some errors of punctuation, along with some prolixity of style and the occasional malapropism. My decision was that, if all such things were 'edited out', this would not give a faithful representation of what the contributor was really like. To imply, in a book on dyslexia, that dyslexic adults never make errors of this kind would have been very misleading, and it seems to me important to respect dyslexics for what they are, and not criticize them for failing to be something different. (The only exception to this policy is that I have made sure that references are set out so as to conform to standard practice.) If readers detect spelling errors or other solecisms, do not blame the copy-editor: she was acting under instruction.

TR Miles
October 2003

Contributors

Joy Aldridge MA, BSc, AdvDip Ed, DipAppSS, is a care home manager for younger adults with learning difficulties

Dave Alexander is an engineer in a family engineering company

Steve J Chinn, PhD, is Principal of Mark College, Highbury, Somerset

Janet Coker is a professional singer

Peter J Congdon, PhD, is Director of the Information Centre for Gifted Children in Solihull

Julian Cox, a former businessman, now serving a prison sentence

Karen Dodd, DipSW, is a qualified social worker

Angela Fawcett, PhD, is a dyslexia researcher at the University of Sheffield and editor of *Dyslexia: An International Journal of Research and Practice*

Dorothy Gilroy, BA, is a former tutor to dyslexic students at the University of Wales, Bangor, and is now doing consultancy work in higher education

Gerald Hales, PhD, was formerly a Research Fellow at The Open University, and now has an independent practice as a psychologist

Sheena Harrison, BA, DipSW, is a qualified Social Worker and a holder of a City and Guilds Diploma in Adult Education

Melanie Jameson, BA, PGCE, DipRSA/OCR (SpLD), is an assessor and tutor in dyslexia and provides a range of consultancy services

Morag Kiziewicz, MEd, is Learning Support Manager at the University of Bath

T.R Miles, OBE, PhD, is Professor Emeritus of Psychology, University of Wales, Bangor

Brenda Millward, was formerly a chef in the Royal Air Force and is now retired

Michael Newby, CertEd, was formerly Head of Science and other departments at a Comprehensive School and is now mentoring children with dyslexia

Lindsay Peer, CBE, PhD, was formerly Education Director at the British Dyslexia Association

Brother Matthew Sasse, FSC, MA, DipSpLD, is a member of a religious order

Roger E Saunders, MA, is a former clinical psychologist who worked in the Baltimore area, and is a Fellow of the Academy of Orton–Gillingham practitioners and Educators, USA

Patience Thomson, MA, MEd, was formerly Principal of Fairley House School, London and is co-founder of Barrington Stoke Publishing Company

Chapter 1
Letter from a mother

KAREN DODD

Dear Mr Miles

I realise that something in print is only a possibility, but feel that it would be very beneficial if you could put something in print as I feel that dyslexia is very isolating and that people do not understand the problems involved.

Writing this is difficult, but I will try to give a condensed account of the experiences of my daughter and I. [Margaret] is my second and youngest child. . . . Little things began to fit into place after I found that she was dyslexic (i.e. didn't learn to ride a bike until 8 years old. Margaret had a stammer, spoke late and had speech therapy No sooner had she started full time school, than she was receiving remedial teaching.

. . . At the age of 9 years I couldn't accept that Margaret's school reports were of a bright happy child who works well and tries hard. I saw a T.V. programme discussing dyslexia and . . . arranged a private assessment for her. I spoke to her remedial teacher about this and this is when I first encountered 'the attitude'. Margaret's remedial teacher had been a very nice woman, helpful and approachable who suddenly went beserk, the real Jekyll & Hyde, I couldn't believe the reaction, she made me feel 3" tall.

I had Margaret assessed and she was indeed dyslexic as was my husband. My husband had always considered himself to be illiterate as he couldn't write at all and had minimal reading skills . . . . I gave the [new] school a copy of Margaret's report and I met with her teacher and the headmaster to discuss what help could be given. Again we met 'the attitude'; we felt interfering parents, over-reacting, trying to tell teacher 'experts' their job. I came out near to tears, I was so angry at the way I had been treated. When I pushed the issue with special ed, Margaret was given 1 hour a week for 12 weeks special ed. Moving houses at an important time in her education was blamed and thrown at me.

Initially Margaret was pleased to find out that she was dyslexic. She said, 'I'm not thick am I mum? I'm dyslexic'. Margaret realised she had a special problem and waited for the special help. The help never materialised and Margaret began to get very frustrated as to 'why no one was helping her'. I

1

requested a formal assessment under the education act but was refused. In view of the private assessment I had I felt their refusal unreasonable and began to write and write. I wrote to MP's, Councillors, County Hall etc.

Margaret's frustration finally snapped whilst doing a national curriculum test. She couldn't do it, but could have no help and she had an outburst in which she threw the textbook, chair and desk at the headmaster who was taking the class.

Margaret moved up a year and her new teacher was worse with 'the attitude' than the last. Margaret was sat on the 'thick' table. Made to learn 20 spellings a week that she couldn't read, had work torn out of her book because it wasn't right. She developed headaches, psoriasis and had to be taken to school crying, kicking and shouting. Things got so bad I considered taking her out of school.

We were now 18 months since Margaret's initial diagnosis – no help – no assessment. I was battling the education dept trying to cushion Margaret, battling the school and coping with my own frustrations. . . . I felt that I was trying to take on the world singlehanded and that everyone was against me. I would feel so confused and isolated I would cry often. My daughter was suffering and I, her mum, felt powerless to help her, I felt so useless.

. . . Margaret has started senior school this term. The school have been very responsive to Margaret's needs so far . . . .

The biggest stress factors for me were the reaction of others, the isolation and the feeling of being a small useless fish, battling alone, the visible mental and emotional turmoil being suffered by my daughter, and the guilt felt at not being able to achieve anything positive for her . . .

People are ignorant to the facts, will not acknowledge dyslexia and will not help these children. Parents are left to battle alone and put the pieces back in their child's life. A battle for the future of all 'Margarets' has begun and must be kept up until children of the future can have their educational and emotional needs met – as all children should.

I hope I have been able to give some insight into the problem. It is very difficult to explain the feelings. I hope you achieve publishing something, every little that brings the issues of dyslexia to light are in my eyes most welcome, it is the only way to achieving recognition of a common problem that causes so much heartache to so many children and their parents.

Yours sincerely
Mrs Karen Dodd

Chapter 2
Stress factors in early education

PATIENCE THOMSON

A measure of stress in life is almost certainly unavoidable and can indeed even be welcome, if it is manageable. It is associated with challenge, with variations from routines that might otherwise become boring, with experiments and new initiatives. It is common to feel anxious when confronted with tests or examinations, yet we still seek qualifications. Considerable stress is involved during the initial period of ineptitude when learning a new sport, but we do not hesitate to do so. It is natural for many individuals to be competitive and ambitious; this necessarily involves stress.

Stress appears threatening only when it becomes pervasive and invasive, when it affects too many areas of our lives and when we have neither the strategies nor the energy to cope with it. With adults, high and undesirable levels of stress can be triggered by insecure social relationships, by a job that is unsuitable or too demanding, or by fear of unemployment, financial worries, social uncertainty or personal failure. We also become stressed when the tasks required of us in our daily lives take an inordinate amount of time to accomplish, are ill-defined or are indeed impossible for us because either physically or mentally we do not have the right tools. A combination of too many of these factors can lead to an overwhelming sense of apprehension, incompetence and confusion, to lassitude, sleeplessness and fatigue. It also invites the victim to resort to escape mechanisms which may temporarily relieve pressure, to fantasy, obsession, rebellion or withdrawal.

Undoubtedly, some individuals are able to cope with stress better than others. There are personality factors involved, but stress management is also a skill that can be learnt. It would be as impossible to protect children from a degree of stress as it would be unwise, because learning to recognize and control it is a necessary tool for survival in adult life. It is the task of parents and teachers and a very necessary part of education to prepare children for stress and to show them how to cope with it. It is also important that levels of stress should be monitored and controlled.

This is sometimes difficult in the case of the dyslexic child, when causes of stress may easily be underestimated or misinterpreted, so that the child is not taught correct strategies. It is quite likely that neither he nor his mentors will understand the nature and implications of his specific learning difficulties, or know how to relieve the accumulating stress that these are causing. This is often particularly true in the early years, before a professional diagnosis has been made. The dyslexic child will also not be exempt from all the natural anxieties inherent for any child in the educational and maturational process. If stress levels become intolerably high, many dyslexic children develop their own inappropriate strategies, becoming disruptive, aggressive, withdrawn or school phobic. There is also evidence that children with special educational needs are less socially confident and more likely than their peers to be bullied in mainstream schools (Thompson et al., 1994).

Every child entering primary school is naturally subject to a degree of stress. There is likely to be some measure of separation anxiety at parting from his or her mother, at being released into a new environment for a considerable period of time daily, among strangers, in unfamiliar surroundings and in a social situation where there is no privacy or possibility of physical withdrawal. Under these circumstances many children take some time to adjust and to gain the confidence that comes from adapting to the school routine, mastering the elements of the working day and reacting appropriately to adults and the peer group.

The normal difficulties of adjustment that face any child are compounded for the child with dyslexia because of certain inherent weaknesses. In the past, when dyslexia was regarded primarily as the persistent failure to learn to read and write, the natural assumption was that dyslexic children would enter primary school with equal confidence and competence to other children. These, it was thought, would be eroded only when they were faced with formal academic tasks. However, more recent evidence suggests that the problems of the dyslexic child begin in the preschool era and that he will enter primary school vulnerable, if not positively disadvantaged.

Dyslexia will, by definition, have some if not all of a range of pattern of difficulties, which will affect their reactions and performance throughout their school career (Miles, 1993). Teachers need to be aware of these diverse problems if they are to make the necessary adjustments that will enable the pupil with dyslexia to be integrated into the mainstream classroom.

There may be problems with visual discrimination, visual sequencing and visual memory, particularly in relation to symbols and their orientation and correct sequential arrangement. A child with dyslexia may transpose letters or syllables within a word, writing 'taek' for 'take' and 'rembember' for 'remember'. He may transpose the words in a sentence, writing 'he come will'. He may omit the vowels in a word as in 'bfst' for 'breakfast'. And he will

not see when he rereads his work that he has made fundamental mistakes.

Such problems relating to recording and reproducing information that is visually presented can also affect the acquisition of mathematical skills. Digits in the answer to a sum may be reversed, and 16 becomes 61. Confused directionality and lack of spatial awareness are common in pupils with dyslexia, and mean that their work will be poorly presented and look scrappy. It will make a bad impression both on the teacher and on classmates, who can be critical and dismissive. Letters and figures may vary widely in size and shape, margins are often ignored, titles omitted and drawings either scrunched up in a corner or inclined to wander off the page. This is why, in teaching a child with dyslexia, competence in word-processing can be extremely helpful because presentation becomes much easier to master and the final results can be made to look impressive.

Right–left confusion is a handicap in mathematics and may extend to difficulties with the concepts 'above' and 'below' (which is also a language problem). Many children with dyslexia, when doing subtraction sums, will arbitrarily take away the top line from the bottom, instead of the bottom from the top, for ease of calculation. The answer to 74 minus 15 then becomes 61. Fractions are a nightmare for them. Incorrect orientation when writing digits can also give rise to errors; for instance if the number 5 is reversed it may be read as a 3 just as 'b's and 'd's are confused when the child is reading or writing.

In the speech and language areas there will, in many cases, be significant problems with receptive and expressive language, evidenced by low scores on the British Picture Vocabulary Scales (Dunn et al., 1997) and the Clinical Evaluation of Language Fundamentals (CELF-3 UK; Semel et al., 2000). Lack of phonological awareness is common in dyslexic children and is a distinct handicap. The child who does not recognize the patterns of letters and sounds, both visual and auditory, in words will be unable to read or spell by analogy. This is a huge disadvantage. Weak auditory blending, poor auditory discrimination and the inability to screen out irrelevant noise or identify accurately sound sequences hamper the effective processing of information presented through the auditory channel. Dyslexic children may also have naming problems which create considerable difficulties when information has to be stored in long-term memory and even greater ones when it has to be retrieved. Dockrell and McShane (1993) wrote that 'The most likely source of the poor memory performance of children with reading difficulties is their already established difficulties in phonological processing' and again 'The working memory system includes a specialized phonological store in which verbal information is retained'. Significantly they go on to say:

> If a printed word cannot be converted into sounds then its sounds cannot be stored; if conversion is slow, then previous sounds may be lost before further processing can occur; if the store is reduced in capacity, then the information

cannot be retained; if the stored sounds cannot be blended, then a pronounceable
form of the word cannot be obtained.

Dyslexic children are often caught up in a vicious circle. They are denied the
opportunity to learn from experience. This is particularly true of reading.
Bryant and Bradley (1985) point out that 'the child who learns to read is
constantly exercising his memory'. They suggest that the poor memory
scores of the unsuccessful reader 'could just as well be the result as the
source of the failure to learn to read'. Muter (1994) suggests that phonological awareness is a powerful predictor of progress in beginning reading.
She stresses, quoting Adams (1990), that the ability to segment words into
their constituent phonemes or syllables, to blend sounds, to recognize
rhymes and to manipulate phonemes by adding, deleting or transposing
them are all good predictors of success in acquiring reading and spelling
skills. If her evidence is borne in mind, it must follow that the child with
dyslexia, lacking phonological awareness to such an extent that he cannot
establish a foundation from which to develop even basic literacy skills, let
alone refine them, falls further behind in his efforts to master those very
reading skills which could improve his phonological skills and develop both
memory and comprehension through practice and experience.

In the same way, writing is a skill that is improved by practice. A child learns
to craft words, sentences and paragraphs or to organize and structure his ideas
through the very act of writing. If he has such technical problems with
spelling, word retrieval or even handwriting that any written work is laborious
and demoralizing, then his skills will improve only at an agonisingly slow rate. A
vicious circle is again created. Frustration builds up and, because there seems
to be no satisfactory solution, stress accumulates. The effort involved may be so
great that the child is worn out long before the end of the day.

In some cases hyperactivity or attention deficit disorder may further affect
the child's concentration and then the outlook can appear bleak indeed.
These difficulties do not develop during the children's school career, but are
often constitutional in origin and present a significant handicap from the
affected child's first day in primary school and even long before.

A reception-class child is soon expected to copy numbers, shapes and
forms, and gradually to remember them with increasing accuracy and speed.
Whereas other children will quickly learn to raise from memory a useful store
of information that automatically relates sound to symbol and word to
meaning, the dyslexic child will search in vain for a key to past learning
experience and fail to make the vital linkages. Visual and auditory stimuli
need to be competently processed, often by linguistic means, to acquire
basic literacy and numeracy skills.

Many pupils with dyslexia experience problems with receptive language.
Efficient and well-developed listening skills and competent information

processing are vital prerequisites for successful accommodation to the school environment. The dyslexic child whose receptive language is vulnerable is disadvantaged throughout his working day. From the moment any child enters primary school, most instructions and explanations, praise and admonishment will be given orally. Effective oral communication between teacher and pupil will depend on that child's ability to interpret language and to respond appropriately.

The dyslexic child may well process what is said to him individually, or to the class, slowly and inefficiently, and his difficulties will be greatly compounded by the distractions going on around him. He may well not be able to screen out irrelevant background noise as a child without his difficulties would normally do. Sounds within and outside the classroom will divert his attention. He cannot automatically focus on the essentials of what he is being told, but may fasten on unimportant or random detail. If, as is likely, he has poor phonological awareness, leading to slow and inaccurate processing of the spoken language, he will be confused about precise instructions, which he will quickly forget, and be reliant upon copying others if he is to accomplish the task that has been set. Anxiety and ensuing tiredness will impede concentration and lead to even more ineffective information processing. The exhausted child may well 'switch off'.

These problems with receptive language may also affect a dyslexic child's ability to participate in classroom discussion. He will be slower to process questions in comparison with the other children, who will quickly have supplied correct answers which, given time, he might well have produced. His discouragement and frustration grow, confidence diminishes and motivation is reduced.

An informed teacher could mitigate the difficulties of the dyslexic child by placing him at the front of the class, by repeating instructions or even by 'buddying' him up with another friendly child who could prompt him when necessary. It is even possible to ensure that the dyslexic child has extra time without interruption from others to answer questions. But to make such concessions, specific learning difficulties must have been recognized.

Unless the teacher is exceptionally knowledgeable or perspicacious, or the parents particularly alert and well informed, it is unlikely that dyslexia will be diagnosed during the first or even the second year of formal schooling. It is more likely that the dyslexic child will be regarded as not particularly bright or as having emotional difficulties. This view will be confirmed when he is slow to acquire basic literacy and numeracy skills. Even when the teacher is sympathetic and helpful, the dyslexic child may be humiliated by the modified programme devised for him.

If receptive language is impaired, expressive language and communication skills are equally vulnerable. Dyslexic children often have word-finding

or naming difficulties, which lead to circumlocution or vague and inaccurate statements. On the surface they may appear articulate, but close analysis of the content of their oral communication leads to the conclusion that they often repeat themselves, miss the point or fail to take account of the reaction of the listener. This develops into a social problem when they bore or mystify their audience, particularly other children who have neither the patience nor the inclination to tease out the thread of a story or argument from the dyslexic child's confused attempts to express his ideas clearly.

Inadequate communication skills are as much a social as an academic disadvantage at every stage of school life. The dyslexic child, struggling to make sense of the conversation of others, to frame his own interventions and to follow the train of thought, often fails to appreciate or even notice body language, facial expression or tone of voice. He fails to anticipate reactions, does not realize that he is inviting anger or criticism, and is aggrieved at the response he receives because he has not recognized the warning signs. Complaints that the dyslexic child is often inappropriate in his language or comments are not confined to school and can equally lead to trouble and misunderstandings at home with parents, with siblings and with the extended family. If dyslexic children are going to have problems with making friends in the playground or with social interaction with adults and their peers, these often start in the early years at primary school. They cannot therefore be entirely ascribed to the frustrations and emotional disturbances of school failure.

There is another contributory factor for many children with dyslexia which often affects social relationships from a very early age. The whole area of motor difficulty as part of the broader dyslexic syndrome has aroused increasing interest and attention over the past few years. Many dyslexic children experience problems with either gross or fine motor control, or both. Some of these problems are often referred to under the general heading of 'dyspraxia', particularly by parents who claim that the significance of these particular difficulties goes unrecognized and that no adequate support is forthcoming. Difficulties with gross motor control have obvious repercussions in school life. The child may have difficulties with eye-hand or eye-foot co-ordination, being unable to catch or kick a ball, a real disadvantage in the playground or on the sports field. In both games and physical education lessons a whole spectrum of difficulty is revealed, because often dyslexic children can neither remember nor interpret instructions as a result of their fallible receptive language skills, or follow them because of weak motor skills. In physical education lessons their lack of co-ordination and poor balance can make them look ridiculous when they try to hop, skip or walk a balance beam; in games, erratic orientation, uncertain body image and left-right confusion mean that they turn the wrong way, run in the wrong

direction, shoot 'own goals' (particularly after half-time) and generally appear to make fools of themselves. They are a liability in any team and often the last to be selected. No wonder that many dyslexic children choose to play the class clown and capitalize on their very weaknesses to attract attention, even if their behaviour attracts criticism or ridicule. Nor do the child's problems end with the formal physical education, swimming or games lessons. Limited time is scheduled for the children to change for the next period. Dyslexic children who display typical symptoms of dyspraxia may struggle with buttons and shoe-laces or put on their clothes in the wrong order. They will often take an inordinately long time to dress themselves while the rest of the class and teacher wait impatiently.

Motor difficulties will be apparent in class, when the child with dyspraxia clumsily brushes the jar of pencils off the teacher's desk, knocks over the paint-pot or jolts the desks of other children, to their considerable annoyance. He cannot stand quietly in line, but will jostle others who naturally push and shove back. If he has poor muscle tone, he will slouch uncomfortably at his desk, wriggle on his seat and distract himself and others by his restlessness.

Problems with fine motor control, even before serious handwriting is required, affect dyslexic children's ability to draw or colour efficiently within the lines. Often they will use undue pressure and their hand will quickly tire; growing frustration that they are not succeeding at the set task will compound the situation and they will give up. Their handwriting may be almost illegible and, because they form their letters so inaccurately, they will not recognize repetitive patterns in words and will spell the same word in many different ways on the same page. All fine motor tasks will present problems as, for instance, those associated with early learning in mathematics such as the manipulation of concrete aids, the counting of beads or the measuring and matching of blocks. What for other children is a task that can be accomplished with practised ease and manual dexterity, while retaining the overall concept of what they are trying to do, becomes for the child with dyslexia a complicated procedure where each step presents a challenge. As in the early stages of riding a bicycle, when to proceed too slowly is constantly to fall off, the child with dyslexia is deprived of the impetus that carries the whole exercise forward to a satisfactory conclusion. In the context of fine motor control it is also worth mentioning that a few of the younger dyslexic children have difficulty in chewing their food and the slowness of their mastication creates problems at dinnertime, when their plateful is halfeaten as others are clearing away. They may want their food mashed or minced. This may be one of the reasons why they are sometimes 'fussy eaters', and invite adverse comment from unsympathetic adults.

The catalogue of dyslexic vulnerability is not yet complete. A large proportion of people with dyslexia seem lost in both space and time and this has serious implications which militate against confident survival in the school environment. Many adults will have experienced the confusion and frustration of asking for directions in a foreign city with little or no know-ledge of the native language. Traffic appears to approach from the wrong direction, landmarks are unfamiliar and the bustling, purposeful crowd is seemingly unwilling to pause to give help or instructions. If people do oblige, they often talk too fast and create further embarrassment. The pupil with dyslexia constantly experiences similar anxiety throughout the normal school day. Most children quickly pick up the geography of a new school environment. The whereabouts of cloakroom, toilets, classroom and hall are soon established. In contrast the dyslexic child is slow to prepare for the next move, follows on behind the rest of his class, is left behind, and finds himself lost, worried and confused.

Similarly, there is an inaccurate conception of time. The person with dyslexia has no intuitive recognition of time past, time present or time future. He may turn up late or early for a lesson, will greatly over- or underestimate the time required for any given task, will be muddled not only as to the day of the week but as to the time of day. One 7-year-old child with dyslexia claimed that there was no order to the days of the week, that the holidays were composed entirely of Saturdays and Sundays and that a whole school week could consist entirely of Mondays. When asked how he could tell which day of the week it was, he said you could usually guess from the teacher's face. No wonder such children, unless their parents are vigilant, fail to bring in their football gear or swimming trunks on the correct day and hence get themselves into trouble. An 11-year-old child with dyslexia who was asked the date of her birthday was embarrassed and appeared not to know 'When was it last year?' 'July 15th.' The teacher could not control the hilarity with which this statement was greeted by the other children. The girl had obviously not grasped the concept that her birthday was on the same day every year. One day I rescheduled a weekly religious education period from the last period in the day to the session before lunch. At the end of the period the entire class of dyslexic children picked up their bags and proceeded to go to the cloak-room, ready to go home, without any sense that it was still only midday. I have often observed a dyslexic child in a craft, design and technology or computer lesson completely absorbed in a task and quite unaware that the hour was up and the bell had gone. When recalled, he was aggrieved and angry, resenting the intrusive need for transferral of attention dictated by a seemingly inexorable and intrusive school routine.

Such sudden focusing of attention in the otherwise distractible dyslexic child, this almost obsessive determination to hang on to any area where

success is possible, leads on to discussion of that major cause of stress for the dyslexic child, frustration. It lies within the very definition of specific learning difficulties that there are pronounced areas of difficulty and vulnerability, but also areas of considerable strength. This distinguishes the child with dyslexia from the child with moderate or severe learning difficulties who is globally affected. There is a wide range of IQs among children with dyslexia, as with any other children. Unlike other children, those with the higher IQs do not necessarily have a better prognosis in terms of academic success. Indeed, their failure to acquire the basic literacy and numeracy skills, essential for academic progress, usually leaves the brighter child more inclined to adverse emotional reactions, which further block his capacity to learn. The inability to capitalize on potential, to express individual ideas concisely, to tell inventive stories plausibly or to communicate original concepts is a major cause of stress.

I have detailed a number of areas within the primary school day where the dyslexic child is likely to feel underconfident, threatened and incompetent. Against this background it is understandable that stress can soon reach disproportionate levels, as the child struggles to achieve in situations where, because of the nature of his specific difficulties, he is seriously disadvantaged. There are too few windows of opportunity when he has a chance to shine, to relax and to redeem his reputation.

From the moment children with dyslexia first enter primary school, they are often a source of puzzlement to their teachers. To brand them as lazy or stupid seems inappropriate, yet their failures in so many areas reduce expectations and the teacher may increasingly assign them less demanding tasks, hoping to preserve their morale. The unfortunate consequence can be that the child with dyslexia who is not challenged may cease to set himself high standards. Low expectations invite low performance. Yet such children are still often aware that they are not truly unintelligent and the contrast between their potential and their performance inevitably gives rise to stress.

Apparent failure at school does not pass unnoticed by the parents, who start to become anxious. In their turn, they too are confused. Often there was little concrete evidence before their child started at primary school that anything was amiss. Some clumsiness, a quaint way with words or failure to remember instructions could easily be ascribed to general immaturity The parents' increasing worries reflect on the child. If there are other siblings without learning difficulties, the parents may be tactful enough not to make direct comparisons, but the child will usually be aware of the discrepancies. A deep sense of unease begins to grow as the child becomes conscious that he is disappointing his family. Stress for the child with dyslexia is not confined to school but permeates home life as well. As it grows it can lead to such manifestations of emotional disturbance as temper tantrums, aggression

and bed-wetting. An element of guilt may be set up in either child or parents, whose management of the child becomes increasingly uncertain. Pressure creates further stress, but acceptance of failure can appear to be demoralizing patronage and a middle way is hard to find.

For parents or teachers of children who are not only dyslexic but also hyperactive or have an attention deficit, and this is certainly a factor in a proportion of cases, the scene is even more complicated and the correct approach even more uncertain. Their difficulties have been concisely and comprehensively described by Barkley (1992). He explains the implications of attention deficit hyperactivity disorder, or ADHD. One of the significant problems is inconsistent work performance. The failure of children with ADHD to stay on task, their impulsive behaviour, disorganization and unpredictable reactions exhaust adults, annoy other children, and impede constructive learning. Almost inevitably they attract negative reactions and will often respond with attention-seeking behaviour, which is unpopular in class and distressing in the home environment. Such children suffer because they are not invited home by others and can be partially ostracized at school, or teased and even bullied by exasperated peers.

This wide spectrum of difficulties extending into so many areas of the dyslexic child's life renders him extremely vulnerable to levels of stress that are unacceptable, inhibiting and even threatening. It is interesting to trace, through case histories, the different reactions of individuals to such stress and to consider how best it can be alleviated.

Until now, for convenience, children with dyslexia have been referred to in this chapter as of masculine gender. In my last five years as principal of a school for 90 dyslexic children of primary school age, the number of girls grew from 12 to 30. The precise reasons for this increase are hard to establish, but it was probably the result of the adoption of a broader definition of learning abilities. The problems of girls with dyslexia can appear on the surface to be subtly different from those of the boys and may emerge at a rather later stage. Some seem to learn to read reasonably efficiently, but for them this is a mechanical decoding exercise and their difficulties lie more in the area of information processing, comprehension and organizational skills – all factors of increasing importance in the later years at primary school. Problems with numeracy skills seem common in girls and are now more readily recognized as part of the pattern of dyslexic difficulty. I shall therefore include girls in my case studies. Pseudonyms will be used throughout.

Bruce

Bruce is the second child in a family of four. He was an early developer, learning to stand at 9 months and starting to talk at a year. He had no noticeable early

articulation problems and his speech was apparently fluent, although his stories rambled, he could never remember names and his jokes missed the point. At almost 5 years of age, he started attending his local primary school. He seemed an active, cheerful, well-adjusted child, although somewhat accident-prone, resulting in frequent trips to the local accident and emergency department. He badly burnt his hand stirring the bonfire with a metal rod and required stitches after a brawl with older children in the park. However, such incidents were ascribed to his impulsive behaviour, his fearlessness and his intense curiosity about the physical world around him. He entered a large reception class of over 40 children. His early failure to make any sort of start with learning to read or write was ascribed in part to lack of individual attention from the teacher in a large and somewhat undisciplined class.

During Bruce's second year at primary school it was suggested that he join a small remedial group. His mother was informed that he was 'not particularly bright' and needed extra help. Bruce was tall for his age and it was at this time that he began to team up with the tougher and rougher elements in his class; there was evidence that he was getting involved in fights in the playground. At home there were temper tantrums, threats to walk out (he would occasionally leave, reappearing somewhat sheepishly a couple of hours later), bed-wetting and sibling rivalry. It did not help morale that his older brother was thriving at school and that his younger sister, still of pre-school age, was a precocious learner. Bruce identified himself as the 'dim one' of the family.

In Bruce's third year at primary school his parents received a letter from his headmaster expressing considerable concern and suggesting that he be referred to the School Psychology Service. Comments on Bruce's problems included the following:

> . . . The need to sound out most of the words. [He appeared to retain very few of the 'look and say' words.]
>
> A habit of seizing on a particular letter in a word and guessing at a possible solution using the letter always as an initial one . . .
>
> The reproduction of a word by indicating the framework, e.g. d l v for 'delivery'.

Bruce was not making progress, even in his small group remedial lessons. He was restless and inattentive in class, unable to stay on task and was distracting the other children.

The Local Authority Educational Psychologist confirmed the Headmaster's identification of Bruce's problems. She established that he was of above-average intelligence. It was subsequently agreed with the understanding and sympathetic headmaster that his parents could take Bruce privately to an

Educational Psychologist with a special interest in dyslexia. She pronounced Bruce's dyslexia to be severe and predicted serious behaviour problems unless specialized help was immediately forthcoming. Private tuition was arranged three times a week and Bruce made dramatic progress. His confidence increased and with it his motivation and attention span. As he learnt to read, it emerged that he was a competent mathematician. Failure to decode mathematical instructions had initially hampered his progress. At home he was calmer, better organized and more relaxed. He started to invite friends back from school and to play more naturally with his siblings.

Bruce's problems were not over yet and there would, in fact, be years of hard work and essential support ahead to ensure that he mastered the curriculum and did justice to himself in the necessary examinations that would enable him to move on through the succeeding stages of his academic career. However, because he was diagnosed early and appropriate help was forthcoming, teachers, parents and Bruce himself acquired the insight into his specific problem, which enabled them to alleviate stress. Sympathetic and properly targeted treatment was forthcoming for his specific learning difficulties as they manifested themselves in different forms throughout his time at school. As was appropriate for an individual with an overall IQ of 128, Bruce eventually went to university.

Anne

Anne was less fortunate. Her problem went undiagnosed until she was a grown woman in her 20s. The following is a quotation from a letter (retaining her spelling) in which she describes her early experiences at primary school:

> So I would like to tell you about my school years. I think I was about seven years old when I became awair that I wasn't learning very much. My reading was very poor untill I was about 11 years and my spelling was awful and my maths were poor. I remember I didn't know my left from my right hand and couldn't tell the time. We were taught these things as a class of thirty children and I seemed to be the only one who didn't learn. So when we had writing I always did a lovely picture and wrote 'This is . . .' or 'The something or other' in big letters to fill up the page. And I remember getting my b's and d's mixed up and so I became good at art and craft and didn't progress in spelling at all. So I was put in the D stream and that was that. . .

> We had a nasty and old headmistress and she was the plague of my childhood she always picked me out and when I couldn't give the right answers she would shout at me and when she was angry she would spit the words at me. She always made me cry and I was so frightened of her. She tried to bully me into getting it right and I really wanted to please her. She would hold flashcards up and i had to say the

words that were written on them. One of the words were Doll and another Ball and I couldn't tell them apart. An so i would guess anf the other kids werld giggle and I knew I was in for it.

So I hated school I hated my tetchers. because they were picking on me and I would tell them so in front of the class. I would accuse them of tearing my picture or of spoiling something I had made. And looking back they were nice everbody liked them exept me.

Particular points of interest in this letter are the evidence of considerable frustration, anger and aggression, the development of inappropriate avoidance strategies and the sense of isolation from other children. They responded naturally to the teacher and mastered with apparent ease even simple tasks which Anne herself found frustrating and impossible. Ridicule alienated her, sarcasm destroyed her confidence, and lack of sympathy or understanding further demoralized her. Anne's schooldays left her stressed and liable to periods of depression. She found it difficult to cope in adult life until, as a result of a chance meeting, she learnt about dyslexia and the pattern of her difficulties fell into place. She set about seeking help.

Kenneth and Terry

Anne was like many children with dyslexia who develop avoidance strategies in the face of the undermining academic and social problems created by their specific learning difficulties. Kenneth, aged 9, simply refused to get up in the morning and lay like a dead weight in bed, equally impervious to bribes and threats. His mother could not dress him, feed him his breakfast or drag him to the school bus. Finally she gave up and waited for the school authorities to intervene. Terry went to school and attended assembly but shortly afterwards would be stricken by stomach cramps. Pale and tearful he would wait to be collected by his reluctant father. Yet if his bluff was called and he was sent back to class he would, on occasion, be physically sick. Not until he received specific help and encouragement and academic progress had started did his genuine pains diminish and finally vanish.

Paul

Paul was 9 years old when he came to us and was a non-starter in reading. At his local primary school he had been the victim of much teasing. At first, when he found himself in an environment where his specific learning difficulties were recognized and remediation was at hand, his new-found confidence converted him into a bully and a rebel. No longer cowed, he threw his weight around. Two years' progress in reading within his first year converted his attitude and his behaviour became tolerable, although he remained wary

and still found it difficult to react naturally to adults and his peers. Being less preoccupied with his problems and better able to concentrate on the task in hand he derived more satisfaction from lessons and was, emotionally, at last available for work.

Others

Edmund had great charm and a talent for 'creative ineptitude'. He avoided work by appearing constantly busy and attentive, but spent an inordinate amount of time drawing careful margins, sharpening pencils or volunteering to run errands.

Christopher, on the other hand, became withdrawn and sulky and was so quiet and unobtrusive that it was scarcely noticed when he skipped a lesson.

Sarah established on the first day of each new class that she was a non-performer, particularly in mathematics. She did this apologetically and with the warmest of smiles, pre-empting reproach and effectively limiting expect-ations.

Roger was rude and disruptive, making it clear to teacher and classmates that the reason for his academic failure lay in his rejection of the entire system.

Alison created a fantasy world for herself into which she retired when under pressure. Her absent expression was usually attributed to a failure to understand rather than lack of attention. The eventual establishment of an above-average IQ came as a great surprise to her teachers.

The problems that each of these attitudes presents to the teacher or parent are as nothing to the difficulties that face the individual concerned. All these strategies are only temporary measures for alleviating stress and anxiety As the child progresses through primary school, the growing realization of the increased pressure that awaits him at secondary school or even of the demands of the adult world begins to trouble him, and panic starts to take hold.

As lessons become more formalized and subject-oriented, the academic difficulties of the dyslexic child become increasingly apparent. Problems with reading and comprehension, with language processing and sequential memory, with spelling and written work intrude more deeply. The older primary age child will be required to use reference books, to research projects, to take notes or extract information from written material. It will be hard for him to remember names in geography or history or sequential processes in scientific experiments.

Lawrence's mathematics is weak because his fine motor skills affect his ability to line up figures. John copies numbers inaccurately because of his weak visual discrimination. Tim still cannot decode mathematical questions

of any complexity because his receptive language and reading skills are vulnerable. Michael has problems with orientation and confuses the signs. Their specific difficulties are different, but failure is the common factor.

For children proceeding to private education, examinations and tests loom as a real threat. The time constraint here is a major factor, with slow language processing skills proving a handicap in revision and essay writing. Pauline, aged 11, wrote her essay on 'shells' instead of 'smells', having misread the question. Realizing to her horror in the last 5 minutes what she had done, she hopefully wrote 'Shells have no smells' as her last sentence. Examinations are stressful for all individuals, but are partly a matter of confidence, and certainly require intense concentration. The additional problems that examinations present to dyslexic children distract them and drain their confidence. This creates such anxiety and stress that underperformance is almost guaranteed.

Academic success for the dyslexic often depends on two vital factors. He must acquire literacy and numeracy skills at a level that will enable him to access information efficiently and express himself in written form. Equally important, self-esteem, motivation and confidence must be preserved because the dyslexic child is almost certainly going to have to work harder than his peers to achieve his potential. Unless basic skills are taught before the child reaches secondary school, the gap between his level of ability and that of his peers will have widened to an extent where catching up will be an almost impossibly long and demoralizing process. Strategies and skills must not only be taught, but practised early, if they are to become automatic and if a child is not to miss the foundation work that underpins the secondary curriculum.

Thirty years ago, when I became seriously involved in the field of dyslexia, I was working with maladjusted and delinquent boys in their late teens. All were of above-average intelligence. I taught them in groups and, twice a week, on an individual basis. My remit was to ensure that they learnt the basic literacy and numeracy skills that they had failed to learn at primary school. Attendance at my lessons was mandatory. Using skills I had learnt in the Dyslexic Clinic of St Bartholomew's Hospital in London, under the direction of Dr Beve Hornsby, it was possible in almost every case to develop these boys' literacy and numeracy skills to a level where they could cope with the everyday demands of adult life and of a simple manual job. Looking back over the often well-documented school records of these boys, it was apparent that problems had already begun at primary school level with manifestations of specific learning difficulties that had hindered academic progress. They had entered secondary school as virtual non-starters. Problems of truancy and non-cooperation created a climate where it was easy to slip into antisocial or delinquent habits. Alleviation of stress at an early age through appropriate

teaching and more resources allocated for support at primary school could well have pre-empted these much more serious social problems from developing.

The parents of the primary school-age children in my school would often ask such questions as 'Is there a cure for dyslexia?' or 'How long will it take for my child to get over his specific learning difficulties?'. The answer can only be that dyslexia is endemic, may be genetic or neurological in origin, and there is no magic cure. There will always be areas that are potentially stressful if they demand precisely the skills and expertise most difficult for the dyslexic child to master. However, there are successful strategies, which can be taught, that vastly improve the capacity to communicate efficiently, to process information, to develop organizational and study skills, and thus to fulfil potential. Modified teaching styles employed by those specifically trained to recognize and remediate specific learning difficulties, and carefully structured and adapted programmes, enable dyslexic children to acquire the necessary basic literacy and numeracy skills to access the school curriculum. It must not be forgotten, however, that there is stress even in the remedial situation, because intense and prolonged effort will be required if the dyslexic child is to 'catch up'.

There is a very fine line between stress that creates challenge and stress that inhibits and constitutes a handicap. The primary school dyslexic child who is taught to overcome his specific learning difficulties will gain thereby a strength and confidence that will enable him to cope with the later pressures of teenage and adult life. The dyslexic child who fails to obtain crucial support in the early stages may well succumb to levels of stress that he can neither control nor understand, which undermine motivation and shatter confidence. He may opt out, with disastrous consequences not only for his educational development but for his future prospects reaching far into adult life.

The last word can most appropriately come from the dyslexic child himself, in this case an intelligent 10-year-old who had been sent to see me, the principal, because he had kicked another child who had taunted him. I sat him down at my desk with a clean sheet of paper to put his side of the story:

A blitixik I think can get angry a tierd of triyng in lessons and they might get there tenshon out on bullying or teasing but just so they can get their stress out, they might fell depresed or upset. They can also give up which is not the thing to do as they can get traped in a bubble and do need help to get out of it. they need help and if any bodyknose a diletic they shod be their friend or cher them up there is no reson that a dislexic can not be treated like a normal person. They do need help in their work but they shod not be treated diferently.

References

Adams MJ (1990) Beginning to Read – Thinking and Learning about Print. Cambridge, Mass: MIT Press.

Barkley RA (1992) ADHI) What Can We Do? New York: Guilford Press.

Bryant P, Bradley, L (1985) Children's Reading Problems. Oxford: Blackwell.

Dockrell J, McShane J (1993) Children's Learning Difficulties. Oxford: Blackwell.

Dunn LM, Dunn LM, Whetton C, Burley J (1997) British Picture Vocabulary Scale, 2nd edn. Windsor: NFER-Nelson.

Miles TR (1993) Dyslexia: The Pattern of Difficulties, 2nd edn. London: Whurr.

Muter V (1994) Influence of phonological awareness and letter knowledge on beginning reading and spelling development. In: C Hulme, M Snowling (eds), Reading Development and Dyslexia. London: Whurr.

Semel E, Wiig EH, Secord WA (2000) Clinical Evaluation of Language Fundamentals, 3rd edn. Sidcup, Kent: The Psychological Corporation.

Thompson D, Whitney I, Smith P (1994) Bullying of children with special needs in mainstream schools. Support for Learning 3: 103–106.

Chapter 3
Stress factors in adolescence

STEVE CHINN

I'm sure that each period in life has circumstances that can create stress, but there has to be a strong claim that the particular clash of adolescence and the demands made by secondary education on dyslexic pupils set up especially potent situations.

In this chapter I look at:

- the expectations that surround adolescents
- the demands of secondary education
- the signs and manifestations of stress
- the role of the pastoral system
- ways of addressing stress.

Expectations

Stress can arise when a pupil feels that he fails to match the expectations of those around him, be they parents, teachers or peers. The list of sources of influential expectations is, for many pupils, quite long. Each source may have different expectations or the pupil may perceive them as different. In addition the pupil may perceive them as conflicting. A pupil may have to adjust constantly to each new expectation and may not, of course, perceive some of them. This uncertainty can easily lead to stress.

In secondary education, pupils are generally expected to be independent in their reading and writing. Communication, particularly communication that leads to evaluation of ability, is largely via the written word. Even with the experience of over 20 years of teaching pupils with dyslexia, the

mismatch between an orally based evaluation of a pupil and his work on paper can be hard to comprehend. In a world where spelling snob teachers correct staff room notices, pupils with dyslexia face an uphill struggle to convince teachers of their true intelligence. (I feel that Howard Gardner's (1983) work on multiple intelligences should be a compulsory inservice for all teachers.)

Triggers for stress can surprise even experienced teachers of pupils with dyslexia. During a recent study into knowledge of basic multiplication tables facts, our Year 7 pupils were asked to answer 10 questions on times table facts. Even though they knew it was for a survey and not a school test, two pupils were in tears by the third question. The study was abandoned!

The foundations for stress can be set at the very start of secondary education, in that the move towards GCSE and post-16 examinations focuses parents' minds on the future. Quite often in interviews with parents of a (severely) dyslexic 10- or 11-year-old boy the conversation turns to eventual outcomes and inevitably to higher education, even though sometimes the assessment of the boy places him in the lower percentiles. Yet this is the ambition, the expectation, the measure of success for which he will have to strive, however inappropriate it may be. It is worth noting that, although ex-pupils have achieved excellent degrees, our first big-earning pupil has made his mark by entrepreneurial and interpersonal skills and not via a university course.

Gauging, constantly adjusting to and interpreting expectations will have a huge effect on stress levels in pupils. Sadly some of these expectations are out of the control of the pupil and even of his teachers and parents. Increasingly, governments are the source of expectations, which are set with little or no acknowledgement of learning difficulties.

As has already been said, secondary education expects pupils to be largely independent in their learning skills. Apart from reading and writing, pupils are expected to have study skills, organize their time and belongings, and be able to revise and hold information in memory. For many pupils with dyslexia, each of these expectations is a problem and a potential source of stress.

The demands of secondary education

In secondary education, pupils move from teacher to teacher, constantly adjusting to different personalities, teaching styles and academic requirements. There has to be an element of negotiation with each teacher and a failed negotiation in one lesson can carry through to the next lesson and beyond. In my experience, pupils with dyslexia, and possibly any disabled pupil, seek consistency and are vulnerable to stress when any routine is changed or disrupted.

No subject is immune to the creation of stress for a pupil, e.g. games can make demands that some pupils know they cannot meet. Perhaps a pupil has to remember a sequence of instructions; perhaps he has to dual task as in controlling the football while remembering the game plan; perhaps he takes a long time to get changed or constantly forgets to bring all his kit. The pupil builds a reputation and then regularly confirms it because his problems are not readily circumvented.

Working in a team situation (not exclusive to games) can also create stress because responsibility to the team's success is a source of peer pressure.

Even very talented sports players can suffer the consequences of stress. A very able javelin thrower was participating in the Independent Schools' Association's national finals. His first two throws were a long way short of his normal distance and his coach could see that the athlete was not coordinating his upper and lower body movements. The stress of competing in a national competition in a big stadium and with a large crowd interfered with his ability to dual task. Quiet reassuring words and some careful rehearsals led to a final, winning throw. The coach had to be aware that, despite the athlete's previous successes and his carefully trained confidence, stress could destroy all the preparation (an outcome that I shall return to later in a different setting).

Not surprisingly, any examinations can be creators of stress. The English education system sets great store by examination and test results. An American friend of mine said how much she admired the English education system, but could not understand how any parent could allow their child to be exposed to such examination pressure.

There is just so much about an examination to create stress, whether it is the pressure of time or the sight of a blank sheet of paper on which to create an essay. And the occasion is exclusive. The pupil has to perform well on that day and at that time. Yet pupils with dyslexia are often labile and usually aware of their fluctuations in levels of performance. This awareness of their own lack of control over such fluctuations will add even more stress to an already stressful situation.

We now bring in an outside consultant psychologist to talk our Year 11 pupils through some relaxation techniques and to review study skill strategies. Even the open discussion and shared experiences of the session help.

I asked an ex-pupil what gave him stress when he was at school. He told me that it was hearing the phrase 'Never mind, you did your best' because it meant that he had failed. He would appraise the challenge, be it an examination question or a history essay or a 400-metre race and, if he felt he couldn't succeed, he wouldn't try. In a research study (Chinn, 1995) looking at the errors pupils made in numeracy questions, I found that the calculation errors made by pupils with dyslexia were much the same as their non-dyslexic peers,

except for the 'no attempt' where the pupils with dyslexia did not even start the question. The comparison was quite startling, with the proportion of pupils with dyslexia avoiding answering questions being far greater than that of the non-dyslexic pupils. (For example, for the question 6040 ÷ 10, the percentage of non-dyslexics making no attempt was 6% but for the pupils with dyslexia it was 40%.) Stress can prevent pupils from taking a learning risk, and risk-taking is an important part of learning.

Coursework time can be very stressful (for parents and teachers, too). Although examinations create stress, the coursework load on a typical Year 11 (age 16 years) pupil in England can create equal levels of stress over a longer period of time. It is possible to manage the timetable coursework deadlines a little, but different combinations of GCSE subjects for different pupils make this quite a difficult task for a school.

Coursework is an obvious area where technological advances have had an impact. The use of a word processor has been such a benefit to many pupils with dyslexia. In the not so distant past, when work had to be handwritten, correcting errors was a necessity but inevitably gave negative feedback. Sadly the 'corrected' version would often have new mistakes. The ease of correction of work on a word processor is almost miraculous and a teacher can suggest a correction, knowing that it is less likely to create stress for the pupil.

Voice and speech recognition via computers is also beginning to impact on the production of written work and thus on stress. I feel that this innovation has received bad or, at best, lukewarm press because people have used it without due regard for its limitations and, consequently, with unrealistic expectations. For some of our pupils, it has been amazingly effective but, as with all innovations and interventions, not for all. Some do not adapt, perhaps because it is too slow or just because, however miraculous it may be to us, they are not computer users. Our philosophy is to work with each individual as an individual.

In Year 9, pupils have to choose some of the subjects that they will study to GCSE level. This can be a time of stress for some because the choice can seem to be very significant and there are influences from several sources adding to the dilemma. Some sound common sense is needed to put the issue into perspective. The basic question to ask is how many grades are needed to open up the next door. Not many pupils need 10 A* grades in 10 very language-based subjects.

Another possible source of stress is the anxiety of being put in a lower set, especially when one of the key deciding factors is ability in written English. A Year 9 pupil left the College to return to mainstream education. Despite reassurances to his parents, he soon found himself in the lower sets and due to take only two subjects to GCSE level. The reality can sometimes confirm the stress.

The prospect of future careers, and indeed of leaving the familiar world of school, can also worry some pupils into stress. Once again expectations come into play. As ever, it is the balance and adjustment that counts. Expectations can be too grand or may start as virtually non-existent and grow appropriately. An ex-pupil started at the College with no ambition and with no experiences to suggest that any expectation was appropriate. Steadily his ability and determination won through and his horizons widened to include sixth form work, then undergraduate work, a degree and then a Masters. But still, for him, writing can be stressful.

In a specialist school such as Mark College we try to provide the correct levels of support for learning at every stage of a pupil's school career. The hardest time to judge this level of balance is in Year 11, the final year in the College. We are trying to finalize our programme of developing independence and at the same time offering support for examinations and coursework, the most stressful time of their school career.

Pupils are ready to move on, yet there is concern that future levels of support will not be the same (or indeed if that would be appropriate anyway), that dyslexia is a lifetime condition, and that stresses will be greater and handled alone or with lower levels of support.

So, in secondary education, there are so many factors, usually interacting, that create stress. The situation is made even more complex by the labile nature of the individual, or circumstances from outside school that can create a reaction to a set of factors that has not hitherto caused a problem.

The signs and manifestations of stress

The signs and manifestations of stress vary between and even within each individual. Outbursts of anger are the most dramatic and tend to generate immediate responses. When I worked as head of a specialist school in Maryland in the early 1980s, we made good use of our 'time-out' room. It was a simple idea to allow a pupil to excuse himself from a lesson if he felt that his stress levels were becoming unmanageable. The culture of the school was such that this was simply accepted by teachers, pupils and administrators. It was not abused by the pupils.

Anger outbursts often result in scenarios that are hard to reverse or forgive. Berne's transactional analysis work from the 1960s has recently been revived by Barrow et al. (2001) and still has some very effective ways of addressing problem interactions between pupil and teacher.

Stress is probably the cause of some of the psychosomatic illnesses that we see in our pupils (some more obvious than others), e.g. there was a 14-year-old pupil who was always 'ill' on games days. We have no direct evidence, but anecdotally we see some asthmatic problems becoming less serious as pupils settle into a more empathetic environment.

Stress can also manifest itself as withdrawal. This could be considered to be more problematic than anger outbursts, in that it can go unnoticed. Pupils may not communicate their worries to others.

One of the explanations for withdrawal and helplessness is attributional style (Seligman, 1996). We were introduced to this construct by a contact in the insurance industry. He worked on the attributional style of salespeople and people who have been long-term unemployed. Both groups experience significant and frequent negative feedback, as do many dyslexic pupils. This experience of negative feedback is one of the reasons that we try to improve the emotional toughness and resilience of our pupils. Seligman encourages 'learned optimism'. He explains that the way a person explains bad events is their explanatory style based on three dimensions: pervasiveness, personalization and permanence, e.g. a pessimistic pupil may think that all teachers are unfair, that he is a stupid pupil and that nothing ever goes right for him. An optimistic pupil will think that one particular teacher is unfair, that he is just not good at the Pythagoras theorem (say) and that maybe he is just having a bad day. Learned-helpless pupils believe that there is little relationship between effort and success. So many pupils with dyslexia experience that particular belief after putting great effort into a piece of written work, only to have it dismissed by an unsympathetic, unaware teacher. The implications of attributional style and consequential stresses for the classroom management of included pupils with dyslexia are considerable.

The role of the pastoral system

Many of these problems will become the responsibility of the pastoral system of the school. Channels of communication are one of the most important parts of any pastoral system. It is so important to collect information, to recognize patterns of behaviour, to notice changes in attitude and, whenever possible, to be pre-emptive. Two of the most important characteristics of effective pastoral staff are the abilities to observe and listen (as opposed to see and hear).

Sadly, many pupils with dyslexia reach the teenage years with very poor perceptions of their own value. They have often been exposed to failure and may have become discouraged and despondent. Teachers can try to repair this damage and certainly prevent more having damage layered on top of existing scars.

Still, we have to remember individual differences. Adolescents will respond differently to similar stresses as they search for their roles in life. The more extrovert personalities appear to cope well with experiences and to handle social situations quite competently, but they may also react impulsively and with little consideration for longer-term consequences. The quieter more introverted personalities may perceive their world as

threatening and thus be less likely to take the risk of being involved in social situations. Although interventions may help the extreme consequences of these personalities, experience suggests that there may be limits to changes in some cases. But on a single incident basis, a careful and appropriate intervention timed correctly can often pre-empt problems. This may simply be a few words of encouragement or an acknowledgement of a recent success.

Ways of addressing stress

A sensible source of suggestions on how teachers could help address the problems of stress is the pupils themselves. Pupils at a Somerset comprehensive school listed the ways teachers could help (Thomson and Chinn, 2001). Any of these suggestions would prevent or reduce stress:

- help being given quietly and discreetly to individuals
- being given more time
- having handouts that summarize work covered in lessons
- marking work in dark colours (and especially not red), tidily
- praise
- working in smaller groups
- teachers who are aware of dyslexic difficulties and care
- grades that show individual improvement
- work being judged for content, not spelling
- access to catch-up exercises.

They also listed behaviours and attitudes that could cause stress, including:

- teachers who go too fast
- being expected to produce the same amount of work in the same time as non-dyslexic peers
- teachers who do not stick to the point and overstretch my short-term memory
- teachers who know I am dyslexic but do not help me (but not being patronized)
- too much copying from the board, and teachers who clear the board too soon

- having test results read out loud
- being told off when I'm asking a friend for help
- confusing dyslexia with stupidity
- being made to read aloud in class.

Appropriate responses to these problems are self-evident, but again the importance of awareness and pre-emptive actions is emphasized.

Finally, I take a brief look from the teacher's perspective. In our ongoing European study into problem behaviours of the included pupil, teachers ranked the four behaviours listed below as highest for pupils with dyslexia. I suspect that these could be the cause of stress for some teachers, but again we return to awareness:

1 having the correct equipment
2 starting work without individual instruction
3 completing written tasks
4 misinterpreting instructions.

Conclusion

When I lecture about the learning problems pupils with dyslexia have with mathematics, I emphasize the importance of being aware of the sources of potential difficulties. Many problems in mathematics can be prevented by proactive awareness. The same is true of stress. There must be an awareness of, and appropriate adjustment to take account of, the factors, the circumstances, the situations and the individual, if the harmful aspects of stress are to be minimized.

References

Barrow G, Bradshaw E, Hewton T (2001) Improving Behaviour and Raising Self-Esteem in the Classroom. London: Fulton.

Chinn SJ (1995) A pilot study to compare aspects of arithmetic skill. Dyslexia Review 4: 4-7.

Gardner H (1983) Frames of Mind: The theory of multiple intelligences. New York: Basic Books.

Seligman M (1996) Learned Optimism. New York: Pocket Books.

Thomson M, Chinn SJ (2001) Good practice in secondary schools. In: Fawcett AJ (ed.), Dyslexia: Theory and good practice. London: Whurr, pp. 286–291.

Chapter 4

Stress factors in the college student

DOROTHY GILROY

The personal counselling element in study skills teaching

This chapter is based on experiences of working with over 500 undergraduates, assessed as dyslexic, who have been given academic and personal support by the Dyslexia Unit at the University of Wales, Bangor, since work with undergraduates was established on a formal basis in 1978. (For a description of this work, see Gilroy, 2000) The student service was originally set up when, as a language-trained tutor, I was appointed to help six students with study skills, particularly essay writing. The service was seen principally in terms of academic support and there was perhaps the underlying assumption that because these students had 'made it' to university (quite an achievement for dyslexic students in the 1970s) they would be fairly confident and able to cope. However, within the first year of its operation a strong need for personal counselling emerged; this need became evident as the relationship between the tutor and the students developed and the students felt able to express their personal anxieties. It became obvious that their feelings, attitudes and motivation were intertwined with the technical aspects of study: problems with study triggered off a whole pattern of anxiety and resurrected underlying insecurities which, in turn, further inhibited their ability to cope with their academic work. Our approach to study, therefore, has always considered the stress factors of the dyslexic student and treated him or her as a 'whole person', an approach that was reinforced by Hales (1994) in a study entitled 'The human aspects of dyslexia'. Over recent years researchers have realized that the personal and emotional effect of dyslexia on academic study is more important than was previously acknowledged (Riddick et al., 1997, 1999; Singleton, 1999).

University students can be self-analytical, reflective and articulate; coming into a new environment, they are also able to look retrospectively at their

28

home and school experiences, and express their feelings about them. A support teacher of students with dyslexia will learn a great deal about the anxieties that many of them have experienced in the past; at an initial interview or after assessment, it might become evident that the balance of the relationship between personal stress and insecurity, and acquiring academic skill, may have to be very carefully considered: with some students their stress may be alleviated by setting to work immediately upon a language or study problem; with other students their stress may inhibit their study and no real academic progress can be made until the student starts to come to terms with his or her personal emotions. Some students may need professional counselling to help them overcome their past disadvantages (Goodwin, 1998; Singleton, 1999).

The specific difficulties of dyslexic students and their need for support may not be readily understood by mainstream subject tutors, who may have little knowledge of dyslexia. They may argue that all students suffer from stress and indeed students with dyslexia fit the general pattern of study stress revealed in Milner (1980), Raaheim and Wankowski (1981), or Peelo (1994). However, students with dyslexia have a specific language disability that may perhaps have caused them much difficulty in their earlier school career (Edwards, 1994; Riddick, 1996), which continues to make them more anxious and more prone to stress; these stress symptoms, in turn, intensify the language and sequencing difficulties caused by dyslexia.

The service offered by the Dyslexia Unit involves study skills support, both group and individual, personal counselling, and help with claiming the Disabled Students' Allowance. In general, registration with and attendance at the Dyslexia Unit are voluntary, although over the years of its existence several students have been admitted to the university on condition that they attend the Unit sessions. Approximately 15 per cent, although being aware of the service, have turned to it only in moments of crisis (a typical comment on the 1994 service evaluation was: 'I did not come in very often, but I always knew that you were there to turn to.').

Students who feel under stress and who need urgent personal counselling may in fact come during the set study group period. For some of them this is the deliberate choice: they will be aware that there are other students present and they may, in fact, have chosen to share their problems with these others. On these occasions the whole group may come together and respond interactively, and the mutual discussion and support can be very positive; there can be a real understanding and sharing of feelings among the students and often some follow-up support is informally arranged. One student described the group as her 'lifeline.'

Most students, however, prefer to see the tutor-counsellor on their own in the Unit where, as with any counselling service, the room is made relaxing

and non-threatening. A student may choose to seek specific help because she is stressed and over-anxious. Another student may come in for a study session but indicate an inability to progress with his work because of underlying stress factors. Very occasionally, their anxieties are so great that they need a point of contact available outside office hours. This may simply involve talking to the tutor over the telephone; indeed one student was guided through the evening before her finals by a series of telephone calls in the course of which she was talked through a panic attack, and offered suggestions on last-minute revision and examination strategy for the following day. A visit to a student's room can be a shrewd indicator of the type of stress a dyslexic student may suffer: her personal belongings may be in total disarray, there can be piles of washing to be done, she might not be eating properly, her work could be hopelessly disorganized with notes and books scattered untidily around. In short, she has lost control of her own coping strategies and organization, and her personal welfare and academic welfare are suffering. Under stress, a student's problems can seem to him or her quite overwhelming; coupled with this a student with dyslexia may not have a very good sense of timing, so the demands upon a tutor–counsellor to offer support at such crisis moments can be quite considerable. It is, of course, to be borne in mind that many students with dyslexia have had very supportive parents or teachers and hence can at times feel isolated at university; equally, parents may feel their own anxieties about how their son or daughter is coping and convey these to the student. Finally, it is important of course to impart to the students that all work of this nature is totally confidential; names are never released without the student's permission.

What has thus evolved from work with the student group is a clear indication of the stress factors that may affect a dyslexic student at university. This stress will now be examined in more detail, looking first at the particular demands of university life and their effect upon the student with dyslexia, second at the more deep-rooted anxieties that may exacerbate the reactions of many students to themselves and their work in this specialized environment; finally some ways in which we might 'manage' the stress of dyslexic students are discussed.

Specific stress factors in study at undergraduate level

University study operates almost entirely through the written word in a very specialized environment; this can therefore place great pressure upon dyslexic students. Gauntlett (1990) indicates that dyslexic difficulties persist into adult life and increase in magnitude in situations that place great emphasis on written language skills. McLoughlin et al. (1994), writing on counselling adults for study and work, have found that a change in personal

or working life increases the likelihood of dyslexia coming to light; this has been shown in the Unit at Bangor by the number of mature students who have returned to learning after several years and who come forward for assessment for the first time. Although students with dyslexia have proved their abilities by being accepted at university in the first place, academically the discipline is more impersonal and more stringent, and certain skills are needed that they may not have used at school (Gilroy and Miles, 1995, Chapter 3; Singleton, 1999, Section 10). Tackling these skills may highlight difficulties that students might have thought they had overcome, or bring to light new difficulties.

Coping with university life, both academic and personal, places demands upon the student to have some structure in his weekly routine. University study can be much more open-ended than school or college work, and students have more responsibility for their own private study. There seems to be more free time to fill in; there is no set homework timetable and submission dates for essays are often set weeks ahead. This may necessitate organizing a study timetable, coping with deadlines, getting to the library and dealing with books on short loan. This can involve planning and time-management tasks which can be very stressful for a student with dyslexia; organizing study also places many demands upon the short-term memory – there is usually much diverse information to process during an academic week. Our students with dyslexia have often described themselves as having 'cluttered brains'. Stacey (1994) writing as someone with dyslexia states:

> . . . our minds are wired differently so that we think in unexpected ways. . . . The result is that we've ended up with muddle in our minds.

This 'muddle' can of course lead to a holistic, lateral, creative way of thinking; however, it can also result in an overcrowding of the brain so that the student cannot sort out the thoughts into clear structures, particularly when stressed. Coupled with this, an analysis of the work patterns of the students in the study group reveals that, in general, dyslexic students have to work longer and harder than their non-dyslexic peer group to achieve the same ends – often written assignments will take twice as long. It is harder for them to catch up by dashing off work quickly; even catching up on a missed lecture may be very difficult because it will be difficult for them to copy out someone else's lecture notes. The awareness of this can at times make students quite bitter. Students may feel that their lecturers do not appreciate the amount of effort they have put into their work – this is often highlighted in laboratory reports, when dyslexic students have performed very ably in the practical but then get a low mark because of the way they have written up the work (Riddick et al., 1997).

Certain aspects of study in higher education can cause dyslexic students stress because they place demands on areas in which they have specific difficulties.

McLoughlin et al. (1994) see the major difficulty for dyslexic adults as being 'an inefficient working memory'. There are also difficulties in processing rapid information and a continuing slowness in reading speed (Miles, 1986). The psychologists' reports on many of our students reveal slower than average reading and writing speeds. As much teaching in higher education is done by formal lectures, note-taking in lectures can therefore prove extremely stressful for a student with dyslexia. Most courses are now structured on a modular system – hence there may be up to 200 students in one lecture, a difficult number for a lecturer to cope with, and lectures may be given at speed, supplemented by the use of overhead projectors or power point; thus there is a large amount of visual and oral information to be processed rapidly and students with dyslexia can easily fall behind. This can lead to difficulties with concentration; the processing involved in intense and rapid reading and writing can tire the brain and the eyes, and dyslexic students often find that they can work only for short spaces of time. At university there is usually a heavy reading commitment, with larger more complex textbooks than were used at school; there is probably not the tutor guidance that was perhaps given on 'A' level or BTEC/GNVQ courses, and some dyslexic students find it difficult to extract information efficiently from their textbooks. They may also have difficulty in coping with the amount of new, unfamiliar vocabulary. Again, lengthy reading tasks can cause considerable tiredness; one student wrote, 'my reading is quite good now but I still find it fatiguing'. Some students may also find themselves faced with having to read aloud; universities are developing 'student-centred' learning where students read tutorial papers or present seminars; this can reawaken the horrors of having to read aloud in class for many students and they find a 'public performance', as one of our students described it, very stressful to cope with in front of a large peer group, many of whom do not know that they are dyslexic.

The difficulties of structuring, organizing and timing also occur in writing tasks. Essays at university are lengthier; they need careful planning and referencing, and an objective academic style has to be acquired. Spelling always remains a major difficulty (Gregg, 1983; Riddick et al., 1997; Hunter-Carsch and Herrington, 2001); in fact some students report that spellchecks make them feel more stressed because they highlight the number of mistakes and can also cause further confusion if the student does not know which alternative correct spelling to choose. Tiredness also leads to poor sequencing and structuring in written communication, which manifest themselves in a marked deterioration in spelling, handwriting and keyboard skills. At certain points in the semester, certain students go through patches of extreme

fatigue where they almost come to a standstill – this can happen after examinations or after an intense period of work.

There are certain times in a university career that are particularly stressful for the dyslexic student. The very early days at university can place heavy demands on memory, organization, orientation. There is the stress of the new environment and a new lifestyle and the anxiety of coping with new names, relationships and activities. Macfarlane and McPherson, 1994, describe 'fresher pressure' on non-dyslexic students as leading to anxiety panic and depression.) There is usually a heavy load of introductory forms to fill in and financial arrangements to carry out. Apart from this there are the demands of the new academic disciplines. Dyslexic students may worry intensely about their new pieces of work, wondering whether they have achieved the correct academic standard and struggling with, for example, the new vocabulary that they are having to learn. The new students therefore need sympathetic support and consideration during their first weeks at university.

When starting university, a student may also face a difficult personal decision, which is whether or not he will, in this new environment, admit to his dyslexia. From a sample of 80 students observed at Bangor, 15 wished to conceal their dyslexia completely. All of these students were diagnosed after the age of 15; perhaps implicit in their wish are bitter memories of school humiliation and fear of 'exposure'. Gauntlett (1990), in a study of dyslexic adults, states that a lack of understanding by many of the people with whom they have come into contact has meant that the 'majority' must continue to conceal their difficulty Out of these 15 students, four had parents who found their child's dyslexia hard to accept, and the students had not been able to discuss their problems at home. Students sometimes state that they have had the dyslexia 'label' firmly attached to them at school and have decided to start again 'incognito' at university; perhaps they now wish to assert more control over their lives and their studies. Others, commendably, wish to make the same start and to move on through the course on equal terms with everyone else. In acute cases not even the friends of these students know that they are dyslexic. This means that they are constantly living with a secret, constantly putting into operation 'avoidance tactics' and constantly worried about the fear of being 'discovered'. This living with concealment must inevitably lead to the build-up of stress whenever a situation occurs in which the dyslexic symptoms are likely to be revealed.

It will be evident, therefore, that it will be a moment of great anxiety when such a student decides to come forward to seek help because he is now having to admit his failure and break down the barriers that he has erected between himself and the world (in fact some of our students talk about 'coming out'). The student is having to ask for help when his very secrecy has indicated that previously he was determined to cope on his own.

To him it can be loss of face or humiliation; one student described it as a 'nightmare' that he 'was trapped yet again by dyslexia'. His stress at this initial stage of a relationship with a tutor may manifest itself in off-putting behaviour, aggressiveness and abrasiveness. He may seem rude and abrupt or he may adopt diversionary tactics, partly to prove again what he can do and partly because it is painful to face up to the problems for which he has sought help.

Perhaps the most stressful time is the examination and pre-examination period. Peelo (1994, p. 32) writes graphically of the fears of non-dyslexic students facing examinations in words that seem equally applicable to dyslexic students:

> They are frightened of shadows lurking at the back of the brain: I'll let everyone down, I'm stupid, I'm a fraud, this isn't going to work. Which leads to even heavier thoughts: I'll fail, I have no future, I'll be humiliated, I'll have no life.

Hales (1990) shows that among people with dyslexia those revealing greatest anxiety are those facing the stresses of examinations and career choices. The revision period is difficult because there is no external structure: the student is 'free' to work on his revision in his own time; there are the notes from the year's work to go through, and often they might not make sense. The student is having to work hard on memorizing and the memory can become overloaded. Fear of the examination itself can place an inordinate amount of stress on a student with dyslexia, and in some universities students have to fight for their own examination provision. There have been cases of students being charged with being a nuisance by asking for examination provision and of being reminded of the financial implications of their extra invigilation. The actual examination period can again be difficult, because students with dyslexia find the pressure of writing, working against time and reading carefully very tiring. In addition it is not difficult for examination fear to lead to a failing complex. A student who has had prolonged failure in the past may easily expect to continue to fail. Sloboda (1990) noted how anxiety about examinations led to a low expectation of future success in non-dyslexic students, and many dyslexic students show little confidence about their future results.

The pressure of academic study can therefore make a student with dyslexia very tense and liable to underperform. Raaheim and Wankowski (1981) point out that susceptibility to high emotionality and consequently greater proneness to reactive depression can be regarded as a powerful factor in academic failure. From observations of the behaviour pattern of the students in our study group over a period of time, it is evident that they experience intense high or low reactions to the success or failure of their academic work; they can become easily upset by negative criticism and react very strongly to what they see as 'hostile' or unfair comments on essays. To

dyslexic students these comments open up old scars. Evans and Smith (1979) evaluated dyslexic clients as being very sensitive to criticism and easily discouraged. Sometimes a student will not hand in any work because she is so anxious about it.

To some extent, however, this type of stress can be self-induced. A dyslexic student may not see that other (non-dyslexic) students have to undergo the acceptance of negative criticism to learn and advance. He may blame everything on dyslexia; we have had several pieces of work sent to us which have been below standard for reasons not necessarily related to dyslexia – poor referencing, irrelevant material, unsubstantiated comment – the student may find it difficult to accept that the marking of these pieces may be justified. This could reflect a state of self-centredness. Dyslexia may be ever-present in the students' minds; it may make them egocentric, and they cannot think out from themselves. As a result, they become quite demanding over their 'rights' and may go bluntly into a tutor's room to seek 'justice'. In turn, the tutor grows more hostile and the stress builds up on both sides. With some dyslexic people this can be linked to a lack of self-awareness – 'we lack the perception of things' (Hargrave Wright, 1994) – which is particularly noticeable when students are under stress.

Many other students exhibit a strong streak of perfectionism which in itself is very stressful; they seem to want to overprove themselves. An obsessive working pattern with impossibly high standards can result; one student asked me to help her improve on her folder of essays – there were in fact three As and two Bs. Another student drove himself too hard in the pre-examination period, worked for extremely long hours and in fact ended up with a much lower class of degree than he should have had. This, again, can happen to any student, but a dyslexic student has a high anxiety factor and it is harder for him or her to put a clarifying structure on an overloaded brain.

Students also experience good days and bad days, as recounted by Susan Hampshire (1981), Eileen Simpson (1981) and Ginny Stacey (1994). 'Bad days' affect the students in various ways, often making them frustrated because their difficulties seem stronger and get in the way of their academic progress. There are days when they cannot use the dictionary or take notes, when they cannot work out the library coding system, when they misread timetables and go to the wrong room. These 'bad days' can be stressful for dyslexic students, because it can make them feel 'different' from their non-dyslexic friends. 'Bad days' may be linked to tiredness, which can be a source of anxiety for students as they realize that they cannot work for long periods in comparison to their peers – students have, for example, reported feeling acute tiredness and subsequent stress in 2-hour group teaching sessions in the Computer Laboratory and felt that they coped far less well than their

non-dyslexic peers. Jean Augur (1985) in 'Guidelines for teachers, parents and learners' lists 21 key points of being dyslexic, one of which is 'excessive tiredness due to the amount of concentration and effort required'.

Anxiety and panic

Highly anxious students are prone to panic, which represents another form of acute stress. The student may panic when faced with tasks in which his dyslexia may be exposed, such as filling in forms in public or (rarely nowadays) writing cheques, which Vinegrad (1994) found to be the most common indicator in the ADO screening test for dyslexia. Students report feeling panic under rapid-processing tasks such as note-taking and, of course, examinations. Once panic sets in, the mind might seize up and the student can do very little (Singleton, 1999). Most students report having experienced moments during examinations when their minds go blank; they have described them as being 'like cotton wool', 'like falling into a muddy puddle', 'like being nailed to the floor'.

An extension to this type of panic-related stress occurs when the symptoms of blankness can go on for a period of time; the student's coping strategy is, in fact, not to cope but to opt out and she can come to a complete standstill. In cases observed, it seems that there has been an accumulation of work with which she cannot cope, maybe a series of deadlines that she cannot achieve. The sequencing tasks involved in sorting out what she has to do are too complex and the student can neither structure nor see a clear pattern so that even the simplest tasks become immense. Personal communication even becomes a burden. Several students have gone through lengthy periods of inertia and inactivity. For example, one student started to sleep heavily and it seemed that this sleep became a means of escaping from the round of tutorials and lectures that he had missed and which had then become too onerous for him to catch up with. At its most extreme, one student negotiated for a complete year off. He needed a total change and relaxation of his system and in fact got a very good degree after returning to university for his final year. This type of stress may be difficult for the tutor or counsellor to deal with because the student may not have the physical or mental energy, or indeed the necessary organizational skills, to come and seek help. It is at this stage that a counsellor may have to take a more assertive role and visit the student at home, or find out what has happened through one of his friends. The counsellor will of course have to weigh up the situation: the student may not be ready to receive help and may wish to be left on his own. In some cases, however, a student seems unable to be guided into any decisions and wants the counsellor to assume a more directive role (Singleton, 1999). This may involve helping the student to prioritize, perhaps by creating an 'action list', such as a highly structured timetable starting with

very short sessions. Students suffering this pattern of stress need careful monitoring, such as reporting to the support tutor on a daily basis.

Acute anxiety shows itself in another, indeed opposite, form, when the student reacts to his difficulties by becoming overactive; his mind becomes confused and he seems unable to structure or unscramble his thoughts: Mueller (1979) discussed the interference of anxiety with the cognitive capacity to study; students with dyslexia can dart from topic to topic in conversation and make illogical jumps in essay writing. Their work gets disorganized and the pattern of stress becomes self-perpetuating. They create disorder around themselves and can see no way out; therefore the disorder in their minds gets worse. Their stress may be reflected in their physical appearance, their eye movements and their body language. It is again important to help the student gain a structure in his work, perhaps even work with him on the details of his day-to-day life pattern.

Personal relationships

Some students with dyslexia can be quite withdrawn and solitary. Hales (1990, 1994) in his work on personality factors in people with dyslexia has found that certain groups of dyslexic adolescents prefer to work on their own, have fewer friends and find it difficult to join in with others. These traits have been shown by some students in the group, particularly when they are under stress; they become quite isolated, in which case their anxieties become intensified because they may not find people with whom they can discuss their difficulties. For other reasons too a student with dyslexia may suffer a sense of isolation. His general dyslexic problems may have led to tensions within the family and to his own feeling of separateness at school (Riddick, 1996). As has already been pointed out, a dyslexic student generally has to work much harder than a non-dyslexic student, and this again cuts him off from some of the socializing so necessary to student life. This can lead to a sense of envy of others; many a dyslexic student has used the phrase 'it's not fair'.

Over the years during which I have worked with dyslexic students I have also noticed a high incidence of illness: two students have had myalgic encephalomyelitis (ME); two have had irritable bowel syndrome; many suffer from skin trouble; and many seem to have recurring throat allergies. These seem to be related to stress. Another indication of anxiety is eating problems, which seem to occur fairly regularly; these can be exacerbated by dyslexia, because when a dyslexic is under stress a visit to a shop or supermarket can be quite a daunting experience. One student lived off bananas and milk because it did not make any demands on her. Two students have developed a stammer under stress.

The point needs to be reinforced that these students are away from any support structures that they may have had at school or home, and perhaps

from a familiar environment where their dyslexia was known and understood. They may have been considered high fliers at school and then may
find themselves in a situation where their dyslexic difficulties are brought out
more intensely. Although the climate of opinion towards dyslexia is changing
in universities, there are still members of staff who are not sympathetic.
Unless there is a dyslexia support tutor, the student often has to fight his own
battles; we have received many telephone calls and letters in the Unit, where
students are appealing for sources of help. I can quote from one such letter:

> . . . fends find it difficult to beie [believe] that I don't get A for exams as I really
> unperstand the metarial given. My letres [lecturers] do not unrerstand the
> problem, and so I wondrer if you had any material to which I could gie them.

Seeking such help can be very time-consuming and is often seen by the
student as quite a humiliating experience.

The effect of past experiences on self-concept

It can therefore be seen that the particular nature of dyslexia coupled with
the stringent disciplines of university life can cause students considerable
anxiety with their academic work. There is, however, a much deeper psychological perspective to the stress patterns of many dyslexic students. There are
certain students with more deep-rooted insecurities that stem from the past,
from having been branded as 'thick', from being ridiculed and misunderstood, from having struggled hard at school without efforts being recognized
(Edwards, 1994). These insecurities may be latent: they create a tentative,
underconfident attitude to work; they can re-emerge forcefully when the
student feels that she is losing control of her work or when she has received
negative comment. It therefore becomes very evident that the emotional
stress suffered in childhood or adolescence has had a very deep-rooted effect.
Kline (1978) spoke of the 'emotional carnage' of adolescents with dyslexia in
a paper which preceded 'Robin's story' (Jones, 1978), a mother's account of
her dyslexic son who committed suicide. Rawson (1988) refers to the 'scars'
(p. 47) left by dyslexia and Stevens (1987) describes the acute underconfidence of the learning-disabled adolescent. Miles (1993) states that most
dyslexic children whom he has met have faced appreciable hardship. Many of
our students have written about their school experiences:

> While I was at school I was educated to feel shame and worthlessness, to feel
> doubt in my own abilities and self-hatred. I was educated to feel small and useless.
>
> During this time my mother was told X is educationally subnormal and will never
> gain any examination grades.
>
> There was a terror campaign waged against me to get me to spell properly.

And from a poem:

> A hundred childehood years
>
> I stumbeld thruoh
>
> clutching at gors yelow flowrs
>
> that promised sunliet
>
> in this boalder-gray clif-egde
>
> of wrieting.

These past experiences may leave a deep scar, the result of which is that many students with dyslexia have a poor self-concept and suffer from low self-esteem. Riddick et al. (1997) found that the average self-esteem rating of students with dyslexia completing a self-esteem inventory was significantly lower than the ratings of the control group. The students with whom I have worked quite often compare themselves unfavourably with their peer group. In listening to a spontaneous, undirected, general conversation lasting about 20 minutes between five students, the following words and phrases were noted: 'hopeless at' (seven times); 'useless at' (five times); 'could never' (three times); 'mess' (twice); 'typical me' (twice); 'never been any good at'. The use of 'never' and 'typical' indicate that the poor self-image may stretch back to childhood and is therefore quite deep-rooted. In answer to a specific-ally directed question following this conversation four out of the five students said that they often felt that they were 'thick'. We can think of Margaret Rawson's description of 'Dyslexia Day in Community Park: there are many individuals present:

> . . . yet perhaps more often than is really comfortable we sense psychological stress, worry, and, in some cases almost palpable discouragement.
>
> Rawson (1988, p. 21)

This is borne out by an interesting perspective that has emerged in the Bangor student group over the past few years; since 1990 the number of mature students in the study group has increased by 60 per cent. Some of these mature students are new assessees, some have been out of education because of their dyslexic difficulties and have re-entered, perhaps through Access courses. Many of these students have lived with their difficulties in the past, suffered from them, but not become aware of them until university and then had to face up to them – yet they entered university with high expectations. For a mature student to be newly assessed as dyslexic can be very stressful; old fears and negative thoughts well up from the past, there is often anger at past neglect, there are worries about being 'disabled', about implications for children, for careers. These students can be extremely

underconfident and hence very anxious; they can also get very frustrated. They contrast with a newly emerging group of 18-year-olds who have benefited from the 1981 Education Act, been assessed at a young age and who have grown up with the knowledge that they are dyslexic. To a large extent they have learnt to come to terms with it and have also developed a more positive attitude. They seek help with their studies but do not suffer the deep-rooted anxieties of these other students.

Developing coping strategies

It is therefore evident that the particular stringencies of university life would suggest that it is advantageous for dyslexic students to have some specialist support. The overall aim of this support should be to alleviate the student's stress by getting him to understand his particular way of working, and hence helping him to feel that he can control his learning metacognitively so that he will approach it with greater confidence: 'The kind of service which actively engages dyslexic learners in dialogue about their styles of thinking, learning and writing' (Hunter-Carsch and Herrington, 2001, p. 173). It is very useful to start with a discussion of dyslexia, which can emphasize the research into the right brain, and indicate that dyslexia is constitutional in origin (e.g. Galaburda et al., 1989) – it is surprising how few students really know very much about what dyslexia is – and look at the positive ways in which students with dyslexia can use their particular skills to learn (West, 1991, appeals particularly to the students). The student should of course be made aware of multisensory techniques for every aspect of his learning. The study skills teaching should emphasize appropriate dyslexia-friendly methods of planning and organization, and help the student to find his or her way of coping with time management and memory and concentration. All students benefit from help with note-taking, both from books and lectures, and various ways of taking notes can be practised. Mind mapping (Buzan, 1994) is particularly useful. Good notes can teach planning and structure and hence lead on to the teaching of essay writing. Into this can be incorporated ongoing spelling and language tuition, for these are often the biggest worries of dyslexic students. Virtually all dyslexic students are now computer literate and there are many new technological aids such as voice-recognition programs and scanners that can be of immense benefit in relieving the student's worries about writing and editing. Dyslexic students need particular help and care during the revision and examination period, where discussion on memory, multisensory learning and work organization can be initiated, the aim of the tutor being to help the student to work efficiently on his own and to prevent him from becoming tired, strained, disorganized. Given this type of study support (see Gilroy and Miles, 1995) many students can forestall or alleviate their stress. Stacey (1994, p. 12) in her article for

other people with dyslexia says 'The good news is that you can learn what you want to when you find the right teacher'.

The role of the counsellor

Into this study skills work will inevitably be entwined a strong element of personal counselling. Ideally, counselling work with dyslexic students would be based on the general theories formulated by Carl Rogers (1951), in which counselling is seen as a 'client-based enterprise' where the student is led to discover his own process and techniques of learning. Counselling in dyslexia has been discussed more specifically by Miles (1988), who distinguishes between 'generalist' and 'specialist' counselling. At times, however, the counselling process may need to move towards being directive, that is, the counsellor becomes a teacher, even an organizer, and provides specific help and advice with the very problems that are causing the student confusion and uncertainty. The tutor/counsellor should respect the student's owner-ship of his work and, if he feels that he needs to assume a more directive role, this should be discussed with the student. I see myself as the student's friend and usually ask him, 'What do you want me to do?' (see also Hunter-Carsch and Herrington, 2001, p. 178).

The counsellor therefore needs to listen with care and empathy to the student's anxieties. There will be decisions to make about how to work with him and how to balance language therapy with restoring the student's self-confidence and battered self-image. As has already been discussed, when a dyslexic student comes to seek help he may be in a state of great anxiety. He may have had endless years of remedial work at school and have thought that he had overcome his problems. If he then receives bad marks at university, he may feel a failure yet again, exposed, vulnerable, inadequate. If he brings a page of error-ridden spellings, or an essay that has been criticized for poor structure, he may desperately need to have help to sort them out, and it will be important for the tutor to do what will offer the most immediate relief to the student. Kline and Kline (1973) cite cases where beginning with language therapy rather than psychotherapy alleviates the stress or reduces the anxiety to a controlled proportion. There are, however, students who cannot face any language work; their morale has been shattered by getting bad marks and they feel out of control. Sometimes they may feel angry and frustrated that their knowledge is not coming out in the way they want it to; someone beginning to teach them more spelling and grammar may make them feel more threatened and even more exposed and out of control.

For these students it is more important to listen to their difficulties and their past insecurities. Many of the students who have used the Unit have said that they have experienced a great sense of relief that at last they can have a

meaningful discussion about the problems of being dyslexic. About one-third of the students have said that they have found real understanding of their problems only for the first time at this level, and that this is the first time that they have spoken openly with someone outside their immediate family. This means that they have had years of school or adult life during which they have been unable to vent their feelings and hence have become accustomed to bottling up their anger and frustration. The 'specialist' approach to counselling is integral to the whole process, because it is the communication of an understanding of what dyslexia is and the effects it has that will create the most meaningful relationship between counsellor and student. Many of the people with whom we have worked at Bangor have said that having someone to understand their anxieties and frustrations was very important. Over two evenings, six university students in the group blamed on stress simple errors such as inability to recall the alphabet, inability to do simple maths, simple mistakes made on the computer. The students were aware of their difficulties and felt that it can be very embarrassing to talk about such 'mistakes' to people who do not understand. Miles (1993) states, from his experience, that many dyslexics need constant reassurance that they are not 'thick' or stupid. Dyslexic undergraduates have a lurking fear that they are not bright enough to be at university; this fear can become dominant when the student starts to feel anxious about his work. Part of stress management, therefore, should be to help the student to see himself in a more positive light; one student was recently encouraged by looking at the degree results of recent graduates – he needed that reassurance. Role-models of successful dyslexic people are also often encouraging.

A further aspect of a more directive way of dealing with the student's stress is to discuss with him how far his difficulties should be communicated to those who encounter him during the academic term. Some tutors do not understand how difficult it is for students to, for example, read aloud in class, or to take tests or orals. They may not have any sympathy for constantly late essay submissions or understand the sensitivity that a dyslexic student might feel. A counsellor can intervene on the student's behalf and hence preclude any further fear of his being put in a stressful situation.

When I first meet dyslexic students I chat to them about being dyslexic and at some stage I indicate to them that they might find themselves prone to stress; I feel that with this awareness they themselves can be more prepared for it, and perhaps more able to cope with it. We often discuss coping strategies. I have implied the value of group work; it can be very positive for dyslexic students to come together as a group and share their feelings. They begin to realize that they are not alone, that their difficulties are experienced by others and that they can discuss mutual ways of coping. Discussion, for example, about their varying memory techniques, can be very useful. So, too,

can a shared sense of humour – they can tell each other the funny things that they have done, whereas they could not laugh at themselves to 'outsiders'. It is interesting to read in Hicks (1990) that, in a study of dyslexic school-children, they said that the quality they admired most in a teacher was 'a sense of humour'.

Relaxation therapies

I encourage the students to practise progressive relaxation; yoga is very useful – it helps to concentrate the mind. We practise deep breathing and practise 'slowing down' – stopping what one is doing and clearing the mind before coping with one immediate task. We have tried juggling. Some of our students have used aromatherapy; some have practised reflexology; all of them listen to music – one student said it created 'a safe sort of little world'. We discuss creative visualization (Shone, 1984). I emphasize the importance of fresh air and exercise (preferably simple, non-competitive exercise such as swimming). I also try to make students aware of the importance of eating regularly. We discuss ways of making lists or flow charts of what needs to be done, and prioritization, the aim being to get the student to take things one step at a time and not to let his mind 'kangaroo' as one student described his overactive brain. Several of our students have developed creative hobbies, such as pottery or photography or drawing, which give them a real sense of escape – and achievement.

In conclusion, it would be useful if every teacher and tutor working with dyslexic students realized the importance of helping these students to maintain a positive self-concept and looked carefully at the links between language therapy and personal support. With greater inner confidence, a student might be able to overcome the stress and anxiety that can become quite inhibiting to his academic progress. It has been sadly illuminating to realize the effect of early struggles and difficulties upon many dyslexic under-graduates and to see how deep-rooted their underconfidence has become, and also how much determination and strength it takes for these undergradu-ates to cope with university discipline. Personal counselling aimed at supporting the dyslexic student as a 'whole person' should ideally be part of every study skills programme at every level of education.

References

Augur J (1985) Guidelines for teachers, parents and learners. In: Snowling M (ed.), Children's Written Language Difficulties. London: NFER-Nelson.
Buzan T (1994) Use Your Head. London: BBC.
Edwards J (1994) The Scars of Dyslexia. London: Cassell.
Evans JR, Smith LJ (1979) Common behavioral SLD characteristics. Academic Therapy XII(4): 425–9.

Galaburda AM, Rosen GF, Sherman G. (1989) The neural origin of developmental dyslexia. In: Galaburda AM (ed.), From Reading to Neurons. Cambridge, Mass: MIT Press.

Gauntlett D (1990) Managing the dyslexic adult. In: Hales G, Hales M, Miles T, Summerfield A (eds), Meeting Points in Dyslexia, pp. 240-4. Reading: British Dyslexia Association.

Gilroy DE (2000) Dyslexia and Higher Education. Bangor: University of Wales Dyslexia Unit.

Gilroy DE (2001) The Bangor Dyslexia Unit. In: The Dyslexia Handbook. Reading: BDA.

Gilroy DE, Miles TR (1995) Dyslexia at College, 2nd edn. London: Routledge.

Goodwin V (1998) Person-centred counselling for the dyslexic student. In: Waterfield J (ed.), Dyslexia for Higher Education: Learning along the curriculum. Proceedings of the Second International Conference on Dyslexia in Higher Education. Plymouth: University of Plymouth.

Gregg N (1983) College learning disabled writer. Journal of Learning Disabilities 16: 334-8.

Hales G (ed.) (1990) Personality aspects of dyslexia. In: Meeting Points in Dyslexia. Reading: BDA, pp. 98-103.

Hales G (ed.) (1994) The human aspects of dyslexia. In: Dyslexia Matters. London: Whurr, pp. 172-83.

Hampshire S (1981) Susan's Story. London: Sidgwick & Jackson.

Hargrave Wright J (1994) Coping strategies for adult dyslexics. Dyslexia Contact 13(2): 6-7.

Hicks C (1990) Dyslexic, retarded and normal readers' perceptions of the qualities of real and ideal class teachers. British Educational Research Journal 16: 199-207.

Hunter-Carsch M, Herrington M (2001) Dyslexia and Effective Learning in Secondary and Tertiary Education. London: Whurr.

Jones FE (1978) Robin's story. Bulletin of the Orton Society XXVIII: 175-81.

Kline CL (1978) Developmental dyslexia in adolescence: the emotional carnage. Bulletin of the Orton Society XXVIII: 160-75.

Kline CL, Kline CL (1973) Severe reading disabilities: the family's dilemma. Bulletin of the Orton Society XXIII: 146-60.

Macfarlane A, McPherson A (1994) Fresher Pressure: How to survive as a student. Oxford: Oxford Paperbacks.

McLoughlin D, Fitzgibbon G, Young V (1994) Adult Dyslexia: Assessment, counselling and training. London: Whurr.

Miles TR (1986) On the persistence of dyslexic difficulties into adulthood. In: Pavlidis GTh, Fisher DF (eds), Dyslexia: Its neuropsychology and treatment. Chichester: Wiley.

Miles TR (1988) Counselling in dyslexia. Counselling Psychology Quarterly 1: 97-107.

Miles TR (1993) Understanding Dyslexia. Bath: Amethyst Books.

Milner P (1980) Counselling in Education. London: Dent.

Mueller JH (1979) Test anxiety and the encoding and retrieval of information. In: Sarason IG (ed.), Test Anxiety: Theory, research and application. Hillsdale: Laurence Erlbaum Associates.

Peelo M (1994) Helping Students with Study Problems. Buckingham: SRHE and The Open University.

Raaheim K, Wankowski J (1981) Helping Students to Learn at University. Bergen: Sigma Forlag.

Rawson MB (1988) The Many Faces of Dyslexia. Baltimore, Md: Orton Dyslexia Society.

Riddick B (1996) Living with Dyslexia. London: Routledge.

Riddick B, Farmer M, Sterling C (1997) Students and Dyslexia. London: Whurr.

Riddick B, Sterling C, Farmer M, Morgan S (1999) Self-esteem and anxiety in the educational histories of adult dyslexic students. In: Dylexia. Chichester: Wiley, pp. 4, 5.

Rogers C (1951) Client-centered Therapy. Boston: Houghlin Mifflin.

Shone R (1984) Creative Visualization. London: Aquarian/Thorsons.

Simpson E (1981) Reversals. London: Gollancz.

Singleton C (1999) Dyslexia in higher education: policy, provision and practice. Report of the National Working Party on Dyslexia in Higher Education. Hull: University of Hull.

Sloboda J (1990) Combating examination stress among university students. British Journal of Guidance and Counselling 18: 124-36.

Stacey G (1994) Dyslexia from the inside. Dyslexia Contact 15 (I): 12-13.

Stevens R (1987) The learning disabled adolescent. SPELD: 3-6.

Vinegrad M (1994) A revised Adult Dyslexia Check List. Educare 48: 21-4.

West TG (1991) In the Mind's Eye. Buffalo, NY: Prometheus.

Chapter 5
Stress factors in the workplace

GERALD HALES

'Hello, this is Smith Engineering. Can I help you?'

'I'm enquiring about the job in today's paper.'

'Oh yes. We're taking names and sending out information. Where do you live?'

'Harmondswyke.'

'Can you spell that please?'. . . .

'Hello, this is Smith Engineering. Can I help you?'

'I'm enquiring about the job in today's paper.'

'Oh yes. We're taking names and sending out information. You have to complete the forms and send them back by next Monday.'

'Thank you.'. . . .

'Hello, this is Smith Engineering. Can I help you?'

'I'm enquiring about the job in today's paper.'

'Oh yes. You have to send in a letter of application.'

'Hello, this is Smith Engineering. Can I help you?'

'I'm enquiring about the job in today's paper.'

'Oh yes. You have to contact Mr Joplin-Smythe at Head Office I'll-give-you-the address-it's-Dearing-and-Cross-Enginecring-Limited-Dearing-House-34-Crescent-Street-Bristol-BS43-SQZ-Have-you-got-all-that?.' . . .

It is the experience of many dyslexic people that being dyslexic creates stress in the workplace. However, any attempt to collect statistics or numbers would almost certainly underestimate the extent of the difficulty because many dyslexic people find that the barriers arise before they can manage to reach the workplace. The scenarios above do not represent anything unreasonable or out of the ordinary on the part of the company. The procedures suggested are not in any sense strange or uncommon. It is for this reason that they tend to create even more stress among dyslexic people, first because they meet such situations frequently, and second because they know that their difficulty arises in circumstances that are not considered strange or difficult. It is not difficult to become frustrated and depressed under those conditions.

Stress is not any sort of inadequacy in the individual or just a temporary reaction to an inability to cope. The reactions to stressful situations are physical as well as emotional and psychological, and continued experience of stress can lead to such problems as high blood pressure and heart disease. An endocrinologist who has carried out major research into the effects of stress upon the body makes it clear that if a stress response is chronic, the constant presence of stress hormones begins to wear down the body's immunological system; whatever part of the body is weakest will show signs of dysfunction first (Selye, 1978).

It is not possible to separate entirely the stress arising from dyslexia at work and the day-to-day problems that are produced. Although this chapter – and this book – addresses primarily the stress aspect, this is inextricably linked to the practical situations with which dyslexic people have to cope. In spite of the common perception that both dyslexia and stress are factors that have only recently become 'popular', we have known for many years that the interaction of these has been a source of a great deal of difficulty in many people's lives (Witty, 1950; Beare, 1975). Not only has this included the aspect of stress and stress reactions, but also lower levels of self-esteem, and a more restricted level of work and vocational opportunities; it will surprise few readers that this often means that the dyslexic worker's economic situation is not always as good as might otherwise have been expected. The following are the main steps in which the stress aspect is likely to come to the fore:

- applying for a job
- interviews
- the first day(s)
- coping with the job (or coping with trying to hide the problem!)
- promotion.

This discussion of the work environment will follow this pattern.

Before you even have a job

Almost all jobs, whether large or small, full-time or part-time, important or trivial, require the completion of an application form. Some dyslexic people find this task so daunting that they do not manage to progress beyond the stage of looking at the form! Why is it a problem?

The reasons stem back to the general underlying difficulties experienced by the dyslexic person. Although it is often true that the major symptoms are seen in areas such as reading, writing and spelling, the problems that arise when doing these tasks are in reality only the external symptoms of what is happening in the brain. Put in its most general form, the problems are those of organization, especially of sequencing. An application form has an organizational structure – quite probably a very rigid one – but the chances of it matching the way dyslexic individuals organize the way that they think are very small! To complete a form, the dyslexic person must try to fit his knowledge into the straitjacket of someone else's structure, and this is very difficult. At best it raises the level of stress; at worst it is cast aside and never done.

We must also not lose sight of the fact that even where the form is completed, it takes a long time to do. Time is a major aspect of most dyslexic people's lives, and performance is frequently a constant trade-off between speed and accuracy This means that to do things accurately they take a long time. For an application the applicant needs time for two reasons:

1. To conceptualize each entry in a manner that suits the form.
2. To ensure that items are being entered accurately.

There is an additional aspect that will affect many dyslexic people; this is the fact that forms need to be filled in with a pen. It is now recognized that quite a large percentage of dyslexic people do not always work best with a pen, and the advent of the personal computer and word-processing has made this even more widespread than it used to be. You can't put an application form in the printer, however, unless you intend to go to enormous lengths to format your responses to fit the preprinted page, and so you are immediately debarred from the method that would create the best impression.

After all, this is one of the major functions of application forms: creating an impression. Although many would deny that this is the primary intention, and that they are meant to convey data about education, experience, skills and knowledge, in reality the overall impression given by an application form is frequently a significant component at the time of short-listing. From the applicant's point of view, an application form has only one purpose – to get you an interview!

What can be done about this? One extremely helpful step would be for employers to be more flexible, more prepared to accept application in different formats. A willingness to accept the same information, but printed out from the applicant's own word-processor, or to consider a general letter of application rather than the specific structure of the form, would alleviate the stress felt by many would-be workers. Of course, application forms request specific information, some of which is vital, but in cases where important parts are missing it is not difficult to follow them up, either during interview or separately. If it is really important that the layout and structure of the form be followed, it would not be too difficult in this high-tech age for employers to supply application forms on disk, so that applicants who wished could fill them in on the computer, but as with the introduction of portable computers in schools, there is frequently a lot of resistance to something seen as 'awkward'.

However, it has to be said that employers often lose potentially good employees because the first step in the process tests their writing and form-filling skills. Yet this is (at this stage, at least) not what is wanted. The employer needs to know about the individual – skills, experience, talents, etc. – and this could be just as easily encompassed within a telephone call, perhaps with a preliminary face-to-face discussion.

Reality dictates, however, that it is usually the dyslexic person who must cope with the procedure, and the chances of having the procedure changed much are extremely limited. There are some options to consider, however: in the first place, it is always helpful to take a photocopy of the form (maybe several) so that the task of completing it can be tried out before producing the final version. It is often useful to enlist the assistance of a friend or colleague, and it is quite possible for the writing on the final form to be his or hers! Where there is no choice but to complete it by hand, dyslexic people should consider whether they find such writing easier in capitals or lower-case letters and stick to one or the other.

Interviews: gateway or barrier?

Interviews create stress and anxiety in almost everyone, so in this respect dyslexic people are not alone. Generally speaking, too, it could easily be considered that the oral, verbal context of the interview situation would be better for dyslexic people than other methods. However, there are two aspects which mean that this is not always true:

1. Some dyslexic people have verbal and speech confusions.
2. Some positions will require participation in psychometric testing.

Verbal dyslexia

Dyslexia is often conceived of as a difficulty with areas such as reading, writing and spelling. This is generally perfectly true, but it is easy to forget, and a potential employer may never have known, that these are only the outward symptoms of an organizational inefficiency in the brain itself. In some people these functional differences also affect speech and verbal output, and so there are those who have difficulty in the oral situation.

We must add to this the effects that stressful experiences have on all of us. When suffering from stress it is more difficult to do things such as carry out detailed tasks requiring high levels of accuracy, be precise over controlling behaviour, or be sure that we give precisely the impression of ourselves that we wish. One of the greatest difficulties faced by the dyslexic individual in this sort of circumstance is that a small number of relatively minor errors will increase the level of distress, thereby increasing the likelihood that errors will be made. In this way the procedure becomes something of a self-fulfilling prophecy, as illustrated in Figure 5.1.

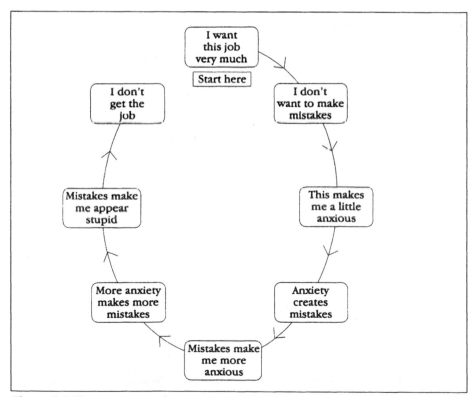

Figure 5.1. The stress conundrum.

Psychometric testing

Psychological evaluations are increasingly being used in the selection process for jobs that have levels of responsibility. In the normal run of events they should not present any applicant with worries beyond the normal anxiety likely to exist about the whole process. They are standardized instruments designed to measure certain aspects of human functioning in an efficient and validated manner. However, for the dyslexic applicant they can raise a number of difficulties.

In the first place many aspects, such as personality questionnaires, are usually of a multiple-choice format, which means that they involve filling in forms again, with the same problems as raised by the application form. Other types, such as verbal reasoning tests, are also commonly used to form some estimate of the individual intellectual potential. On a practical level, if the response sheet is designed to be read by a computer, the printing on it may well be in quite faint colours, and this can make it less clear for the dyslexic applicant to see which answers go where (to say nothing of the effect it might have on some colour-blind people). However, there is a point here for the professionals, too. In many dyslexic people their pattern of functioning means that they will not produce scores on a verbal reasoning test that do justice to their true intellectual position or potential. It is recommended that for people with this type of difficulty, a non-verbal test should be used. However, the stress position can be encountered either way, because if dyslexic people do not say that there is problem they will be faced with a difficult and inappropriate test situation, whereas if they do make a declaration they have the anxieties arising from doing that. The worry then is that they are seen to be awkward, that they ask for 'special treatment', that they give the tester difficulties because non-verbal materials may not be available, and that such matters might result in them being less likely to succeed in the process.

Finally, it must be remembered that interviews require instant responses. The individual is expected to provide reactions, explanations and opinions immediately, but in many areas of life dyslexic people need to take a little time to consider the data and formulate a response that truly reflects their understanding. Often a slow reaction in interview is taken not as a sign of deep thought about the matter in hand, but as an indication that the individual cannot cope as well as others. This is often inaccurate and generally unfair, and the dyslexic candidate knows that, of course; but that knowledge does nothing to reduce the level of stress either!

Taking up the offer: challenge or opportunity?

Many people might be forgiven for thinking that if the individual manages to get through all this and be offered the job, all the stress will disappear in a

cloud of euphoric relief, and so it almost always does – temporarily. However, the day comes when a new job must be started.

Taking up a new position is stressful for us all. There are new things to learn, new procedures to adopt, new people with whom to establish relationships and a new culture of day-to-day work. The dyslexic person, though, has the following added factors:

1.   Coping with all this and the dyslexic mode of operation as well.

2.   Stress arising from either telling or not telling people about the dyslexia.

Dyslexia is at its worst when the individual is in 'learning mode'. As the difficulty is one of organizing, remembering and using information in the right manner, time to consolidate and work through the information learned is very important. This means that situations where more and more information is fed into the system are the hardest of all, and this is exactly what happens (to us all) during the first few days in a new job. It is also why the situation of education or training is frequently particularly hard.

There are many things to 'take in'. This is fairly obvious when we are talking about such elements as company procedures, specific demands of the job, how equipment works, and so on; but it is also true in less obvious ways, such as remembering everyone's name, getting used to a new timetable of the day's work, and even finding out how to use a telephone system or input the code for the photocopier! Often it is the unwritten procedures that are more crucial to day-to-day harmony than the official rules. Knowing that Albert always sits in that chair, or that only Millicent does his typing, are the stuff of which smooth running is made, but are totally non-obvious to the newcomer. Although all newcomers will be forgiven once (or maybe twice) for getting it wrong or forgetting the details, the new dyslexic employee may find it especially difficult to internalize these aspects of life, which are not, after all, clear and obvious, and the tolerance of others for apparently stupid lapses will not last long.

It is in this context that the decision will have to be made as to whether to tell people about the dyslexia. It is clear that in an ideal world making the difficulty clear is a good idea. Not only will employers and colleagues not be able to make allowances for it if they do not know about it, but if they are kept in the dark they are not available when the dyslexic individual needs help, assistance or advice. However, there is much evidence that this ideal world is not the world in which most of us live and work, and it is understandable – if regrettable – that some dyslexic people decide that it is wiser to keep their own counsel. It does, of course, increase the stress factor once again, as the new employee is placed in the position of not only having to

cope with the difficulties of learning the new job, but also having to do it as a dyslexic person, and additionally working things so that that fact is hidden from everyone! This is a substantial mental juggling act and can easily lead to anxiety levels far in excess of what would otherwise be expected.

We should not underestimate the emotional reactions in this situation. Change is stressful and frightening for us all, but the level may be much greater for the dyslexic person. There may be real fear: fear of failure, fear of ridicule or fear of exposure as 'inadequate' in some way. It may well take the new dyslexic employee much longer than everyone else to internalize the fine points and become fully part of the team.

Doing the job

All the factors mentioned so far are temporary; they are hurdles that it is necessary to climb over, but once over them the individual does land on the other side. Having landed, though, there is then a long-term situation to be faced – that of actually doing the job, hopefully with as much success as everyone else.

The fact that the individual has managed to pass through the selection procedures, survived the interview and settled into a new position does not mean that the task is over or the difficulties solved. Here we should separate the practical aspects of the person's working practices and the aspects that relate to the person him- or herself. The dyslexic worker is not a deficient piece of office equipment that takes a time to get going, but once it is properly installed all the problems go away. He is a person, with all the reactions, idiosyncrasies and personal perceptions that this implies. We see this, among other things, in the attempts made to compensate for the situations in which the individuals find themselves. Gauntlett (1990) reports that:

> Language learning difficulties were found to have been an interactive influence on the development of the individual's personality. Highly significant differences were found indicating that the dyslexic adult is intelligent but retains an open mind when problem solving and as a lateral thinker is capable of producing unorthodox results.

In the results of research into the personality structures of dyslexic people carried out by me, a very high score was found on a measure of dominance, something that increases steadily from childhood (Figure 5.2). The pattern found among the dyslexic adults in that study indicates that they are independent-minded and assertive but also solemn, unconventional and rebellious. In the report of that work it was suggested that this is not surprising, because they need a level of assertiveness – perhaps even stubbornness – to cope with the difficulties they find in life (Hales, 1994).

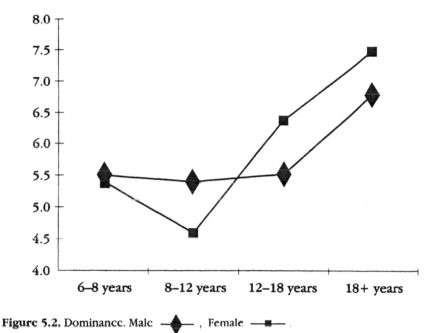

Figure 5.2. Dominance. Male ——◆—— , Female ——■——
The normal figure for non-dyslexic people is 5.5.

It is largely recognized now that the dyslexic pupil or student needs specific strategies to be able to pass through education; in the same way, the dyslexic adult needs strategies to cope with working life – although this is not yet so commonly recognized. Many of the strategies that could be interpreted as 'work skills' are often an extension of 'life skills', because the differing parts of the dyslexic person's life interact just as they do for everyone else.

This is important in terms of the wider question of 'coping', because it is not only the dyslexic person who has to 'cope', but those who work with him as well. Indeed, this can sometimes be the most major factor; people with all types of disability often say that their real disability is other people and their attitudes, and in this respect dyslexic people are no different. Co-workers and superiors will frequently exhibit the common misconception that dyslexic-type errors indicate a low level of competence or intelligence, and the constant worry that they might be 'caught out' by someone with entrenched (erroneous) ideas about the problem is a source of high anxiety levels for many. Even when matters are explained, this does not always lead to understanding or improvement. Klein (1990) wrote:

> Although many dyslexics are highly articulate, they often take and use language literally. they do not appear to be able to make the implicit explicit, or know how to get others to do this.

Explanation is an interesting and often difficult area for the dyslexic person. There is an implicit assumption by many people that because an individual possesses a condition, they know precisely what to do to fix it. This is in addition to the concept that it can be 'fixed' in the first place. The closest that most people's personal experience comes to that of any disability is illness; but illness, generally speaking, can be treated and ultimately gets better. There is an extrapolated expectation by many individuals that the dyslexic person is in a similar situation, and if only they were able to do the right things the problem would be eliminated.

To a certain extent elimination of as much of the problem as possible is the aim, but 'elimination' is achieved by the introduction and use of strategies that enable coping. The competent dyslexic adult has not cured the problem, but has learned how to bypass and circumvent some of the most obvious difficulties it raises. However, it falls to the lot of the individual to explain this to colleagues and others – including the boss – and once again the onus for containing the difficulty and doing what is necessary falls on to the shoulders of the dyslexic person.

In this respect, the results of a good and complete assessment are frequently invaluable. Psychological assessments to establish the details of the dyslexic person's functioning are relatively common at school level and not infrequent for students at college or university, but it is more rare for adults to need the results of a recent assessment. Nevertheless, such a procedure can provide not only accurate details and information, but can also be useful in providing objective third-party data that may be more readily believed and respected.

It has been stated earlier that the most common conception of what dyslexia means is that it affects reading and writing. This being so, many work colleagues will not be completely surprised at errors in things like spelling or writing, although it is often found that they do expect them to diminish over time. This phenomenon is seen with children, too, and it derives from the fact that most people's experience of not being able to do things leads to the necessity of practice, and if a skill is practised it does tend, usually, to improve. However, although it is true that a great deal of practice may improve the dyslexic person's functioning to a limited degree, lack of practice is not the cause of the problem, and improvement by this route is unlikely. Once again, the task of explaining all this falls upon the shoulders of the dyslexic worker, and once again it is necessary to expose personal difficulties in a public forum.

Earlier in this chapter, the difficulty of application forms was discussed. It should be remembered, however, that there are other sorts of forms throughout a great deal of working practice. Many employees are in a position of needing to complete such things as the following:

- order forms
- expenses claim forms
- internal requisitions
- accident record forms
- stock control forms.

People at a more senior level may be provided with more sophisticated forms, such as:

- performance reports
- financial data
- extracts from the customer database
- planning projections
- records of meetings.

This aspect is also frequently complicated by the fact that often such information as financial data is provided at a meeting (with no notice and chance to read it through beforehand) in small, poor-quality print from a high-speed printer; this can often mean pages and pages of rows and columns of figures which are supposed to be digested accurately and on the spot!

Apart from these specific situations, practically everyone needs to be able to cope with the following:

- payslips
- tax forms
- holiday records
- important notices
- diaries.

However understandable it is that someone with dyslexia should have difficulties with written material, there is still a level of embarrassment that never goes away entirely. This is important in terms of the individual's self-image, and self-image is important because it permits (or denies) self-respect among colleagues. Each one of us has an 'image' of ourselves within us – that something that each of us recognizes as 'me'. Of course it may be true that the image is sometimes out of step with reality, occasionally greatly so, but it is thus that we all manage to cope with our various imperfections and

inadequacies on a day-to-day basis. It is, however, important that each one of us has an image that it is possible to live with on a day-to-day basis; and a constant necessity to call this into question, or frequently being reminded that all in the garden is not rosy, will undermine the individual's self-image, self-esteem and self-confidence. If an individual begins to believe that he really is inherently inadequate, he will ultimately behave as if that were true. If that happens, not only will the individual suffer but the employer will not have best service from a valuable employee.

Although practicalities are important, we must not lose sight of the dyslexic person's right of choice. Some situations really are extremely difficult for a particular individual, and the decision that such a situation should be avoided might well be the best way of dealing with it. No one can know that except the dyslexic person, but such a decision can often need negotiation with the boss. This is in itself an anxiety-producing situation for most people, but where the individual can easily appear as if asking for favours or special treatment the stress produced can be high. This must be balanced with the stress produced by continuing to be placed in situations in which it is difficult to function properly, or hard to carry out the task adequately.

Onwards and upwards

As time passes, the dyslexic employee, like most others, considers the future, and the future frequently involves some version of promotion. This immediately raises the spectre of training, examinations and interviews–areas that produce a high level of stress among dyslexic people.

In some respects life becomes easier once the individual becomes more senior. Apart from anything else, it is quite likely that there will the provision of a secretary, an assistant or at least access to someone in the typing pool. This means that it is possible that some of the practical tasks can be delegated to another person in whom the dyslexic individual can have confidence, probably with whom some rapport can be established. However, this relationship must be treated very carefully, and there is always the worry that you may be thought stupid or incompetent because you cannot do apparently simple things that a much more junior employee can carry out easily and swiftly. And, of course, this position is usually reached only after a considerable time and the acquisition of some seniority. For the working individual, starting out on a career life can be very difficult; assistance is frequently needed but by no means always available, and for many people this position necessitates enlisting the help of relatives, family, friends and perhaps work colleagues either to advise or perhaps to carry out tasks. This scenario can produce stress on all sides – not just in the dyslexic person. There will be a degree of extra work for the other people who are helping the dyslexic ones

on top of the tasks they already have to do; there will be the necessity of maintaining the relationship, probably with constant explanation about the nature of dyslexia (some people are quite willing to help for a few days or a few weeks, but become puzzled when they realize that this is an ongoing situation), and there may be a degree of 'cover-up' if the dyslexic person is requesting help for things that ought to be done by them and the boss must not find out.

Avoiding tasks that cannot be done, perhaps by seeking out someone else to do them, does apply not only to small day-to-day matters. It is important that employers realize that there is a possibility that a dyslexic employee will avoid larger situations, such as training courses and examinations, that are difficult and do so by not seeking promotion opportunities. It should be the responsibility of the employer under these conditions to monitor progress and discuss the matter with the member of staff if it appears that chances are being turned down. This is not entirely philanthropic, of course, because a better-trained and qualified employee can be of greater benefit to the operation of the enterprise. It does need to be approached sensitively, however, as the idea of training will raise in the minds of many dyslexic people memories of experience at school, which may have established a fairly strong negative attitude to learning. Even in an employee who appears to have confidence, who is good at the job and who generally seems to be coping well, it is frequently true that this is a recent phenomenon. Although such an individual may have confidence and coping skills now, this was by no means always true. Such techniques are learned slowly, and the remembered experience of school and education is that the dyslexic position created stress, and the stress increased errors. As in all of us, the past experience influences present behaviour.

If it is agreed that training is appropriate, practical assistance in coping with the requirements is necessary; how this is done depends on how the training is done, but for internal training opportunities there would be much value in an employer (or the training division of a large company) seeking advice from others who do have experience of the ways in which dyslexic people learn. The dyslexic employee must have support and help throughout the whole process: offering an opportunity is the beginning of the process, not the end.

It is worthwhile for employers to remember that avoiding the difficult tasks is only one side of the coin. The other approach is to look for abilities, rather than disabilities. A person employed and perhaps promoted will have been placed in that position because of things that he or she could do, not in spite of things that he or she could not do. It is valuable to take this concept further. The level of understanding of a dyslexic person is the same as it always would have been; it is the practical aspects of performance that are

affected. Therefore, although it is likely to be very hard for them to carry out detailed tasks relating to language and information processing, such as extracting information at speed from complex documents, or correcting drafts of reports, their ability to contribute to wider contexts will be much better. As with all employees, they will function best if placed in a position in which they can utilize their personal abilities, and participation at levels such as policy-making and planning frequently shows a grasp of data not evident in the more mundane tasks.

So where does it all leave us?

Stress is increasingly being recognized as something that must be addressed, and this is true whatever the cause. The fact that in some cases, such as dyslexia, the cause is reasonably obvious can make it easier for everyone, but there is a note of caution here. Where there is an apparently obvious reason for stress it is sometimes too easy to make the link between cause and effect. With a dyslexic employee suffering from stress, there is an obvious assumption that the individual's experience of the combination of the disability and the work environment initiated the stress reaction, and of course this is highly likely to be so in many cases. The fact that it is obvious, however, does not necessarily make it right, and it is important that, especially if the stress symptoms are significant, other possibilities are investigated. These can range from other stress-producing psychological states, other life experiences or even physiological factors such as illness or an incipient tumour.

In practical terms dyslexia is a real disability. However, there are some differences between dyslexia and other disabilities. For one thing, it is invisible; it is not alone in this, of course, but there is a tendency for people to consider things to be 'real' only if they can see them. Thus, the individual with dyslexia never gets quite the sympathy extended to the blind person or someone in a wheelchair. In some ways the official symbol for disability – the wheelchair – does not always help. Dyslexia also stands out from other types of handicap because of a specific pattern of experience of the problem. In most cases of disability, there is a particular dysfunction that can be diagnosed and specified. The effect of this is to render it impossible – or at least, very difficult – for the person to carry out certain tasks, but with the capacity to do things in other fields much the same as it would have been without the problem. Thus, the deaf person can do anything that does not require hearing, the blind person can do anything for which sight is not essential, and the individual in a wheelchair can do all those things that do not require walking about. In dyslexia, however, there are important differences. On the one hand, the individual has a pattern of difficulties that makes it very difficult (and in some cases even impossible) for him to acquire and use a specific set of skills

and, on the other, the manifesting symptoms are those that are frequently seen in other more commonly recognized categories of human functioning: specifically, those who are of low intelligence, have poor skills or are bone idle! This aspect has been recognized for many years, and is commented upon in the Kershaw Report, published in 1974 (Kershaw, 1974).

One aspect that is frequently ignored, or at least given less importance than it should, is that of fatigue. A dyslexic person has to cope with the effects the disability has on functioning, but it is very easy to fall into the trap of believing that this happens only in relation to work, or school, or writing, etc. The organizational inefficiencies in handling information apply to everything in life, of course, and the fatigue arising from it therefore also happens all the time. This aspect of dyslexia is not obvious, but it is important, not least because over time it may have a profound effect on the individual. When someone has to work harder than others to reach the same level in everything, it creates a considerably higher level of pressure and fatigue, and often this is accompanied by the extra burden of being considered not to be working hard enough – or, at least, not as hard as everyone else! This situation is immensely frustrating, and can affect the individual profoundly, and can be a major cause of stress as a component of dyslexia.

There are two levels upon which stress in relation to dyslexia may need to be addressed: one of these concerns attempts to alleviate the difficulties engendered by the dyslexia, and the other is in the area of treatment of the stress. For the dyslexic person the two go hand in hand and may well both be needed; in both cases it is better to seek professional guidance rather than risk getting it wrong. This does not mean, however, that there is nothing that can be done. Far from it; in most cases much can be done to alleviate the stress arising for the dyslexic individual in the workplace, and, if the stress is eased, then not only is life a good deal better for the individual, but the entire environment becomes a much happier and more productive place for everyone concerned.

What should employers look for?
- Someone who is apparently much more anxious than the job warrants.
- Someone who avoids particular situations, such as never at staff meetings, or never writes memos.
- Any pattern of absenteeism.
- Refusals to take training.
- Unwillingness to consider promotion opportunities.
- A greater level of fatigue than seems to be likely.

Dyslexic employees should do the following:

- Work out the implications of telling people about their dyslexia.
- Plan beforehand how they will explain it and what they will suggest.
- Try to organize their working lives to minimize the most stressful situations.
- Arrange to 'get away' from time to time to consolidate data.
- Realize that stress is involved – not just dyslexia – and learn something about managing it.
- Make sensible choices.
- Seek co-operation and help where necessary: don't be too proud.

Employers of dyslexic employees should do the following:

- Understand that dyslexia is nothing to do with intelligence or ability.
- Realize that some alterations of working practices may be necessary (although these will lead to improved performance).
- Allow time for short breaks to consolidate information.
- Know that, for many dyslexic people, life and work are a trade-off between speed and accuracy; both are usually not possible at the same time.

Conclusion

There is a great deal of dyslexia about; indeed, as research continues it becomes increasingly apparent that there is probably more in the population than was thought. This means that there is an increasing likelihood that employers will meet dyslexic workers – and indeed most companies probably employ some already, whether they know it or not! We are therefore not addressing a minor difficulty that can be largely ignored, but something that exists in major proportions and affects a substantial part of the adult and working population.

Making proper provision for dyslexic employees is not, therefore, something that is simply good, decent and human, although it is those things, of course. It is something that facilitates the performance of a large number of competent and experienced individuals and enables them not just to work, but to work up to their full potential. In many cases where the dyslexia has not been declared, it may be that the stress symptoms are the first to become apparent, and initially there may be no apparent reason why a particular employee should suffer from stress. There are many reasons for stress, of

course, and it is important that all possible causes are investigated. These are not mutually exclusive: in a number of instances there might be a combination of other factors as well as dyslexia.

There have been many myths generated about dyslexic people, but we now know that the truth is that dyslexia is independent of practically every other factor. Dyslexic people are not intellectually deficient, they are not odd and they are by no means inadequate workers. They may have to organize their lives differently from others, but that does not mean that they perform less well. Indeed, in many instances it will be found that the problems that they meet are little different from those met by everyone else – but they are exaggerated and made more obvious.

Some years ago the 'Fit for Work' campaign used the slogan: 'Disabled workers are good workers'. This could easily translate into: 'Dyslexic workers are good workers'. It is much more true, however, if we can make it: 'Stress-free dyslexic workers are very good workers.'

References

Beare D (1975) Self-concept and the adolescent L/LD student. Journal of Texas Personal and Guidance Association 4(I): 29-32.

Gauntlett D (1990) Managing the dyslexic adult. In: Hales G, Hales M, Miles T, Summerfield A (eds), Meeting Points in Dyslexia. Reading: British Dyslexia Association

Hales G (ed.) (1994). Dyslexia Matters. London: Whurr.

Kershaw J (1974) People with Dyslexia. London: British Council for the Rehabilitation of the Disabled.

Klein C (1990) Learning support: A different slant on teaching adult dyslexics. In: Hales G, Hales M, Miles T, Summerfield A (eds), Meeting Points in Dyslexia. Reading: BDA.

Selye H (1978) The Stress of Life. New York: McGraw-Hill.

Witty P (1950) Reading success and emotional adjustment. Elementary English 27: 281-96.

Chapter 6
Dyslexia and the law

MELANIE JAMESON

An exploration of the nature of dyslexia will reveal numerous ways in which people with this condition can be at a disadvantage when they are required to process information at speed under stressful conditions – such as in the courtroom. Fortunately, well-informed and concerned professionals can help to lessen the impact of this disability.

Introduction

As dyslexia essentially impacts on the processing of information (both written and spoken), people with dyslexia can clearly be at a disadvantage in conditions that place heavy demands on them in terms of language and working memory; a prime example of this must be encounters with the legal system in general and court appearances in particular.

This chapter focuses mainly on the dyslexic as defendant. It is based on experience in the courts, advisory work for the Adult Dyslexia Organisation on legal matters, consultancy undertaken for the Law Society, and experience in preparing documentation for disciplinary hearings and employment tribunals dealing with claims under the 1995 Disability Discrimination Act.

How then can professionals in the legal system seek to redress this disadvantage? The first step must surely be to become informed about a condition that can affect one out of every 25 people appearing before the courts. Once one is aware of the likely areas of difficulty, appropriate responses can be put into place and, ideally, embedded in disability policy. Typical problem areas and ways of accommodating them are outlined at the end of this chapter.

No response to dyslexia is complete without bearing in mind the fact that it is known to overlap with two other syndromes: developmental coordination disorder/dyspraxia and attention deficit disorder. The former is concerned with motor skills and co-ordination, and includes a range of associated social and emotional difficulties. The latter, as its name implies, concerns attention span, distractibility and listening skills, and can give rise

to a range of behavioural problems. Finally, depression is not uncommon – in fact many of the adults and students with dyslexia with whom I work have been or are currently being treated for depression; this is yet another contributory factor adding to an overwhelming accumulation of difficulties.

Stress and the courts

As a specialist in adult dyslexia I have been called as an expert witness on several occasions; this has given me opportunities to observe dyslexics under stress in court proceedings. Two cases that exemplify the devastating effects of stress are those of CJ and MT which came before the magistrate's court.

The offence with which CJ was charged was, in itself, an illustration of the effect of stress. Caught speeding on the way to work, he was asked to blow into a breathalyser (although it was only 8am) but found himself quite unable to blow, only to perform the opposite action and gasp for breath. He was then charged not only with speeding, but also with the more serious offence of obstructing the police. Strongly advised to plead guilty, CJ reluctantly accepted that he would gain a police record. It was only after discussing the incident together that it became clear that there had been no wilful obstruction on CJ's part; on the contrary, he had been struggling to comply with the officer's request knowing that he had not consumed any alcohol, but the harder he tried to breathe into the breathalyser the more impossible it became.

The matter came before the magistrates with a changed plea for the obstruction charge: it was now incumbent on me to show that dyslexia could be a 'reasonable excuse' to explain why this involuntary non-cooperation had taken place. By coincidence, one of the specific points at issue was highlighted by Dr Anthony Clare in a Radio 4 programme on stress, in which he stated that 'stress affects muscle control and breathing patterns'.

CJ's performance on the day enabled me to witness how a normally sociable and chatty individual can be rendered almost speechless by the stress of questioning in court. A slight delay between hearing something and understanding it meant that CJ was unable to give an immediate response, but suffered a 'penny dropping' delay before being able to work out what the question was getting at. Sometimes his answer would reveal that he had missed the point, sometimes pronunciation difficulties would cause him to stumble or he would produce spoonerisms (recalling the crude depiction of dyslexia by the media). Being aware that he was making a poor impression, his stress worsened until he was barely audible.

Moreover, CJ had a short attention span, so he found it increasingly difficult to concentrate; one saw him narrow his eyes in an attempt to stay focused while he had clearly reached mental overload and was unable to

think clearly. Afterwards, although he won his case and was just charged with speeding, CJ could only comment: 'I went completely to pot there!'

At this stage, it is worth emphasizing that an expert witness is not an advocate – a role that specialists of dyslexia at times may find themselves drawn towards, but which undermines their function, namely to provide impartial and reliable information about a specialist area.

The second individual, MT, seemed unable to express himself without striding about the room (despite requests to stay still), using his whole body in an attempt to help the words out. His assessment showed literacy difficulties typical of dyslexia, but also many dyspraxic characteristics; these included weak visuospatial skills, clumsiness/poor motor co-ordination, disorientation and poor posture. Unable to confine himself to the small space designated for those giving evidence, he paced with wild extraneous arm movements. There was no problem with volume in MT's case; in fact his voice was overloud and his discourse rambling and often inconsequential, as though he were trying to avoid the question. He was unable to use words with any precision and so experienced great difficulties with verbal expression; this eventually caused him to weep with frustration. The oblique line of questioning worsened the situation as did the compound nature of some of the questions. Although he had prepared by making a few notes, he was quite unable to make sense of them in this distressing situation.

MT was charged with driving under the influence of certain substances. His doctor testified that the drugs he was on to help alleviate his long-standing depression would not affect his driving skills. Part of my evidence was to state that MT was unable to pass the standard test of sobriety for drivers because he was incapable, in any circumstances, of bringing his finger from a distance in front of him to touch his nose or of walking along a thin line, placing one foot in front of the other. The doctor carrying out the tests reported that MT was 'ponderous and slow, asking for all instructions to be repeated'; this is regarded as an indication of being under the effect of alcohol or some other substance but could also be interpreted as the struggle of an individual, with a weak short-term memory and tendency to misinterpret information, who though under great stress was attempting to ensure that he had correctly grasped what was required of him.

We can well imagine the problem an individual with dyslexia might encounter when having to mirror a movement, accompanied by instructions referring to left and right, demonstrated by someone sitting opposite. The failure to succeed in such a test, designed to assess fitness to drive, was another black mark for MT. The final comment in the doctor's report was: 'MT was unable to accommodate his vision.'

In conclusion, MT displayed severe language processing difficulties, which are typical of someone with dyslexia and/or dyspraxia under stress. In

earlier interviews left/right confusion occurred and, although he heard requests made by police and the police doctor, he did not necessarily understand what he was expected to do. Furthermore, 'poor accommodation' has been described as a visual correlate of dyslexia (Evans, 1996).

A high-profile case

In January 1998 Richard Branson came before the courts to make his case in a high-profile libel and counter-libel action. His dyslexia was not public knowledge at the time but his performance gave many clues. *The Times* report of the case describes Branson as 'um-ing and ah-ing', 'wrestling to remember events and dates' and drying up completely at one stage. He could only stutter: 'I'm sorry, my mind's gone blank . . . what on earth . . . I can't remember what the, what do you mean?' Speaking about it afterwards Branson commented: 'as a family we often just can't get our words out.' There could not have been more of a contrast between his hesitancy and confusion and the competent businessman who had set up and run at least 200 businesses.

Getting the message across

The experiences related in this chapter serve to show the types of problems that arise when dyslexia or dyspraxia (or both) combine with stress to aggravate a criminal charge or to undermine the individual's performance in court.

Preparing supporting documentation is a specialist area. The individual will need to have confirmation that she or he has dyslexia; this will usually be the report from a diagnostic assessment. It is important to refine the superficial understanding of dyslexia as a reading and spelling problem by explaining that it is fundamentally one of information processing, generally exacerbated by a weak short-term memory and often characterized by the failure of certain routine skills to become automatic. It is far preferable for the authorities to realize in advance that a person with dyslexia may well perform badly in court when information has to be processed rapidly, inferences grasped, and responses given promptly and concisely.

In the cases discussed above, it was also necessary to draw attention to the associated symptoms of impaired motor co-ordination. From this stage, one can proceed to the fact that these areas of difficulty are considerably augmented if the individual is under stress. In many cases, the assessment report will not bring out key factors relevant to the case, or document the effects of stress. As we are all prone to stress to a greater or lesser extent, it is necessary to make the point that the disruptive effects of stress are more severe in people with dyslexia compared with non-dyslexics, and can considerably impair their ability to cope. In CJ's situation, for example, I challenged the accusation that he *would not* comply with police

procedures and provided evidence to back up my assertion that he *could not* comply.

Illustrations of stress in specific learning difficulties literature include examples of problems in 'getting your act together'; the author of *Dyslexia – How would I cope?* wrote: 'My hands won't do what my brain tells them' (Ryden, 1992). In his publication 'Personality Aspects of Dyslexia', Dr Gerald Hales (1990) refers to high tension and anxiety leading to compounded difficulties and impaired chances of success. Dr Harry Chasty (ex-head of the Dyslexia Institute) stated: 'A dyslexic appears completely incompetent in situations of stress.'

'Two strikers' and the courts

A change in Government policy has resulted in many people on non-custodial sentences being returned to the courts, to the dismay of the Probation Service. It used to be the case that, when the third breach of the conditions of an order (now called a Community Rehabilitation or Community Punishment Order) occurred, the individual would be reassessed by the courts. When this was reduced to two breaches, many offenders fell foul of the new regulation, which was designed to illustrate the toughness of the Government's stance on crime.

Reformers maintain that the prison population now contains a proportion of 'two strikers' who should not be there. Failure to attend a session or keep an appointment as stipulated on the order is an example of a breach – this recalls an item on most adult dyslexia checklists (Vinegrad, 1994): 'Do you mix up dates and times and miss appointments?' In fact the 'no show' rate is so high that compliance officers have now been brought in. The number of agencies involved entails travelling to different venues and being 'processed' by an increasing number of professionals who may not be aware of any special needs or circumstances. The pre- and post-programme assessment procedure (designed to evaluate progress) is a gruelling 100-question psychometric test battery. Many offenders need help to read the questions.

OD is a case in point; he was given a Community Rehabilitation Order that required attendance on an Addressing Substance-Related Offending programme. He first turned up at the wrong place, assuming that his course was being delivered at the place where he had undertaken the assessment. This was ironed out but the following week he mistook the day and again missed his session. Whether this was a genuine mistake or the result of a growing disillusionment with the programme is not known. OD was unable to read much of the programme materials and did not like to keep asking for help in front of the group – especially as all the sessions were videoed (this is done to check that group leaders deliver courses in a consistent manner, but it must be off-putting for people who already feel embarrassed that they

require extra help). Even though he received one last chance, it was only a matter of time before OD slipped up again and was facing the stress of another court appearance. His failure to follow the import of the questioning and his inconsistencies, together with his breaches, convinced the magistrate that a custodial sentence was appropriate.

Employment tribunals

A particular consideration arises when supporting people who are making claims under the 1995 Disability Discrimination Act: the definition of disability is quite specific, excluding anyone who is not severely affected. The individual's dyslexia must have a 'substantial and long-term adverse effect on his ability to carry out normal day-to-day activities'. On several occasions I have been asked to supply supporting documentation for employees with dyslexia who are making claims under the Employment section of the Act; these claims have challenged the employer's failure to make 'reasonable adjustments' to accommodate dyslexic difficulties in the workplace, or alleged unfair dismissal.

Unfortunately, prolonged difficulties at work have often led to stress-related illness; it is therefore doubly debilitating that the (ex-)employee also has to face the additional stress of appearing before a tribunal. Having your competence probed and your areas of weakness exposed is a damaging experience, aggravated by the protracted nature of such hearings, some of which have dragged on over more than a year, involving experts on both sides testing and re-testing the complainant. (Fortunately this system has now been revised so that one 'neutral' expert is employed by the tribunal.) It is therefore advisable to try to resolve complaints through the Questions Procedure (DfEE, 1998), whereby the complainant fills out a questionnaire to which the respondent must reply within a given time limit.

Supporting witnesses and plaintiffs

Compared with tribunal and court hearings, it is much more straightforward to provide a 'covering note' for a plaintiff or witness. An example of such a situation occurred when a woman called as a key witness to a break-in contacted me because she knew that her dyslexia would make it very diffi-cult for her to present her evidence clearly, and respond promptly and effect-ively to questioning. She feared that the inevitable anxiety would further undermine her. After an interview and a study of her dyslexia assessment, it was possible to draw up the document below, which could then be circu-lated through her solicitor in advance of the hearing.

To whom it may concern.

Re: Ms P

Case: xxx

Ms P experiences certain difficulties that are characteristic of dyslexia, namely

- a weak short-term memory;
- auditory processing difficulties, i.e. she experiences a delay between *hearing* something and *understanding* it;
- word-naming problems, i.e. using inappropriate words at times either in error or because she cannot recall the correct word.

The above problem areas are exacerbated by stress, making aspects of functioning, particularly relating to memory, very difficult. We are concerned that Ms P will only be able to function effectively as a witness if these factors are taken into account during the forthcoming hearing.

A general outline of the implications of dyslexia is included with this document. Ms P can supply a copy of her dyslexia assessment, carried out in 1998.

In some cases, it appears that solicitors have relied on their own superficial and anecdotal knowledge of dyslexia rather than the documentation that has been supplied to them. As a result, some of their clients struggle to cope with a situation that is impossibly stressful for them. LS, a dyslexic seeking compensation for work-related injuries, was in this position.

Her request for help (dictated to her partner) contained the following record of her experience:

I have found the whole legal and medical process in connection with my accident and unfair dismissal claims extremely complex and stressful. This has been compounded by my dyslexia, and I am now suffering from bouts of depression. I have tried to make my solicitor aware of my dyslexia and how it affects me, but I have found that my dealings with her, and especially the medical examinations and interviews by specialists (on both sides) extremely distressing. Attempts to explain my dyslexia have often been met with examples of successful dyslexics such as Duncan Goodhew or Richard Branson - look how well they've done. Consequently, I feel I have not been able to give a clear account of the events and their impact on my life, and I am very aware that those I'm dealing with have little or no understanding of, and respect for, my disability. I find the whole process both exhausting and dispiriting.

The following examples illustrate some of my experiences:

- One of the specialists (who claimed to know about dyslexia) enquired of me early in our meeting 'I gather you have a dodgy memory?'. He was obviously basing this on notes which he had received from other specialists who had examined me. I found this very offensive and it had a major influence on how I was able to handle

the subsequent examination and questioning. I felt very pressured and that I was being bombarded by questions. He made it clear that I was entitled to leave if I did not want to continue with the interview and examination, but this only added to my anxiety because I felt that had I done so, this would be misconstrued by others.

• Another specialist mentions in his report 'during the interview it was often impossible to obtain a clear history . . . she appeared to have difficulty comprehending the questions posed and frequently replied "what do you mean?" she seemed extremely anxious . . . [she] gave a history which was extremely confusing and often blamed this on dyslexia and short term memory. However, although the history given was not always clear there is no obvious exaggeration when compared with the contents of the medical records.'

• The third specialist (who represents my insurance company) comments 'Ms S appeared to be far more nervous and anxious at this examination than at my last examination and it is probable that her dyslexia is tending to become worse. She also appeared to lack confidence . . .'.

As you anticipate, my confidence in the whole process and in particular in the individuals involved, has disintegrated. There seems to be little or no recognition that the stress of the legal and medical process due to the difficulties in the process stemming from my dyslexia (especially overload, memory, putting myself over, low self-esteem and lack of confidence) affects my ability to make my case. Moreover I have found the manner of some of the specialists at times both unprofessional and patronizing.

When required to fill in forms, I have pointed out that I am dyslexic and find them extremely intimidating and very difficult to fill in. It has now become clear to me that due to my dyslexia, some responses on my forms were not accurate of my experience, because of misunderstandings on my part.

LS had always faced particular difficulty tackling written material as a result of aspects of visual discomfort/Meares–Irlen syndrome (the condition is described below). When forms and documents were placed in front of her for comment during one of these interviews, LS could not admit to being unable to tackle them properly, being all too aware that she had already made a poor impression.

LS's letter concluded:

I am very concerned that I will not be able to put myself over as I would have wished in the forthcoming hearing. I now realize that in the last hearing I failed to understand at the time what some of the questions were seeking to establish.

In the face of prolonged difficulties, in particular the failure to gain appropriate understanding of and provision for her dyslexic difficulties, she has abandoned her attempt to gain redress.

Visual discomfort/Meares–Irlen syndrome

It is worth briefly touching on this subject, because struggling with unaddressed visual discomfort will heighten stress and make reading more problematic. Typical symptoms experienced when reading include headaches or eye strain, the blurring or shifting of print or a 'glare' from white paper that obscures the text. MT described print as becoming blurry and indistinct and found that his sensitivity to bright lights led to headaches. Other individuals are hampered by frequently losing the place, omitting and misreading words, and become exhausted by the effort needed for reading. It should be emphasized that people with dyslexia do not have a monopoly on these symptoms; some migraine and epilepsy sufferers report similar problems. A visual processing checklist is a good way of screening for these difficulties (Jameson, 1995).

It is now well established that certain types of visual dysfunction, not always picked up by routine eye tests, can be regarded as visual correlates of dyslexia (Evans, 2001). Ideally, an optometrist specializing in dyslexia and light sensitivity will identify and correct any visual problems and may prescribe tinted spectacle lenses, but both the cost of this treatment and a general lack of specialist knowledge mean that many individuals struggle unnecessarily. As regards the courts, visual discomfort could cause additional stress for affected individuals who have to cope with written materials and/or exposure to fluorescent lighting.

Ways forward

Disseminating awareness throughout the professions involved in the criminal justice system is a starting point in enabling individuals with dyslexia to give a proper account of themselves in the courts, despite their disability. The following summary is part of an awareness document, designed to highlight dyslexic difficulties that could arise during police questioning, interviews with solicitors or during court appearances, and outlines appropriate responses. The full article was published in the *District Judges Law Bulletin* and circulated within the Disability Unit of the Crown Prosecution Service (Jameson, 2001).

Implications of Dyslexic Difficulties

It must be emphasized that dyslexic difficulties vary considerably from person to person and in their severity. One should be aware of the following possible problems and make allowances:

- Difficulty in understanding oblique or implied questions
- An inconsequential style of discourse; at times it is difficult to grasp the point being made

- A limited attention span and/or high level of distractibility
- Poor recall of dates and details (this may give the impression of unreliability)
- Particular problems estimating the passage of time (this could be important when giving evidence)
- Difficulty presenting a sequence of events in a logical, structured way leading to possible inconsistencies
- Incorrect sequencing of number and letter strings (such as car number plates)
- Inaccurate references to left and right
- Particular susceptibility to the effects of stress.

The following accommodations are recommended when delivering *spoken information* to an individual with dyslexia:

- Allow thinking time before pressing for a response
- When reading information back, insert pauses after each section to allow the information to be internalized
- When providing complex information (such as explaining one's rights) first introduce the topic, then give the details, then summarize if necessary
- Be aware of a likely limited attention span and the possibility of mental overload.

The following points relate to *written information*:
- Be aware that some people with dyslexia have considerable difficulty extracting the meaning from written material despite being able to read adequately
- Sometimes reading difficulties can be compounded by perceptual problems that cause the print to appear to move or blur
- Written material should be well spaced and of a reasonable font size (not below 12 point) and justified *left only* – it is then much easier for a dyslexic person to keep the place
- Bright white paper may appear to 'glare', obscuring the print; for this reason it is to be avoided
- Whole phrases in capital letters are harder to decipher because the normal shape of the word is no longer apparent.

Conclusion

Although some people with dyslexia manage to provide clear evidence as a result of well-developed oral skills, many are very vulnerable. Aggressive questioning and what comes through as attempts to trip people up or entrap them on details of their statements will not lead to justice being done in vulnerable cases.

Solicitors and barristers are two of the many professions that appear, on the whole, to have little awareness of dyslexia, yet their daily work can have a decisive impact on the lives of individuals. It is therefore up to dyslexia

specialists and organizations to promote a proper understanding of dyslexia and to support individuals who come before the courts. In addition, certain changes are also called for in order to accommodate key dyslexic difficulties, not least in the expansion of the role of 'responsible adults' (as outlined in the Police and Criminal Evidence Act) who support people taken into custody regarded as having a 'mental impairment'. The dyslexic community rejects this category as applying to them, but clearly needs support to cope with the stresses of the criminal justice system. Furthermore, it is to be hoped that a greater awareness of disability issues arising out of the ever-widening implications of the Disability Discrimination Act will enshrine this provision.

References

DfEE (1998) The Disability Discrimination Act 1995 – Employment Provisions: The Questions Procedure. London: DfEE.

Evans BJW (1996) Visual problems and dyslexia. Dyslexia Review 8(1).

Evans BJW (2001) Dyslexia and Vision. London: Whurr.

Hales GW (1990) Personality Aspects of Dyslexia: Meeting points in dyslexia. London: British Dyslexia Association.

Jameson, M (1995) Visual Aspects of Dyslexia, revised 1998 (available from the author at 1 Brook Street, Lancaster, LA1 1SL).

Jameson M (2001) Dyslexia in the Courts. Law Bulletin 13.

Ryden M (1992) Dyslexia: How Would I Cope? Revised edn. London: Jessica Kingsley Publishers.

Vinegrad M (1994) A revised Adult Dyslexia Checklist. Educare 48.

Chapter 7
Stress factors in gifted dyslexic children

PETER CONGDON

Before venturing to consider the nature of stress factors experienced by gifted dyslexic children it may be helpful to clarify the subject of giftedness itself. Briefly, 'gifted' can be used as a general term to cover two major groups of children, namely those of outstanding measured intelligence and those who demonstrate exceptional ability in a particular area. The latter are sometimes referred to as 'talented' children.

High or superior intelligence may refer to those children who, in traditional terminology, record an intelligence quotient in the region of 130 or more. We say 'in the region' of 130 because, even if the notion of a 'quotient' in this sense is legitimate, it would still not be suggested that the figure of 130 should be used as a rigid cut-off point. If, for instance, on a properly administered test of intelligence, a child's profile of scores indicates that he or she is operating in most areas at the 130 IQ level then, in spite of the overall score which may fall somewhat below this level, he or she may well be considered as intellectually gifted. What is important is not the IQ itself but how that global result was arrived at.

Nor should we make the mistake of lumping together all children of high or superior intelligence. There is evidence that individuals scoring in the highest ranges of the intelligence scale, i.e. IQ 150+, may have very special needs. George Bernard Shaw once stated that his education was interrupted by his schooling. Unless we are prepared to consider children of very superior intelligence as special cases, then Shaw's criticism may be equally applicable to the education of a very important, if numerically small, group of children in our schools today. We should try to provide for the needs of children of high intelligence and also for those of very high intelligence. However, in the present context, we are not only considering the plight of intellectually gifted children but such children who are also experiencing a degree of dyslexia. Americans sometimes refer to this group as conundrum children or those of dual exceptionality. On the one hand, they have special

needs on account of their giftedness and, on the other, they require special attention on account of their learning difficulty.

It is widely agreed that children who experience a degree of dyslexia often demonstrate outstanding abilities in certain areas – in particular spatial, mechanical, constructional and artistic talents; and it has been surmised that such abilities reflect an unusual balance between the two hemispheres of the brain. It is believed that the very dominance of these 'right hemisphere' abilities can result in a corresponding depression of the language abilities that depend on the opposite or left hemisphere. Dyslexia can be seen, therefore, to arise from a brain difference rather than from a brain defect.

A number of researches both in Britain and abroad have highlighted a particular pattern of scores that dyslexics often manifest on the Wechsler Children's Intelligence Scale (Wechsler, 1992). The pattern is sometimes referred to as the ACID profile. The four letters A, C, I and D refer to the initial letters of the Wechsler sub-tests Arithmetic, Coding, Information and Digit Span. If an individual records low scores on these tests relative to her or his other scores then it may result from the fact that she or he is experiencing difficulties in coping with certain aspects of language. His Arithmetic may be low because he suffers from the problem of dealing with symbolic language. His score on the Coding test may be low because this measure demands automatic responses to arbitrary symbols, and this is very similar to what is demanded by reading and spelling. He records a low score on Information because basically this is a general knowledge test and development in this area may have been depressed by poor literacy skills. Finally, the Digit Span score may be low because this is a measure of the ability to remember items in sequence – another ability that is crucial to the processes involved in mastery of written language.

When considering the overall depressing effect that scores on certain sub-tests may have on a child's global IQ, then an examination of the scores on the other tests becomes imperative as a possible indicator of the child's intellectual potential. It is this very examination that can highlight the intricate way in which dyslexia and giftedness are often related.

In a study of 160 cases of dyslexia (Congdon, 1989) it was discovered that, of the 115 whose verbal or performance IQs did not reach the superior level, no less than 36 (29 male, 7 female) recorded scores on three or more sub-tests which were equivalent to superior scores. Of these 36 some 15 in fact recorded scores on four or more sub-tests at the superior level. These findings, therefore, not only further confirm the existence of the many exceptional intellectual abilities to be found in a population of dyslexic individuals, but also highlight the kind of pressures such individuals experience in the development of their functional intelligence. It is common for a child with dyslexia to show an uneven profile of abilities. For a gifted dyslexic child this very unevenness may be of exceptional proportions and cause

correspondingly greater disturbance in both the child's mental and emotional growth.

A wintry climate of opinion

The gifted and dyslexic individuals have often been faced with what can only be termed a 'wintry climate of opinion', and this arises from a general failure to understand the two conditions. In the past, dyslexia has been misconstrued as a middle-class syndrome or an excuse for low ability or poor motivation. Giftedness has equally been misunderstood. There has been a general failure to identify and stretch the abilities of gifted children, and the attitude that such children have been born with a silver spoon in their mouths and should learn that they are not the only pebble on the beach has been prevalent in a society that glorifies the average. The situation can become particularly stressful for an otherwise highly intelligent child who is experiencing problems with basic reading, spelling and writing, and who is largely judged on the standard of these. Gifted and dyslexic individuals have been among the most neglected in our educational system and the child who falls in both categories may be at a total loss.

Pre-school and infants: the signs emerge

Many gifted children appear as pre-school children to be bright and alert and able in all kinds of areas, and their parents, who may feel at times that something is not quite as it should be, nevertheless assume that the child will make progress when schooling begins. With such children, valuable time has often already been lost before they go to school.

Some parents may have tried teaching their otherwise bright child with conventional methods which may have brought success with other siblings but which now appear to produce few positive results. The lack of success with the written word, even at this very early stage, can produce the beginnings of an aversion towards the subject. Parents may well blame themselves as being inadequate in the teaching process and feel that all will be well when the child goes to school. Years later, when they learn about the condition of dyslexia, they may recall these early failures.

Until they start school, intellectually gifted children have every reason to believe that they are perfectly normal and at least the equal of their contemporaries. Many have been well ahead of their peers in language, in walking and in general social development. Some may have astounded adults with their precocity in certain spheres. Then suddenly these children come face to face with inferiority and failure in an aspect of life that appears to be important for reasons that they cannot understand. Reactions can vary. Some lose interest and adopt negative and avoidance attitudes. Others may try

harder, spurred on by their teacher and parents, only to discover that the greater effort does not produce the longed for results. A feeling of disillusionment and mystification sets in. Until then the child had been told he was clever and he believed it. Now he develops doubts in himself. The teacher's attitude may not help. As most intelligent children learn to read quickly, it is all too easy for the teacher to infer that the child who conspicuously fails to read is either lazy or dull, in spite of a superficial brightness. In the former case, with the child being driven beyond his capacity, there is little hope of developing a constructive relationship between teacher and child, and both soon find themselves at cross-purposes. In the latter case, the child may be written off as not worth a great deal of trouble. The pre-school or infant stage can witness the emergence of attitudes that can affect the child's development for the rest of his school career and beyond.

Transfer to the junior stage

By the time the child transfers to the junior stage of education he may already have been tagged with the 'lazy' or 'dull' label. It is at this stage that the educational pressures begin to increase, with more emphasis on the 3 Rs, and in many places the 11+ examination is still casting its shadow. It is also at this level that self-awareness begins to show, and young gifted children are often precocious in this respect. The failing reader has to cope not only with his own self-doubt but also with the knowledge that poor progress 'far from being a secret shame, often becomes a public failure' (Gaines, 1989, quoted by Pumfrey and Reason, 1991). For the gifted dyslexic individual who previously may have had high aspirations for himself, this period may be particularly traumatic. Like any other children with learning problems, he may act out in a variety of ways. These may take the form of temper tantrums, aggression or destructiveness. Many gifted children want perfection and are satisfied with nothing less. If they cannot reach the high standards they set themselves, they sometimes destroy what attempts they have made, or refuse to participate in the activity any longer. Some retreat into themselves or resort to day-dreaming or 'playing dumb'. Other manifestations of emotional disturbance arising from the problem are enuresis, stammer, sleep-walking, asthma and various physical symptoms, such as vomiting and recurrent abdominal pains for which no physical cause can be found. The situation is not helped when attempts are made to treat the secondary symptom rather than the primary cause, which is an underlying learning difficulty.

As a result of the various pressures on them, together with their continued failure in basic scholastic subjects, many intellectually gifted children who are also dyslexic have little idea of the extent of their high intellectual potential. This has become only too apparent to me and, as an educational psychologist specializing in the assessment of such children, I have noted their

responses to such questions as, 'Did you know that you have high ability?' or 'Did you know that you have high intelligence?'. Some would beam and reply 'Yes, I am good at this, that or the other'. Many, however, would react with confusion and disbelief and reply, 'So I am not thick or stupid' or words to that effect. Responses of this nature remind us that there is little systematic documentation of the views and feelings of dyslexic children themselves. Publications tend to concentrate on personal accounts by dyslexic adults or on parents' descriptions of the plight of their children.

Parental pressures

The parents of young gifted children often, and not unreasonably, have high aspirations for them. They see their offspring as superior to, or well above, the average and not unreasonably expect a high standard of attainment when they enter school. When this is not forthcoming, the disappointment and disillusionment can be traumatic for both parent and child. Nor is parental distress necessarily proportional to the extent of the disability. This may relate to values, ambitions, hopes and knowledge (Knusson and Cunningham, 1988). I have known parents dismiss serious cases of dyslexia whereas others will over-react to mild or moderate cases. When their child fails to live up to expectations the disappointment can be marked.

Reactions towards school and the education system also differ. Although some parents accept their child's shortcomings and its consequent effects, others automatically blame the teachers and so deny the necessary collaboration which is an indispensable requisite to their child's education. Gifted dyslexic children can find themselves under a particular strain. Many of their outstanding abilities are recognized by their parents, but ignorance concerning the condition of dyslexia can result in those same parents becoming vexed, angry and unkind towards the child, whom they see as careless and poorly motivated. Some children are the victims of bullying by disappointed fathers. At the other end of the scale, excessive anxiety on the part of loving and caring parents can have equally adverse effects. The children may react by attention-seeking behaviour. Too often they become aggressive and antisocial. It is of interest to note that a large proportion of juvenile delinquents have reading and spelling difficulties, and many of these have undisclosed talents in certain areas.

Transfer to secondary school

Late identification compounds emotional problems. Often the child's learning difficulties are not recognized until late in the primary stage of education. This is frequently so with the gifted dyslexic child, who may be adept at employing other abilities to compensate for or to cloak inadequacies

with written language. By the time the problem is recognized and remedial help is beginning to take effect, the child is then faced with the traumatic experience of being transferred to a secondary school. The secondary school may be much larger and impersonal and the curriculum is more formal and demanding. It thereby places an extra strain on what are precisely the child's weak points, namely reading, writing and organizational skills. This is the time when new subjects and new areas of knowledge are introduced. The learning of foreign languages takes on greater importance. An intellectually gifted child normally approaches such a time with enthusiasm and interest. However, for one who has a history of dyslexia, this stage may mean only more frustration, more failure and, in some cases, more exposure to ridicule.

It is at the secondary level that emotional symptoms and behavioural disorders arising from an underlying learning problem often take on a more antisocial form. Truancy, not unknown at the junior level, becomes more prevalent, and the same is true of stealing, pathological lying and the drift into more destructive gang activities. For particularly sensitive individuals, deep emotional disturbance, depression, fantasy-building and other neurotic signs are manifested. Adolescence, with all its turmoil, is enough without the extra problem of dyslexia. However, the outlook need not be completely bleak for the adolescent. At this level many discover for the first time that they are dyslexic and they experience a sense of relief when it is explained to them. Yet coupled with the sense of relief there may also be an element of despair, anger and bewilderment. The intellectually gifted child may experience a deep sense of injustice. Being aware of the responsibilities of those in charge of his education, he may well ask, 'Why didn't the school or the local education authority identify the problem before and arrange appropriate help?'.

Dyslexic children who come from families who view school involvement as of little consequence may happily contract out of any attempt to achieve. Such children may find that, although they cannot become literate, there are other socially acceptable school or out-of-school activities and they concentrate on becoming competent in these. Gifted athletes, musicians, artists and builders are to be found in this group.

Towards the end of their schooling it is natural for children to look forward to what will happen when they leave school. As intellectually gifted individuals, they might legitimately have expected a demanding and stimulating career. The knowledge that this may now be barred to them owing to their problems with basic literacy is likely to produce anxiety and frustrations, and increase emotional tensions, and these can be exacerbated by the realization that they are disappointing their parents' career expectations for them. For many technical and virtually all 'white collar' jobs, some evidence of having passed examinations is required. This may well be merely a routine and the employer may well set little store by it. However, the candidate who

has no certificate to produce may be deterred from applying. When he does make an application he is likely to be asked to do so in writing. Whether this is done on a prescribed form or in a letter of his own composition, he will find it difficult to present himself in the best light. He will be vulnerable to revealing the limitations of his literacy skills and his educational attainments, and it is these which, in the public mind, are normally associated with ability. The gifted dyslexic child, like any other, will be at risk of being eliminated before she or he is considered for interview.

For those dyslexic individuals who are able to take written examinations, it is fair to say that they can now be offered special consideration or dispensation. This may take the form of extra time or having someone read the question to them. However, there are some who choose not to take advantage of such arrangements. Some may see it as an unfair advantage over other candidates with whom they wish to compete on equal terms. Others are dissuaded on account of the fact that details of the dispensation may appear on any certificate that they may be awarded, and this would therefore reduce its value.

Management

Careful management is essential for all dyslexic children if they are to reach their potential, and this is especially so for gifted dyslexic children, who may have much to offer in a wide variety of areas and yet whose limitations with written language may hold them back, with tragic results. To prevent this happening, early identification and appropriate help are essential. Ideally this should be done either at the pre-school level or when the child first enters school. It is unrealistic to talk about a 'cure' for dyslexia, but a great deal can be done to help the child reach a standard in written communication that will facilitate progress in other areas.

It is paramount that parents, teachers and the child should work together in an atmosphere of trust. Gifted children are often capable of a high level of understanding of a problem at a comparatively young age. It can be explained to them how it is possible to be clever in many ways and yet still have difficulty with reading and spelling. Often the diagnosis of dyslexia and the use of the term itself can be helpful in making it easier for both parents and child to come to terms with the negative aspects. For the parents, it offers reassurance that no shortcomings on their part have been responsible for the child's difficulties, whereas the children recognize that they are not just 'dull' or 'lazy'. Susan Hampshire, the gifted actress, writes:

> If 1 had known what was the matter with me and why 1 couldn't read, would everything have been easier just because my difficulties had a name? Yes, it would. To know that it was not a disease but a disability, a condition that could be improved, would have made all the difference.
>
> Hampshire (1981)

The guide *Dyslexia: Towards a better understanding* (Congdon, 1981) was purposely written to help young able dyslexic children to understand their learning difficulty. It is written in the first person in simple conversational language and contains many cartoon-like illustrations together with examples of famous people who were dyslexic.

Opportunities should be given for allowing the use of alternative means of communication wherever possible. This can include oral or spoken language as well as the use of up-to-date technology. Many dyslexic children show an aptitude for computers and word processors and this should be exploited by offering early training in touch-typing.

The possibility of help in alleviating the condition of dyslexia provides an optimistic outlook. What one can hope to achieve can be substantial and for the intellectually gifted and talented, who can compensate in all sorts of ways, the future can indeed be bright. For such children, like any others, it is important to emphasize their strengths while not overlooking their weaknesses.

References

Congdon PJ (1981) Dyslexia: Towards a better understanding. Solihull: GCIC.

Congdon PJ (1989) Dyslexia. A Pattern of Strengths and Weaknesses. Solihull: GCIC.

Gaines K (1989) The use of reading diaries as a short term intervention strategy. Reading 23(3): 141-5.

Hampshire S (1981) Susan's Story. London: Sidgwick & Jackson.

Knusson C, Cunningham CC (1988) Stress, disability and handicap. In: Fisher S, Reason J (eds), Handbook of Life Stress, Cognition and Health. Chichester: Wiley.

Pumfrey PD, Reason R (1991) Specific Learning Difficulties (Dyslexia). London: Routledge.

Wechsler D (1992) Wechsler Children's Intelligence Scale. Sidcup: The Psychological Corporation.

Chapter 8
Stress factors within the family

ROGER SAUNDERS[1]

Indeed, when there is a 'dyslexic in the house' it can create considerable stress. At times these feelings can become so immobilizing that the family becomes near the familiar 'dysfunctioning stage'. At other times, in contrast, a mild-to-moderate reaction can mobilize the family around 'the cause' and bring all the members into a more harmonious relationship.

Several factors come to mind to create the degree of stress in the dyslexic family: the age of the person (child or adult) when first discovered, the facilities for educational treatment, and the 'excess emotional baggage' that the various members of the family have endured before the awareness of dyslexia as an added 'burden'. For example, for whatever reasons, a marriage that has been strained for years can be unable to cope further with the necessary requirements that the dyslexic condition in one or more members of the family can necessitate. Moreover, in some instances the re-education process can take so long and be so arduously demanding that the parents' patience can be tested to the limit.

---

[1]The author apologizes for the reference to the masculine. The use of 'he or she', 'him or her' seems grammatically clumsy and boring to the reader. Although statistics may be changing, it is generally assumed that in the population of dyslexic individuals there are four times as many boys as girls. It is hoped that none of the dyslexic females has been offended by this masculine reference. They are just as important, and at times, because of fewer girls with the problem, can experience even greater stress. Although I have no hard evidence, I have often felt that if it is the mother who is dyslexic there can be greater stress in the family. The mother, often because of her freer work schedule, is the parent who initially goes to the school for conferences. Entering the educational institution or building, a black cloud of memories of early fears and frustration can descend, reducing the mother to being unable to communicate appropriately. The administrators and teachers observe her high level of anxiety and unknowingly remark, 'No wonder the child is upset, look how anxious the mother is'.

Having been involved in the field of dyslexia for well over 40 years, the writer chooses to share personal experiences which he has known, clinically, from many families, many of whom have been followed from childhood, through marriage, to their own children, creating a 'third generation' of data from observations. Some attempt will be made to classify the traditional family constellations and their reactions to stress. These categories will range from the involvement of the grandparents, the parents, their children, the child and/or his siblings.

Grandparents

A grandmother often feels that the daughter-in-law had turned a 'deaf ear' to her as she tried to share some of her own early experiences encountered in rearing the child's father. The grandmother's memory may be remarkably challenged and brought back to light when she observes her grandchild's learning style, or specifically the non-learning of critical skills. She well remembers their startled reaction when a highly verbal child began to fall behind and/or to exhibit significant symptoms that were later classified as 'dyslexia'. Now armed with all of that wisdom, she is aware of the possibility of a genetic link between her husband's style of learning and that of her son and that of her grandson. Her daughter-in-law might subtly or overtly refuse the grandparent's concern and send the message 'Don't butt in'. The daughter-in-law can be blinded by these warning signals because she observes only her very successful husband (and father-in-law) and has no clue to the personal history of how his parents had met the challenge of his educational needs in youth. The grandmother's intent, remembering her husband's and son's experience, is to 'soften' the emotional response to the frightening evidence when her grandson exhibits similar patterns, knowing that very special needs must be met head-on. Tact and diplomacy on the part of the grandparents are crucial to keep the 'lines of communication' open and to avoid being 'tuned out' by those who need to listen the most.

Parents

When the couple first met, courted and were married, the father's painful emotional scars of the past were possibly well healed. Moreover, anxieties had been reduced and the stress of those earlier years forgotten. On the other hand, his wife might have observed that when her husband is under some experience requiring the use of reading, and particularly expository writing, he can become anxious. Not uncommon is an out-of-character 'blow up' exhibited when he innocently asks her how to spell a word and she retorts, 'Look it up', or 'I spelled it for you yesterday, why can't you remember it?'. She is not aware that these are continued symptoms of his dyslexic learning

condition and the residual feelings of stress encountered from his early educational years.

Living with a dyslexic child, who, in spite of the parents' best efforts continues to fail, can gradually become more and more stressful until the reality of the learning style has been properly addressed by a professional diagnosis. Before this discovery, the parents have struggled with their youngster without being mindful of the unique characteristics or the style of a dyslexic learner. Usually they have been discouraged with the child and have run the gamut of questions: 'Is it our fault?', 'What have we done wrong?', 'Why can't he learn?', 'Why is our adorable child having a personality change – for the worse . . .?' Searching for answers, naturally they have turned to educational administrators and teachers with whom to share their dilemma. Seeing the frustrations of the parents, the teachers attempt to deal with the parents' feelings, fears and anxieties, rather than looking closely at the child and searching for clues as to what is really wrong. Example after example springs to mind, particularly of the child who is reasonably successful in the early grades, but, when the academic demands for reading and writing and comprehension become greater, can gradually begin to fall behind. Uninformed teachers blame either external or internal factors for a child's failure to learn.

The external factors are when the blame is placed on the external environment, such as: 'The parents are not supportive', 'The parents are expecting too much', 'There is too much confusion at home', 'The parents are stressing other things more than academics, such as sports, drama, art, music, etc.', 'The parents need better control of their children'.

As for the internal factors, the child is blamed, with statements such as: 'He doesn't pay attention consistently', 'He's too involved in other activities (sports, girls, car repairs, etc.)', or 'He is unmotivated, lazy, emotionally immature, etc.'. Blaming the external and internal factors, and communicating these to the parents, does little to reduce the stress that parents feel when the child continues to fail. Usually it increases the guilt, as when one mother of a dyslexic son was blamed for influencing and/or damaging her developing fetus because she stretched and hung draperies during the sixth month of pregnancy. Seldom does the teacher look at the educational 'system' and place blame thereon, and certainly she does not heap stress and guilt on herself, by exclaiming, 'Not my fault, I am a certified teacher', 'I have had good training, and the other children are responding well to my teaching strategies'. Therefore, the stress intensifies until there is proper recognition that this is a child with learning patterns that are different from the norm.

In some families this scenario is not as stressful because, in some instances, it is not unusual for parents to have had some awareness of the nature of dyslexia; therefore, when symptoms first occur they quickly search

for realistic explanations of the child's failure. Although the stress factor in this case is limited, concern and stress do occur when parents ponder about, 'What's going to happen in the future?', and, in particular, when they cannot find adequate educational facilities to offer some 'prevention' of the symptoms before they become crippling or undermine proper educational growth. Moreover, parents might have learned from their own experiences and their observations of other children, as well as their neighbours' children and their siblings' children. Hopefully, emphasis on public awareness of the early signs of dyslexia, or that it 'runs in families' (the genetic cause), has allowed parents to observe other children who have shown some delay in the acquisition of language at an early stage, and wonder what lies ahead. Even 'non-verbal' children have forewarned their parents to be more or less prepared for this dilemma of achievement in the more formalized teaching experiences. Moreover, they have been aware that a child has shown less interest in 'books', or in learning the alphabet, and sometimes a delay in the efficient use of the pencil and/or crayons. On the other hand, they have also seen extraordinary strength in the manipulation of visual-spatial relationships, such as taking toys apart and putting them back together, extreme creativity in building with blocks, talents in motor coordination, music, dance, and other strengths that are out of harmony with the lack of interest in the educational routines, and demonstrate much higher talent than their same age peers.

Marion Welchman, of the British Dyslexia Association, has in her lectures clearly illustrated what happens within the family and with the siblings when one sibling has the dyslexic condition. First she draws a circle on the board and says, 'This is the normal family circle, all living in harmony with each other'. Then she draws a little hump on the circle and says, 'This represents one sibling who has dyslexia, undiagnosed'. Then as she begins to talk about the necessary management and attention required to address the needs of the dyslexic child's problems, this 'hump' becomes larger and larger, and pretty soon is in itself as large as the family circle. This clearly illustrates the tension that can be created in the family when the parents must begin to focus more and more on the sibling (or siblings) who have a different learning style.

The parents must also face the financial burden which, in itself, adds extra stress to the family's budget, and face the burden of scheduling for extra time for homework, extra trips to the tutor, etc., and the list becomes never ending.

Sib-ship stress

With the more affluent families, the parents may enrol their child in a school, the curriculum of which is designed especially for the dyslexic learner. This

can create great sibling rivalry because these schools have built into their philosophy and curriculum the idea that one of the first steps towards rehabilitation is to create an environment in which the child becomes a successful and enthusiastic learner. This can create disharmony with a sibling who is struggling with the traditional educational system that lacks creativity and personal attention. Many extremely gifted siblings could certainly profit from the type of originality or creativity involved in the dyslexic educational system; however, unless the state school has 'classes for the gifted', these children go with their needs unmet and can become sour and less enthusiastic about educational pursuits – jealous of their sibling.

Another condition that becomes more and more stressful to the dyslexic student is when a sibling, two or three years younger, equally bright and linguistically facile, exhibits none of the typical dyslexic symptoms, sits quietly, observing the teaching of his dyslexic sibling during the homework period or during tutoring, and begins to 'catch on' to reading quite spontaneously This puts the older sibling's 'nose out of joint'. Parents struggle to give 'equal time', but this is difficult because they are aware that the older child has greater specific needs for survival in the educational system than the younger child. Even grandparents can begin to favour the dyslexic child, trying to ease burdens for the entire family by remembering when they had walked in the same footsteps of the parents in the years past.

Stress reducers

The greatest stress reducer comes after the awareness of the condition, when the child, with the proper teaching, begins to learn. Although this might occur quickly, it may take longer. It is not uncommon for the parents to recognize that not only is the child making academic progress, but, as many, many have exclaimed, 'Thank goodness, we've got our little boy back'. This means that the therapeutic intervention in the academic area has also resolved some of the fears and frustrations (and stress) that the child was feeling as a result of academic failure. Actually, many untrained teachers continue to 'pound away' at teaching strategies that are inappropriate, and the dyslexic child has begun to experience what I term 'academic abuse'.

The awareness of the dyslexic learning 'condition' is the first step leading towards the proper treatment. This comes about through diagnosis by an experienced clinician. The in-depth discussion should help to erase the 'bad labels', or blame, of the external and internal accusations.

The diagnostic process should not be hurried as it can be for a minor medical problem. For example, in a very short time a paediatrician can see a 'red throat' and give an appropriate prescription. However, the diagnosis of dyslexia, at whatever age, starts with an explanation of the strengths and weaknesses from the traditional intellectual assessment. This should be

explained thoroughly. Often a 'visual' is helpful. The clinician draws the graph of the intelligence test, labelling average, above average, superior, below average', etc. Also, it helps to draw a traditional bell-shaped curve marking these categories while placing the 'grade levels' underneath. This shows the discrepancy between where a child with normal learning ability would be placed and the levels achieved by the dyslexic child. For example, a child in the third grade with superior intelligence should be reading at around sixth grade or higher, whereas the dyslexic's reading may be barely 'grade level'. From personal experience I believe that the strengths of the dyslexic are usually in the cognitive, 'thinking' areas, such as commonsense reasoning (comprehension), abstract thinking (similarities) and possibly oral vocabulary development. The non-verbal tasks that require the manipulation of visual-spatial materials can also be a strength. The explanation of the differences in the memory system can help a child understand his dyslexic style of learning. An extremely important part of this evaluation is the in-depth family history. Examining arduously the levels of achievement of parents, uncles, aunts, cousins, etc. can bring relief to a puzzled child, because, when he hears that his favourite uncle or highly admired first cousin is also dyslexic, he gains courage to feel that his future is bright. The thrust of such an interview should be explained in the language the child understands and the intent of the outcome should be that the child leaves the office feeling, 'It's not my fault'.

As Margaret Byrd Rawson (Editor Emeritus of *Annals of Dyslexia*, published by the Orton Dyslexia Society) says, 'Diagnosis without treatment is criminal'. Therefore, the next step in reducing the often blinding stress is an educational prescription that addresses the 'different' learning style. Available facilities for this prescription may vary. Some local public educational facilities are able to accept a diagnosis and deal appropriately with the child's needs. However, most are not. Therefore the parent must search for other resources. Private tutoring in or out of school, home teaching or a transfer to a school (boarding or an independent day school) specializing in the education of the dyslexic child can be an option. Finances play a big part in this selection, as mentioned earlier. This added burden, while reducing the stress on the dyslexic student, can shift some additional stress to the family's lifestyle, perhaps limiting lengthy vacations or family excursions, etc.

Answers to the unanswered questions 'How long will he need help?', 'Will he make college?', 'What of his employment future?' can be a stress reducer if the clinician has years of experience and can assure the parents of other children, who, when given proper day-by-day management, have succeeded. Rawson (1995) is very reassuring for parents pondering these questions. Also parents must be reassured that they can have confidence in their own judgement because they have proved their adequacy as parents by having searched

arduously for the right answers to their original question of 'Why can't he learn like others?'. Hearing this from a professional lowers their fears and anxieties about, 'What of the future?'.

Magnifying strengths is a 'must' for preserving the integrity and 'self-opinion' of the dyslexic at any age. 'What are you good at?' is often a surprise question because the child has had teachers who only observed and mentioned what he is 'bad at'. Learning that because one is a 'bad speller' does not make one a 'bad person' is the message to get across.

Often the financial stress can be reduced by the parents searching for opportunities for earning additional income. Also, learning how to help other dyslexic individuals by taking courses for tutors or teachers has helped many mothers to have greater insight into her child's dilemma about learning. As one socially prominent mother said, 'I am tired of pouring pink tea at the women's socials; I would like to learn how to help my Johnny and many others like him'. And she did – and many other mothers joined in 'the cause' from her enthusiasm, which gradually led to the formation of a local branch of the Orton Dyslexia Society, to a special summer camp, to college courses for teacher's credit and to an international conference on the topic of dyslexia. A recent newsletter from a school in Seattle, Washington, which specializes in the education of dyslexic children, quoted a letter from a mother:

> No one knows better than me the value of education and the cost of not achieving one, and there's no price I can put on the education he is receiving at [his present school]. For a child like him it is truly a gift of life, a chance to succeed and hope to overcome nearly insurmountable barriers.

Many mothers overcome the long-standing guilt that they have borne for feeling that they were at fault, by shifting their stress energy into a more productive experience through becoming active in organizations devoted to furthering the understanding of dyslexia. Parents can be 'movers and shakers' when their purpose is just and clearly defined.

Reducing stress in relationship to one's employment also requires understanding and management. For example, the bright, creative, personable, likeable employee who is advancing up the 'company ladder' may be frightened that the next step up is a 'desk job', which places great emphasis on reading and writing. In many such instances, the selection of a competent secretary has allowed the freedom for him to continue in his area of strengths and expertise and not be hampered by the 'paper and pencil work'.

Often parents reduce their stress over the fear of job inadequacy by magnifying their own strengths or, if possible, by becoming employed in their area of strength, such as building, selling, designing or gravitating

towards jobs that rely on good 'personality' traits rather than those demanding academic prowess. Off-duty recreational activities such as sports, gardening, home repairs, etc., or pursuing talents in art, music, design, etc., have been a 'saving factor' to many parents burdened with the stress of living in a dyslexic family.

Studying the lives of past and current successful and famous dyslexic individuals is important. Lloyd Thomson's (1969) article can be a great boost to dyslexic individuals fearful of their future. One dyslexic teacher developed a question and answer format in which she listed the accomplishments of these great people and had the students guess to whom this referred. Currently, seldom does a day go by that one does not hear of a successful dyslexic person who has just 'come out of the closet'.

In summary, stress in the family is a real emotional experience for everybody. Stepping stones taken one at a time can keep stress from becoming an insurmountable 'stumbling block' to the future of the dyslexic learner and his family.

References

Rawson MB (1995) Dyslexia Over the Life Span: A fifty-five-year longitudinal study. Cambridge, Mass: Educators Publishing Service.

Thomson L (1969) Language disabilities in men of eminence. Bulletin of the Orton Society 19: 113–18.

Chapter 9
Stress: the hidden side of dyslexia

LINDSAY PEER

We have come a long way in the identification, assessment and remediation of dyslexia over the past few years. There are local education authorities (LEAs) and schools now claiming that they are proudly employing dyslexia-friendly practices. People openly use the word 'dyslexia' in conversation with little fear of stigma. It is generally recognized that an individual may be highly able, yet experience weaknesses in the acquisition of literacy. There are people with dyslexia who speak candidly of their greatly enhanced creative skills alongside areas of considerable difficulty.

However, we have a long way still to go. Some schools are aware of the need for specific methodologies in the teaching of literacy and numeracy, and that becomes the major dyslexia focus for them. Other schools offer little provision and employ staff who have not been offered awareness training. More worryingly, these same staff are often unaware of dyslexia specialists upon whom they can call for guidance and support. The situation is therefore patchy – with many children being played as pawns in a game of chess. Appropriate support offered to them is often dependent on where they live, the age at which they are identified, and the financial resources determining the level of provision that they (do or do not) receive.

It comes as no surprise to me that even better provision focuses primarily on success in the areas of literacy and numeracy, because schools are being driven by the need to achieve, as is measured by and publicized through the 'league tables'. In order to achieve in such an environment, pressure is inevitably placed on head teachers, who in turn place pressure on their class-room teachers. The individuals who are ultimately under the greatest pressure are the children themselves. What happens in an environment where children and their teachers are greatly pressured? They are taught for success in the examination system – the only thing that matters – and in the process are *tested to death*. An exaggerated term? Read on . . . .

90

Case 1

Dear Lindsey,

I thought you might like to know about our own personal experience regarding stress and dyslexia with our 8-year-old son – while in a mainstream school, undergoing bullying and intense feelings of worthlessness, he planned his suicide (he was going to hang himself from his climbing frame). Fortunately he told his older brother that he couldn't take anymore and that it would be best if he ended his life this way. Our very understanding family doctor removed him from school until his Statement was complete and he could be educated in an appropriate environment. While he was away from school someone had to be with him at all times because he was so very depressed. Once he settled in a specialist ASC for dyslexics, and he became understood he has returned to the happy, confident child he once was before having to go to school, he is slowly beginning to believe in himself again, but his confidence is still fragile, even two years on.

I hope this will be of some help to you, as you can imagine we as a family have very strong feelings about stress and dyslexia.

The stress caused by inappropriate handling and mismanagement of children with dyslexia is considerable, and affects parents, teachers and children alike. Sometimes the children 'act out' their frustrations and at other times they suffer in silence. So many adults are unaware of the stresses that these children experience – and the results can be most profound.

It is not unusual for children with dyslexia to find themselves the victims of bullying. As education director of the British Dyslexia Association, I have had the privilege of running 21 'family days' throughout the country over the past few years. At each one I have held a session entitled 'Let's Talk' for children aged 12–16. In each and every one of those random groupings of young people, at least one child, if not several, has spoken about being the victim of bullying. This may be in the form of verbal abuse – sometimes by staff and sometimes by parents – and other times by physical abuse in the playground or on the way home.

Case 2

Dear Lindsay,

I have a personal anecdote regarding my then 10-year-old daughter, now 11, X. X was verbally bullied mercilessly by another girl in her class for over two years. X perceived this bullying to be due to the fact she is severely dyslexic and was called names like dyslexic freak, dumbo, thicko, stupid and worse names she did not like to repeat. One particular evening after an intolerable day at school we sat in her bedroom and she lay on the bed crying. She held out her hands like a pair of weighing scales and lifted them up and down alternately saying that she didn't know which was the heaviest weight, the dyslexia or the bullying! Thankfully she

is now at secondary school with a Statement attending a dyslexia provision within a mainstream school. She has just had a marvellous first interim report and is not being bullied. She still takes a bit of stick from some children in the mainstream but nothing she isn't coping with, long may it last. Through all this she has never lost her enthusiasm for learning and always tries 100%. We her parents take our hats off to her, don't know if we could be so resilient!

And what is the effect on the parents? Living with children who are existing in a state of stress, experiencing fear, demotivation and low self-esteem has its own stresses. Many of the parents will have experienced dyslexic-type difficulties themselves when they went to school. For them, dealing with their children's difficulties may well be a re-enactment of the same problem all over again. Many of them tell me how they feel when they enter a school to talk on behalf of their children – the feelings of nausea, the feeling of choking, the fear of reprimand.

Case 3

Dear Lindsay,
If you want a case study talk to my oldest, Y. If he is not stressed then I am. I have two other children on the [Dyslexia Association] books who have tried suicide who I can put you in touch with if you want.

There is often an assumption that in adulthood the problems of dyslexia disappear – that people will have come to terms with any difficulties and will get on with their lives. People have told me that they assume that computers are the answer to all the problems of adults with dyslexia – a simple solution indeed, if that were the only difficulty.

There are, however, many problems that adults with dyslexia experience – accepting the difficulties, having to explain to employers and having to explain to spouses. Many adults with dyslexia will not have been identified while at school and as such will come to the realization of their condition only much later in life. This is sometimes through listening to programmes on the radio, sometimes through their own children's identification and sometimes through their own adult studies. It is rare, as yet, for an employer to understand sufficiently and encourage the worker to seek assessment and then provide the support that is needed; employers are eager for the job to be done and are less caring of an individual's specific needs.

Case 4

Dear Lindsay,
On the radio recently there was a programme about twin sisters; one was a bright

and successful twin and the other twin struggled. Years later and after treatment for horrendous mental health problems, including attempted suicide, the struggling twin finds out she is dyslexic.

Case 5

Dear Lindsay,

Z, aged 20 in his second year at University, was having an identity crisis, doing the wrong course and living with the wrong people. Over the New Year we noticed a certain stuttering in his speech which his younger brothers particularly did not tease him about, recognizing all was not well.

He returned to the University and over the telephone his speech got worse, to the extent that I could not understand what he was saying. Through a friend of his I established that I would be coming up the next day to see him. On my arrival I found he had been to see the university counsellor who had not been able to understand anything he said. We know a doctor in the area who we went to see that evening and who arranged for him to be admitted the next day for tests – brain scans etc. He was also referred to an important but useless psychiatrist. Wherever we went, Z insisted on making the arrangements, buying the bus tickets etc., which caused huge confusion because the bus drivers could not understand him.

The tests showed nothing but I knew that, as a very sensitive and initially badly mismanaged dyslexic, speech was his most important means of communicating and thus, surely, this was his plea for help. He came home for a bit and went to a very good psychotherapist who referred him to a colleague near his University. Unfortunately the arrogant psychiatrist who said he could do it himself blocked this. Finally the speech returned and it has not re-occurred. I still feel pretty angry with the psychiatrist blocking what would have been a marvellous opportunity in many ways.

Even in the year 2002, when science, policy and practice have changed so much there are still stories of very late identification – and that by chance.

Case 6

Dear Lindsay,

Jade was a happy toddler who went downhill after starting school. Throughout primary school there were reports that she exhibited problems concentrating and didn't read much. No one ever suggested that she went for an assessment to try to identify the reasons for her difficulties. She struggled hard at secondary school, and finished with a good range of GCSEs; A-levels were another problem. By coincidence, a cousin was identified as being dyslexic and this proved to be the catalyst for Jade being assessed; she was 17. Now she understands why she has a problem remembering things and writing slowly. She currently feels more positive and is choosing subjects and provision that better suit her needs.

Case 7

Sometimes, unfortunately, the ultimate can happen. A year ago, I received a letter on my desk from the mother of Nicholas. This was the sort of heart-breaking letter that puts the fear of God into the parent of any child who is experiencing difficulties. Nicholas, after years of suffering, had taken his own life – enough had become enough. The beautiful child, who had so much to live for, no longer wished to live. Dying had become easier than surviving.

I have had many conversations with Eileen, the mother, and she has agreed to write a piece for me for the following reason:

> I am writing this letter because I don't want what happened to Nicholas John to happen to any other parent's child. If I can help just one other child with dyslexia or learning difficulties then I hope that Nicholas's struggles were not in vain . . . I tried my best for him all my life, and in his death I find myself still trying. It is all I can do. I love you Nicholas John. May you rest, at last, in peace. Mum.

I hope that the reader will look at this in relation to the issues of stress, demotivation and low self-esteem – the areas that as parents and teachers we need to look out for. Dyslexia and other specific learning difficulties are not only a function of difficulties in reading, spelling or the processing of language at speed. Individuals are affected throughout their lives. It is our duty to identify and manage such learners appropriately, ensuring that no one even considers taking their own life again. In the year 2002, we know too much to allow that to happen.

Eileen tells me:

> We realized that something was terribly wrong when Nicholas went to nursery at the age of 3. His older brother had attended the same nursery and could count, write his name and socialize well with the other children. In contrast Nicholas spent most of his time in the Wendy House, sleeping. Sleeping was one way that he could escape the world; that went on throughout his life. The nursery teacher told me I was 'wasting my money sending him there'.

> One day he came home at the age of 7 and asked me why he hadn't been selected for a part in the nativity play. He had asked for a part and the teacher had replied 'You can't read, let alone read lines'. He then asked me 'How do you read lines mum?'. It broke my heart and I went to the teacher who said that he wasn't like his elder brother, he was just lazy.

When Eileen spoke to the headmaster and told him that she was worried that he might have dyslexia, she said that he told her that 'It is fashionable to have a dyslexic child'. At 16, at a parents' evening, his father was told that 'He is lazy and won't concentrate'.

A week before he left school at 16, Eileen says that the teachers came to her and said that they were worried that he had no qualifications. When she said that she had been asking for help throughout his school life, they offered classes to help. Too little, too late.

His mother tells me that the night before he died he called her and said that he was a failure . . . that he was doomed to fail because everyone puts so much emphasis on reading knowledge and not the person behind it, their hearts and their skills.

The stories are heart breaking and should make all of us sit up and think. There are many people who think of dyslexia only as a reading and/or writing problem. The truth is that it is not. Curriculum success is seemingly what counts in school – the road to success for the individual and the institution. However, we are dealing with human beings who are often fragile and vulnerable. For them the ramifications of failure are enormous, as are the everyday stresses that these learners, their parents and teachers live with on an everyday basis.

Overwhelming stress on the part of child and teacher

Llewellyn and Hogan (2000) have shown us how the personal attitudes and expectations of educators can affect the way that they interact with different learners. It was found that if the educator had a good relationship with the student the disability was perceived as being less difficult. It was also found that if the student with a disability became aware that educators or peers held negative perceptions of them, this had a negative implication for self-belief. We must not underestimate the power of self-belief. The best teaching in the world will not be effective if learners do not believe that they will succeed.

Teachers at schools are under a great deal of stress. A huge amount is being asked of them today and they suffer constant scrutiny. That said, the vast majority care a great deal about the children in their care and wish to do the best that they can to encourage their pupils to learn and feel a sense of achievement in themselves.

Teachers cite lack of support, constant changes, imposed curriculum innovation and lack of non-contact time as just a few of the pressures (Dunham, 1992). Add to that the need to learn about and be competent to deal with the range of special educational needs with which they may have to deal in their classes on a daily basis, and the pressures grow. Hinton and Burton (1992) suggest that the stresses arise from an imbalance between 'perceived demands' and 'perceived capabilities'. As a result there is a feeling of lack of success, possibly a similar feeling to that of children with dyslexia

who experience a lack of success on a daily basis. No wonder that teachers are leaving the profession if that is the case. But what choice do children with dyslexia have? They do not have the option of changing jobs . . . they have to remain in school! Teachers need the support of the school management if they are to succeed. If they are to manage successfully that which is being demanded of them within a philosophy of inclusion, they need to have a structure set up whereby they can be given the support that they need to work well with learners with dyslexia and their families. Children with dyslexia do succeed, but they do need an appropriate environment in which to blossom.

Dyslexia-friendly schooling

For many years there was a belief that the only way children with dyslexia could be educated was in special schools or through one-to-one specialist teaching in mainstream schools. Essentially this was at a time when the group of specific learning difficulties was little understood and there were strong opinions bandied around about the description and manifestation of the various conditions. At that time, children with dyslexia rarely had their needs met within mainstream education. There was a high level of frustration experienced by teachers, parents and pupils – educational targets were rarely met and the level of self-esteem seen in many of those children was very poor.

Research and practice have moved on from this position and, in a few places in the UK, most children with dyslexia are now receiving the support and appropriate teaching that they need. In those places, improvement is felt by all and parents work closely together with their children's teachers. These are in the few LEAs and specific schools that have taken on the ethos and philosophy of 'dyslexia friendliness':

> Whilst 'the special educational needs friendly school' is the ideal descriptor to work for, this document focuses on dyslexia in the knowledge that many of the strategies which can be used to help this group also enhance the learning of other children with a variety of needs.
>
> City and County of Swansea (1998)

For the inclusion of children with dyslexia in mainstream schooling truly to work, there is a need for schools to adopt ways of managing the changes necessary to fulfil the requirements of a fully inclusive policy. Upgrading the skills of all staff and appropriate resourcing are key, as is the need to share good practice where it exists. The alternative stance, by definition, will mean exclusion for those with needs that are different to the norm.

In the foreword to the *Dyslexia Friendly Schools Resource Pack* (British Dyslexia Association or BDA, 1999) David Blunkett, the then Secretary of State for Education and Employment, stated:

> As I know from first hand experience, dyslexia is not something a child grows out of and when it goes unrecognised, it can be the source of much misery, frustration and underachievement.
>
> It is equally important that we recognise that the effects of dyslexia can be alleviated by using appropriate teaching strategies and committed learning. Teachers need to know how to identify children who have special educational needs and how to provide for such children effectively once they have been identified.

For an LEA to become 'dyslexia friendly', an approach centred on the following key elements is fundamental:

- Working in partnership with parents and voluntary organizations, the production of clear expectations and good practice guidelines accepted by parents and schools
- Awareness raising and continuing professional development for staff
- The provision of BDA-accredited training for at least one teacher in most, if not all, schools
- Specialist support for schools to ensure quality improvement and appropriate provision.

To make this work, there has to a commitment on the part of leaders in schools in addition to an LEA commitment. An inspiring head teacher can ensure that all staff work together so that all their special educational needs (SEN) children are fully included. The SEN adviser in Swansea LEA, Cliff Warwick, states:

> Where schools have implemented the dyslexia friendly schools charter on a planned basis it has quickly become clear that there are wider benefits, including improvements in literacy across the curriculum, better teaching of literacy for all pupils, greater awareness of individual learning needs and the use of more varied teaching strategies.
>
> City and County of Swansea (1998)

Being an effective school and being dyslexia friendly are two sides of the same coin. Effective schools enjoy strong leadership, value staff development,

and pay close attention to the quality of learning and instruction. These are schools in which all children are important, regardless of ability or difficulty.

Within a philosophy of inclusion, we need to ensure that children with dyslexia have their differences recognized and addressed, and that they are known for the qualities that they have and not for their difficulties. When science and good practice have taught us so much, someone needs to be made responsible for ensuring that these children have their needs met. There is most definitely an issue of accountability.

In my work, I have had the privilege to meet some of those inspiring head teachers who have led their schools through a process of change, ensuring that all children achieve educational successes as well as social inclusion. Undoubtedly, there will be a few children whose needs are so severe that, despite everything that has been provided, both on a personal and whole-school basis, improvement does not happen. In those cases there may well be a need for a special school that is better geared to meet their needs. If all parties in leadership see the benefits to all of the true meaning of inclusion, the number of these children should be very small.

There is a need to change attitudes and philosophy of all staff in schools if we are to work effectively with children with dyslexia, their teachers and their parents. There are some shining examples around the UK where the cycle of frustration and low achievement has been broken, where success and a feel-good factor are experienced by all those involved. Furthermore, it has been shown that methods used for working with children with dyslexia will benefit many more in the classroom. Even those with the most severe needs can be well supported and make excellent progress. As Reid and Hinton (1996) state:

> Dyslexic children can provide the teacher with a considerable challenge but this can be met by specialist and trained teachers. If the school system, however, is not supportive, this challenge can seem insurmountable adding to teacher work stress, but with adequate school supports the difficulties associated with teaching dyslexic children can be overcome.

Let us ensure that this challenge is met by all, and that educational inclusion does not become a lottery depending on where people live.

Acknowledgement

In completing my contribution to this book, I wish to thank those who have contributed their heart-rending stories to me and have allowed me to share them in the public arena. It is left for me to say only that, like his mother Eileen, I pray that Nicholas John should rest in peace, and hope that, in the shadow of his death, there will be a light for others. When we know so much

about dyslexia, awareness-raising must take place and provision must be made so that no child with dyslexia will have to face unnecessary stress and suffering again.

References

British Dyslexia Association (1999) Achieving Dyslexia Friendly Schools. Reading: British Dyslexia Association.

Dunham J (1992) Stress in Teaching, 2nd edn. London: Routledge.

City and County of Swansea (1998) Dyslexia Friendly Schools – a good practice guide. Swansea: City and County of Swansea.

Hinton JW, Burton RF (1992) Clarification of the concept of psychological stress. International Journal of Psychosomatics 39: 42–43.

Llewellyn A, Hogan K (2000) The use and abuse of models of disability. Disability and Society 15: 157–165.

Reid G, Hinton JW (1996) Supporting the system – dyslexia and teacher stress. In: Reid G (ed.), Dimensions of Dyslexia, Vol. 2, Literacy, Language and Learning. Scotland: Institute of Education, pp. 393–402.

Chapter 10
Deadlines – collision, confusion, collapse

MORAG KIZIEWICZ

This is a good time to be writing about dyslexia and stress. It is early in a new year marked by the usual and particularly virulent flu infections and we are entering the end of semester exams in the University in which I work. Stress levels are extremely high among students and staff as we share the pressure of meeting points of assessment for course modules and units.

I write, as a dyslexic myself, both from the perspective of my personal experience of dyslexia and stress, and from my knowledge of the perspective of the dyslexic student attempting to address these difficulties and for those seeking to support them. I look at the underpinning factors that magnify stress for dyslexic people through the impact of the deadline on the dyslexic experience and draw on case studies from my work as Learning Support Manager.

Collision

Deadlines tend to cluster at the end of semesters and, if you are a student with dyslexia, you may have been given an extension of time to take account of the extra time needed to read and to write your course work. This extension may have taken you over a holiday period. However while you have been busy completing this course work you have not had much of a break nor an opportunity to revise for the exams.

Exams can be a bête noir for everyone, but for dyslexic students they can be hell. There are reasons for the additional stress specifically experienced by dyslexic students. You may have experience of exam failure as a dyslexic student and have extreme difficulty in understanding why it is hard for you to remember the content and to express the answers in the time available, to demonstrate your knowledge and understanding of the subject in a way that your lecturer can read and understand. You have experienced frustration and often feel misunderstood. Your anxiety increases as you attempt to read your

lecture notes which, if you have not had the support of a note taker or learning support tutor, will be scattered and incomplete, often illegible. You find it hard to focus on component modules as your mind ambles across different aspects of the course you have been studying, people you have met and things that have happened. It is likely, as the words before you blur into what seems an impossible mess, that these excursions will distract you sufficiently to day dream about something, anything, else – until you realize with a start that another day has flown by.

As the time available to complete your work rapidly and unforgivingly decreases so your anxiety and stress levels rise. You find it increasingly difficult to prioritize. Should you concentrate on finishing this piece of course work or preparing for that exam? As the stress levels rise it becomes increasingly difficult to find the information you need. Books and papers are scattered everywhere and, although you have learnt good strategies for colour coding and organizing your work, it becomes impossible to find the essential item you need. This leads to intense frustration, anger and grief.

The collision of subject areas merges in your mind and you find you cannot even remember what you read a minute ago. In fact you begin to doubt you have learnt anything at all. Although these experiences may appear on the surface to be the same as those that apply to everyone in this situation, there are specific factors that relate to dyslexia and magnify the stress for dyslexic people.

The collision factor is represented by the deadline. The very notion of a boundary to knowledge is anathema to a dyslexic. To meet several boundaries at the same time becomes a chaotic and tangled experience. The experience remains true for a dyslexic working adult required to attend meetings at specific times in different places, to catch trains and to meet deadlines for delivering lectures or papers. Difficulty with being in the right place at the right time, with knowing what date or day it is and with closing one discussion or activity in order to meet the next commitment are significators for dyslexia, and such demands do not create a natural environment for a dyslexic. In our time ordered time based world most dyslexics are fish out of water.

Not all dyslexic students are fazed by exams, and some cope by being ultra organized. However a dyslexic adult may have developed good coping strategies, they may be early for everything, double check every day on their commitments for that day, focus weeks ahead on what they need to revise and where they need to be when, and still run foul of this difficulty if something goes out of place, for example a pen or keys. Many adults will have non dyslexic support in the form of a secretary or spouse to help them to meet the requirements of time order. Others will have chosen the independent route of self employment or entrepreneur to give themselves enough flexibility to avoid most time ordered demands.

It is not accurate or sufficient to say dyslexics cannot manage in a time based world – we need time order. Imagine the chaos of an airport that went with the flow. Indeed, I have met a dyslexic air traffic controller who is exceptionally competent and able to manage the extremely stressful and highly time ordered demands and spatial skills required for this job. We need to explore what supports dyslexic inclusion in that world and how we can address the stress that time order inevitably engenders for the dyslexic person.

Confusion

If a sequential time ordered world is not one in which the dyslexic thrives then we need to question why some dyslexic people (Richard Branson, for example) evidently thrive very ably indeed and maybe we can learn from their strategies and from understanding what apparently causes the magnified element of confusion and stress in dyslexia.

One item of knowledge leads automatically to a connection with another and layers of information overlap and merge together. In dyslexia separating these layers is specifically difficult and when these areas have to be separated out the whole mode of thinking involved with dyslexia becomes tangled. If one strand is pulled the entire knot can tighten, apparently irretrievably, and if the wrong strand is cut the whole can unravel into a chaotic pile.

This way of thinking becomes particularly difficult to communicate clearly in writing and this is very evident in dyslexic sentence structure. The stress involved with this difficulty is magnified again if the individual does not know that they are dyslexic and therefore why they are having an intense difficulty that is evidently not shared by peers. The dyslexic individual whose dyslexia has not been identified will suffer from extreme anxiety when needing to submit written work to deadline.

Dyslexic students with whom I have been working have given me permission to use their experiences, the names have all been changed.

> Mark came in to the Learning Support office late one evening. He was anxious and nervous. Mark suffers from a severe skin condition and this was his first approach to Learning Support. He was having social and learning difficulties which he believed to be caused by his skin condition. We talked about the nature of his difficulties, he was a first year undergraduate student and he described a project which he could see very visually, and talk about in some depth, however he was finding it very difficult to write the required report. We discussed his physical difficulties and the relationship with stress, and then discussed his learning styles and preferred method of working. I referred Mark to the Medical Centre and also suggested the Quick Scan report, which is used as a screener, as a means to identify his best way of learning.

When we met to consider the report, which had picked up signs for dyslexia, Mark was extremely distressed. He felt he could not tell his family that he may be dyslexic, and was extremely concerned to ensure that nobody would know. The positive aspects of dyslexia were emphasized, however the experience was highly distressing, but also cathartic for Mark, who said he had always felt there was 'something different about him'. We talked about his early learning experiences, and also about the fact that he thought his father, who had recently been made redundant, was probably dyslexic too. Mark felt his A levels had been a terrible struggle and he was thrilled his results had enabled entry to University. We arranged to meet again the following week, and to give him time to consider the report before deciding what to do.

Mark began to appear in the Learning Support office on a practically daily basis. He demonstrated significant attachment needs and it was evident that he was anxious and isolated and in need of considerable support. Another meeting established that there were a number of factors influencing his heightened anxiety: fear of his family's response, financial pressures, fear of his department's response, and magnification of a difference he already felt due to his skin condition. He decided he would like to be referred to an Educational Psychologist for an identification of dyslexia, and was also referred to Student Money Services and to the Student Counsellor. We discussed strategies for managing his family communication and his sense of isolation, and he was given additional learning support tutor sessions.

Throughout the first year Mark received regular learning support and the stress and the resulting skin condition abated as the dyslexia was identified and Department support was put in place. At the end of the first year Mark had been able to meet the deadlines for submissions and exams, and his anxiety receded with the increased sense of acceptance and achievement. He still has some anxiety as he approaches exams and project submission deadlines and is showing occasional attachment needs, however he feels well, his skin condition is far less severe than in his first year, and to date there has been no repetition of the extreme anxiety and stress evident in his initial approach to Learning Support, and throughout the identification process.

David Pollock (1999) addresses the issue of identity. He proposes that earlier identification of dyslexia, increased support for students with dyslexia in Higher Education and wider access for mature students may all have a bearing on an individual's sense of self. He quotes Ivanic (1998), and supports the social construction model of identity, discussing the construction of the sense of difference and being 'other' as a consequence of difficulty with reading and writing. He goes on to suggest that this experience has the potential for becoming compounded and further magnified as a result of a student's experience on entering higher education and again on identification and assessment of dyslexia.

In addition to the confusion, self blame and stress that arise from not knowing you are dyslexic, there is often a history of academic exclusion.

Fred is an adult male European graduate student who owns a successful business in his own country. He was referred to Learning Support by the Students Union Academic advice and welfare office (Aware) who were supporting Fred in a request for a review of his exam results. Initially Fred's difficulties had presented as a result of personal pressures and Fred was seeking a review of his failure to pass the first semester exams on this basis. The Aware office work closely with the Learning Support Service and felt that there may be an underlying learning support issue affecting Fred's difficulties on the course.

I had initial discussions with Fred around language and structure of written work, and recommended we screen him for dyslexia. The results led to a longer discussion around his academic history. This was an emotional discussion for Fred, he reported having some difficulties in his first degree, in his home country, and added that he had 'not felt so bad since he was a little boy at school' referring to how he felt in the University at the present time. The discussion with Fred on the full dyslexia report was also highly charged emotionally and Fred felt a lot of grief around the diagnosis of dyslexia and in relating this to his life history. However he reported that 'since the first appointment I felt I was not alienated from all. To go in agony where you feel you do not have a friend in the world'. He reported finding and understanding the nature of his difficulties and finding acceptance was highly emotional, but also liberating.

The review procedure was an extremely stressful experience for Fred, however the dyslexia report was accepted by the Department and supported a successful outcome to the review. Fred was given a resit opportunity for his exams, with alternative arrangements and learning support tuition in place. Fred needed both counselling and learning support tuition to manage the stress of diagnosis and review. After his resit exams, during a visit home, he found that his younger brother had also been identified as dyslexic and was now receiving support at school.

Fred failed one of his resit exams, and was offered substantial additional course work for that component of the course. This added considerable pressure to Fred in managing to complete his other course work in addition, on time. He visited the Learning Support service regularly and had regular Learning Support tuition. The Learning Support staff were aware of Fred's complete commitment to the course and the hard work he was undertaking during this period, however the Department felt he had 'disappeared' and students and staff reported they hardly saw him. In turn, Fred felt communication with the Department was extremely difficult, and reported feeling very anxious about any communication to and from the Department. He also felt that some individual staff displayed apparent prejudice towards him as an individual, and towards dyslexia.

After some communication difficulties, which were negotiated with the help of the Learning Support Service, Fred was awarded an extension of time in which to complete his final project. Fred was successful in gaining his Masters degree, however he is excessively grateful to the Learning Support Service for their support, and still feels an outsider within his department. Further meetings with Fred have begun to deal with his early bullying experiences in school by teachers about which Fred had never spoken to anyone before. Fred said 'the best thing I have got from my study here has been in learning about my dyslexia'.

Fred and Mark's cases also demonstrate the social isolation and stress that can result from: a combination of the additional time required to work in academia with dyslexia; for reading and comprehending written material; for structuring a piece of work, and for the sense of 'otherness' common in disability issues. Mental health forums have identified the high level of mental health difficulty and depression associated with disability issues. Dyslexia can appear to be less marginalizing and less isolating than other disabilities due to the relevant ease with which everyday activities can be conducted, for example cooking and socializing. Many dyslexic people demonstrate high level social skills, however this can often be a coping strategy and the experience of 'otherness' and 'difference' is commonplace. Helene Cixous (in Susan Sellers, 1996) discusses 'keeping the other alive and different' and it is helpful for dyslexic people to meet the understanding and acceptance of others as well as to know and understand themselves and play to their strengths. Isolation, low self esteem and exclusion are well understood as major contributory factors in stress.

Memory loss or memory confusion is another significant stress factor in dyslexia. The difficulty in remembering dates and names, particularly when needing to recall these in viva or written submission under time pressure causes intense anxiety and distress. It is a common misunderstanding that exams are a measure of memory, however most exams are intended to be an equitable method of confirming that the work submitted is genuine evidence of the individual's own knowledge and understanding of a subject. Many dyslexic individuals believe they have a poor memory, due to the difficulty in recalling details at speed, and often fail to give required details in written submissions.

This in turn can lead to self doubt. Most dyslexic individuals appear to have exceptionally good long term memory. In exercises with students I have found that dyslexic students long term memory is often more detailed and extensive than those who are not dyslexic, however those same dyslexic students can demonstrate real difficulty with recall under pressure, and with their short term or working memory. This leads them to believe they cannot remember at all.

> Karen is an international graduate student and part-time tutor. She attended a staff development session about dyslexia, which included some memory recall techniques in which I ask the group to revisit an early childhood experience. She approached me afterwards to discuss the session and explained she could not usually remember anything from her early childhood, however this session had brought some memories out. We talked about her early experience and the possible impact of trauma or change on recalling early memories. We also discussed her learning style and area of study for her science based PhD.
>
> Karen's dyslexia was identified and when we met to discuss the report we discussed her academic achievement, Karen is a high achieving 'A' student. She

referred to my description of different learning styles and said she had such difficulties with certain components of her course she sometimes thought she was stupid. She also felt she had always had difficulty with her memory and avoided exams whenever she could.

I recommended some memory recall exercises, which include drawing. When she brought the drawings to me she was in tears that were a mixture of joy and sorrow. She said it was like discovering her past.

Karen has worked with the learning support tutor on the history of stress, rediscovering her memories and developing her understanding of the impact of dyslexia on her life.

In working with students on memory recall techniques, I have developed visual tools and liken the memory to a fish tank. The fish are the information stored in the long term memory, the surface of the water is the working memory and the air in the tank is short term memory for immediate recall. Helping dyslexic students to recall (or 'fish out') the information stored in their long term memory can be a pleasurable experience for student and tutor. The student rediscovers belief and confidence in themselves as they realize and recognize for themselves how much information they have absorbed and understood, and the tutor has satisfaction of helping the student to calm the working memory (the surface of the water) sufficiently for information to be retrieved. Under exam conditions the stress and anxiety of working under time pressure causes the working memory in dyslexia to become very disturbed and the 'fish' of information to scatter and dive for cover. It is vital that dyslexic students learn stress relieving techniques prior to undertaking exams. This is not always sufficient, however, to address dyslexic difficulties with exams.

Malcolm is an international Chinese student and he was extremely distressed when he first approached Learning Support, having failed his exams. He explained that as the elder son of illiterate parents he had major family responsibilities and had been under considerable personal stress, which had affected his exams at the end of the second year. He explained that he had managed to successfully pass his A levels in one year of study in England, which was followed by his entry to University. We discussed the fact that his department thought that many of his difficulties were due to his use of English, although he had passed the required level for use of English prior to commencing his course. Malcolm's spoken English was at that time very stilted, especially when distressed. We talked about language, structure and processing issues and his early academic experience. Malcolm was a mature student who had previously worked as a nurse, he reported feeling very isolated and was evidently frightened by the academic staff and fearful of talking to them. Anti-depressant treatment had been prescribed by the Medical Centre.

Malcolm's dyslexia was identified and a review enabled him to stay on campus in suspension and repeat his exams the following year. During the year in suspension, Malcolm became more positive and confident and came off the anti depressant treatment he had been prescribed which he felt had significantly affected his performance. He was generally happier and well, and the Support team felt confident of his progress until the date for the exams approached. The Director of Studies requested that Malcolm contact his lecturers for details of the exam content changes. Malcolm became highly anxious as contact with his Department was re-established, and as the date of the exams grew nearer, Malcolm was showing increasingly evident signs for stress.

The support tutor had subject expertise in Malcolm's discipline and a high level of confidence in his knowledge and understanding. Malcolm was a visual thinker and used visual techniques to recall information. In exercises it was clear that he had a comprehensive grasp of the subject area. Writing was slow and Malcolm was given additional time and the use of computer for the exams.

Malcolm had four exams in close succession. By the final two exams it was quite clear that the effects of stress and dyslexia were having an effect. He was exhausted and the Learning Support team were concerned for his welfare. Malcolm worked hard and conscientiously in preparation for the exams and was given stress relieving techniques, however there was particular anxiety in the multiple choice paper, in which Malcolm found it hard to sequentially order his answers. The results were given as fails, and the exam results were lower than his previous results. Malcolm returned to his home country at the end of the academic year, following extraordinary personal commitment, without completing a degree.

One of the speakers at the Genius in the Genes Symposium at the Green College Oxford (Arts Dyslexia Trust, 2000) described how, as an undergraduate student at Oxford, he had repeatedly failed his exams, year on year. His ability was recognized by his tutors and he was given support and several resit opportunities. He described the dyslexia within his family and explained that his concern was that such 'opportunities to have one's ability recognized and supported despite an inability with exams was no longer available in contemporary education practice'. Surely an academic system that cannot find an alternative way of assessing a student's abilities is failing academia as well as the student, and is causing uncounted misery for individuals within such a system.

The confusion in sequencing, the difficulty with ordering thoughts and content significant in dyslexia, is not representative of a lack of ability or understanding. Indeed, as in Malcolm's case, it can represent such a high level of information storage in the memory that processing the information in timed exam situations is an impossible task. To address the stress this engenders we need to reflect and reconsider our understanding of exams as being the only way of assessing and ensuring an individual's own work.

Collapse

I was talking about writing this chapter to some dyslexic students over a cup of coffee, asking them what they thought of the title. They laughed in recognition and gave me more examples of the stress they are currently undergoing as they prepare for their exams. One student, who was told by an educational psychologist when her dyslexia was identified that she was not University material, is in her final year and heading for a 2:1 degree while coping well with a high degree of personal stress; another has successfully completed her first degree and is now undertaking post graduate study. The third member of our group was quieter, and almost tearful, 'I think I am at the collapse stage' she said.

We met later to discuss and address her difficulties. For many students the collapse stage is reached as pressure is heaped on pressure until the 'final straw' stage is reached. The final straw does not need to be particularly heavy, nor in its self particularly difficult to sort out. However the accumulated overload of work pressure, exhaustion and attempting to keep all information in the short term memory for fear of not being able to retrieve it is overwhelming and leads to the stage of breakdown and giving up. This is the stage most likely to result in failure to retain the student. The student has attended all lectures, submitted course work, attended support sessions, learnt enabling software, and is simply unable to find yet more energy to revise and ready herself for the exam stage.

One aspect of this collapse is fear: fear of failure, fear of derision and fear of loss. The student has had a history of this experience and would prefer to avoid undergoing it again. She finds it difficult to believe dyslexia is the cause, prejudice towards dyslexia being quite evident in her Department. She blames herself for being 'weak, too tired, unable to function'.

Perhaps more than most of us dyslexics need duvet days. The amount of energy consumed by the level of processing involved is intense and good rest in a safe environment is the most effective way to address this stress. It is difficult, however, for the dyslexic person to relax, for fear of losing or forgetting that which they know, for fear of not waking up in time, for fear of never getting up again; but they can, they will and they do! The courage and persistence of dyslexic students in the face of adversity never ceases to amaze and impress me.

Another element to the collapse stage can be the perfectionist principle – the three P's of Perfectionism, Procrastination and Paralysis. Many dyslexics will have a common experience of receiving work covered with red lines and corrections, or of having a teacher refuse to mark their work because they cannot make sense of it. This tends to have the effect of creating in the dyslexic a need to present a perfectly prepared piece of work. Hours will be spent doing draft after draft, ensuring the information is ordered and clear. In

so doing editing becomes a peculiar function of gradually reducing long and descriptive sentences that the person might say, to short summaries that use few simple to spell words and have brief sentences that cannot be grammatically incorrect.

This piece of work then fails to give the whole picture the student wishes to present, and so the student procrastinates, going over it again, and again, doing something else, watching tv until ultimately the student collapses and in despair gives up the struggle. The good enough principle needs to be learnt, and the freedom to express thoughts, however messily, and to trust in the component ideas, needs to be encouraged.

Finally, collapsing too is permissible, re-creation is just that.

Dead line

Every day, as an adult dyslexic, I am confronted by my difficulties and by my strengths. I have learnt good coping strategies over the years, understand myself and my abilities and am nevertheless confronted by daily hurdles of time keeping, finding things, meeting sequential demands. Humour is one of my coping strategies, forgiving myself is another.

I use my holistic skills to take the overview, and synchronicity, that meeting point of times and events that happens apparently without effort, entirely naturally when intuitive skills are being fully utilized, and can flow and connect when I need to with immediate time demands. I trust my knowledge and know the information I need is in my mind and will flow out when I need it to. I remind myself that the ability to forget is an essential part of human survival, knowing that if we all remembered everything all of the time we could not survive.

I am a good manager and when I am under stress and have deadlines to meet, as I have now, and am overloaded with what is in my short term memory, I can give myself permission to say no to some demands in favour of making time for my creative thinking process. I respect myself and find that others respect me too.

Would it have helped me to have known, when I failed English O level, that I was dyslexic? I had teachers who believed in me and wanted to query the result, and I lost faith in exams then. I retook the exam and got a grade 2, but instead of becoming a writer, which was my first love, I left the academic system in favour of the arts base. I had a good education, was taught stress management in my twenties and have an exciting and varied life and career. Yes, it would have helped my self esteem, helped me to understand my difficulties and yes, I would have stopped apologizing for myself and aimed higher.

My regret is that in our current assessment system we lose so much creative thought to the regimen of the clock, and so much creative writing to

the insistence on sequential delivery. This is clear in poetry and other modes
of non sequential expression.

> In the unmade essays he rushes to meet
>
> A deadline tide coming in
>
> In the sentence some things are hidden
>
> Water slapping on stone

Kiziewicz (1997)

Hope

So how do dyslexic people overcome the distress that is created by being a
round peg in a square world, or to return to my earlier metaphor, a fish out of
water? They become amphibian. We learn from the heightened stress and
pain that dyslexic people experience and work towards addressing their difficulties.

In our research for the Webb Project, developing access to Higher
Education for people with dyslexia (1997–2000) we found three strands
needed to be plaited together to achieve good results: Identification,
Intervention and Institution Issues.

In identifying their dyslexia, students learn they are round pegs and work
with their strengths rather than their weaknesses. They find solace in identifying and confronting the reason for, and nature of, their difficulties. They
recognize the influence on their past and present experiences and gain
support for forgiving themselves, for grieving, healing and recovery and
developing a new self esteem. I describe it as finding, making and holding
four inches of their own territory in which they can firmly stand when chaos
or criticism looms.

Mark, now in his final year, has learnt to manage his workload and to anticipate the pressure points. He has developed methods for ordering and
locating his work and has more confidence and support from his department
in presenting some of his work in alternative format, for example
photographs. He no longer shows the attachment needs evident in his first
year. He has good friendships within his peer group and has a sense of
humour about the occasional conflict in group dynamic situations when
different ways of working reveal themselves.

In intervention students learn to incorporate new ways of working and to
use all tools available, from enabling technology to recording lectures, from
electronic diaries to the support of a good and organized friend to enable
them to succeed. Learning Support tutors aid the students in developing the
coping strategies that suit them, whether these are visual, organizational or

structural and to develop their understanding of different learning styles. Karen collected her PhD last summer and as she shook the hand of the University Chancellor she was beautiful, radiant: Fred calls it being reborn.

Addressing the institution issues enables students to negotiate pathways, including alternative arrangements for assessments, and to gain support from their department. Dyslexic members of staff feel more able to disclose their dyslexia and the culture within education becomes a learning environment rather than an assessment minefield. Yesterday I met two dyslexic students over coffee: the current semester exam results are out. One has achieved a 60% pass rate having had to resit the year and learn coping strategies. One was disappointed that he had 'only' passed 6 modules out of 8, having entered University via an access course. Exams will never be the best method of revealing dyslexic ability, of assessing their knowledge and understanding of a subject. Enlightened educationalists are working on alternative approaches, but in the meantime it is the only, albeit clumsy, method we have of ensuring institutions are assessing an individual's own work.

Dyslexic people cannot measure their own ability by their exam results. Perhaps a truer measure for their success is the quality of their lives, their working and social relationships, their contribution to society and ultimately their well being in a 24x7 working world. Malcolm has blended his western education with Chinese approaches, is completing a degree programme in a Chinese University and is contributing to the growing understanding of dyslexia in his home town at the same time. I am writing this chapter and living a creative life. The stress experienced by dyslexic people is magnified when they are asked to perform to their weaknesses, the joy is experienced by others when dyslexic people are encouraged to work to their strengths.

Acknowledgements

My grateful thanks to: the students at the University of Bath for their courage in sharing their experiences and for teaching me, the staff of the Learning Support Service for their commitment, and to Dr Mary Haslum and Iain Biggs at the University of the West of England and Professor Tim Miles for their patience, clarity and support.

References

Arts Dyslexia Trust (2000) Genius in the Genes symposium. http://members. sniffout.com/adt

Ivanic R (1998) Writing and Identity. Amsterdam: John Benjamins.

Kiziewicz M (1997) Kimmeridge. In: Caddy D (ed.), Dorset Waters. Blandford Forum, Dorset: East Street Poets.

Pollock D (1999) Dyslexia and identity: some experiences of undergraduates who are dyslexic. In: Dyslexic Learners: A holistic approach to support. Proceedings of conference on dyslexia support. Leicester: De Montfort University.

Sellers S (1996) In: Helene Cixous, Authorship, Autobiography and Love. Cambridge: Polity Press.

Chapter 11
Living with dyslexia: a personal account

DAVE ALEXANDER

At five years old I did not understand the words stress and dyslexia. It wasn't until I was twelve that dyslexia was mentioned but I had experienced stress every day at school and now know that I am dyslexic for life.

I find it difficult to explain how my differences compared with my school friends. My only thought is that it felt like being a tourist abroad – most things were strange to me yet it seemed everyone else was getting on. At an early age I had no sense of time – days of the week and months of the year were confusing. Stress was felt whenever my slowness in reading and difficulty in writing were tested.

I was marked out as different because I was stuck on the same reading book. Despite help with reading every night, my school friends moved onto other books and I just couldn't. I hated being asked to read aloud – I would panic and become even more confused over the words. Whatever I did I just could not get the hang of reading.

You may be expecting me to say I was bullied at school or called names. I was not – this claim was left for the teachers. I remember looking back how one teacher said there was no such thing as dyslexia, I was just 'thick'. School therefore was not enjoyable – I lived for the weekend when I could ride my motor-bike. My grandfather bought me my first bike at five and every weekend up to about 14 I enjoyed motor-cross. This was something I could do and do well. Other boys used to watch the tricks I could do and I soon had a reputation for going faster and jumping higher than others. Motorcross made me feel confident – my dad said it was good for my self-esteem.

Junior school was not good for my self-esteem – in fact I hated school. At 11, I sat an independent school test and failed. Only then did teachers say to my parents that there could be a problem called dyslexia. Their advice was to see an educational psychologist, which we did.

Looking back, I didn't enjoy any of these tests and changes; moving school was stressful but I could not go to the secondary school where all of my

friends were going because of LEA boundary changes. Hence the stress of another exam; often I was sick before exams. I would get migraine headaches and sometimes be physically sick in the days before the exams. Many times I stayed at home but still no one at junior school tried to help – I was left to sink.

The exam at the college didn't go well and hence more test with the psychologist. It seemed like another teacher – a bit cold and not always making himself clear on what he wanted me to do. A day long test in Oxfordshire recorded I was dyslexic and I felt relieved; I was not thick. His advice was that I could catch up the lost ground on my reading and writing and the college was willing to accept me because they have specialist teachers for dyslexic students.

At college, I met Dan. He was dyslexic and my best friend. We attended 'dyslexic classes' together, shared the same sense of humour (this was to get us in trouble from time to time) and struggled to do school work together. Mrs Middleton was my specialist teacher – by this time I needed a lot of convincing that any teacher could help me. Again I struggled, this time with a label but I did not enjoy school. Exams were very stressful, trying to copy from the board was stressful (I often used to phone Dan to compare notes on what homework we were meant to be doing) and it was stressful not being able to convey my thoughts into print. However, I realized I was far from thick and thanks to the support of my parents and my belief in myself, my future will be working for myself. I am putting plans together to create an internet mail order company to further my other passions – motor-bike racing and snowboarding.

School was not a good preparation for me. I still experience stress – no more so than when I had to undergo the theory exam for my driving test. To help, I used a CD Rom and after a lot of effort passed first time; the first real exam I succeeded at. However, despite being a good driver I failed the practical. This was because at a roundabout I could not determine my right from my left and feeling stressful, made the wrong turn from the examiner's instructions. However, I did pass on my second attempt.

Driving has also provided another example of stress. One night I was stopped by the Police in a routine check. Everything was OK but I became confused over my date of birth and had to provide my documents at the police station. I collected the documents but didn't read that my temporary cover note had expired – the desk sergeant threatened me with court action. But after a lot of going backwards and forwards, the matter was resolved.

No one can really know what it is like to be dyslexic unless you are dyslexic. I still feel like a tourist abroad and anything to do with reading and writing can be stressful. Despite school, I am confident in my own ability and my future success – to that end I owe it to my parents for their belief in me. In case you are thinking, I haven't written this – I dictated my thoughts and had it written for me. Trying to write would have been too stressful!

Chapter 12
Disruptive dyslexic cycle of stress

JOY ALDRIDGE

I feel a small 'pen sketch' of my dyslexic background may be of help to the reader. I was 38 years old when first diagnosed as being dyslexic. Born after the World War II into a poor working class farming family, the middle of seven children. My early educational life was traumatic and fearful not to say stressful. My older sister had the unenviable task of 'dragging' me by the hand to school. She has often recounted the day I sat in the middle of the main road causing the stoppage of lorries and cars.

In an effort to get the message across of just how much I dreaded going to school. I have a keen memory of my early school experiences, aware that my classmates displayed no difficulty with understanding the symbols the teacher wrote on the black board. In fact they did it with ease, but they made no sense to me and 'how out of place' it made me feel. Throughout my school life from the age of four and a half to fifteen, I had an intense dislike of reading aloud. Which in some classes could be quite frequent, on such occasions it was quite usual for the teacher to start at the front of the class and gradually work round the room with every child taking their turn to read a paragraph aloud from a specific book. I use to try and work out how many times it would take for my turn to come around. I was never able to follow the script because I was too busy flicking through the following pages trying desperately to work out what paragraph I would be expected to read and then try to work out what the words said. As it got closer to my turn I would feel my heart pounding, my face going hot and red and my stomach churning and say a silent prayer for the ground to open up and swallow me up. My attempts were more usually followed by sniggering and laughter, to this day I strongly dislike reading out aloud and the idea of public speaking.

Due to my social/class background the teachers expectation of my ability and performance was low to say the least. So no one seemed to care that I had great difficulty with learning to read and write which personally caused

me a great deal of unhappiness and distress, because I so longed to be able to read and spell. With the net result that I went through my school years and early adult life with a poor self image and low self esteem and being extremely shy. However I did excel on the sports field. I was also at a very early age quite naturally gifted with a needle and thread, having made and designed my older sisters bridesmaid dresses at the age of fourteen. That I left school at fifteen with no academic paperwork was of no little surprise or concern to anyone but my self. What followed was low paid work and later marriage.

On the death of my beloved father, with two children and later a third, my son was experiencing specific language problems, having not said baby sounds until the age of three. I wished to know more about my fathers experience in the war, to which end I enrolled in an 'O' level modern history class, with no thoughts of taking the exam, just to gain an understanding. I got carried away with the flow of the class and managed a 'C' in the exam. Having made friends with another mature student at her persuasion I enrolled in English Language gaining a 'B' which equally surprised the tutor and myself. I don't think any exam result will ever taste as sweet as that one. Sociology 'O' and 'A' level followed, with the teacher in the sociology class advising me that the way my mind worked I might be more suited to degree level study. The advice coincided with the need and desire to find out more about language and the learning process to help understand my sons learning needs. It was at this point in my life, despairing of ever getting the appropriate help at school for my son who by now was six years old, I stumbled by chance on a book by Tim Miles about Dyslexia. Up to this point in time I had not been aware of dyslexia. Autism had been ruled out and he had been diagnosed as suffering from a specific language disorder (aphasia). On completion of Tim's book I paid to have a full assessment for my son. When in receipt of the report I gave a copy to the schools educational psychologist, only to have the report thrown back at me across the table with the words 'its irresponsible for someone to write a report like this of someone so young', that there was no such thing as dyslexic, by now he was seven. My behaviour that followed and the resulting advise changed the path of my son's life and my own. I wrote to Tim Miles, seeking advice I sent a copy of the report. Tim replied, gave me his home phone number and during the course of two phone calls gave me guidance and advice in respect to what I could do to help improve my son's present circumstances and that which would help him to reach his potential. To this day, my son and I owe Tim Miles a great debt, the like of which can't be repaid.

I enrolled with the Open University, not with the aim of gaining a degree, just to gain what knowledge I could. One day towards the end of the course, I took a step back and looked long and hard at the Tutors comments and asked myself 'was it possible that I too could be dyslexic?' Once the question

of my own dyslexia had come to rest in my consciousness I needed to find out the truth about myself. To which end I again wrote to Tim Miles in North Wales to ask if he would be prepared to do an assessment.

On a damp autumn day before the break of dawn I journeyed from Reading Station to North Wales. The person who made the journey down was not the same person armed with a dyslexic statement who returned the early hours of the following day and a few days away from my first of many O.U. exams. I remember Tim being just as pleased with the results as I. I recall him looking around the room and pointing to the books lining one wall and saying 'if you had not been dyslexic you could have achieved this', his advice being to grow a tough hide and study to the level I felt I could cope with taking into account the level I was reading and spelling at. Before I left Dorothy Gilroy gave me some very valuable advice too and has kept in touch over the years encouraging me. On leaving Bangor University, with a feeling of a great weight being lifted from my mind I felt exhilarated at the idea that I was not stupid after all, but bright and dyslexic. Negative early learning experiences flashed through my mind, such as experience of learning to drive under verbal instruction and the instructors expressed frustrations especially every time he said take the next right turn and I would signal left and turn left. It was disastrous trying to learn three point turns under verbal instruction. I only started to develop the skill when the instructor gave up on verbal instructions and left me to work it out myself. He did blame me for his premature greying hair on numerous occasions. Had he and I known then that I had a left right confusion, life would have been much easier for us both. We forget the stress a dyslexic can cause others.

As a postscript, my son is a well-adjusted young man. After being told at the age of four and a half that he would not do well at 'normal school' and being informed that ESN School might suit him better. I am pleased and proud to report that when he left his state school he had gained 9 GCSE's, 4 at 'C' and above, one being an 'A' in Drama. He also achieved a BTEC National Diploma in Leisure Studies, having achieved several merits within the course.

When asked if I wish to make a contribution to this book about dyslexia and stress, my first thought was to write about the stress suffered by not having been diagnosed dyslexic. I have decided to give focus to the extra stress in my working life, which is the direct result of being dyslexic.

Dyslexic stress in my working life

Minute-taking

The organisation that I work for has no regular minute taker, which means in certain situations such as reviews and meetings, it falls on me to take the

minutes. In such situations I find it difficult to be selective about what is being discussed. This can result in choosing between two different strategies:

- being selective and losing some of the discussion
- trying to write down everything word for word and attempting to sort out the jumbled mess of unformed incomplete words straight after the meeting to produce something reliable and for my secretary to type.

Whichever course of action I choose it is anxiety and stress provoking above that of non dyslexics. Thankfully I now have a good secretary, who has learnt how to read my notes better than I can, which I am extremely grateful.

Report writing/exams

Like most dyslexics I use a 'dual track' thought process when writing:

- The creative ideas of what I wish to say
- Listening in my mind's eye to the sounds the words are making and then try to produce these sounds in the correct order to form words. Hoping that the finished product will be readable after three or four rewrites.

After such periods of prolonged concentrated writing I always experience the feelings of mental and physical fatigue and painful headaches. As we know from studies of stress (Coleman, 1988; Patel, 1992) that stress can cause physical 'unwell' symptoms.

Meeting/case conferences

There are two problems in relation to my dyslexia which present as a problem in such situations:

- If people talk too fast I can miss some of the debate
- Difficulty of holding on to an idea which I need to hold in my short-term memory, which we know has an inherent weakness and the ensuing difficulties of having to wait my turn to speak when needing to speak immediately an idea presents itself. I am faced with the dilemma of risking losing the idea and waiting my turn to speak or butting in to say what is on my mind.

This can (and quite rightly) be viewed as being impolite and even antag-onizes other people, especially the person being interrupted. It looks and feels unprofessional which again is stress proving. Added to which if someone makes a derogatory statement about such behaviour it further adds to the anxiety and stress. Secondly, one can employ the strategy of writing the idea down as it comes to mind. Again to be able to do this a dual thought process is required which results in missing some of the debate while writing.

I could take the easy less stressful option and let my contribution be lost, but, that leaves one feeling frustrated and inadequate and of a feeling of not doing my job as well as I am capable of. For dyslexics in a professional setting there is no way of avoiding stress since they cannot afford to take the easy path, we always have to walk the bumpy road in ill fitting shoes. By the very nature of our dyslexia we will suffer more stress in such situations in the workplace. The fact that the dyslexia handicap is hidden to view from others actually only compounds the stress suffered.

What has contributed to my stress level has been the need to constantly use various coping strategies on a daily basis, especially in my working environment. Also how a 'bad' day can be so disruptive and stress provoking when in the pursuit of the most basic and simplest of activities. What follows is a short account of a 'bad' dyslexic day.

Disruptive cycle of dyslexia

On visiting a shop to purchase a household item for one of the group homes at work that needed to be delivered by the stores transport. The assistant asked for the address of where the item was to be delivered, a simple enough question one might think for someone who goes regularly to the address, that is only the case if you are non dyslexic and not having one of those dyslexic days. I first gave her the name and number of the wrong house, quickly tried to correct the position, but I could see clouds of doubt crossing her forehead. On the second attempt I got the house name and road correct, but as soon as the number had crossed my lips I began to have doubts that this was correct. I took a deep breath and told her I thought the number was wrong, but I could not remember if it was 108 or 109, this did not help my situation. I could then see the storm clouds of doubt gathering across her face. In an attempt to get it right the next time round, I asked permission to phone the house concerned to check the house number. On using the phone I misdialed (didgets in wrong order), I made my apologies to the unknown person on the other end of the line, in full view of by now a quite confused sales assistant. On my second attempt I got through to the correct number and asked the care officer on duty for the house number, she expressed some surprise and I could hear her

chuckling to herself as I replaced the phone. On completion of the sale, when I was about to leave the shop I asked the sales assistant for a receipt, saying she had not given it to me. She was adamant that she had and prompted me to search my bag, whereupon I found it in a side pocket, I had no recollection of her giving it to me, or of my own actions of putting it in my bag. The non verbal interaction which I could see taking place between the sales assistant and her colleague did little to help my self-esteem. I reminded my self I was not stupid, just dyslexic and that I had tomorrow to look forward to, and that with luck my mental processes might be more 'conformists' since past experiences told me that this was just the beginning of a disruptive dyslexic day.

I would like to be able say that such an occasion as described is rare and that it happened at the end of a particularly busy day. This was not the case, it was the first task of my working day and the beginning of the week. It was one of those unexplained days when my dyslexia makes it's self known to the outside world in a 'mega-phone' way. I don't know why I have days like this, but at such times I can be particularly clumsy, knocking into things, walking into door frames, spilling drinks etc. One such stressful experience; when in a large DIY shop purchasing tins of household paint, I don't know how I misjudged the lifting of a very large tin of paint from it's shelf, but suddenly other paint fell to the floor landing on my foot and bursting. I was not a pretty sight – knee deep in paint unable to see my shoes or legs. I was quickly ushered away by several staff to start the arduous task of cleaning me up, on such occasions hand blow dryers can come in very useful for drying cloths. To say that the staff were kind to me is an understatement. Also more recently when in the dentist chair, I pick up a tumbler of mouthwash and dropped it, after the dentist cleared up the spillage with me mumbling apologies, only to repeat the incident again minutes later. I always make sure now that I pick the tumbler up with both hands with great care under the watchful eye of the dentist.

If I had not been aware of my dyslexia I am sure by now I would have begun to suspect some kind of brain disorder starting to show. Such disruptive days are compounded by the fact that when experiencing them, I desperately want to use some kind of adjustments or strategies to get some kind of balance. I don't know if the awareness creates an underlying anxiety which in turn sets up a cycle of disruption, but I do know that such times are very stress provoking. I see the disruption cycle as consisting of the following:

- poor co-ordination
- information accessing problems
- loss of confidence to produce the correct information
- lowering of self-esteem
- increased anxiety
- feeling stressed
- experiencing the physical symptoms of stress (such as headache).

For me personally I don't experience an isolated 'black-spot', if it's a bad day it's a bad day, like riding a storm, just hang in and try to get through the day without too many problems.

Without such committed people who have made dyslexia awareness their life's work, so many of us dyslexic's would still be perishing by the wayside of academic life. I don't know if I will ever make up my lost days of learning, but I am still trying to and feel privileged that many have made it possible.

What for me continues to be a source of frustration is the difficulty with the recall of names (people, places and things), which can also be detrimental to others as well as myself.

Of all the aspects that are stress provoking, I find it to be the interlink of the hiddeness of the handicap with the experience of the tiredness, through the constant need to use strategies to produce and perform at a 'normal' level. This is especially stressful on a 'bad dyslexic day' when I can't string more than a few letters together in the correct order and can't finish my answers without having to go back mentally to the beginning. If you have no picture of words in your mind, every word you write has to be spelt out letter by letter mentally whilst writing.

Physical stress

Due to poor coordination and in an attempt to aid my letter formation I have always held my pen over tight, as with typing I press the keys too heavy, and have much difficulty trying to control the mouse of a computer. I have been experiencing tendon problems with my writing hand and wrist. I have worn a brace on it and received hospital treatment of injection. This did relive the problems for some months.

Unconscious baggage

We need to recognise that dyslexics early school life can still have some measure of impact at times in later life. Such as a 'bad dyslexics day' when you feel the old stupid self is lurking in the shadows waiting to trip you up over the words, your mind plays hide and seek with the sounds of words and you can't find the right ones no matter how hard you try.

In spite of the lateness of being diagnosed dyslexic and sometimes momentary sadness at the loss of so much positive early formal academic experience, I have managed to claw my way up the academic mountain as a mature student and I still continue with my quest for knowledge. I have to date managed to gain whilst also working, a Diploma in Applied Social Science, an Advanced Diploma in Special Needs in Education, a BSc. and a M.A. in Education. I would dearly love even at this late stage to do a PHD in Education. I can in all honesty say that all the feelings of exhaustion and

accompanying stress are well worth the sense of achievement and the knowledge gained. Never the less, what I quickly acknowledged and took fully on board very early after my diagnosis was that the path to knowledge and greater mental freedom would be stoney, long and difficult (if not some what familiar). I knew that I would tire quickly, but the knowledge that the diagnosis gave me and the accompanying advice were like much needed refreshments along the journey. If a dyslexic is fortunate to survive any early setbacks, the learning experience is definitely character building, which help shape and mould a resourceful person. Moreover, dyslexics learn very early how to live with added stresses on a daily basis, which makes them fit for many kinds of work.

As a footnote, I would like it acknowledged how supportive The Open University has been with my (dyslexic) learning experience. However, this most positive and fruitful experience would not have been possible without the lifelong work conducted by Tim Miles, Ved Verma, their team and others working in the field of dyslexia. Especially their individual belief dyslexics have many hidden abilities and how they install immense faith in people, with regards to what is possible. More over Tim, Ved and others have broken down so many barriers in the process of educating and informing people about the dyslexic condition and thereby helping to reduce their stress. I for one (and I am for sure countless thousands of other people) will be eternally grateful for all their work. Thank you all.

References

Coleman V (1988) Stress Management Techniques. London: Gold Arrow Publications Ltd.
Patel C (1992) Understanding Stress. London: Hodder & Stoughton and Consumers' Association.

Chapter 13
Dyslexia without stress

MICHAEL NEWBY

Some people believe remediating the basic problems dyslexics face gets rid of problem traits and the dyslexia as well as any existing stress. But in reality dyslexics are part of an alternative cognitive spectrum consisting of those who learn and think in ways which aren't fully synchronized with the majority learning mode (Hynd and Cohen, 1983, pp. 121–127). Yet this alternative grouping generally tends to be adaptive and broadly creative.

However, dyslexia is mainly viewed in negative terms, since research into those cognitive states where divergence from the norm causes initial and/or long-term problem traits, concentrates on those same negative traits. Dyslexia over the last hundred years has accumulated very many negative connotations. It remains broadly true that most experts on dyslexia have not only avoided studying positive traits but also didn't value any insights dyslexics had about dyslexia (Miles, 1993, pp. 237, 296). But the best way to counter problems and stress is to view each individual holistically. That way we can use positive attributes as a foundation for educational and/or mental-health progress. Too often Local Education Authorities only appear to see problems not the child and also tend to prioritize cost saving before aiding children.

Education has become a succession of standardized attainment tests (SATs) and other markers which are used to produce league-tables of performances in the basics. Pressure is exerted on schools to meet set academic targets, with financial and educational status depending on pupil performances. Stress has become a constant threat to both pupils and professionals. This generates even greater stress in alternative minded children struggling to meet set formal targets in the basics.

Today education is over-emphasizing the basics and ignoring the fact machines can now perfectly perform those very same basics. It also downgrades creativity which is the main trait that separates us from new generation of 'intelligent' machines. Everyday PCs can be programmed to accept orally dictated data and instructions telling the machine what to store and what to do including reading books. Machines do this with total

accuracy. Users now accept machines will automatically remove human errors by offering alternative wording, re-structuring sentences and correcting spelling and grammar.

Yet even as machines extend their performance beyond the basics, those who are initially unable to match machine accuracy are now experiencing increasing levels of bullying. Some teachers resent having their schools' league-table positions lowered by educational underachievers whilst some schools take to finding ways of either removing or driving out academic under-performers.

Stress in dyslexics is intensified because tensions increase when they experience scholastic failure in educational systems that undervalue their range of positive traits such as being creative, inquisitive and highly motivated.

My grand niece, by marriage, at primary school was diagnosed as being a spelling dyslexic. Because of cost cutting the local education authority decided not to offer her any extra help at all. For nearly a year her class teacher and most of her peers took to bullying my grandniece 'for letting the class down'. She became so stressed she sat down and wrote this poem at home.

> My blood bubbles and burns,
>
> I go bright red,
>
> My hands and forehead
>
> Are wet with sweat.
>
> I erupt like a volcano
>
> and bite back
>
> At the things they said.
>
> I don't think what I am saying
>
> I just say the first thing
>
> That comes into my head.

The first verse is a good description of the high blood pressure generated by severe stress. Again I had to rebuild her confidence and her mother again had to remind the school her daughter was dyslexic as well as pointing out how badly she was being treated. My grandniece is now doing well.

Such bullying is returning education to the time of Hans Christian Anderson. He wrote his autobiographical tale, *The Ugly Duckling*, in order to point out that he, the bullied ugly duckling, had really been a cygnet who became a swan. Anderson, the one time school dunce, overcame his initial dyslexic difficulties by letting his imagination fly until eventually he learnt to use a swan's quill to write down his flights of fancy. This is why neither teachers nor parents should view a child having initial problems as being the problem, but should instead seek out their positive attributes and build progress around them

Rawson (1981) stated dyslexics were a diverse group of adaptive thinkers. West (1991) produced data which supported Rawson's viewpoint in his study of famous people who had been educational underachievers, Miles and Gilroy (1986), in their study of dyslexia at college, noted dyslexic students very often had advance understanding of both English and Maths despite still having problems with basics (pp. 4 and 57). Miles (1993, p. 237) suggested that dyslexics may display 'an unusual balance of skills' and that research into their talents has been largely neglected. He also suggests that traditional intelligence tests often do not do justice to a dyslexic's full potential.

In fact the true potential of such educational underachievers can't be measured by standardization in either academic or IQ tests because such tests are designed to precisely measure the majority's performance.

Preschool it is quite common for these children to be either orally and/or creatively advanced. Many parents are aware of this higher potential in dyslexic and other alternative learning children. But this awareness causes stress in parents when they find that their children, rather than remaining equal to or ahead of their peers, enter a cycle of academic failure at school. No matter how well parents conceal concern about their child's educational progress, nearly all such children will become aware of their parents' worries. This then intensifies each child's own stress about not being able to keep up with their peers at school. Yet such children still retain the potential the parents recognized preschool.

The key to avoiding/reducing parental and child stress is for both to accept that any initial academic setbacks are the result of alternative mental maturation/educational development. Both should also accept that when thoroughly encouraged and correctly educated such children over time really will develop their 'unusual balance of skills' in ways which cannot always be foreseen. Thus a dyslexic mother of twins found her dyslexic daughter who at first was academically behind her twin brother and also was so clumsy she 'tripped over air' by secondary level was producing above average work including art. Educationalists and other professionals should accept it is perfectly natural for people who belong to cognitive minorities to develop

giftedness in ways which diverge from the expected norms. Without such a shift in attitude these individuals will continue to find it difficult to reach their full potential within educational systems designed for majority thinkers and will continue to become stressed.

West (1991) in his chapter on Mathematics, believed that a minority of children learn maths in reverse order; that is they leave the basics until last whilst concentrating on learning advance mathematical patterning etc. Certainly at college my daughter outperformed her maths tutors, in some advanced areas, before she fully grasped the basics.

Over the years I have seen many other children unexpectedly flower in the areas causing them initial problems. Both as teacher and parent, since 1964 I've found that alternative learners progress better academically and creatively under a childcentric, imaginative and broadly based curriculum. This way they can explore the more advanced and stimulating work they need, even as they struggle with aspects of the basics. I even took a class of nine year olds, from the roughest council estate in Sunderland, to use university equipment and observe experiments in the Geology and Botany Departments at Durham. Joseph, a boy who lived in a council house where windows were regularly smashed during family rows, a few weeks later brought in a tiny fossil shell preserved in flint. He had found it amongst the pebbles beside the school's sports field.

We really must accept that rigorously and systematically teaching basics first just isn't inherently right for all children. However, this isn't the same as claiming basics shouldn't be taught to dyslexic and other underachievers but rather sometimes, basics should be secondary to more advance work in areas which spark these young underachievers interests.

Dyslexia is partly the outcome of rigid educational systems. In pre-literate eras most oral and visual creatives were highly valued as communicators and teachers. Dyslexia and most other types of academic underachievement only exist in literate societies. But in our age of powerful computer chips such negative definitions are both wrong and outdated particularly since the formal teaching of literacy and other basics isn't fully effective. It isn't adaptive and diverse enough to develop more unusual forms of giftedness. Moreover today, an over-concentration on the basics is concentrating on what have become machine skills. The fact is remedial education for intelligent underachievers will never be fully effective, unless and until it also develops each individual's imagination

Pumfrey and Reason (1992) recorded research showing that the first crucial step in remediation is to restore each individual's self-esteem. This reduces stress. Government plans, to make so-called 'failing' children attend extra academic classes outside school hours, are flawed because they will

lower such failing children's self-esteem and are a retrograde step. In the 1940s we were taught basics every morning. This was an era when inner-city schools were almost entirely given over to vocational courses. In the 1960s as a teacher I found there many areas where literacy and numberwork still took up the morning. Ministers are also planning to shift all those they percieve as being non-academic low performers onto non-academic vocational courses from the age of 14. This will invariably include many children who have far wider potential as well as too many inner city children.

I've always found pupils of all ages and students progress much faster when I explain, in age related terms, the how and why their brains find some aspects of learning a problem. Explaining why Anderson wrote the tale of *The Ugly Duckling* as well as detailing some other famous people who have succeeded despite having early learning problems also aids the restoration of self-esteem. It's particularly helpful to talk to underachieving children about your own academic problems. Problems shared are problems halved.

My reading strong but otherwise fully dyslexic grandson, age 7, once his self-esteem had been restored ceased to suffer from school phobia, frequent tears, retreat to bed as soon as he got home from school and constant claims he was too ill to go to school the next day. As well as field-trips and doing scientific experiments, I have always taught art and poetry writing to all those I aid as part of enriching their experiences Since this grandson has discovered he can paint and write creatively, he has grown even more confident and now happily goes off to school. This is the first poem he wrote which helped him to regain his confidence and self-esteem:

The tiger

Fur like autumn fern

with night sky stripes

and yellow crystal eyes

with sharp, diamond-hard teeth

and tongue as red as fire.

Prowling for its prey

on quiet, soft paws

with claws hidden;

camouflaged

by swishing, curving bows of grass

sneaking closer and closer.

Then pounce to kill

with paws that rip

murdering for food;

wild, dangerous and deadly

the tiger purrs as it eats;

but the sun turns it to gold

beautiful to look at.

Instead of remaining well below average in spelling my grandson is showing improving scores on standardized tests. But such formal measures of improvement don't mean all his initial academic problems have disappeared. His written work, whilst increasing in complexity and length, often contains a spate of errors.

Teachers, lecturers and parents need to keep in mind that the greater the number of logical sequences alternatively-minded individuals have to deal with the more likely it is that errors will arise. Thus children may learn to perform well when tackling a limited number of times tables and/or spelling lists, but will malsequence each time such lists and other formal work exceed the critical mass of sequences/list learning they can cope with. This is why so many dyslexics, seen as being remediated, remain prone to error. Unfortunately too many regard such continuing errors as resulting from being careless and/or lazy rather than a continuation of the malsequencing associated with dyslexia.

Maths is the subject in which my grandson produces the most frequent errors. We keep up his mathematical interest levels partly by encouraging him to continue to enjoy the mathematical games available on the internet. We also encourage him to explore any advance mathematical concepts which attract him, such as symmetry and problems involving logic. This is the same route followed by my daughter and grandnephew which ultimately led them to formal success. We also offer him pieces of advance information in other areas. Before and after going to museums/interpretative centres to see a small selection of exhibits/interactive displays etc., we show him selections of linked visual material. He also used a kit to cast a few hieroglyphs in plastic to make such objects as badges.

Even infant school children can learn academic details, though the aim is to enhance their interests not formally recall data. Machines recall data with the utmost accuracy. We know my grandson does take in knowledge details because, long after a visit to the Science Museum's earthquake displays, he wrote the following two lines:

volcanoes exploding

across the world circling

Adults will find enrichment methods will also aid their underachieving children. However, they should also remember that such activities as hockey, football, cricket, chess, visiting airshows and the theatre etc. are just as important as stimulating children in data based subjects. But above all else thinking of dyslexics and other underachievers in more positive terms will give them the best chance of developing giftedness. If we believe in our children they are much more likely to believe they can achieve.

Because Dyslexia is a negative name, with very many negative traits associated with it, I believe it should be viewed more positively. Since they are a group which learn in ways which appear strange but are really just alternative, I have renamed dyslexics 'allomaths' (Newby, 1964). In fact one might describe all those, who belong to this minority spectrum as being allomathic. That would allow many conditions such as the autistic, stutterers, epileptic and even psychotic hallucinators to be more positively viewed instead of being always defined by their negative traits.

Dyslexia without stress is brought about firstly by keeping a child's belief in themselves high thus strengthening their self-esteem. Next positive traits should be used as a foundation for turning problems into strengths. Children and their teachers should accept that this takes a variable amount of time and that any continuing basic errors aren't signs progress isn't being made since, correctly encouraged and taught, the individual will continue to explore advanced aspects in areas causing problems.

Finally, childcentric and creative enrichment-education also helps to minimize stress. Enrichment allows the child the freedom to develop their curiosity, in any degree of detail they wish without being constantly frustrated at school because they have to precisely follow a way and order of learning which is alien to them. If this isn't possible, then the parents are left with the sole responsibility of encouraging wider interests over weekends and holidays. As I noted this will involve a range of activities from helping parents with such skilled tasks as cooking and car maintainance to visiting nature reserves, museums, historical enactments and the theatre; searching the internet for interesting sites; as well as using stimulating books and videos. By doing this parents will further strengthen such positive traits as curiousity, creativity, empathy and humour. Where schools and parents jointly utilize enrichment methods children are least liable to become stressed and are more likely to reach their full giftedness.

We really also need to change the public's negative perceptions of dyslexics' and other cognitive minorities to one of being an adaptive and innovative spectrum. Otherwise, when the majority turn to genetically

altering or selecting which embryo they allow to go full term cognitive minorities will largely become extinct. Even genetic pruning of mental illness has the same dangerous potential for damaging the innovative side of the human race.

References

Hynd G, Cohen M (1983) Dyslexia: Neuropsychological theory, research and clinical differentiation. New York: Grune & Stratton.

Miles TR (1993) Dyslexia: The pattern of difficulties. London: Whurr.

Miles TR, Gilroy DE (1986) Dyslexia at College. London: Routledge.

Newby MJN (1964) Creative work with remedial groups. Remedial Education 44: 194-198.

Newby MJN (1995) Allomathia: a new name for dyslexia. Dyslexia 2000 2: 8.

Pumfrey PD, Reason R (1992) Specific Learning Difficulties: Dyslexia, challenges and responses. London: NFER-Nelson.

Rawson MB (1981) A diversity model for dyslexia. In: Pavldis GTh, Miles TR (eds), Dyslexia Research and its Application to Education. Chichester: John Wiley & Sons.

West TG (1991) In the Mind's Eye. New York: Prometheus Books.

Chapter 14
The positive and the negative

BROTHER MATTHEW SASSE

People often say to me: 'I *sometimes* forget people's names but usually don't find it a problem.' If it only happened *occasionally* to me, I would find it easier to laugh it off. But it has happened too frequently in the past, causing me great embarrassment. So I am at great pains to avoid that situation by following detailed strategies, like writing out a list before I go to a meeting with people I have not seen for some time, and having that list easily access-ible in my pocket. This is just one instance of how my dyslexia puts pressure on me.

A dyslexic's bedroom

In my case, dyslexia means lack of organization. My room tends to look like a bombsite. Yet I know where everything is, because it's not all tidied away out of sight, but is all on view so that I can put my hands on it at once. This habit has its drawbacks however, because if I need to cross the room at speed, that's not always possible! Then I'm inclined to get angry with myself because I am keeping people waiting. Also, if anyone opens the door, the room looks somewhat intimidating, especially as they can't usually sit down because even the chair is piled high with books and papers.

Some strengths

Being right-brained means that I know intuitively how things work which is not always welcome. For instance, if I manage to start a car first go after somebody else has nearly drained the battery in their efforts to get it started, my 'favour' more often than not results in a mixed reception of thanks and frustration. It might have been more tactful not to intervene! It can also be frustrating for others that I dislike reading through operation manuals or leaflets from cover to cover; I prefer to 'dive' right in and follow my instinct. This is particularly true when adjusting or mending digital watches; I prefer to experiment until I have worked out how they function; it is usually quicker!

School and university

They say that schooldays should be the happiest days of your life; that was certainly not true in my case. It was not a total nightmare but I soon learned to take precautions. Precise strategies were quickly evolved but working twice as hard as my peers usually enabled me to come out with reasonable marks, so I decided that was a 'price' I had to pay! The best, undetectable avoidance strategy was a serious stomach-ache fifteen minutes before I had to leave for school. Otherwise it was necessary to plan ahead where I would sit for the lessons in which I always had difficulty, however hard I tried. The best place was out to the side near the back where I was not in the teacher's line of sight. But I had no solution to FRENCH DICTATION! I always scored nought out of ten, or even minus marks, which never failed to aggravate the teacher, who was a Frenchman himself. He seemed to take it as an insult both to his home country and to his teaching ability. As so many dyslexics find, after a point, the harder you try, the worse it seems to get. I often ended up in tears! While trying to correct errors, I just spelt them differently but still not correctly. Then it wasn't only the teacher who became frustrated!

It was at university when the pressures of my dyslexic difficulties very nearly brought me to my knees. I could not keep up with the essays. The thought of everything resting on a week of final exams after three years' work became intolerable. In one term I had lost a stone in weight, the doctor suggested tranquillizers and I was about to ask, for a third time, not to complete the course. Luckily I found a senior tutor who managed to convince me that, as I had survived till now, the university authorities must consider I was worthy of a degree, so it was just a question of persevering to the end. The stress that I suffered then was the worst I have ever experienced.

Writing

Writing letters has never come easily to me. As a child I needed plenty of persuasion to write Christmas thank-you letters. The final, convincing motive was that, if they were not written, I would probably not receive many presents for my birthday in the middle of January. Also it took me over four months before I sat down and faced the task of writing this short article. Frequently I say to friends: 'If you ever receive a letter from me, FRAME IT!!!, because you are unlikely to get another one!'

Reading

Reading still presents me with a few problems. When reading a newspaper with anyone else in the room, usually I find I cannot concentrate. On a 'bad day', I can read a paragraph three times and still not remember the gist of it,

although I know perfectly well what every word means. On a 'good day', I can take it in at the first attempt. As I live with a community of religious brothers, I am not at liberty to take the newspaper out of the reading room. Result: Frequent Frustration!!

As a child I remember how adults would recommend 'GOOD BOOKS' to me. Generally it took me twice or three times as long to read a set text for an exam or one of those 'GOOD BOOKS'. One of my favourite sayings at that time was: 'I - - - HATE - - - "GOOD - - - BOOKS".' On one occasion the pressure became too much for me. So I put on my black shoes, lay on my bed and kicked up and down the wall, leaving great, black marks right up the wall.

Strategies that work

One of the strategies that helps me to live and work effectively is a series of set routines. Each of my pupils has his own, personal zip file with always the same eight things in it, like a triangular pencil with a rubber at one end, a six-inch ruler with their name on, a notebook for spelling rules, a cardboard file for used worksheets etc. As a teacher, even my pencil case is transparent and has a cardboard partition inside, so I can see at a glance if anything is missing; because I know that, on one side, are two pens and two pencils, and on the other side are five pens or markers.

My briefcase also has a strict layout inside that rarely varies. The result is that, even if I am in a hurry, I soon notice if anything is missing, before I close the case and go to my next lesson. Before I leave the house or classroom, I go through a set routine of checks so I do not leave things behind.

I learnt the importance of this early on in my working life as an adult. Once, I took to the cinema a pencil case with three gold-topped pens in it, which had been a present for my 21st birthday. While I was there, I bent down and they must have fallen on the floor. I did not check my pocket before I left the cinema, only discovering my loss when I returned home; they were never recovered. I was devastated and I could not afford to replace them. It taught me a salutary lesson and nowadays, before I leave anywhere, I always check my inside pocket to see if my three pens are there. Keeping to these routines serves to slow me down, which means that people may have to wait until I'm ready, having completed all these checks. Often people become impatient and this is hard for me, so sometimes I do not bother. Occasionally I pay the price and forget something like my umbrella, as I did when I dashed away from a British Dyslexia Association meeting last year.

Some more positives

Dyslexia for me has many positive sides to it. I'm sure it's made me a more efficient problem solver. When others are, at first, 'stumped' when presented

with a new problem, I can 'dive' straight in and apply a series of possible solutions until I find one that works. Problem solved! Life for this dyslexic can present a series of difficulties due to short-term memory, poor concentration etc. which may be stressful. But it can occasionally be quite rewarding, as when you arrive at a novel solution to a problem, which no one else has thought of, like my word index. It has been published in every edition of Alpha to Omega by Beve Hornsby since the 1990's, and should make accessing the spelling rules that much easier. Being dyslexic myself has usually proved reassuring for my pupils; to be able to truly empathize with them can often be a turning point in their struggle with their specific difficulties.

Chapter 15
A letter

SHEENA HARRISON

Dear Tim,

A, by now, very belated reply, hope its not to late for the book. How are you? The tips you gave me have proved to be useful . . . .

Now stress and dyslexia, it becomes a permanent companion that swiftly overwhelms at times. My experience is a two layered one, pre knowing and post knowing.

Pre-knowing. I was considered to be a 'highly strung', a b – – – – y nuscience, perhaps a hyperactive child in todays terms, both at home and at school. As being tied to a chair at 3/4 yrs by the teacher – to make me sit still, examples.

At 14/15yrs, I had my appendix taken out, as a last resort, the GP considered I was 'playing my mother up' and my appendix pain was described as being psychosomatic and a result of my nerves at being in the grammer school.

Anxiety and panic were a constant in my childhood, as I lived with the blight of being a scholar with writing, spelling and computational difficulties, not to mention a memory you couldn't rely on. My mother, a nurse, used to consider I needed medication to 'calm me down' and intermitently, make me go to steep, especially at exam times and for the 11+ exam.

Anxiety overwhelmed me at exam time. In the 2nd year Juniors I rember being only able to put my name on the page. Similarly at the 'O' Level exams, I achieved 2 'O' Levels passes – History and RE. Work to was to prove to be a nightmare of waiting to be found out to be an incompetent.

I have suffered with day time stress incontinence since early school days. It remains to this day a problem that continues to puzzle medical professionals and yet again my symptoms do not fit their 'normal' typologies. I don't own up to this aspect of stress to many Tim. I bit my nails to as a child and today bite the skin around my nails.

I personally believe today that the overwhelming levels of anxiety created by the daily ignominies and embarrassments of being a dyslexic functioning in society, fuelled my abusing myself with prescribed medication and

135

alcohol. The verbal beratings for unexplainable errors to parents, teachers and peers, the constant 'showing ups' in shops, on public transport and in other public situations as the dyslexic dysfunctioning outed eroded my self-worth and self-esteem. A psychatrist once described me as having a 'slight' inferiority complex.

I was prescribed Valium a number of times, as a treatment for my dry scalp which my GP considered was attributule to stress. When I stop awhile and reflect, I have been offered treatments for conditions that have been ascribed to stress most of life, by the medical profession.

Eventually, despite medication, GPs' prescribed to relieve anxiety, I turned to alcohol to anaesthetise the resultant levels of anxiety. I used alcohol Tim for fifteen years to 'help' me deal with life people and social interactions, in ignorance of the dyslexia and dyscalcula that flaws my daily social functioning's.

Post knowing, at 45 years of age, that I was a person with both dyslexia and dyscalcula. Uncovered at Bangor University by the specialist help made available at the Dyslexic Unit, I was to discover the levels of stress that being involved and exposure in education produced in myself and preversely being a belated academic success. I sought counselling and was given 'Beta Blockers' by my GP who, when I presented myself when the 'panic attacks' and the resultant fibrillation's, were beginning to be a daily trail, in my first year.

His comment was 'what do you expect as a dyslexic Sheena' as I expressed my puzzlement at him considering I needed this type of medication. Despite not wanting to take medication, the daily poundings of 'abnormal' stress levels forced me to considering the 'docs' advice, relief followed as the cycle of panic attacks were reduced. At least till exam times.

Today I have an awareness of the holistic persuasiveness, the affects and effects of having dyslexia compounded by having dyscalcula. This has enabled me to develop a range of strategies for dealing and coping with my levels of stress. It still catches me out when I get over tired or anxious about me in work and educational situations. I am at present receiving counselling and have had to 'look at' the effects of being a person with dyslexia and dyscalcula and their impact on my life. I have recently worked with a group of Post Truamatic Stress Disordered ex-service personnel and have observed the extreme effects of long term truamatisation. The similarities have struck me, although I realise they are not as extreme for me. The social dysfunctionality also is, in them exaggerated, but nevertheless comparable to my own experiences and those I have known with other dyslexics. I am working with one at present who has been severly afflicted socially & functionally since adolescence. She is almost like the 'wolfe child' – been locked away and not

been allowed to have a normal adolescence. Kieth – – – has done the testing & she has proved to be severely dyslexic & dysculic.

Lots of caring thoughts and special heartfelt thanks for your work and concern for advancing knowledge.

Sheena

Chapter 16
I am a singer

JANET COKER

I am a singer. before all els I am a singer, my hole being sings. I am also a wife a mother gardener, window cleaner, cooke house cleaner, painter decorateor, you name it I will have a go.

I am a diselexeix I am a diselexic singer, wife mother gardener ect, ect.

Being diselexicc has maid me at time's very angry very frustrated and has resulted in countless humileations. You eather go under or become stronger with each ocation. Laughter is a great healer I have red and said some helarious things quite serilesey, turn to laugh at yourself and outhers will laugh with you and not at you.

When I was a little girl I was concidered very backward I could not read or spell or write legilbeey, but I could sing, I would go into the lockel woods and filds and sing my hart out.

If the music is growing out of your sole, you cant stope it. Do not get stuck behind dots on paper words you cant reed. Make sounds, thrilling vibrations, take of into the realmes of your own emagination blow your horn, strum your gitar, crash your cords or cress each note of your piano

The pure joy of making music be it with voice or insterament is with out limit. make music go for it sweep aside barriers buld your own bridges

I am a singer before all els I am a singer

Chapter 17
How has dyslexia affectered me?

BRENDA MILLWARD

I was asked to write an article on how dyslexia has effected me. I have been trying to remember, but it is difficult because I accepted that I was slow and lazy, what I did not accept is when I was told that I did not try, all I wanted to do is please the teachers. I DID TRY but I did not know how to try harder. Even now I can feel the anger at anyone who said it to me, when I told them I did try then they told me I was cheeky and I got into more trouble. Now when I look back I think that I gave up trying and I just accepted the way I was.

I think my troubles go way back before school. We were a very poor family as was most of the people who lived around us so we accepted the way we were, some family's were far worse off than us. It is only when you have grown up and moved on that you can look back and see that you were different. At school I was picked on because I was untidy and scruffy. I was classed as under priverlidged and was made to drink two bottles of school milk a day and I hated it, at home we had stelarized milk, school milk had cream on top and it tasted sour by the time we got it. I was also made to stand in a row with six other children to have a tablespoon of malt and cod liver oil it only humiliated us but I suppose it was intended to be good for our health but not the damage it would do to us mentally.

When I now look back I can see how much school I lost; I was born in 1936. So I was only 3yrs old when the war started, I think I was 4yrs old when I started school, I can remember the teacher smacking me because I was late. That was my introduction to leaning.

I was a very shy person and I could not talk very well at four I had five older brothers and I think they did my talking for me, I know I could not sound my Rs I would say Bian and Deik.

Instead of Brian and Derek and any thing with R and L in it I could not get my tongue round it such as library. I think I found. It was less trouble not to talk much at school then I did not have people laugh at me. Mind you when I

did start talking nobody could stop me. I now think I had all my confidence knocked out of me having five brothers who always thought they could do everything better and quicker than me. I never really got the chance to build up my confidence.

As I lived in Birmingham and lived near the ammunition factory's such as Lucas, Wilmot and Breadon, Singer, and the large factory of the Ford land rover the airport also Coventry we had a lot of air raids, so spent a lot of our school time in the air raid shelters. We did not get proper lessons the teachers read us stories and poems, which I loved.

I had trouble with my feet and went to hospital three mornings a week so I missed nearly all my Basic English maths history and geography that we had in the mornings. So really I was in trouble without being dyslectic.

So that is a bit of background. I think the biggest feeling of inadequacy that I felt was not being able to help my two sons with their homework not even the basic spelling, and numbers. Sums are even now a nightmare for me I get upset trying to do very simple figures

The other big disappointment was not to be able to train and go to higher positions in my career. I had the chance to go to train as a supervisor in the P/O canteen also school meals. I trained as a cook in the airforce it was on the job training and exams where questions that gave you three choices and you ticked the one you hoped was right and then you had your practical assessment. Then if you passed, you went from AC woman to leading aircraft woman and then Senior AC woman. I could not become a corporal because of my education but it was very frustrating to have someone in charge of you because they had a school certificate but where awful cooks and supervisors.

I decided to try to get my chef's diploma and enquired at the Thomas Danby College. At this time they had changed the structure of exams and you where assessed on your course work. This was no good to me as I had four Years of catering behind me that meant the first year and second year I was too advanced but I needed the assessments of those years to do the final year. So it was decided that I would do a different course and I did a City of Guild Flour and sugar design.

Lucky for me at that time, the two-year course was based on the practical and theory work together. I got such a good mark on my practical that it covered my lesser grades in theory and still ended up with 86% which I was very proud as it was the first certificate that I ever got.

Had I done this course a year early I could have become a teacher of cake decoration, but the year I finished my course the education department changed their structure and you then had to do a years teacher training before you could teach, Oh well such is life.

My mind keeps jumping about, as I am typing something else drifts through my memory, playing card games or board games I dreaded going to

parties and meals at friends for some reason they always wanted to play games. Cards where far worse and I soon realized that people lose their sense of humour when playing, they play to win and if they unfortunately got me as a partner I soon felt the antagonism from them.

Another was if I got an idea to write to someone or to do something I would get very upset because I could not carry it out. Oh the sheer frustration I have felt over the years.

Telephone directories and dictionaries are a nightmare for me they really make me feel inadequate. Taking messengers especially over the phone I cant remember them even as I write them straight down.

Dyslectic 2

Beginning to understand me

An incident happened at college this week that really made me aware of being dyslectic. I had spent the whole of one class and three quarters of another doing a mock exam. I checked and rechecked my work I saved as I went along. Something in my head kept saying numbers so I went to the beginning and numbered the first page. When I felt I had checked my work to the best of my ability I called Angela over and she started going over my work. It started off fine and then we came to a sentence where the last word of the sentence came on the line bellow, and the next sentence came under that line. Angela was explaining to me about this when I said that I had taken a sentence out of there and moved it elsewhere. But I had not corrected the space So she asked me to get my letter back, and disaster, there was the finished article but I had not saved as CLAIT 1 and 2 or changed the other numbers as I had made all the changes to my work.

I can't say how badly I felt about doing the work all over again, it was not the typing, or moving the work around, it was the copying of the work which is the most difficult thing for me to do. Even a simple word my mind can alter the letters about, but the worst of it is that I don't see it.

It is the same with the keyboard, I go to type a letter and I can't see it. I know this sounds odd I can touch each key and still not find the letter and then suddenly it is there, so it takes a lot of time copying a piece of work. Also I can type a sentence and when I have finished it somehow I have changed the sentence to read slightly differently. Some one who is not dyslectic could type the same work in far less time.

I understand in exam work we all have to be the same, but is there anyway, once we have proved we can type, and the tutor is satisfied with our typing, however slow we are, that the basic letter for working on could be on

our computer? Then we could spend more time leaning to **use** the computer and less time copy typing.

Another incident came up this week. My husband has Parkinson's and a friend was helping him to fill in some forms for disability allowance as he has difficulty writing with his right hand. This is the reason I wanted to lean the computer so I would be able to write letters, as he has always done mine. As I was listening to the questions it made me realize how I have been handicapped all these years I did not even understand the question and I could no have filled in a form, and this is something I could not have done with a computer. Listening to them trying to answer the forms made me feel completely inadequate. I felt sorry for my husband the way questions are asked it made him feel awful.

This is when we are so grateful for friends and colleges that help us.

Chapter 18
A personal view of stress and a dyslexic professional musician

Exploring how stress can both invigorate and disable a performer and how the insights of dyslexia research can enable the performer to cope with stress

MICHAEL LEA

Professional music making is notoriously stressful. Recognizing that Gillingham (Gillingham and Stillman, 1969) used teaching techniques which matched those that have enabled me to make my way as a professional musician, led me to think that there are many insights for musicians to be gained from studying research into dyslexia.

Perhaps too, studying musicians might have many insights for the further understanding of dyslexia, in particular the study of dyslexics with compensating skills involving a high degree of multi-spatial awareness.

When I first learnt about dyslexia some 15 years ago, I soon noticed the importance of being aware of the concept of paradox in trying to understand the effects of dyslexia. Thus one dyslexic might have a great deal of difficulty finding their way when travelling, whilst another might never ever be lost, having an exceptionally good sense of direction. The dyslexic might have this perception of themselves, which they believe implicitly and act on accordingly; however, objective study might demonstrate a more complex and sometimes a different view.

So it is with the musician, whose self image might be of being 'good' at sight reading. That musician might consequently be relaxed about performing at sight in public even though objective study might show

missing notes. In the opposite case the 'poor' sight reader might actually be playing more notes. In either case appropriate reassurance and support from teachers, conductors, colleagues or from the musician, him or herself, is important to allowing the neurological connections to work smoothly, in this case to facilitate sight reading skills.

It is the continuous involvement of the mind in every stage of performance that enables a musician to play. As Galamian (1962, p. 5) writes 'The foundation upon which the building of technique rests, lies in the correct relationship of the mind to the muscles, the smooth, quick and accurate functioning of the sequence in which the mental command elicits the desired muscular response'. He adds 'What counts is not the strength of the muscles, but their response to the mental directive' (Galamian, 1962, p. 6). I would suggest that because stress directly affects all parts of the neurological system that it is intimately involved in performance at all times. I suggest that it is significant how that stress is perceived and used, and that it is significant by the degree of its presence and its absence.

When I eventually discovered Gillingham I was immediately struck by the close similarities between the Gillingham method for teaching dyslexics literacy skills and the instrumental teaching that I had received to become a professional musician. When I arrived at the Guildhall School of Music in 1965, I was unable to produce written work. My thoughts did not come out in linear order. My handwriting was illegible in a thin squiggle where many of the letters looked similar, so that errors in spelling were not noticeable. I wrote fast on every other line so that I had plenty of room, though never enough, for corrections, additions and for whole sale crossings out. I could sign my name so that the bank accepted it. Even after a number of tries at writing an envelope, letters did not always arrive. I had not known it then but I was dyslexic.

At the Guildhall I had good music teaching and was able to start the process of constructing a thought out dependable technique. The teaching involved having individual lessons where my teacher helped me construct a technique which would stand up to the stresses of professional playing. He passed onto me age old principles of how to play and adapted them to fit my particular physique and musical approach. I learnt to play in time and in tune, first time through, in highly competitive and pressured situations. I learnt to explore and express musical ideas in my own way and with others.

It is perhaps self evident that playing a musical instrument engages many senses simultaneously. The feel of the hair of the bow on a particular part of a string being connected directly by sound to the ear, enabling all kinds of adjustments to be made spontaneously. The complex processes involved require the pupil to learn in a structured way. Where that pupil wishes to make his living as a professional musician, then the most basic matters have

an enhanced importance. It is this kind of detail that Gillingham goes into, using multisensory techniques and a structured approach to teach literacy skills.

To look at one detail. Consider playing a scale on the guitar. It might be that as well as fingering the correct notes with precisely defined movements in the left hand, that the musician is to use only the first and second finger alternately to strike the strings with the right hand. In order that this becomes second nature to the performer, this complex process is broken down into its constituent parts. The pupil might practise with the right hand only on open strings. It helps the pupil to say out loud 'Two One Two One Two' the words matching the fingers on the right hand as they strike the string alternately. This is first learnt at a slow speed using a metronome. This speed needs to be so slow that there is time to think of everything. Once that slow but successful speed is found and with it the successful coordination, then the speed can be allowed to increase. When the notes of the scale are added in the left hand, slowly at first, counting out loud in time with the right hand establishes the thought behind the process of playing this scale - which in this case is to use two fingers in the right hand alternately, starting with the second finger. The words combined with the action enable learning.

This teaching is surely remarkably similar to the techniques detailed by Anna Gillingham and Bessie Stillman to help dyslexics. Perhaps this is not surprising as making accurate and dependable neurological connections is the common thread. An example of this parallel learning system is Gillingham's principle of SOS - Simultaneous Oral Spelling. As the pupil writes each letter of a word, the pupil simultaneously sounds out the name of the letter. In doing this the pupil feels the pen on the paper and the associated movements of fingers and arm, simultaneously hearing the names of the letters and using the tongue, lips and voice to say the letters. This combines to produce a strong neurological message imprinting the correct spelling of a word. The actions are reinforced with the words

There are many occasions when it is useful to say things out loud whilst playing, to reinforce learning on a musical instrument. For example counting time out loud during complex rhythmic passages. Another example is naming notes out loud when playing scale intervals on one string i.e. fifths - A, E, B, F#, C#, G# etc.

Repetition is another important element to this learning style. To establish correct patterns, my music teacher taught me to repeat things correctly three times in succession and then move on. Repeating things correctly three times in succession is also part of Gillingham's teaching. I would suggest that these parallels extend throughout both learning styles.

These techniques are necessary to enable the musician to function under considerable stress. This stress might result from personal experience that

the musician carries with him. The stress might be connected to the conditions in which the musician is working. Where ever the stresses come from, the late Dr Ian James demonstrated that a musicians life involves working at severe levels of stress. In 1997 he presented the results of a world wide questionnaire to the conference on Health and Musicians at York University. In a weighty aside to the conference he said, 'this is a deeply unhealthy profession'. In the Abstract that accompanied his presentation he writes 'The survey shows that levels of anxiety and depression are unbelievably high. Furthermore, the survey shows an association between many of these stressful factors with psychological and physical problems.'

In presenting the result of the FIM survey to the conference, Dr Ian James listed ten causes of the most severe stress, ten causes amongst many others detailed in the questionnaire. These are the perceptions of musicians in the survey:

1   The conductor who saps your confidence

2   Incompetent conductor

=2   Having problems with an instrument

4   Playing an orchestral solo

=4   Illegible music

=4   Disorganized rehearsal time

7   Incompatible desk partner

8   Having medical problems which affect work

9   Making a mistake when performing

10   Inadequate financial reward

10   Worrying about finances in the event of accident/sickness.

I would suggest that the first 7 of these causes of stress have direct relevance to the dyslexic musician and also number 9. There were no papers on Dyslexia and Music at the 1997 conference in York so the connections between dyslexia, music and stress were not discussed as far as I know.

I am sure that as research is carried out into dyslexia and music that many insights will emerge that will help aid understanding of some, if not many of the stresses that are to be found in professional music making. For instance to understand how dyslexic traits might make for difficulties between desk partners: take my earlier example of one type of dyslexic who might have a poor sense of direction that results in that person following a particular and clearly defined route to a destination, whilst another dyslexic has an over view of where to go and feels free to follow any route as appropriate on that

particular day. If these two are desk partners in an orchestra, one might obsessively mark the part with bowings, and even fingerings, to the great irritation of the other or vice versa, one rubbing out all markings which the other needs. This might be an exaggerated example, however there are many situations where tiny differences become magnified, perhaps when playing in a 'picky' acoustic where small tendencies to differ, or even the risk of a difference of approach, might be enough to cause great stress.

The principle of the 'grasshopper' approach of some dyslexics being potentially incompatible with the 'earth worm' approach of others can be applied in all kinds of ways. The dyslexic who speaks in a disjointed fashion leaping from one idea to another sometimes missing out the important connections that might help the methodical listener follow the train of thought. The other way round is that the methodical approach might be deeply irritating to the other. The dyslexic who misreads, or misses entirely, social signals might offend the highly socially aware dyslexic who in turn might be seen as an overly smooth manipulator and held in contempt. My suggestion is that these opposite effects, which paradoxically can be both dyslexic, which can cause stress between people in normal circumstances, can be the source of intense stress in the high pressure world of professional music making

Fortunately in this structured musical world there is room for all, provided sufficient musical signals are picked up and the notes are played. To cope with the stresses between musicians within orchestras, there are strong formal ways of behaving. These unspoken invisible lines can cause great offence if crossed, however these structures give a feeling of safety to all concerned and also allow great freedom. These formal politnesses exist around the world and in different times. They are immediately recognizable to fellow musicians, enabling different strong characters to coexist, to combine their individual ideas and make music together.

I can report that being a professional musician for all the difficulties, is a rewarding life. It provides a unique opportunity to explore, from the inside, with like minded people, the works of the masters of the past and the present. Bringing to life the notes on the page that even the greatest composer is limited to writing, is endlessly fascinating and deeply creative. I suggest that as a performing musician you are part of the creative process alongside the composer, providing the light, the brush strokes and the energy that a composer can only hint at.

I suggest that professional music making is a multi spatial world that is ideally suited to a dyslexic. It is the multi faceted link between the ear and the sound; the links between the feel of the music, the hall, the ensemble and the instrument, that are so important. In this positive environment stress adds definition and intensity to what is happening. To put the bow on the string

and pull out a particular sound at a particular time with the accuracy of a surgeon using a scalpel, when there is only one opportunity to do this and everyone is depending on you, is worthy cause of much admiration, and makes possible great musical expression. This positive outcome is perhaps a middle way where, on one hand the stress is not disabling and on the other there is enough stress to concentrate the senses, and thus the performance.

References

Galamian I (1962) Principles of Violin Playing and Teaching. Englewood Cliffs, NJ: Prentice-Hall Inc.

Gillingham A, Stillman BE (1969) Remedial Training for Children with Specific Difficulty in Reading, Spelling and Penmanship. Cambridge, MA: Educators Publishing Co.

Vail PL (1990) Gifts, talents and the dyslexias: wellsprings, springboards, and finding Foley's rocks. Annals of Dyslexia 40: 3–17.

Chapter 19
The stresses of a dyslexic enterpreneur

JULIAN COX

I never really considered my dyslexia to be much of a problem until I started up in business, if I'd of known then what I've' learnt since I would have never started out on the venture. During my school and collage days I had always had problems with the written work but as most dyslexics do, I'd developed fantastic and sum rather odd coping strategies that got me through.

Even though I detested exams and was always scared of failing and being labelled a failure I'd pass, my marks would never be marvels and when the results came through I always had that deep down gut feeling that I could of done better. I knew the answers but when it came to writing the answers the words and the spellings escaped me, the pages were full of scribbled out miss spelt words, it looked a mess.

Eventually I found a niche it the job market which suited me just fine. I started work on a large Luxury Motor Yachts out in the Mediterranean, it met my demeanour nicely and it meant I could put my childhood passion of boats and sailing into practice. I soon gained a very professional reputation and job offers flooded in, within 18 month I was skippering a large sports-fishing boat in the Med' and was then offered a job as First Officer on a very large private yacht, which resembled a small Cruise Ship than that of a yacht. The position held a lot of responsibility it was very much a hands-on position that entailed a little paperwork, for this I honed my copping strategies. that I'd developed over the years. At first I would dread filling in the Ship's Log when on watch, but I soon planned a head and before I went on watch I had a good idea of what I was going to write and developed set sentences of different circumstances, It worked. I recently asked and ex-captain that I'd worked with for over four years and he had no inkling of my dyslexia.

It was an extremely enjoyable career working on some of the worlds finest yachts, it took be all over the World visiting many of the Worlds most scenic and glamorous places.

For some reason I decided to take a brake from this enjoyable line of work and start-up a business, it seamed like a good idea at the time!! My plans sounded so simple and foolproof, the Business Plan was collated and then presented to the bank and with the blink of an eye I had the managers full backing. I was ridding high on conflidence the ugly issue of dyslexia seemed totally insignificant. The initial foundations of the company were laid I brought an off-the-shelf Limited Company via my accountants and then started up a French company, the plain was to export English foods to France and sell them through our own shops in Southern France, I say 'our' as I had a friend that was going to become a partner and run the French operation.

Within months the companies were trading and a regular freight service was running between Portsmouth and Nice supplying the necessary food stuffs to the shop and hauling freight from Southern France to all over England. The freight was a very profitable side line that off set the food freight costs but, it is was extremely complicated. Once trading started it soon became apparent to me that I was struggling with this brilliant idea of mine. In the early days my mother who was registered as the company secretary would help with the documentation, this help was invaluable but unfortunately she had little free time to spare and even less as the business expanded. The rapid expansion was a major problem for both companies and my self as the work load grew due to the shop's increasing popularity with the English and French customers. We were soon supplying bars, restaurants and other French shops with English goods all along the Côte d'Azur. The demand for both freight and food was far beyond our expectations and within six months we had opened a separate French freight office and within eleven months a second larger shop.

I became increasingly burdened with the bureaucracy that lay behind importing and exporting (bearing in mind this was pre-EU day's when we were part of the Common Market and before 'true' open trading between France and England existed). I was now in at the deep end and totally out of my depth, the paperwork mountain was growing and the English office soon became awash with unanswered mail, I simply couldn't face the numerous forms and letters that needed my attention, the paperwork from the Customs and Excise alone was enough to fill a small filing cabinet.

The personal stress was becoming increasingly evident, I start to look haggard, I was drinking and smoking heavily at this stage. Then things when from bad to worse my business partner's marriage was braking up and he decided to leave France and go back to sea, well it was easy for him as it was my money that was invested and not his. Suddenly I had to be in two places at the same time whereas before I would spend about a fifth of my time in France but now I had to divide my time between the two countries. Before I thought I was in at the deep but now my feet were being bound together.

I'd found the English bureaucracy hard to contend with, but now I had the French bureaucracy too and of course it was all in French! My spoken French was fare from fluent and my written French was non existent, it was all beyond my abilities. Yet, somehow I managed to keep the shop trading and the freight rolling, you may wonder how! Well it was easy, I simply left all the paperwork and concentrated my time on trading, for me that was the easiest way of dealing with such matters.

Dyslexia is often described as a word blindness and believe me when your staring at a French document, it like staring at a sheet of scribble.

As with all business you get a few problems from time to time, I certainly had my fair share of them. The first being severe smoke damage to the French shop and office when an adjacent office caught fire. Then two separate motorway accidents, the French delivery van that was on leased got written off in an accident and then a large twin axle, four ton hired trailer and the entire cargo of antiques got seriously damaged whilst en route to England., on both occasions the company driver wasn't responsible. These three accident cost the company many, many thousands of pounds and put an increasing financial strain on both companies and once again produced vast quantities of form filling. Even though I was owed thousands of pounds from the insurance companies I couldn't face the paperwork that went with it, so I left it unclaimed. Some people may find this hard to comprehend and think its laziness it wasn't I used to work extremely long hours, I found the harder I worked the easier it was to forget the outstanding paperwork.

Within months of taking over the French company I soon new that in reality it wasn't going to workout I now had two paper mountains to contained with now, I quickly learnt that written correspondence plays a vital part in commerce and not all situation can be dealt with face to face or over the telephone. It now seemed that everyone on both sides of the channel was keen for me to contact them it was normally for unpaid bills that lay in the mass of paperwork.

It was in a 'Catch 22' situation, to fold-up was a solution but not an option, after all how could I face the reams of paperwork that went with it? Continue trading and the situation keeps growing, what a dilemma. At this stage I was so stressed-out it was impossible for be to make a logical decision I guess this is why I thought the easiest way out was to just carry on going.

It was shortly after the third accident that finial demands, court summonses and letters of complaint started landing on both French and English doormats and I still continued to ignore them.

At this stage the anxiety that I felt as a teenager during exams regularly came back to haunt me, the beads of perspiration, the sticky palms, the dryness in the mouth and that unforgettable tightness in the stomach became daily experiences, I loathed mail deliveries.

When I started running the French end I was in at the deep end with my legs bound together and it wasn't long after that sharks started nipping my heals.

My drinking along with the permanent anxiety and the increasing stress got the better of be and I was now in hospital having a kidney removed but like many stubborn dyslexics I didn't know when to stop. Two weeks latter I was back in France with another bank loan and new ideas. On my return I discovered the manageress had stolen tens of thousands of Francs during my absence. I now knew that the recovery of the business was totally beyond my capabilities. Then one day out of the blue I decided to give the staff one months paid holiday, I lockup the shops and left keys with the senior cashier and then went to say with some friends in Brittany for a few days which ended up being three carefree months working in my friends boatyard, no mail, no telephones, it was carefree time, though very superficial.

A few months before these carefree days at my friends boatyard I had started negotiations with an Englishman who had approached me about buying the business. He had friends already living in Southern France running an English video business and wanted to do something similar. This seamed to be the answer to all my problems, sell the business, pay off the bank loan and go back to sea. For a brief period things look sunny again, however this it soon became very clear that I was dealing with a crook, a very heavy handed crook who had a very nasty track record.

My carefree months in Brittany got shattered when out of the blue I received a very threatening phone call from the crook. My problems came flooding back to me, Brittany was no longer my sanitary I had been found and worst of all I was being threatened, blackmailed by a crook.

I eventually returned to England never realizing just how stressed-out and desperate I'd become and naively presumed that on my return the mountain of unopened letters would of disappeared, of course it was still there waiting for me. The paper mountain was now gigantic, there where pages and pages of faxes and numerous answer phone massages awaiting by attention, I guess this was my 'finial' braking point and tragedy was lurking around the corner and struck with vengeance.

I had been home for about five days and still I'd touched nothing, not one envclop opened, not one phone called answered. I just spent the time helping my parents in the garden, shopping with a girlfriend and generally avoiding anything to do with the business but at the back of my mind it continued to haunt me, I lay awake at night looking for solutions, trying to think of a way out. I knew deep down it was way, way beyond my abilities but somehow I had to end this nightmare.

Laying in bed in the early hours and came up with a solution, I could bum all the existing papers and simply start again but this time deal with them as they arrived one-at-a-time instead of letting them build-up.

So this it what I did, at the time it seemed such a simple and easy solution when your in the midst of a server 'mental breakdown' anything to case the stress seems straightforward and simple. For a dyslexic that loathes documentation and has paper mountains in every corner of the office this option seamed even more appealing. By destroying the dreaded VAT forms, tax returns, bills and the odd letters of complaint would ease the burden, it was a simple case of, 'out of sight out of mind, destroyed 'full stop'.

My action on can only be described as 'utterly' reckless, I brought petrol into the house to use as fuel because I thought I'd need it I didn't! I didn't have any real plan of what I was going to do all I remember is that I just wanted to destroy and bum the paperwork, but my disorganized approach brought utter chaos to the situation and before I knew it I found my self in a state of utter confession, it all got out of controlled, I was out of control. My next real memory is that the house was on fire, alarms ringing and people shouting, it was 'Hell'. It, was shear chaos and I had started it.

During the fire my Mothdr sustained serious bums and sadly died a few days latter. Whilst I was in hospital with minor burns and breathing problems I was arrested my the police and latter charged with, intending to damage property and causing the death of my mother.

During the police questioning.

From the very beginning I admitted that I'd caused the fire, I'd started it, it was all my fault though at that stage I could remember very little of what had actually happened. I was indeed in a state of server shock, I was also suffering from smoke inhalation and still depressed.

Before I knew it I was charged with arson and murder! But, as far as I was concerned it had all been an accident, a terrible, terrible accident. I'd tried to explain my story to the police, well as much of it as I could remember. However they weren't interested in spending time with me to determine what had actually happened they just wanted a story that fitted their preconceived ideas. I was bombarded with question and they continued to giving me their preconceived versions of the events, for a dyslexic this form of questioning definitely isn't very conducive. I found it horrendously overwhelming I continuously found myself being misunderstood because of my inadequacy at the time to explain my self coherently, I was continuously fighting their suggestive questioning. All I wanted was to see my family and sleep.

It's nearly twelve years since that tragic night and I'm still haunted by the events, I can honestly say hand on heart that I've give many hundreds if not thousands of hours of thought as to what happened and what lead up to the very tragic events and it's only now with *hindsight and a very* brief understanding of psychology and some extremely good counselling over the years that I'm now able to take a constructive look back.

I could easily sum-up and say that I suffered a sever 'mental overload'. It can easily be compared to the household PC when that too jams-up. I think this was the same with me for the brain literally had to much information to process because of the various demanding pressures that the business required but, unlike the PC I didn't have a 'reset' button to press!

However, I adamantly believe that my dyslexia was directly associated with my mental illness and the tragedy that lead to my incarceration.

It's only a dyslexic or somebody with an in-depth knowledge such as an expert in the field of dyslexia that will ever come close to understanding the frustrations and difficulties that dyslexic suffers. It is very easy for a person to announce that their dyslexic when really it was a lack of schooling/teaching, parental upbringing or another form of learning difficulty/disability. Just because they have reading and writing difficulties they are quickly, often to quickly call or labelled dyslexic.

Over the course of my imprisonment I've come a crossed many 'true' dyslexics though I have never openly admitted to my peers that I too am dyslexic, though an enigmatic of a dyslexic. I label myself enigmatic because many dyslexics are frighten of learning because it involves using skills that they literally don't posses, reading is just a mass of indistinguishable characters, written work is simply distressing, to even contemplate the writing of a short sentence provokes a sweat. Hence they soon develops a history of truancy and behavioural problems and the children quickly become delinquents.

Unlike most dyslexics I really enjoy learning though it takes more time for me to absorb the relevant information I enjoy studying and the class work that goes with it and at heart I'm a bit of an academic but, when it comes to the written work there is no compatibility, it's like putting a square wheels on a bicycle, they go round but it's extremely bumpy, slow and quite inefficient.

So, here's a person that has an IQ well above average, enjoys learning, very ambitious, extremely keen to take on any new challenge and is well spoken, but he's a 'true' dyslexic. How is that frustrating or what!!

To prevent being 'labelled' and being deeply embarrassed in front of friends, colleagues and peers over the years I've adopted many Copping Strategies to mask and to manage my dyslexia. These strategies have been formed consciously and subconscious and were conceived and honed from a young age. My coping strategies were so refined that even my long-term girl friend had no idea of my dyslexia, it was only my mediate family that knew and only my mother that was aware of the severity of my dyslexia.

I'm certain that if the original jurors at by trial had had a full representation of the effects and problems that a dyslexic suffers and a true picture given of this 'enigmatic Dyslexic' i.e. 'Me', the out come would of been quite different.

Looking back in hindsight with twenty, twenty vision I should never of started such an ambitious project, I should of known and more importantly understood my personal limitations, 'Yes' it was a brilliant idea but not for me, not for this Dyslexic.

Unfortunately during my spell in business I let many people down, I started the venture with such good intent but it turned sower and ended in such tragedy. I'm extremely envious of today's dyslexic entrepreneur for they can truly benefits from today's technology, computers with sophisticated spell checkers and programs that can scan and read the text even when its in a foreign tongue. For today's dyslexics, dyslexia is no longer a dirty word its now being understood and commerce is slowly becoming dyslexia friendly unlike that of yesteryear. I now manage my dyslexic by trying to avoid the stressful situations and limit by workloads when the stress mounts I prioritize the work and slowly nibble away at the important jobs, its simple 'Dyslexia Management'.

Foot-note

I haven't tried to explain the events In full as it would require reams of paper and to be quite honest I don't want to provoke the haunting memories. There are many controversial views about the events and my behaviour and many so called 'facts' that became rather incriminating. I've now grown beyond exhorting the validity of the so called facts my arguments have proven futile. However, my case has always been described as an extremely 'Bizarre Case 'from start to finish which is about the only thing the defence and prosecution could agree on. Bizarre is an appropriate word to use as it also describes nicely the Dyslexia disorder and the behaviour of Dyslexics.

Chapter 20
Individual case studies and recent research

ANGELA J FAWCETT

In preparing this chapter for the 2nd edition of *Dyslexia and Stress*, I have taken the opportunity to evaluate the current situation in dyslexia, and its potential impact on children with dyslexia. There is both good news and bad news. First, the good news. Public awareness of dyslexia has increased since the first edition was completed in 1995. The education system is now more accessible for children with dyslexia, and it is possible to identify difficulties early, in order to cut into the cycle of failure and stress traditionally associated with dyslexia. In education, and increasingly in employment, there is an awareness of the needs of dyslexic people. However, the bad news is that further evidence (Nicolson et al, 2001) now confirms the extent of the difficulties in learning in dyslexia. In terms of long term skill learning in dyslexia (Nicolson and Fawcett, 1993,) we have derived our square root rule for the increase in learning time in relation to the complexity of the task (Nicolson and Fawcett, 2000). Second, we have investigated the most basic learning via conditioning of eye-blink in dyslexia (Nicolson et al 2002), to show problems in the most fundamental processes. Consequently, we are now in a position to know exactly how difficult learning can be for dyslexic children, even when conditions for learning are as near perfect as possible. It seems that despite our success in reducing external stress for people with dyslexia by increasing awareness of their difficulties, the internal stress of being dyslexic will prove more difficult to resolve.

In this chapter I present the stories of some of the children and adults I have worked with over the last 20 years, starting with the history of my own son Matthew in his struggle to achieve his potential, including his struggles and successes at University and beyond. I have found this interesting in terms of the developmental "niche-finding" model described by Boetsch and colleagues,(1997), in which the shift into adult life may foster more constructive experiences and internal processes. Then I consider the underlying causes of the stress dyslexic children suffer, in particular the stress which can

be engendered by misperceptions of the level of application of the dyslexic child. I illustrate this with some case studies of dyslexia across the age range from pre-school to adult. In the second half of the chapter, I relate this to our own research, which revealed the extraordinary efforts needed for dyslexic children to achieve in a wide range of the most basic skills, even those unrelated to reading. For further information on stress and dyslexia, see Rourke et al., *Psychiatric Annals* (1991) special edition on learning disabilities; for reviews of socioemotional functioning see Little, (1993), and for depression and emotional difficulties, Wright - Strawderman and Watson (1992) and Lamm and Epstein, (1992). More recent material can be found in Barbara Riddick's insightful 1996 book on the social and emotional consequences of dyslexia, *Living with Dyslexia*. Further insights into the difficulties experienced by dyslexic people come from two US sources, Vail, (2001) and Guyer (1997), while some of the more unfortunate consequences of mishandling dyslexia can be found in Edwards, 1994.

However, I should emphasize here that many of these more negative outcomes should now be viewed from a historical perspective, although the adults who experienced a less supportive regime are still affected by their experiences. Recent changes in educational policy, which are still evolving in 2003, mean that children with dyslexia are likely to be identified earlier so that appropriate provision can be made to limit the negative effects of their dyslexia, and allow them to express their strengths. The material that follows should therefore be seen as a cautionary tale, pointing to the need for continued vigilance, to ensure that children are not exposed to misunderstandings of their dyslexia. This compounds the stress associated with being dyslexic, in struggling to acquire the skills needed for a successful life.

Stress and dyslexia – a family history

From a personal viewpoint, it was particularly apt that I should be asked to contribute a chapter to this book on dyslexia and stress, because my first involvement with the media was in a television programme about stress in early childhood, in the Baby and Co series chaired by Miriam Stoppard. In the early 1980s the emphasis was on issues such as additives and congenital disease, including in this case dyslexia. The producer's brief was to find a child whose problems had been identified in the first year of school, as a result of a stress reaction. This led them to my son Matthew.

As many readers will know, my original interest in dyslexia was inspired by Matthew, who was first diagnosed as dyslexic at the unusually early age of five and a half. As a small child, Matthew was clearly bright and enquiring, with a challenging mind, great confidence in himself, and tremendous enthusiasm for life. When he started school, he became withdrawn and

introverted, to the extent that his first teacher questioned whether or not he could speak. Despite his assurances that life had never been so good, it soon became clear that something was badly wrong. This culminated in many broken nights, where Matthew woke crying with pains in his legs There were also reports of his poor progress at school. Following his referral to the children's hospital with suspected rheumatoid arthritis, Matthew was referred to the clinical psychologist for investigation of his cross laterality. In Matthew's case, the discrepancy between his intelligence in the top one percent and his inability at this stage to recognise a single letter was particularly striking. At this stage he had been at school for around nine months, in a fairly formal environment, where the children were expected to be able to write their name on arrival. Matthew could not even hold the pen, and was still undecided whether to use his right or his left hand!

The diagnosis of dyslexia transformed Matthew's life, and his relief was palpable. He explained that he had been particularly concerned by the flash cards which the teacher held up, which other children read with ease. He had assumed, therefore, that he must be stupid. After a weekend with us trying to learn 'Come' (one of the most frequently recurring words in the Ladybird first reader), Matthew could tell us that it was a four letter word, that it came at the beginning of a sentence, and it must therefore be either come or here, but he still could not read it! The sequence of letters seemed to be useless to him in his attempts to identify the word. The unexpected communication failure between Matthew and his teacher meant that he lost any opportunity to convince her of his intelligence, by revealing the depth of the discrepancy between his spoken and written language. In response to the stress of the school environment, where he was continually asked to perform tasks which he found impossible, Matthew had produced a characteristic response. This response, based on the need to hide his difficulties and appear the same as the other children, in its turn increased his feelings of anxiety and fear of failure. After diagnosis, for the first time for many months, he regained his talkativeness, and would approach strangers on the bus, as before, but now to confide that he was dyslexic, and this simply meant he had to try harder to reach the same level as the other children.

I had foolishly assumed that a diagnosis of dyslexia would in many ways alleviate the stress in itself. Certainly, Matthew had become aware that there was a reason for his difficulties, and no longer saw himself as stupid. However, as any parent can tell you, the identification of the problem is just the beginning of a long slow battle for recognition. The first stage for the family is coming to terms with the problem and the acceptance that there really is a difficulty. Too much time and effort can be wasted in simply denying the situation, which in itself hampers the development of the dyslexic child.

In my search for an explanation for Matthew's difficulties, I had considered (and dismissed) the possibility of dyslexia, because initially, I found it difficult to equate what I read of dyslexia as a language-based deficit with my own verbally able child. Rather than showing language difficulties, Matthew was fascinated to the point of obsession with the subtle nuances of meaning in the English language. Nonetheless, if you examined his language more carefully, it was obvious that he experienced some early difficulties in the pronunciation of polysyllabic words, coupled with some confusion over their application. To illustrate this, as a small boy of around 5 years old, he had some difficulty in pronouncing elbow and shoulder, producing 'oboe' and 'soldier' as his best attempts. Not only that, he continually mislabelled the two, which led to some confusion when he fell over and hurt himself. Problems such as these suggested an underlying deficit beneath his apparent competence.

Matthew needed to be re-assessed as dyslexic at age 7, because he had been diagnosed before he had shown a discrepancy of 2 years between his chronological and reading age. In terms of literacy skills, by this stage, when prompted with the letter 's' at the beginning of a word such as 'says', he still failed to recognise the letter 's' at the end. His written performance was even worse, so that his teachers described him as the brightest boy in the class, but able to write less than the little Chinese boy who could not speak English. At this time, a placement in special school was considered, but the local junior school decided they were prepared to take Matthew, despite his difficulties. It was an uphill struggle to ensure Matthew reached the appropriate reading level for his age, but we were fortunate enough to receive help from a friend, a junior school teacher with a belief in the merits of a structured approach. He taught Matthew on a voluntary basis for two hours each week, from his sixth birthday, until he reached secondary school, and in the process developed a lifelong interest in the anomaly of dyslexia. The work he set involved Matthew laboriously completing several exercises at home each week, always pitched at his level of understanding to maintain his interest in the task. As a young child, there were times when Matthew resented the level of committment involved in this work, when other children his age were playing. The turning point came after about six months of instruction, when we took the gamble of allowing Matthew to decide for himself whether to continue with the lessons or not. Fortunately, he opted to continue.

Junior school

Nevertheless, Matthew's slowness in producing the work he was set and his difficulty in following instructions at junior school nearly undid all the good work which had been achieved. Following a difficult term with his first teacher at junior school, who was naturally enough irritated by Matthew's

vagaries, he developed a stammer. During this year, the educational psychologist came into school to attempt to resolve a situation which was becoming increasingly stressful for Matthew. His teacher believed that he simply refused to complete his work. In a one-to-one situation, in an empty classroom at break, he achieved much more, and therefore it was assumed that he could maintain this level if he wished, in the normal classroom situation. By the end of that year, his teacher admitted that she had misunderstood Matthew's problems, and assumed that he was being difficult when he failed to follow instructions. By this stage, she had realised that Matthew was a co-operative boy, with a wide knowledge base, who could produce the correct answer orally. However, she no longer felt able to question him, because his stammer embarassed the rest of the class.

At this stage, Matthew first encountered the sponsored spell and the written examination. The children were asked to learn 150 words, appropriate for children aged 7–11, and to collect sponsors. Matthew became sick with worry at the prospect of this test. I therefore contacted the school to check whether participation was compulsory. The head was very reassuring, and said that no-one need collect sponsors, but of course they must all attempt the test. For the first time, I took the decision to keep Matthew away from school for the test, but we sent the sponsorship money to add to the school funds. This seems to me to be a useful illustration of the way that the education system can fail to understand the problems of dyslexics. Following this sponsored spell, Matthew found it difficult to cope with the weekly 20 spellings, and the educational psychologist negotiated with the school to allow him to opt out for a few weeks. The responsibility was left with Matthew to opt in again when he felt able to cope. Within three weeks, much to our pride, he had started again, but with 10 simpler spellings, so that he had some hope of achieving them. This was by contrast with the spellings he had struggled with, the list of topic words, which at Easter included Mary Magdalene, Judas Iscariot and Gethsemane, and at other times included champagne and shampoo in the same list. Interestingly enough, my husband tried out the Easter list on his colleagues at work, and only one adult out of twenty in an office environment gained full marks. We adopted a similar strategy of shielding Matthew from the first formal exams, when he was just 8 years old, which were taken in the hall under examination conditions. For many weeks prior to the exams, his teacher had warned him that he would get nothing in the exams. On this occasion, Matthew had become very anxious, and complained of sickness and sore throat. This time I checked with our local doctor, who found the whole system of testing such young children barbaric and recommended that I keep Matthew at home. These were the only times when we allowed Matthew to stay away from school, to avoid humiliation which we felt would be counterproductive.

Matthew's problems were compounded in the second year of junior school by his experience of a very pleasant but over zealous teacher, who sent home nine pieces of homework some nights, in her efforts to ensure that Matthew had completed as much work as the rest of the class. Matthew became anxious, and started trying to get up very early in the morning in order to complete the work. At this stage, we decided that it might be appropriate to change schools, and send Matthew to a school that was a little less formal. However, the situation was defused by intervention from the newly appointed head, who dictated the work to Matthew and wrote down his response, thus completing the allocated work in 30 minutes. There then followed two of Matthew's happier school years, with teachers who understood and liked him. By the time he reached secondary school, his reading was adequate but slow, but he needed a further year in the Special Needs class to improve his writing and spelling skills.

Living in close proximity to the problem, I was inevitably faced with constant exposure to a whole series of dyslexic vagaries, such as confusion over times, days and even the general organization of life. The pervasiveness of the deficit, in fact, again led me to question whether the problems we were dealing with could be dyslexic in origin. Most striking of all, in retrospect, was the clumsiness which led to a constant series of accidents ranging in severity from the regularly spilled drinks to a suspected broken back! But at the time, it was the simplest manifestations of dyslexia which appeared the most puzzling, in particular the problems with even the simplest rote learned material. To illustrate this, at junior school, Matthew constantly muddled breakfast and supper (because you eat cereal at both), and he only grasped the difference when explicitly taught that breakfast was the first meal in the day, because it is then that you break your fast.

Secondary school

At secondary school, Matthew continued to exasperate his teachers with his forgetfulness, until they realised that this was just one manifestation of a more generalised memory problem. The school operated a fortnightly timetable. Matthew, however, could never work out whether it was week one or week two, and anyway he had lost his timetable. At this stage, of course, pupils no longer have desks, and need to bring the appropriate books daily. Matthew's response was to fill his large bag to overflowing with every book he possessed, and then delve fruitlessly in its depths for the appropriate books. Moreover, he would spend many hours completing his homework, only to leave it crumpled in the bottom of his bag, because he could not find the pigeon holes to hand the work in. A memorable instance was the occasion when, having been sent home for a forgotten book, he simply

forgot that he had put some sausages under the grill and set fire to the house. Strangely enough, Matthew's response to this near disaster endeared him to his teachers, and from that stage forward he had reached a turning point. The special needs teacher, a woman with a very clear understanding of dyslexia, set up a support system for Matthew, which for the first time allowed him to do himself justice. He simply reported to her each morning, and she checked that he had handed in his homework. At the end of the day, she checked that he had copied down his homework correctly. This recognition that his efforts to achieve were hampered by his memory difficulties tranformed the situation for Matthew. Just how much progress we had made became evident during his GCSE's, when one of the more resistant members of staff exclaimed 'That boy has difficulties- he does tremendously well!', in response to my query about the regularity of presentation of his homework. This is not to say that everything became perfect, and Matthew now admits to the odd day where he pretended to be sick, presenting me with a mixture of orange juice and flour, to justify his claims. It seems to me that it is simply not possible for even the most motivated child to constantly maintain the degree of effort and concentration necessary to become a successful dyslexic.

'A' levels

With considerable support from school and home, Matthew had largely overcome his reading difficulties by the time he reached GCSE level. His spelling remained relatively poor, and the speed of his written work significantly slower than other children of similar ability. Nevertheless, with extra time allowances for GCSE, he achieved laudable grades, and went on to tackle A levels. Here he chose subjects which place an unacceptable burden of written work on the majority of students, not simply those who are dyslexic. He decided to take English Literature, History and Sociology, despite the fact that he was still considerably slowed down by the effort required in reading and writing. However, because his reading skills were improved, the issue of whether or not extra time should be allowed in his examinations was less clear-cut. The school put him in for extra time, on the grounds that they recognised his dyslexia. A short questionnaire was sent out to all the teachers, who agreed that, although his performance was not always exemplary, he was generally a conscientious student who should be allowed extra time because he was still slow to complete his work, and continued to have considerably more difficulty than others of similar ability. In the event, the educational psychologist who dealt with the case found more evidence of emotional difficulties than dyslexia, based on the stammering. This was despite a letter from the clinical psychologist who diagnosed the dyslexia to the effect that Matthew's emotional difficulties were a consequence of his learning difficulties. Consequently, Matthew was denied the extra time to which he should have been entitled as a dyslexic.

Not only this, he had completed half his exams before a decision was reached, and each day faced the uncertainty this failure to reach a decision engendered. The consequent level of stress was unacceptable at a time which is already stressful enough for a candidate with no disability. A subsequent appeal and re-assessment confirmed his original diagnosis of dyslexia, but could not raise his grades in the English exam, which he only half completed. If parents with our level of knowledge and experience in the field of dyslexia were impotent in this situation, how much more difficult must it be for less knowledgeable parents to obtain their rights? Overall, however, the story has a happy ending, with Matthew achieving grades that allowed him to take up a place at university to study politics and philosophy

Matthew as a student

Having been offered a place to read Politics at university, Matthew was subsequently offered the opportunity to apply for a 4 year Master's course in Russian and Politics. This involved learning Russian, working in the Kremlin for one year, and writing a dissertation in Russian, with guaranteed employment in Russia after graduation. Matthew was very keen to try this, and so I advised him to write to the department outlining his dyslexia, and explaining that he had never taken languages, having been taken out of French to do extra English. Somewhat to my surprise, his department thought that this would be an interesting experiment. Despite our misgivings, we made sure that Matthew had all the specialized equipment possible to help him, including a computer program which allowed him to translate material from English to Russian and vice versa. Sadly, this was not to prove enough to get him through the course. Matthew had the Russian alphabet pinned up around his bed, but he had the same problems learning it as he originally had in learning the English alphabet when he was 5 years old.

By the end of the year, it became very clear that Matthew would fail, but he was desperate to avoid retaking the year. He knew that he would never be able to face starting again. Matthew had been determined not to seek any further concessions for his dyslexia and had not notified the dyslexia support service at his university. When he tried to discuss the problem with his head of department, he found himself unable to speak because his stammer had returned, and so he was referred for counselling for stress, rather than sent to the dyslexia tutor. At this stage, having allowed Matthew to make his own decisions, I decided that I needed to intervene, and contact his Politics tutor, because it seemed wrong that he should be penalized for the sake of an experiment, which was to my mind, misguided. Throughout this time, he had been achieving good grades for his Politics, despite the fact that he was concentrating on the Russian. It was therefore agreed that he could pass the first year, as long as he promised never to take Russian again. Following this

unsatisfactory period, he sought out the dyslexia tutor, and received hypnosis which transported him to a sandy beach when the stress became too great. Space precludes a full discussion of Matthew handing in his dissertation in May when the deadline was March, because he had mixed up the months! However, Matthew finally graduated with a good 2.1 in Politics from a reputable university. Much of his success to my mind could be attributed to his development as an autonomous learner, prepared to take full responsibility for his own development.

Matthew in employment

In terms of the adult outcomes for Matthew, it seems to me that his current career is a good example of the reduction in stress and rise in self-esteem that Boetsch and colleagues (1999) note for adults with dyslexia who are successful in 'niche-finding'. Matthew has been working as a journalist with the Ethical Consumer, a journal which researches ethical issues in relation to large companies. The format is ideal for someone with difficulty completing work at speed, with a long lead time between issues which come out six times a year, coupled with a firm deadline to be met. The support system within the organization is strong, with workers living and working together, and subscribing to a belief system based on ethical principles within a non-profit voluntary organization run as a workers' co-operative. The mutual support an organization of this type provides is an ideal work environment for Matthew. In some ways it may seem ironic that Matthew has chosen a career which emphasizes research and the written word. However, he always had an academic bent, which made it doubly frustrating for him when he proved unable to express himself adequately in writing. Matthew is preparing to move away from this supportive environment, having developed his skills in computers and started to work on a freelance basis setting up computer systems for charities such as Oxfam and Amnesty International. He is currently setting out in pursuit of his long term plan to work for the Peace Corps in South America. Having previously undertaken a short term placement in Mexico, Matthew is hoping that he will be offered a full year, if he is accepted following intensive training and three months living with a family in Guatamala to learn the language.

My need to research dyslexia

In my efforts to deal with the pain I experienced during Matthew's struggle to become literate, I returned to a technique which had always worked for me during my schooldays, in this case immersing myself in study of dyslexia. It had soon become evident that, at least in Matthew's case, the dyslexic deficit was expressed in a whole range of areas more generalized than the traditionally accepted reading, spelling and language. At the same time I was

well aware that the most difficult part of coping with any handicap lies in accepting and coming to terms with a range of possible outcomes. Therefore, I set out to research the condition systematically, in as wide a range of children with dyslexia of similar age as I could find. Eventually, I found myself armed with a battery of anecdotal evidence of generalized deficits in other children with dyslexia - for instance of clumsiness and difficulty in rote learning - gleaned from my dialogues with parents, teachers and children. It seemed that I was not alone in noting these bizarre manifestations of the problem, and clinicians in the field had a range of similar observations to report. On the other hand it was clear that perceptions of dyslexia, unfortunately, remained very much dependent on the viewpoint of the observer. This is illustrated by a series of vignettes on the child with dyslexia, drawn from interviews with parents and teachers and from school reports.

The teachers

Unsympathetic head (of 7 year old)

He's not dyslexic – he's just a silly little boy who won't concentrate for more than 10 seconds: what he needs is a good kick up the backside!

Exasperated (but supportive) teacher (of 14 year old)

This year Mark has put in the very minimum of effort. He arrives at lessons ill-prepared, his homework is rarely, if ever, handed in and his work is scrappily presented. He is his own worst enemy!

The parents

Baffled parent

Alan just keeps losing things – he put his coat in the locker so it wouldn't get lost, but then he lost the key, and now he can't even remember which locker it was – he'd lose his own head if it wasn't joined on!

Depressed parent

The depressing thing is that although we've gone over the word 20 times this weekend, he still doesn't seem to be any better at spelling it!

Desperate parent

He's been in the remedial reading group for 5 years now, but I'm sure he's reading worse now than when he was 8 years old.

My need to understand the enigma of dyslexia led me to return to study as a mature student, and altered the whole course of my life. An attempt to impose some meaning and order on such apparently disparate phenomena as these led me to the formulation of my research hypotheses. The theoretical implications of this research will be discussed later in this chapter. First, however, I shall discuss some of the major issues in diagnosing a child as dyslexic.

To label or not to label?

Readers of this book will all be familiar with the reluctance in educational circles to label children as dyslexic, in case the child shelters behind this diagnosis and uses it as an excuse for failure. Having read my own family history, it should come as no surprise to the reader that I do not subscribe to this view. It is important in such cases to consider the alternative labels which may be wrongly applied to the child: these range from stupid, not very bright, a late developer, over-anxious, or emotionally disturbed, to lazy and lacks concentration, or even in the worst case scenario, aggressive, unco-operative and difficult. These labels offer no solutions. A diagnosis of dyslexia, by contrast, provides not only a description of the range of symptoms but also a prescription for how to help the child to overcome their difficulties.

Readers may also be familiar with the well-worn concept of 'reading readiness', and 'late developers'. This school of thought suggests that, like potty training, it is better to wait until the child is ready, and then they will simply make up the lost ground in their own good time. The problem is that reading is not a bit like potty training, mainly because it is not an all or none experience. Reading is based on the interplay of a large range of subskills, all of which must be in place before progress can be made to the next stage. The child who fails to achieve fluency in tasks such as letter naming, falls further and further behind, until it becomes impossible to make up the backlog. Unfortunately, the corrosive effects of this failure can damage the psyche irretrievably, producing the 'Matthew effect' (Stanovich, 1986), culminating in both depressed achievement and depressed self- concept. The longer the problem goes unrecognized, the greater the potential effects. Research suggests a steady deterioration in the prognosis for reading, directly related to the number of years before dyslexia is diagnozed (Strag, 1972). On the other hand, the majority of children whose dyslexia is identified at around the age of 6 to 7 reach the appropriate reading level by the time they reach secondary school. In common with other researchers in the field, we have found convincing support for the effectiveness of early intervention (Nicolson et al, 2000, Fawcett et al, 2001). Nevertheless, we have also found a small 'core' of children who do not accelerate in response to short term

intervention, and it seems likely that these non-responders are the children with dyslexia within our intervention groups.

Sources of stress

It is hardly surprising that life is stressful for a dyslexic child who is failing within the school system. One might assume, however, that the situation for successful dyslexics, with no overt reading difficulties and minimal spelling problems, might well be very different. Quite the contrary. My experience and interactions with a range of adult dyslexics, including my own husband, strongly suggests that this is not so. Whilst the plight of the low-achieving dyslexic is more severe, life for any dyslexic remains fraught with difficulties. Is this simply because they are still carrying the burden of their earlier struggles? The most plausible explanation is that there can be more than one source of stress. For underachieving dyslexics, there are external pressures from school and home to reach an acceptable level of literacy. However, there is an added source of stress for dyslexics, whatever their level of achievement, namely the sheer amount of effort needed just to keep pace with life. A useful analogy here might be that of the dyslexic constantly running on a treadmill, just to stay in one place in a range of skills that others acquire with ease.

The remainder of this chapter I shall divide into two parts. First, I shall address the role of external pressures from the school and home as a contributory factor in the stress dyslexics suffer, illustrating this with some case studies. Then I shall go on to describe some of my own research, which attempted to quantify internal sources of stress in dyslexia, in particular the amount of effort required just to achieve normal performance. This research explains the fragility of the skills acquired in dyslexia, the problems in concentration identified in dyslexia and the good and bad days which have been so widely documented. However, firstly, let us consider external sources of stress.

It is tempting to assume that the education system must take the major responsibility for the stress that is suffered by children with dyslexia. Certainly, as I shall go on to show, lack of understanding of the problem within the teaching profession has meant that children with dyslexia traditionally suffered more than was necessary. Naturally enough however, failure to understand dyslexia is not the fault of the teacher, but attributable to problems in training teachers adequately in the recognition of dyslexia, despite the efforts of the British Dyslexia Association and the Department for Education and Skills to increase awareness within current teacher training. However, changes in provision based on the 1995 Code of Practice mean that dyslexia is now recognized in young children, and support can be provided in school for children 'at risk' of failure. Nevertheless, dyslexia remains an

exasperating anomaly, - why should a child who appears to be verbally able show such inordinate difficulty in grasping skills that other children acquire with relative ease? I think we have all been guilty at some stage of responses of this type. Possibly more deleterious for the child, is an underestimation of the child's abilities, coupled with access to only a restricted curriculum within the special needs class. Of course many teachers are particularly skilled in detecting the type of anomalous performance that characterizes dyslexia. Others, despite training in the warning signs, tend to underestimate the incidence of dyslexia., Unlike many of the other developmental disorders, such as autism, dyslexia is relatively common, with around 5 per cent incidence regularly identified in Western countries (eg. Badian, 1984; Jorm, Share, Maclean and Matthews, 1986). This means that every classroom will contain at least one dyslexic child. After lecturing to a group of teachers, it is not unusual to witness their reassessment of pupils with whom they have worked in the past, coupled with a belated realization that these children were classically dyslexic.

An interesting reflection of teachers' perceptions may be the fact that, particularly in America, attention deficit hyperactivity disorder (ADHD) and/or hyperactivity is also commonly diagnosed in conjunction with dyslexia. The basis for this diagnosis is typically the Connors Behavioural Questionnaire, derived from teacher's impressions of the application children show within the school (Holborrow and Berry, 1986). Consequently, many positive indicators of attention deficit are based on factors such as the inability to complete work within an allotted time period, and therefore it is hardly surprising that children with dyslexia tend to show a more consistent deficit than other children. This has led to considerable unease in the UK regarding the specificity of the current DSM-IV criteria for attentional deficit (Reason, 1999). The Dunedin epidemiological study, for example (McGee and Share, 1988) found about 80 per cent of 11 year olds identified as ADHD had dyslexia, which led the authors to argue that for these children their attentional deficits were really secondary to their learning disabilities. Even in this country, therefore, the concept of the dyslexic child with poor concentration and short attention span has become something of a stereotype.By contrast with this interpretation, our own research (Nicolson and Fawcett, 1990), which I describe in greater detail later in this chapter, shows that children with dyslexia actually input considerably greater resources in all skills, not just literacy skills, to achieve the same level of performance as other children. In basic or primitive skills which form the building blocks for more complex skills, they even show deficits in comparison with younger reading age controls (Nicolson and Fawcett, 1993; Fawcett and Nicolson, 1996). Despite all their efforts, they are often less successful in literacy skills, which demand the smooth interplay of a range of basic skills. Misinterpretation of these

efforts as laziness or lack of attention increases the frustration of the dyslexic child, and could well provoke confrontational behaviour in one personality type, or depression in another.

This brings us to the second potential source of stress: the parents. Although many enlightened parents would defend their offspring at all costs, there are others with less knowledge of education who take on board any negative perceptions of the school, and endorse them. The situation for a child who is misunderstood at school and at home is particularly stressful. For many parents, the difficulties their child suffers are an unpleasant reminder of their own experiences in school, The feelings of ineptitude and frustration that they suffered at that time, when the education system was less sympathetic to dyslexia, may render them impotent to deal with their current situation. My own husband for example, has painful memories of one teacher's instructions to 'Stand in the bin - you're rubbish!'. The smell of cooking, new paint and disinfectant that permeates most schools can still bring back his feelings of sickness and fear.

However, it is also worth emphasizing here that the child's own perceptions may play a role in their difficulties. It may not be simply the failure to learn within the school environment which places such stress on the child with dyslexia. There is a body of evidence now accruing which suggests that differences in the brain organisation of children with dyslexia may predispose them to problems with organizational and social skills (see, for example, Rourke and Feurst, 1991; Badian 1992). In terms of emotional stability, the literature suggests a threefold increase in psychiatric diagnoses in children with dyslexia (Duane, 1991), in particular of conduct disorder and depression. Of course, it is difficult to establish whether this is a cause, an effect or simply correlated with dyslexia. However, it might be argued that these problems are natural sequelae of the years of failure, or the need to constantly strive to achieve even average marks within the school system.

Finally, an additive factor in the stress engendered by dyslexia, is the guilt which all those involved in this situation may suffer. The teacher may blame herself for her failure to achieve any worthwhile improvement in the skills of a child who is clearly bright. The parents experience guilt because they have inadvertently passed their difficulties on to their child, and they themselves do not have the necessary skills to help them. Sensing these undercurrents, the child may blame himself for letting down both his parents and his teachers. This guilt can easily turn to anger and blame for each other, rendering the situation untenable and potentially explosive.

In the case studies that follow, you will note that there is an imbalance between males and females - this is because typically four times as many boys as girls are diagnosed as dyslexic (although see Shaywitz et al. (1990) for a more equal distribution, and Miles et al. (1998) for an explanation of the

difference between reading disability and dyslexia). I shall attempt to show that dyslexia has repercussions throughout life in terms of stress for dyslexics at all levels of achievement. Let me illustrate this for you.

The pre-school child

There is evidence for a strong hereditary component in dyslexia, from both a genetic, and possibly also an environmental viewpoint. In fact, there is between a 14 and 17 percent chance of being dyslexic if your mother or father is dyslexic (Pennington, 1991). The child I describe here, Adam, is the second child in a family of three. The father, (a dyslexic student, to whom I will return later in these case studies), and the eldest daughter are also dyslexic. Adam was typical of a certain type of dyslexic child, slow to develop language and with speech problems in articulation which were identified pre-school and resistant to speech therapy. He presents as a pleasant but confused small boy, very willing to learn, but with difficulties in almost every aspect of language and literacy. His failure to benefit from speech therapy led to a referral to our department for testing. Despite the fact that his problems were clear to the majority of professionals who came in contact with him, his teacher was not unduly concerned about his progress, and it was decided that the parents were being overanxious. It was also necessary to wait for Adam to fall two years behind in his reading before dyslexia could be diagnosed. In the interim, since the breakdown of his parent's marriage, the decision has been taken to conceal the family history of dyslexia from the new school. Given that there are now presumably emotional difficulties consequent on the split, it is not clear how this child will progress, and his lack of skill in language may well be interpreted as indicative of low potential. When the family moved to another city, the child was lost to the research panel, and no further information is available on the long term outcomes.

The junior school child

Jacob

Jacob's difficulties were originally diagnosed at the Dyslexia Institute, when he was aged 8 years and 6 months, and around two years behind in his reading and three in his spelling. There was a marked family history of dyslexia, his grandfather had left school unable to read and write, his mother had experienced difficulties, and all six of his cousins had been diagnosed as dyslexic. His family had experienced considerable difficulty in obtaining any recognition of Jacob's difficulties from his school, because the area in which he lived was fairly mixed in terms of socio-economic intake. It was therefore suggested that his performance was not necessarily the worst in the class.

The stress he had endured had resulted in Jacob losing all his hair. He found it particularly galling to be consigned to the remedial class, because he realised that many of the other children were simply not very bright. By secondary school age, he had made intense and successful efforts to overcome his reading difficulties, although his spelling was still dire (see Thomson, 1984 for a comparison of reading and spelling problems). When I retested him again at the age of 15, he continued to show problems with speed of processing and short term memory, to the extent that his scores on the IQ tests had dropped. This was not because Jacob had deteriorated in real terms, simply that he had not made the expected improvement with age. Jacob was not allowed to attempt GCE, because he was not considered to be of the appropriate calibre, despite the efforts he and his parents made to obtain recognition of his difficulties. We last worked together when Jacob was around 17, when he developed problems with kidney failure and dropped out of my research panel. He has since made some unsuccessful attempts at further education, and is currently looking for work.

Benjamin

The effects of stress on Benjamin were in many ways similar to those on Jacob. Benjamin and his older brother both had problems in literacy, but their mother, an ex-teacher, had put in considerable effort to help them with their reading. This meant that parental concern over the boys' progress was dismissed, because there were other children in the class with similar or greater problems in reading. Benjamin was more severely effected by the attendant stress than his brother, and lost over a stone in weight. By the age of 7 plus, Benjamin was unable to write his own name, and begged to change it to Ben. The situation came to a head following a school trip to a police station, which Benjamin had clearly enjoyed, when his teachers claimed that he simply refused pointblank to write a thank you letter. By this stage Benjamin had changed from a compliant and delightful boy, to a stubborn and angry child, and the school became confrontational about his refusal to complete his work. Eventually, he burst into tears at home, admitted that he was simply unable to write the letter, that he realized that he wrote like a baby and knew that he was different from the other children. He finally completed the letter by copying his mother's writing, thus resolving the issue for the time being. However, nothing had yet been done about the underlying problem. In the following year, he became more and more withdrawn, lost a stone and a half in weight, and suffered from blinding headaches, attacks of weeping and reluctance to attend school. This led to a referral to the children's hospital, where Benjamin was given an EEG and a brain scan. There was no evidence of any medical problem. The situation was resolved when his parents had both the boys tested for dyslexia at the local Dyslexia Institute, and removed them from their local school to place them in a more

sympathetic environment. Here Benjamin flourished, regained his lost weight and began to enjoy school. By the age of 11, he was second in science within a highly academic environment, but nevertheless, he still shows a motor co-ordination problem with his handwriting. He continues to maintain these skills in science, and is currently studying medicine at university.

Dominic

Of course, not all children react to stress by becoming withdrawn and introverted, and losing their hair or stones in weight. It is possibly just as common, dependent on the basic personality of the child, to adopt a 'devil may care' response to failure. In many ways it is possible to save face amongst your peer group by pretending that you do not care whether or not you succeed in the school setting. Taken to extremes, a dyslexic child may develop behavioural problems, as a consequence of a sloppy approach to work as a smoke screen to hide the fact that he cannot cope. This was the case with Dominic, who had reached the age of nine before his problems with literacy were diagnosed. This was undoubtedly because they were masked by even more severe behavioural problems. I first met Dominic when he was withdrawn from school for poor behaviour and came into the Psychology Department. His school complained that Dominic found it impossible to concentrate and disrupted the other children with his antics. Dominic presented to an adult as an appealing boy with an impish sense of humour and prodigious skill in drawing. There was no trace of problems in concentration as he produced a whole family of space monsters for me. However, it was particularly striking that when he wished to name these monsters, he needed an adult to spell even the simplest word. This led me to question whether or not Dominic might be dyslexic, and to raise the issue with his father, a psychologist who was dyslexic himself. The situation came to a head when Dominic ran away from school, and started to walk the four miles to his house. His teacher followed him in the car and returned him to school, where he threw mud in the playground. When his teacher asked him to stop this, Dominic responded by throwing mud at her and was subsequently expelled. In Dominic's case, his school had been unable to identify the real cause of the problem, because he had used bad behaviour as a smoke screen to hide his inability to cope with literacy skills. Even his own father, a skilled and sensitive clinician, could not put his finger on the underlying difficulties, possibly because he was himself dyslexic. A full test of Dominic's abilities showed that he was a boy of superior intelligence with severe difficulties in literacy. Since this diagnosis his behaviour has settled down, although he needed to move to several schools, including one for children with behavioural difficulties, before he found one that was sympathetic to his dyslexia. Dominic successfully studied media at sixth form college, and is now a graphic designer.

The adolescent

Of course, not all dyslexics are so successful - which brings me to my case study of stress in adolescence, John.

John

I have worked with John since 1985, when he became one of the first members of my research panel, during his placement at a special school in Sheffield. At 10 years old, John presented as a pleasant outgoing boy, with extensive difficulties in the area of language and literacy. His score of high average on the WISC test was probably an underestimate, because he was slowed down somewhat by his tendency to verbalize when completing each task. His reading was around three and a half years behind his chronological age, which meant that he had barely started. John had problems in almost every area which has been implicated in dyslexia; he had visual problems, he stuttered, he was extremely nervous, and some of his movements were clumsy. John was a boy who did not tolerate fools gladly, and would challenge me as an experimenter to justify the tasks I asked him to complete. He had a wry sense of humour, and the ability to laugh at his own shortcomings. Following several years of remediation at the Dyslexia Institute, John had made impressive gains in his literacy skills, and had even improved his scores on the intelligence tests. He had always had a good measure of support from his parents, and his school and the individual teachers were all sympathetic. In fact his level of support was exceptional. However, the attendant stress and the amount of effort that he constantly needed to input into his work to try and achieve his potential took its toll. By the time he reached GCSE level, John suffered a nervous breakdown, and was simply no longer able to maintain the level of effort needed to keep up. From that date onwards, John no longer took part in my research panel, moreover the decision was taken to drop anything which could be a potential source of stress. Later, John regained some of his confidence and successfully completed a youth training scheme in horticulture. Nevertheless, his parents remain concerned that he may never obtain work.

Adult students

The problem is, if anything, potentially greater for the dyslexic student than for other A level candidates, although the Disability Discrimination Act has proved a major factor in levelling the playing field for dyslexic students. Most universities now make special arrangements for dyslexics that are less dependent on evidence of reading difficulty, but recognize the effects of spelling deficits. However, the amount of effort required to successfully complete a degree with dyslexia is stressful in itself.

The two cases I present here are very different in outcome, although in many ways the students involved were similar in their approach, in the type of difficulties they shared and even in their previous careers in nursing. They were both of superior intelligence, with a glaring discrepancy between their verbal and written skills.

Connor

Connor was a mature student in the Department of Psychology, whose problems were identified when his essays were graded unsatisfactory because of his grammatical errors. Following a WAIS test (the adult equivalent of the Weschler test for children), I established that Connor's intelligence was in the superior range, and that his errors were not ungrammatical, but dyslexic in nature. I confirmed this by asking Connor to read back his work, to check that he appreciated that he should use 'the' rather than 'to' before a noun. Connor showed the typical absent mindedness and organizational deficits which characterize dyslexia. This may be attributed to the difficulties such students have in working memory, which leaves them less spare resources to deal with the organization of life. This was illustrated perfectly by Connor's marks in the first year statistics exam. Despite the fact that statistics was not one of Connor's strengths, even he was dismayed by the low marks he had achieved. On enquiring about this, he learned that only one of the two papers had been submitted and marked. The other paper was subsequently retrieved from his statistics workbook, where it had languished ever since Connor had completed the exam and failed to hand it in. The paper was so poorly presented that it was quite clear that it had not been tampered with in any way, and therefore Connor managed to scrape through when it was eventually marked.

At this stage Connor made a decision which in retrospect he was to regret. He had spent many years fighting down the feelings of inadequacy to which dyslexics typically fall prey. As a result of his experiences in education, Connor was embittered, and felt that he had been denied his rights. Moreover, he knew that he had areas of weakness, but he was less confident that he had areas of strength. He was therefore reluctant to disclose his problems, and adopted a defensive policy of trying to hide his difficulties. He had never suffered any problems in motivation, and adopted the policy of simply working harder and harder in order to achieve the grades he needed. This technique had paid of well as a mature student at A level, where he had given up any attempts to lead a normal life to dedicate himself to working in the day and studying at night. However, Connor failed to realise quite how dense the workload would be in his chosen field of law. As a lawyer, he decided that an acknowledgement of his dyslexia might carry a stigma, and therefore he did not seek the allowances to which he was entitled. As a

consequence, he failed to complete his papers, obtained a 2.2., which limited his options as a barrister, and went on to fail his articles at the first attempt. Eventually, he admitted that he was dyslexic, and obtained the grades he needed on a resit. However, Connor suffered for many years from his attempt to deny his dyslexia, and after completing his articles was unable to obtain employment which used the law degree he fought so hard to achieve. Recently, he has found work in his area of expertise as a lawyer representing underprivileged members of the community.

Richard

By contrast, Richard, the father of Adam, whom I described earlier, was much more successful, and another clear example to me of successful niche finding. If anything, his problems in literacy were greater than Connor's and consequently in his early career he had actually failed his nursing exams. At this stage he decided that if he was not good enough to become a nurse then he would become a doctor instead. Rather than denying his difficulties, Richard has used the system wherever possible to enable him to achieve his potential. The stress that he suffered in the remedial class at school had made him angry, and it is this anger which carries him through and underpins his determination to succeed. Achieving his medical degree involved studying for many more hours than others of similar ability, and counterbalancing low marks on essay based exams with full marks on multi-choice exams. The major difficulties he then faced were in coping with the potentially confusable names of drugs. He dealt with this by using his disabled students allowance to purchase a computerised organizer which interfaced with his computer. Richard is now a successful consultant gynaecologist. The frustration he continues to face is the fear that his children, in particular Adam, who is the mirror image of Richard as a child, will suffer as he suffered in school. Richard is not alone in the anger which his treatment in school has engendered. I shall never forget a potential PhD student, who achieved a first in psychology, whose parents had fought against his placement in a special school for children with moderate learning difficulties. His first instinct was to seek out the teacher who had described him as slow, and confront her with the evidence of his success.

Adults with dyslexia in employment

Of course, the problem for adults with dyslexia is by no means confined to students. The difficulties faced in school, where the emphasis is placed on subjects in which the dyslexic is disadvantaged, may be compounded in the workplace. The problem here of course is not simply one of literacy, but the speed and efficiency of processing. It is now recognised that a major

component of dyslexia is a weakness in handling rapidly presented information (Tallal, 1974; Wolf, 1991; Nicolson and Fawcett, 1994). It may well be that, given ample time, the dyslexic adult can process accurately, but under conditions which are resource intensive, involving high memory load or integration of material from diverse sources, they are at an extreme disadvantage. This may be evident in mundane tasks, such as trying to integrate the information on television programmes from the newspaper, in order to decide exactly what to watch at 8pm, bearing in mind possible overlaps between programmes, and regional variations. For some adults, it may mean that they need to devise mnemonics to help them remember seven or eight figure numbers which are beyond their memory capacity. In other cases, however, the consequences can be potentially disastrous. This brings me to the case of Simon, the British Rail signalman.

Simon

Simon was an adult in his 40s, who had worked on the railways all his life, predominantly as a signalman. The difficulties he had experienced in learning to read and spell were no problem to him in managing a hand operated signal system. In fact, by this stage, on any simple test of single word reading, Simon no longer had problems which would be diagnosed as dyslexic in type. However, problems arose when the railway signal system had become computerized. Instead of taking responsibility for a handful of lines, Simon was suddenly asked to monitor thirty three lines, with trains represented on a vast overhead illuminated map. Furthermore, to compound his difficulties in co-ordinating this mass of information, he was expected to remember eight figure numbers for the individual trains, well beyond the capacity of the majority of people. In addition he needed to make split second decisions on which line to route the trains, based on very small initial letters, 'f' for forward, 'n' for normal and 'r' for reverse. Awareness of his own shortcomings and the stress this engendered had reduced Simon to a state of imminent breakdown. Following the King's Cross rail disaster, he suffered daily nightmares that his tardiness or errors could precipitate a similar major crash. When he came to me for counselling, I advised Simon that the tasks he was attempting placed unacceptable demands on his processing capacities. Armed with a diagnosis of dyslexia, he approached his employers and was able to make a sideways move into management, which capitalized on his experience, whilst avoiding his areas of weakness. This was a most successful resolution of an issue which might well have ended in tragedy.

The theoretical basis of stress in dyslexia

The suffering which was endured by dyslexics in the school system and the attendant psychological scarring is hard to quantify, but it can impact on the

motivation, the emotional well being and possibly the behavioural stability of the dyslexic. In many ways, it seems to me that the dyslexic is working constantly at the limits of their endurance. Many of us will be familiar with the situation where, under constant pressure, an excellent memory and the most organized personality suddenly gives way, with the effect of switching off a computer. For even the most over-stressed academic, this happens just once or twice a year, when conditions become intolerable. I believe that for dyslexics this must be at least a daily occurence, if not more. In many ways, of course, this may be related to confidence, in that for most of us a belief in our own ability to cope carries us through. For the dyslexic (or even the mature student I might suggest from personal experience) this knowledge is less certain and more vulnerable to breakdown under stress. In order to break out of this destructive cycle, what is needed now is a better theoretical understanding of dyslexia. This has the potential to defuse the guilt and blame, and allow the child, the parents and the teacher to concentrate on the most important task, improving the skills and thereby the self-concept of the dyslexic. It must be recognized that dyslexia represents a difference in brain organisation, (Galaburda, Rosen and Sherman, 1989) and that as such, dyslexia cannot be cured but simply remediated. Consequently, children with dyslexia grow into dyslexic adults, whether or not their reading difficulties have been overcome. Reading is just part of a constellation of difficulties, which impinge on the performance of the dyslexic throughout their life. (Miles, 1993). Until recently, Tim Miles was unique in attempting to identify these positive symptoms of dyslexia with his Bangor Dyslexia test (Miles, 1982, 1997). Once it has been generally accepted that dyslexia is a constitutional, often hereditary condition, based on a difference in brain organization and processing mechanisms, it becomes possible for teachers and researchers to look out for early signs of difficulty, and thus break into the cycle of dyslexic failure, before motivational deficits have a chance to set in.

In fact, children with dyslexia obligingly enough seem to have something within their range of deficits to interest researchers from every conceivable background. Consequently, theories for the cause of the dyslexic deficit are many and varied, and a good deal of time has been spent in trying to establish which one of these theories is correct. Following early evidence of visual difficulties, one of the major achievements of the last 30 years was the identification of deficits in language skills, (Vellutino,1979), and the refinement of the phonological deficit hypothesis (Snowling et al, 1986; Stanovich, 1988), which is arguably the consensus theoretical belief of most dyslexia researchers from a psychological background. More recently, problems with visual skills have been re-established as a potential cause of the dyslexic deficit, specifically the threshold for the detection of flicker, (Lovegrove et al, 1990), which has been linked via an interdisciplinary project to

neuroanatomical abnormalities in the magnocellular pathway (Livingstone et al., 1991).

From a theoretical viewpoint, a programmatic series of experiments from our own laboratory has gone a long way towards revealing one of the underlying causes of dyslexia. In the process, it has revealed the full extent of the stress children with dyslexia and adults suffer in their attempts to produce normal performance, and the strengths of the compensatory strategies which allow them to succed in so many areas. I discussed dyslexic children's inexplicable difficulties with skills such as rote learning the months (see Miles, 1993) with Rod Nicolson, and we decided that their underlying problem might be one of automatization failure. This would mean that it was difficult for a dyslexic child to become expert in any skill, and Rod suggested this might best be tested experimentally using motor skills. This led us to challenge the dominant hypothesis that dyslexia is essentially a language based problem, and consider instead that it might be a more generalised deficit in the acquisition of skills.

Working from the premise that reading is a learned skill, and that all skills, whether cognitive or motor, are learned in the same way (Anderson, 1982), we first examined automaticity in children with dyslexia. In the process of learning, the novice has to concentrate on each individual part of the skill they aretrying to acquire. An analogy commonly used in describing the development of automaticity is that of learning to drive a car. At first it is necessary to concentrate on each individual component of the driving process, to the exclusion of all others. The expert driver is able to collapse these subskills into a fluid subroutine, leaving plenty of of spare capacity for navigating and anticipating the vagaries of other drivers. We already knew that the children we were working with, by definition, had problems with their literacy skills, and so in our search for a skill which is not typically impaired in dyslexia, we decided to test motor skill, and in particular the most highly practised skill of all, simply balancing on both feet.

Many parents of children with dyslexia recall that their children were unusual in their early years — slow to walk, slow to talk, rather clumsy, maybe a bit accident-prone. These anecdotal reports were distilled by the late Jean Augur into a set of 21 key points (Augur, 1985). As expected many of her points reflected lack of phonological skill. Equally notable, however, were consistent problems with motor skill. Indeed, motor skill problems accounted for Augur's first five points, together with 'Difficulty carrying out more than one instruction at a time' and 'Excessive tiredness due to amount of concentration and effort required'. Interestingly enough, this is one of the earliest acknowledgements of the amount of effort children with dyslexia need to input in all areas of their life. Living with the problem, like

Jean, I had reached similar conclusions, but as a psychologist felt the need to check out and quantify my theories.

At the time that we started the balance tests, there was no compelling evidence of motor skill deficits in children with dyslexia after the age of nine to ten (Rudel,. 1985, although see Haslum, 1989). However, the problem for an automatization deficit hypothesis (DAD) is that it is really far too powerful. It would predict that children with dyslexia would be unable to walk around, or even stand up. We argued that children with dyslexia obtained their near normal performance after this age by simply working harder, our Conscious Compensation (CC) hypothesis. My own familiarity with dyslexia had convinced me that children with dyslexia could obtain the same results, but by very different means from their non-dyslexic peers. This had been confirmed for us by an in-depth analysis of the reading skills of members of our dyslexic panel who performed at around their chronological age level on single word reading. Any more sensitive tests of literacy revealed that, despite their apparent competence, these children were devoting significantly more resources to the task, were slower in their reading performance and more able to use context, overdependence on which has been noted by other researchers (eg. Stanovich et al, 1985).

Based on these observations, the task we selected to test the motor skills of the children with dyslexia was a dual task, specifically set up to reveal any subtle deficits in balance. The results were consistent with our conscious compensation hypothesis, showing that although the children with dyslexia could balance quite well when just balancing, they were severely impaired when asked to balance while counting. The control children, by contrast, were not affected by the need to perform the tasks concurrently, and there-fore their balance was automatic, whereas the dyslexic children's was not. We went on to replicate these results, producing a design where we used three groups of children with dyslexia and three groups of controls, allowing us to measure the effects of age and dyslexia on performance. We used a variety of secondary tasks, finally selecting a blindfold balance task as the easiest to interpret.

Despite the support that this series of tests gave to our DAD hypothesis, they were not designed to illuminate whereabouts in the automatisation process the deficit arose. At this stage, we therefore started a long term training study with the older children, to determine how easily they learned a motivating computer game involving navigating round a Pacman maze. From this study, we found that the children with dyslexia started off very much worse than the control children, in terms of both speed and number of errors, but learned as fast, although they had difficulty in eliminating their errors. However, it is well known that children with dyslexia have problems with left and right, and therefore some of their problems could be explained

in these terms. As a control, therefore, we ran a further long term training study, where the children were matched on their baseline speed of performance on simple reaction times (SRT) to a flash or a tone, with hand or foot. When we put the two tasks together to create a novel choice reaction task (CRT), we found that the children with dyslexia were initially significantly more slowed than the controls. Despite the fact that they then learned the task as well as the control children, they never reached the speed of each individual baseline component, whereas the controls, by contrast, could speed their CRT performance after practice up to the level of their SRT performance. Extrapolating from these results shows that if skills take around 100 hours to master, it would take a dyslexic child around 1000 hours (10 times as long) to reach the same level. Note that the longer the time taken for a normal child to learn the skill, the greater the predicted decrement - so that for a skill which takes a normal child 400 hours, it would take a dyslexic child 20 times as long, and so on (Nicolson and Fawcett, 1993). In recent analyses, we have called this the square root rule (Nicolson and Fawcett, 2001). A similar, but more pronounced, pattern was found for error elimination in the Pacman training, with children with dyslexia making more errors after 10,000 trials than normal children after a 100 trials! These figures are really quite astounding, and have profound implications for teaching children with dyslexia, if you remember that learning a complex skill can take anything up to a 1000 hours. They suggest that it is essential to help the children as early as possible, before bad habits develop and mistakes are perseverated. The most efficient technique would be to identify the children as soon as they start school, and give explicit training from the very start.

The realization that the major problem for children with dyslexia lay not in learning a task but in the very poor baseline from which they started led us to our next programme of experiments. Here we set out to examine a range of primitive skills, everything that anyone had ever considered might be impaired in dyslexia, plus many more besides. Our reason for choosing primitive skills was that we needed to prevent our dyslexic panel from applying their efficient conscious compensation strategies to boost their skills. Moreover, by this stage, we had decided that even the efficiency of the panel's reaction time performance was achieved by a strategy of vigilance and anticipation, which a closer examination of our data confirmed. And so the skills we examined here included psychometric, phonological and working memory, balance and motor skills, and speed of processing. Our results revealed hitherto unsuspected deficits across the range of skills (full details of which are provided in Fawcett and Nicolson (1994 a, and b, 1995). Arguably, our most striking findings overall were that the 17 year old dyslexics were rarely achieving any better performance than our 8-year-old controls. It has previously been emphasised that much more may be learnt

from comparison with their reading age controls than their chronological age controls (Bryant and Goswami, 1986). Here, however, we were finding that our dyslexic 17 year olds were performing at the level of children around half their age. In terms of our driving analogy, learning skills for our children with dyslexia was somewhat akin to continually driving through a foreign country. It is possible, but at the expense of constant vigilance and an unacceptable cost in resources.

Naturally enough, these results caused consternation amongst the dyslexia community and practitioners working in the field. However, it is worth emphasising here that this evidence for a generalized deficit does not mean dyslexics are simply stupid. Quite the reverse, in fact. We believe that the cognitive system (including intelligence) is functioning at normal or above normal levels, as witnessed by the high achievement levels of many adults with dyslexia (West, 1991). It may well be, in fact, that these children start off with a constant struggle in acquiring literacy, and then simply carry on fighting throughout their adult lives to reach heights to which others cannot aspire

One of the more heated ongoing debates revolves around the role of intelligence, that is whether there are any differences between children with dyslexia, whose failure is surprising, and slow learners, whose failure is not (e.g Siegel, 1989). We recently started to compare the performance of our dyslexic panels with children with intelligence levels of around 70-85 on the WISC test at diagnosis. Our overall aims here were twofold: first, to establish whether or not the phonological deficits identified in dyslexia were found in children of low ability; and secondly to see whether or not our series of screening tests were capable of differentiating between dyslexics and slow learners. Interestingly enough, the slow learning children had difficulties in the majority of the primitive skills we tested, although their balance performance was not necessarily as impaired as that of the children with dyslexia by the addition of a blindfold. Similarly, they showed a different profile on the SRT, showing little effect of the addition of a choice reaction on their poor baseline SRT. The pattern of results obtained, however, was not yet distinctive enough to reliably discriminate the two groups, but they pointed the way to further research.

Existing theories for the cause of dyslexia were not able to handle all the results from our primitive skills battery, although all these theories contribute substantially to our understanding of dyslexia. Moreover, even our own automatization deficit hypothesis, although a useful characterisation of the pattern of deficits shown, is mainly descriptive. At this stage, we sought to link our own theories back to the underlying neurophysiology. Consideration of the pattern of deficits we had identified led us to consider the potential role of the cerebellum in dyslexia. Until recently, the cerebellum has been

largely dismissed from consideration, despite the fact that it is well-known that it is involved in motor skill. The fact that the cerebellum has evolved to an unprecedented size in humans compared with other primates, was largely explained in terms of bipedal walking. A series of experiments has now suggested that the cerebellum is critically involved in learning, not just in motor skill, but also in any task which demands 'language dexterity' (Leiner et al, 1989), which seemed to us to be an excellent description of the deficit in dyslexic performance. This involvement of the cerebellum in language was found even when only memory is involved, without any overt articulation to introduce motor skills (Paulesu et al, 1993). Working on this premise, we presented a series of tasks to our dyslexic panels, performance on which have been found to characterise cerebellar patients (Ivry and Keele, 1989). To our excitement, we identified a similar dissociation in dyslexia to that identified in the cerebellar patients, namely a deficit in time estimation but not an equivalent control task, loudness estimation. In work funded by the Medical Research Council, we set out to investigate basic cerebellar skills, assuming that there would be subtle manifestations of deficit which must be unmasked by dual task manipulations of task complexity. Somewhat to our surprise, we unearthed problems in a range of basic cerebellar tests drawn from a post-war medical book, based on the deficits found in patients with wounds to their cerebellum (Dow and Moruzzi, 1958).

Finally, we set out to quantify the relative size of the deficits in all the primitive and cerebellar skills in our panel, (using standard scores to compare the performance of each child with the mean and standard deviation of their control group) to establish which of the existing theories was best supported by the data. We found, as we had always suspected, that actually all the theories were right! There were problems in phonological skills, memory, speed, balance, and cerebellar tasks (Fawcett et al, 1996). However, the strongest and most consistent deficits were in phonological skills and balance, particularly the simpler cerebellar tests. These included simply pushing a blindfold child in the back with one finger, and noting their response, a task which is particularly straightforward to both administer and score. The size of the cerebellar deficits and the incidence amongst our dyslexic panel were amongst the highest in our battery of tests, equivalent to the spelling deficits, which typically were more severe than the reading deficits. Interestingly enough, we found a similar pattern of results in the boys at Mark College, a school for dyslexic boys in Somerset, having mounted an expedition to test around half of their 80 students. However, these boys had made considerable strides in their phonological skills, confirming that the phonological deficits are amenable to good remediation techniques (see Fawcett et al, 1999). Further research indicated that slow learners also show problems with speed and phonology, but that they did not show the pattern

of poor muscle tone which we have found in our dyslexic population (Fawcett et al, 2001). For a recent review of the cerebellar deficit and the causal chain which links the cerebellum to phonology via articulation, see Nicolson et al, 2001.

Based on these findings, we put together a screening test for positive signs of dyslexia, which may be applied in the first term of school. The DEST test (Nicolson and Fawcett, 1996,), is based on positive indicators of balance, speed and cerebellar deficits, coupled with the well known phonological deficit. The exciting thing about our test is that it taps natural skills, rather than taught skills, is independent of home and school training effects, and above all is non-threatening. As a lifespan test, it can therefore be applied not only to children before they fail to learn to read, but also to adults who are relatively skilled in literacy. The results of our survey (Nicolson, Fawcett and Miles, 1992) suggested that this would be welcomed by the dyslexia community. This was confirmed by the interest our early screening test has engendered. The Psychological Corporation published the DEST test, as well as the DST and DAST, for school children and adults respectively. They have now become best-sellers, and a new test for nursery children, the PREST, was published in 2001.

Finally, let us consider what the outcome might be in terms of stress reduction if children at risk for dyslexia could be identified via whole school screening in reception, or before and support provided to prevent their failure. Matthew is an interesting case in point, because, of course, his problems were identified exceptionally early. Nevertheless, he continued to suffer stress, which at times became insupportable. However, at this stage understanding of dyslexia in young children was not sufficiently advanced to ensure appropriate provision in school. Many of his early difficulties could be attributed to his attempts to hide his dyslexia, because he mistakenly feared that he might be stupid. From that stage on, he was given the help he needed to progress, but not necessarily the understanding. Whilst we encountered excellent teachers who gave Matthew every support, despite their lack of knowledge of the condition, we also encountered teachers who misunderstood. Despite the recognition of his difficulties, at every open night some teacher would express surprise that Matthew was dyslexic. For a child like Matthew, who manages to overcome their reading problems. the ability to interact well with his teachers is critical. It is essential to enlist their aid and their sympathy for the condition, rather than arouse their irritation by apparently slap-dash work. Similarly, it is crucial that the parents adopt the right mix of support and encouragement, and maintain their equanimity, despite the scepticism they may encounter within the education system. How much easier it would all be if the knowledge of how to handle dyslexia equalled that of sensory deficits in the early school years. It is not so many years since

children with visual or auditory deficits were condemned to years of failure, before their condition was recognised. Hopefully, identification of dyslexia will soon become as standard as the eye test all children are routinely given at school entry.

We have moved a long way forward in the intervening years between publication of the two editions of *Dyslexia and Stress*. For the first time, we can potentially sidestep the cycle of motivational deficits which permeated the previous system. An index of how far we have progressed is that I now sit on the selection panel for the Medical school, formerly seen as the last bastion of resistance to concessions for dyslexia. With new developments in research and their application to education, I am confident that although life must always entail some element of struggle, we can ensure that children with dyslexia are able to express their potential freed from the debilitating consequences of their literacy difficulties.

References

Anderson JR (1982) Acquisition of cognitive skill. Psychological Review, 89, 369–406.

Augur J (1985) Guidelines for teachers, parents and learners. In M Snowling (ed). Children's written language difficulties. Windsor: NFER Nelson.

Badian NA (1984) Reading disability in an epidemiological context: Incidence and environmental correlates. Journal of Learning Disabilities, 17: 129–136.

Badian NA (1992) Nonverbal learning disability, School Beahviour and Dyslexia. Annals of Dyslexia, 42, 159–179.

Boetsch EA, Green PA, Pennington BF (1998) Psychosocial correlates of dyslexia across the lifespan. Development and Psychopathology. 8, 539–562.

Bryant P, Goswami U (1986) Strengths and weaknesses of the reading level design. Psychological Bulletin, 100, 101–103.

Dow RS, Moruzzi G (1958) The Physiology and Pathology of the Cerebellum. Minneapolis: University of Minnesota Press.

Duane DD, Gray DB (Eds.), (1991) The reading brain: the biological basis of dyslexia. York Press, Parkton MD.

Duane DD (1991) Dyslexia: Neurobiological and Behavioural Correlates. Psychiatric Annals, 21, 703–708.

Edwards JH (1994) The Scars of Dyslexia: eight case studies in emotional reactions, Cassell, London

Fawcett AJ, Nicolson RI (1995) Persistent deficits in motor skill for children with dyslexia. Journal of Motor Behaviour, 27, 235–240.

Fawcett AJ, Nicolson RI (1994a) Persistence of phonological awareness deficits in older children with dyslexia. Reading and Writing: An Interdisciplinary journal. 7, 361–376.

Fawcett AJ, Nicolson RI (1994b) Naming speed in children with dyslexia. Journal of Learning Disabilities, 27, 10 641–647.

Fawcett AJ, Nicolson RI, Dean P (1996) Impaired performance of children with dyslexia on a range of cerebellar tasks. Annals of Dyslexia , 46, 259–283.

Fawcett AJ, Nicolson RI (1999) Performance of dyslexic children on cerebellar and cognitive tests. Journal of Motor Behaviour. 31, 68–79.

Fawcett AJ, Nicolson RI, Moss H, Nicolson MK, Reason R (2001) Effectiveness of Reading Intervention in Junior School. Educational Psychology, 21

Fawcett AJ, Maclagan F, Nicolson RI (2001) Cerebellar tests differentiate between poor readers with and without IQ discrepancy. Journal of Learning Disabilities, 34, 2, 119–135

Galaburda AM, Rosen GD, Sherman GF (1989) The neural origin of developmental dyslexia: Implications for medicine, neurology and cognition. In AM Galaburda (Ed.) From Reading to Neurons. Cambridge, MA: MIT Press.

Guyer BP (1997) The pretenders: gifted people who have difficulty learning. High Tide Press, Homewood, Illinois.

Haslum MN (1989) Predictors of dyslexia. Irish Journal of Psychology, 10: 622–630.

Holborrow PL, Berry PS (1986) Hyperactivity and Learning Difficulties. Journal of Learning Disabilities, 19. 426–431.

Ivry RB, Keele SW (1989) Timing functions of the cerebellum. Journal of Cognitive Neuroscience, 1, 136–152.

Jorm AF, Share DL, McLean R, Matthews D (1986) Cognitive factors at school entry predictive of specific reading retardation and general reading backwardness: A research note. Journal of Child Psychology and Psychiatry and Allied Disciplines, 27: 45–54.

Lamm O, Epstein R (1992) Specific reading impairments – are they to be associated with emotional difficulties. Journal of Learning Disabilities, 25, 605–615.

Leiner HC, Leiner A L, Dow RS (1989) Reappraising the cerebellum: what does the hindbrain contribute to the forebrain? Behavioural Neuroscience, 103, 998–1008.

Little SS (1993) Nonverbal learning difficulties and socioemotional functioning: A review of recent literature. Journal of Learning Disabilities, 26, 653–665.

Livingstone MS, Rosen GD, Drislane FW, Galaburda AM (1991) Physiological and anatomical evidence for a magnocellular deficit in developmental dyslexia. Proceedings of the National Academy of Sciences of the USA, 88: 7943–7947.

Lovegrove WJ, Garzia RP, Nicholson SB (1990) Experimental evidence of a transient system deficit in specific reading disability. Journal of the American Optometric Association, 61: 137–146.

McGee R, Share DL (1988) Attention deficit disorder-hyperactivity and academic failure: Which comes first and what should be treated? Journal of the American Academy of Child and Adolescent Psychiatry, 27, 318–325.

Miles TR (1982, 1997) The Bangor Dyslexia Test. Cambs: LDA.

Miles TR (1983) Dyslexia: the pattern of difficulties. London: Granada.

Miles TR (1993) Dyslexia: the pattern of difficulties. 2nd Edition. London: Whurr.

Miles TR, Haslum MN, Wheeler TJ (1998) Gender Ratio in Dyslexia. Annals of Dyslexia, 36, 27–55.

Nicolson RI, Fawcett AJ (1990) Automaticity: a new framework for dyslexia research? Cognition, 30: 159–182.

Nicolson RI, Fawcett AJ (1994) Reaction Times and Dyslexia. Quarterly Journal of Experimental Psychology, 47A, 29–48.

Nicolson RI, Fawcett AJ (1993) Children with dyslexia acquire skill more slowly. Proceedings of the 15th conference of the Cognitive Science Society, University of Colorado, Boulder.

Nicolson RI, Fawcett AJ (1996) The Dyslexia Early Screening Test (DEST).: The Psychological Corporation: London.

Nicolson RI, Fawcett AJ, Miles TR (1993) Feasibility study for the development of a computerised screening test for dyslexia in adults. Employment Department. Report OL176, Employment Department, Sheffield.

Nicolson RI, Fawcett AJ, Moss H, Nicolson MK, Reason R (1999) An Early Reading Intervention Study: Evaluation and Implications. British Journal of Educational Psychology, 69. 47-62

Nicolson RI, Fawcett AJ (2000) Long-term learning in dyslexic children European Journal of Cognitive Psychology,12, 357-393.

Nicolson RI, Fawcett AJ, Dean P (2001) Developmental dyslexia: the cerebellar deficit hypothesis. Trends in Neuroscience 24: 506-509

Nicolson, RI, Daum I, Schugens, MM, Fawcett AJ, Schulz A (2002) Eyeblink conditioning indicates cerebellar abnormality in dyslexia. Experimental Brain Research, 143: 42-50.

Paulesu E, Frith CD, Frackowiak RJ (1993) The neural correlates of the verbal component of working memory. Nature, 362, 342-345.

Pennington BF (1991) Diagnosing Learning Disorders, New York; Guilford.

Reason R (1999) ADHD: A psychological response to an evolving concept. Journal of Learning Disabilities, 32, 85-91

Riddick B (1996) Living with dyslexia: the social and emotional consequences of specific learning difficulties. Routledge, London

Rourke BP, Feurst DR (1991) Learning disabilities and psychosocial functioning: A neuropsychological perspective. New York: Guildford.

Rudel RG (1985) The definition of dyslexia: Language and motor deficits. In FH Duffy, N Geschwind (Eds.) Dyslexia: A neuroscientific approach to clinical evaluation. Boston: Little Brown.

Shaywitz SE, Shaywitz BA, Fletcher JM, Escobar MD (1990) Prevalence of reading-disability in boys and girls - results of the Connecticut Longitudinal Study. Journal of the American Medical Association, 264, 998-1002

Siegel LS (1989) IQ is irrelevant to the definition of learning disabilities. Journal of Learning Disabilities, 22, 469-479.

Snowling MJ, Goulandris N, Bowlby M, Howell P (1986) Segmentation and speech perception in relation to reading skill: a developmental analysis. Journal of Experimental Child Psychology, 41: 487-507.

Stanovich KE (1986) Matthew effects in reading Some consequences of individual differences in the acquisition of literacy. Reading Research Quarterly, 21, 360-407.

Stanovich KE (1988) The right and wrong places to look for the cognitive locus of reading disability. Annals of Dyslexia, 38: 154-177.

Stanovich KE, Jacob RG, West RF, Vala-Rossi M (1985) Children's word recogntion in context: Spreading activation, expectancy and modularity. Child Development, 56, 1418-1429.

Strag G (1972) Comparative behavioural ratings of parents with severe mentally retarded, special learning disability, and normal children. Journal of Learning disabilities, 5, 52-56.

Tallal P, Piercy M (1974) Developmental aphasia, rate of auditory processing and selective impairment of consonant perception. Neuropsychologia, 12, 83-93.

Thomson ME (1984) Developmental Dyslexia: Its nature, assessment and remediation. London, Edward Arnold.

Vail PL (2001) Treating the whole person: Emotion, denial, disguises, language, and con-
nectedness. In Fawcett AJ (ed). Dyslexia:Theory and good practice. Whurr, London.

Vellutino FR (1979) Dyslexia: Theory and Research. Cambridge, MA.MIT Press.

Wechsler D (1976) Wechsler Intelligence Scale for Children Revised (WISC-R). Slough,
UK: NFER.

Wechsler D (1986) Manual for the Wechsler adult intelligence scale – Revised UK. edition,
Sidcup, Kent: The Psychological Corporation.

West TG (1991) In the mind's eye. Prometheus: New York.

Wolf M (1991) Naming speed and reading: The contribution of the cognitive neuro-
sciences. Reading Research Quarterly, 26, 123–141.

Wright-Strawderman C, Watson BL (1992) The prevalence of depressive symptoms in children with learning disabilities. Journal of Learning Disabilities, 25, 258–265.

Chapter 21
Some final thoughts

TIM MILES

Several of the contributors to this book have commented on the increase in public awareness of dyslexia that has taken place in Britain since the first edition was published in 1995. There are, indeed, grounds for optimism. One's impression is that there is now less defeatism about the possibility of teaching literacy skills to those who, for whatever reason, have found the acquistion of literacy difficult. As public awareness increases it is likely that many of the kinds of events described in the first edition will become less frequent, such as the harrowing experiences of Karen Dodd in trying to get help for her daughter, Margaret. Similarly it may well be that the unkind remarks cited in this book and elsewhere, for instance, saying to a dyslexic child, 'Stand in the bin – you're rubbish', or the lack of understanding shown by the head teacher who said, 'He's not dyslexic; he's only a silly little boy', will in the future, as Angela Fawcett suggests in Chapter 20, be regarded only as cautionary tales as to what *not* to do rather than reports of what is currently happening.

It would be wrong, however, for me to gloss over the darker side of the picture. Lindsay Peer, in Chapter 9, tells of two cases where suicide was contemplated and of one, the case of Nicholas, where this actually happened. At a recent conference organized by the British Dyslexia Association, Nicholas' mother was brave enough to address the assembled audience and tell them about the tragedy. Lindsay speaks of 'every parent's nightmare' – the fear that something similar should happen to their own child. One can only hope that increased understanding of the stresses experienced by people with dyslexia of all ages will prevent such tragedies from occurring in the future.

Another example of real tragedy is the case of Julian Cox (Chapter 19). Further details of what happened will be found in Cox (2001). When his business ran into difficulties, it seems that he was confronted by a mass of letters, some of them threatening court action, which simply overwhelmed him. It is, of course, well known that most dyslexics are slow readers, and his awareness, at least implicit, of the time that he would have needed to deal with the letters one by one was too much for him. The desperate expedient

of setting fire to the papers, like many aberrations on the part dyslexics, is at least understandable, given the stress that he was experiencing. Very sadly, in the ensuing conflagration his mother lost her life. What one must particularly deplore is the lack of understanding of dyslexia on the part of the legal system, which found him guilty of murder, i.e. *deliberate* killing of his mother, and then rejected his subsequent appeal.

These tragic events are, indeed, possible when dyslexics are put under excessive stress. It should be remembered, however, that in both these two tragic cases there was a *combination* of a large number of adverse factors, and the likelihood of their recurrence in the same or similar combinations is small. It goes without saying, however, that any case of *threatened* suicide should always be taken seriously, and even if the threats are not carried out the extent of the sheer despair experienced by some dyslexics should never be underestimated.

To turn to more pleasant topics, Brother Matthew Sasse speaks of 'the positive and the negative' aspects of dyslexia, and it is of course essential when one is giving advice to people with dyslexia to encourage them not to undervalue themselves. This is, indeed, a theme that runs throughout the book, and Brother Matthew is here speaking for all of us. In my own case, I would take care when I carried out assessments to let the children or adults see for themselves what they were capable of. I was able to do this because of my knowledge of what to *expect* from a dyslexic of a given age. As in intelligence testing, one has to discover the limits of what the individual is capable of; I would make clear, if I expected failure, that I was not necessarily expecting success. I also made a point of giving them items that were likely to tap their strengths at abstract reasoning, and as a precaution against possible failure I would sometimes say, 'Would you like to try this really difficult one?', perhaps explaining that it was intended for older people. Then little would be lost if they failed, but it would be a real boost to their self-esteem if they succeeded.

Like Brother Matthew, Michael Newby is very much concerned to emphasize the positive aspects of dyslexia. To make his point he proposes that we should make what philosophers have called a 'conceptual innovation' (Harzem and Miles, 1978). By re-describing or renaming some phenomenon, we are promoting a different view of it. Michael points out that the word 'dyslexia' has all sorts of negative associations, and he proposes that in place of 'dyslexics' we should speak of 'allomaths', i.e. those who have a different style of learning from the majority. 'Dyslexia without stress' (the telling title of his chapter) can be achieved if parents and teachers recognize that some children have different learning styles from others, that 'slogging' at the basics of literacy and numeracy is not the right approach for some children, including dyslexics, and that it may sometimes be profitable to put them on

to more advanced work, such as visiting science laboratories or art galleries, even when they are not secure on the basics. It is particularly important, he suggests, to provide the environment in which their 'positive' skills can thrive.

Michael also refers to the stresses that can arise from well-intentioned efforts on the part of the Government to improve literacy standards – head teachers may pressurize their own staff, and the staff may in turn put inappropriately heavy pressure on pupils. The use of league tables may, indeed, act as a spur to some who would not otherwise have made so much effort – and this is true also of the teaching and research assessments in tertiary education. One of the sad consequences of league tables is that schools are under pressure to spend time and resources on those candidates who are at the margin between passing and failing, and this could be to the disadvantage of dyslexics who would have been capable of learning if appropriately taught, but at a given time appear to be well below pass level.

There is the further problem that emphasis on passing tests leads to an overvaluation of rote learning, at which people with dyslexia tend to be weak, at the expense of understanding and creativity, at which they may well be strong.

In view of this, it seems to me essential that those who formulate Government policy should consider the needs of distinctive groups, of whom dyslexics are one. What is particularly required is the concept of 'value added'. What should be taken into account in evaluating teaching success is not so much the end product as such, but the amount of change in the desired direction – including improved confidence and self-esteem, which has been brought about. In the case of dyslexics such a criterion would be more informative and therefore fairer. A dyslexiic may arrive at secondary school or college with qualifications that seem unpromising for the future. A school or college that restores self-respect to students with dyslexia should not be judged to have performed 'worse' than another school or college that started with promising material and obtains higher overall grades at A level or degree level.

I do not have the space to comment in detail on the many other insights from both the dyslexic and the non-dyslexic contributors, but it may be of help if I highlight a few of them. Dave Alexander describes how his skill as a cyclist contributed to restoring his self-esteem. Brenda Millward points out how even kindly intentioned actions – in her case providing a group of underprivileged children with cod liver oil – can be stressful if they involve picking out some children as being 'different'. Michael Lea reports on the ways in which the multisensory methods originated by Gillingham and Stillman for the teaching of literacy skills are also of value in teaching pupils to learn musical instruments. He also reminds us of the many differences between

one dyslexic and another; for instance some dyslexics are able to find their way about a maze of streets and others are not. One of the curious things about describing people as 'dyslexic' is that, despite these varied manifestations, there is still a recognizable underlying pattern.

Morag Kiziewicz speaks with feeling about the stresses imposed on dyslexics (and, indeed, others) when they have to meet deadlines. She also raises the very interesting issue of whether there might be better ways of assessing the skills of dyslexics – ways not requiring large amounts of reading, writing or rote learning and not imposing timed conditions.

Lindsay Peer, in addition to giving us the heartbreaking account of Nicholas and the two cases of threatened suicide, has emphasized the need for 'dyslexia-friendly' schools, and it is to be hoped that this concept will gain wide, and eventually universal, acceptance. Melanie Jameson has reminded us how very vulnerable a dyslexic person can be when he or she is involved with the legal system – whether as defendant or claimant. As Melanie points out, slowness in processing symbolic information is a characteristic of dyslexia that persists into adulthood and may create the wrong impression in all kinds of different ways.

Angela Fawcett's chapter seems to me a remarkable example of how humanity and compassion can be combined with scientific rigour. Her chapter is the only one in the book that provides information on any large scale about any systematic research. It is all too easy to assume that such and such is a characteristic of dyslexics, without troubling to ask how many non-dyslexics also behave in the same way. This is why the concept of a control group is important, and why in dyslexia research it is often useful to compare dyslexics not only with control individuals of the same age and background, but also with control individuals who are at the same reading level; this is because it is important to separate out effects that are not associated with dyslexia as such but would occur in any child who had the same amount of reading experience. What she and Rod Nicolson termed the 'square root rule' is a fascinating step in trying to quantify the amount of time and effort that a dyslexic need in order to achieve the same results as a non-dyslexic. According to the square-root rule, a skill which takes a non-dyslexic 100 hours to acquire will take a dyslexic 1000 hours (10 being the square root of 100 and $10 \times 100 = 1000$).

Some readers may be interested to hear about some recent techniques that are currently being explored in the area of stress management. Suppose you are stressed about something – you feel anger at the way in which you have been treated, or oppressed by the load of work confronting you, or worried at the thought that you may not be 'up to' performing a particular task, or suppose some of life's seemingly minor annoyances are 'getting you down' – the long queue in the supermarket, or the frustrating wait in the

traffic jam. The suggestion is that you should relax yourself, focusing, perhaps, on your breathing or on the space occupied by your body, or concentrate all your attention on imagining the beauty of a simple object such as a nut. These are all things that you can do in public without anyone knowing that you are doing it!

When you are thoroughly relaxed, you should not try to *deny* your anger or your frustration – it is unrealistic to pretend that they are not there. When you come out of the 'relax' mode you are then free to decide whether to *act on* them – and there is now the chance of you making a more rational and less damaging decision than you might otherwise have done.

At a recent conference I heard a reference to the stresses caused by 'oughtism' (the homophone of 'autism'), which means being weighed down by guilt over the things that, according to either yourself or others, you 'ought' to have done. This, of course, is one of the themes in the chapter by Steve Chinn (Chapter 3). Here Steve speaks of the stresses that can arise among dyslexic adolescents if they feel that they ought to meet their parents' expectations but through no fault of their own are unable to do so. Similarly, when Dorothy Gilroy in Chapter 4 reports how members of her group of dyslexic students reported themselves as 'hopeless at . . .', the suggestion would be that, in relaxing, they do not concern themselves over whether it is *true* that they are hopeless at this or that, but that when the relaxation exercise is over they reflect on what they are able to change, and to learn to live with what cannot be changed.

At another conference on stress, use was made of the analogy of 'ripples'. One can think of events that occur in the life of a dyslexic as setting up ripples similar to those that occur in a lake or pond. Adverse treatment may produce quite strong 'currents' and, whatever the treatment, it sets off ripples in a number of directions – in the family, at the school, in the workplace – the effects, for good or ill, being far wider than one might initially suppose. When a dyslexic masters his or her first book ('Mummy, I can read') the consequences may 'rub off' on relationships as far afield as those at father's place of work.

Laughter, of course, is one of the best antidotes to stress. Where there was dyslexia in the family, some of the happiest families I have met were those who were able to laugh at the mishaps and vagaries that regularly arise when one or more members of the family are dyslexic. To laugh *at* dyslexics is criminal; to laugh *with* conveys empathy and understanding. I recently made the acquaintance of a dyslexic student who could never spell the word 'colour' correctly; when on one occasion she actually did so, the tutor wrote 'hurrah' in the margin.

It is, of course, a very basic principle when one is helping people to change their behaviour that one ignores as far as possible the 'unwanted'

behaviour and gives high praise for any behaviour, however minimal, that is in the right direction.

There is no doubt at all that in Britain at the present time dyslexics can succeed academically, and it is good news that research findings are now influencing social and educational policy. Much, however, remains to be done, and whether families live in an area where there is adequate provision is still something of a lottery.

If dyslexia is misunderstood the consequences, as we have seen, can be tragic - and let us hope that in the future no one will suffer as Nicholas and Julian did. That said, however, the central message of this book is one of hope: there is now increased understanding and with it the possibility that our society will come to respect dyslexics for what they are, rather than denigrate them for not being something else.

Acknowledgements

I am grateful to Dr Lindsay Peer for giving me many helpful suggestions when I came to write this final chapter and to my colleague, Dr Paul Elliston, for giving me the opportunity to experience some of the techniques for stress management at first hand.

References

Cox JHA (2001) From inside prison. Dyslexia: An International Journal of Research and Practice 7(2): 97–102.
Harzem P, Miles TR (1978) Conceptual Issues in Operant Psychology. Chichester: Wiley.

Index

Printed in the United Kingdom
by Lightning Source UK Ltd.
124906UK00002B/193-201/A